AF394280

HITLER AT HINTERSEE

GERHARD BARTELS
THE BOY IN THE PHOTOGRAPH

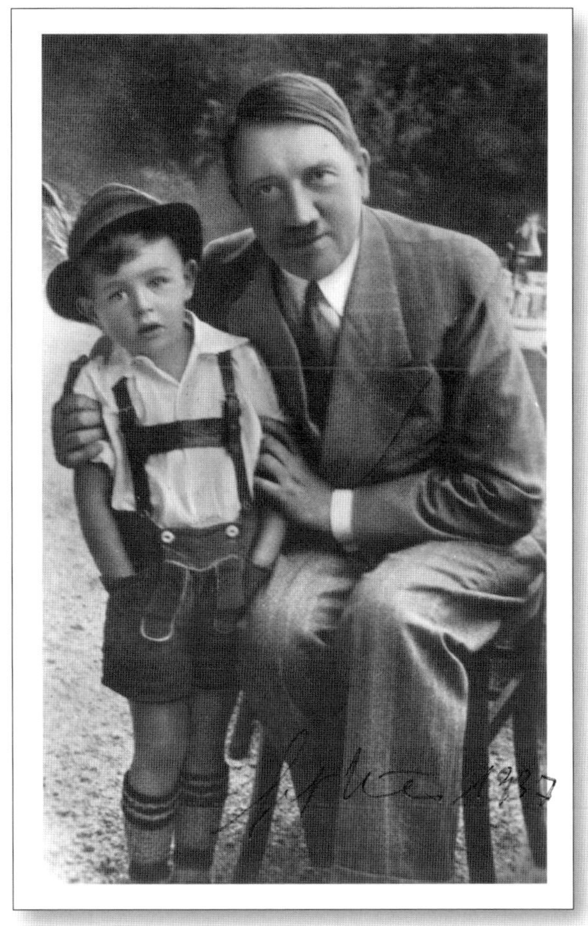

JAMES WILSON

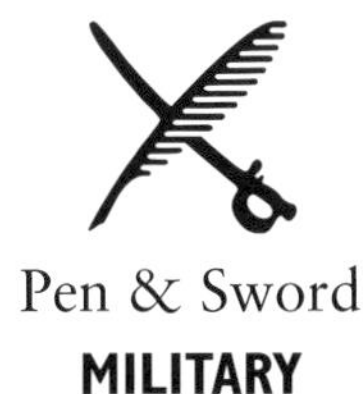

Pen & Sword
MILITARY

First published in Great Britain in 2024 by
Pen & Sword Military
An imprint of Pen & Sword Books Limited
Yorkshire – Philadelphia

ISBN 978 1 03610 083 4

A CIP catalogue record for this book is
available from the British Library

Typeset by Mac Style
Printed in the UK by CPI Group (UK) Ltd, Croydon, CR0 4YY.

Pen & Sword Books Limited incorporates the imprints of After the Battle,
Atlas, Archaeology, Aviation, Discovery, Family History, Fiction, History,
Maritime, Military, Military Classics, Politics, Select, Transport, True
Crime, Air World, Frontline Publishing, Leo Cooper, Remember When,
Seaforth Publishing, The Praetorian Press, Wharncliffe Local History,
Wharncliffe Transport, Wharncliffe True Crime and White Owl.

For a complete list of Pen & Sword titles please contact

PEN & SWORD BOOKS LIMITED
47 Church Street, Barnsley, South Yorkshire, S70 2AS, England
E-mail: enquiries@pen-and-sword.co.uk
Website: www.pen-and-sword.co.uk
or
PEN AND SWORD BOOKS
1950 Lawrence Rd, Havertown, PA 19083, USA
E-mail: uspen-and-sword@casematepublishers.com
Website: www.penandswordbooks.com

Contents

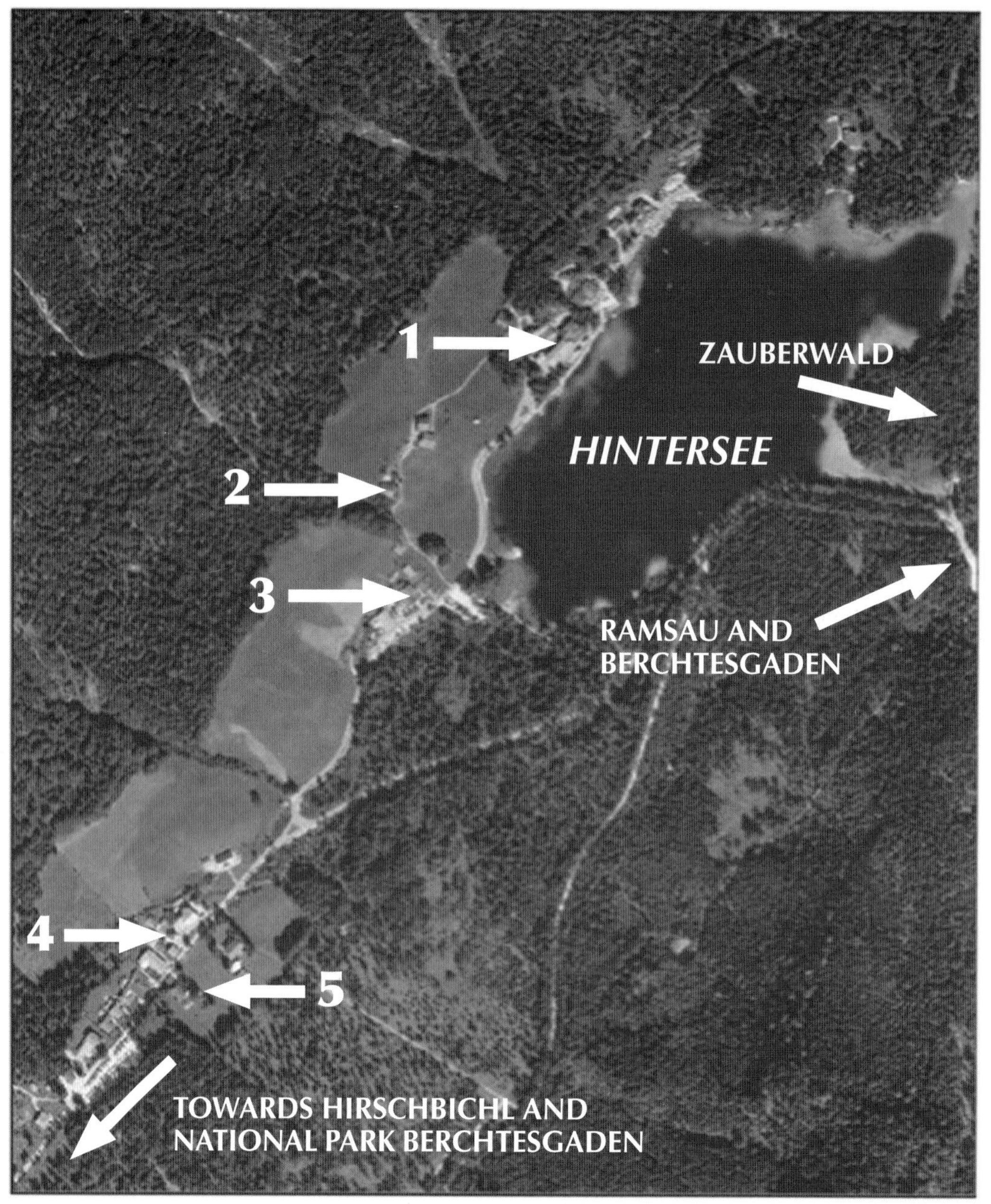

Map of Hintersee

This map shows the location of particularly relevant buildings and nearby areas.
1 Hotel Post   **2** Seehäusl (formerly Meister house)   **3** Bartels Alpenhof
4 Gasthaus Auzinger   **5** Altes Zollhaus (formerly Fritz Todt house)

Introduction

It has to be said that the passage of time has done little to diminish public interest in the subject of Adolf Hitler; in fact it's probably fair to say it has only increased. The number of books and documentaries ranging from factual to speculative on the subject seems to increase year on year. I myself have spent over thirty years researching and studying Hitler's relationship with Berchtesgaden and the Obersalzberg area; this region that was so very important to the Führer on a personal and little understood level. During his time as Chancellor, Hitler spent approximately one-third of that time on the Obersalzberg, initially in Haus Wachenfeld, then later, following reconstruction and enlargement after which time the building was generally referred to as the Berghof. Therefore Hitler spent more time here than anywhere else.

Everyone knows of the Kehlsteinhaus (Eagle's Nest) the teahouse on top of the nearby Kehlstein that the Party presented to Hitler on the occasion of his 50th birthday on 20 April 1939. However the Führer only visited this masterpiece of engineering and construction fourteen times. These official visits took place between 1938 and 1940. Hitler did make a number of unofficial and mostly unrecorded visits to the Kehlsteinhaus, perhaps six in total. He much preferred to make a daily visit to his other, and certainly lesser known teahouse situated below the Berghof at Mooslahnerkopf. This became something of a daily ritual when the Führer was on the Obersalzberg. Accompanied by a select few, Hitler would stroll down across the valley to Mooslahnerkopf to enjoy Austrian cakes and pastries and relax for an hour or two before returning to the Berghof. While period photographs of the Kehlsteinhaus are not uncommon, images of the teahouse at Mooslahnerkopf are rare indeed.

Both buildings survived the air raid of 25 April 1945 unscathed. Earmarked for destruction in 1952 the Kehlsteinhaus was spared due to the intervention the District President, Karl Theodor Jacob. The Mooslahnerkopf teahouse was not so lucky, the building was torn down due to its association with Hitler and his all too frequent use of it. The remaining ruins were finally removed in 2007.

So, who is Gerhard Bartels, and why was he photographed with Hitler? Let's first deal with who Gerhard Bartels is. Well he's my friend; I've known 'Gerd' since 2004. That first meeting came about by complete chance. I was in Berchtesgaden and had been told about a local man, Tony Resch. Tony sold old postcards of Berchtesgaden and the surrounding area. Well that was why I was there after all, so having acquired his telephone number I spoke to Tony and told him what I was looking for. He assured me he probably had something I'd be interested in. Tony came to our hotel that evening carrying a number of large photograph albums. As I went through the albums I drew Tony's attention to a particular postcard. It was a Hoffmann image showing Hitler seated with his arm around a young boy. I remarked that I already had this image and was about to move on when

Tony said that the little boy in the photograph was still alive. Well I could hardly believe my ears as Tony continued to tell me that he knew the man, Gerd Bartels, and that he lived at Hintersee, about half an hour away.

Before making that trip to Berchtesgaden my publisher had mentioned how helpful and interesting a short interview with a local person would be, particularly someone who'd lived through that time and how it would be good for the book I was working on. I'd already made some enquiries in that regard but nothing had surfaced, and yet, here I was, looking at that postcard. I bought some postcards from Tony and he gave me some more information on Gerd Bartels. Next day I telephoned Bartels Alpenhof at Hintersee and asked to speak to Herr Bartels. I explained why I was in Berchtesgaden and asked if I could come to Hintersee and 'have a chat' as I put it. Herr Bartels had no objections and we agreed we would meet at Alpenhof the next day.

Hintersee is a beautiful, picturesque area on the edge of the Berchtesgaden National Park. I arrived at Hintersee with time to spare before our scheduled two o'clock meeting the following day so I had time to take in the beautiful Alpine scenery surrounding the lake. As two o'clock approached I made my way to Alpenhof which turned out to be a typical Bavarian style hotel. On approaching the entrance I noticed the year 1938 crafted in wrought iron and fixed above the main door. A member of staff greeted me as I walked into the hallway. I said who I was and explained I had an appointment with Herr Bartels. I was taken through to the kitchen where I was introduced to Gerd Bartels. We shook hands and Gerd suggested we continue talking in the dining room where it would be quiet. Gerd is a tall, thin man with a kindly face and softly spoken. He was wearing a long green apron with traces of flour on the front of it. This was the first interview I'd done and I was a little unsure and a little nervous. But there was no need, Herr Bartels was warm and welcoming and almost immediately asked if I'd like something to drink, a beer or a coffee. I thanked him and said I would prefer coffee. He immediately asked a member of staff to bring two mugs of coffee.

I explained why I wanted to speak to him and thanked him for agreeing to meet with a complete stranger. We'd been talking about mundane, everyday things for a few minutes when Herr Bartels excused himself and left the room. He returned carrying a folder from which he produced a number of documents and photographs. One document told how civilian and military staff from the Obersalzberg had arrived at Hintersee soon after the bombing of the Obersalzberg complex to take over the hotel. The photographs were period postcards showing Gerhard Bartels when he was a small boy with Adolf Hitler. In showing me these things I felt Herr Bartels was at ease in my company and the conversation began to flow effortlessly. Needless to say I got my interview with a local person, better than that, I'd spoken to the very man who'd been the 'poster boy' in a number of photographs taken with Adolf Hitler back in the 1930s.

Since that time I've visited Gerd Bartels every time I've been in the area. My wife and I spent Christmas 2007 in Bartels Alpenhof where we enjoyed walking on the frozen lake. That Christmas Eve, Gerd invited us to join him later that evening on a visit to the small church in Ramsau about ten minutes drive from Hintersee. He was going to visit the graves of his parents in the churchyard there. This is a traditional Bavarian custom where family members gather to light candles on small Christmas trees placed on the graves of past family members. I considered it a great honour to be invited along on something so personal to Gerd.

While we were in the graveyard we were treated to a thunderous barrage created by the *Weinachtsschützen* (Christmas Shooters). This is a centuries old tradition. In pagan times people would rattle chains and ring bells to drive away evil spirits while at the same time attempt to reawaken nature in the dark, gloomy months of winter. The tradition has survived, and while altered and adapted it now plays a part in Christian belief. On 17 December at exactly 3:00pm the firing of short-barrelled, large-calibre pistols and small cannon herald the impending arrival of the baby Jesus. The ritual ends at midnight on 24 December. Throughout this period the incredible noise of the shooting echoes around the Berchtesgaden valley at 3:00pm daily. It really is quite an experience.

Following my retirement in 2014 my wife and I moved to Berchtesgaden where I spent three seasons working as a tour guide specialising in Third Reich history. During that period I sometimes brought small groups to Alpenhof where, to their delight, Gerd would come and sit with us and chat to the group about his life. On many of these occasions he would appear wearing his signature green apron. Gerd still works in the kitchen of the family-run business where, amongst other things, he continues to make his delicious Pflaumkuchen and Apfelstrudel.

Now let's look at why, when he was a little boy, Gerd was chosen to be photographed with Hitler all those years ago. Adolf Hitler made his first visit to Berchtesgaden and the Obersalzberg in April 1923. Hitler had come to visit his old friend and mentor, Dietrich Eckart. Eckart, who knew the area well, was in hiding. He was wanted for questioning by the police in connection with articles published in *Auf gut Deutsch!* (In plain German!) an anti-Semitic periodical of which Eckart was editor. While in Berchtesgaden, Eckart, now using the name Dr Hoffmann, made every effort to keep his whereabouts secret. Hitler, for his part, was using the alias Herr Wolf. 'Wolf' was an old nickname of Hitler's and now he used it in an effort to avoid leading the authorities to his friend's location. At the end of his visit, Hitler was, in his own words, 'completely captivated' by the region. This visit in 1923 was just the beginning of a relationship between Adolf Hitler and the Berchtesgaden area that would last until his death in April 1945. Hitler would return to the region time and time again.

Following his imprisonment for his part in the failed Beer-Hall *'Putsch'* (Revolt) that took place in Munich on 9 November 1923 Hitler returned to Berchtesgaden. Having already spent considerable time on the Obersalzberg, Adolf Hitler rented a typical Bavarian Alpine style cottage on the mountainside in mid October 1928. Haus Wachenfeld, situated close to Hotel zum Türken, offered fabulous views across the valley towards the imposing Untersberg. Hitler was putting down roots; the Obersalzberg had cast its spell on him. In these beautiful and peaceful surroundings Hitler could relax and conceive a strategy that would see the Nazi Party achieve political success and ultimately power in Germany.

Berchtesgaden is about a thirty-minute drive from Hintersee where the Bartels family lived. There was a hotel at Hintersee, Hotel Post, owned by Isidor 'Dori' Weiss (1892–1941). During the First World War, Dori Weiss had been Hitler's sergeant for a time. The two men were on friendly terms and when he was in Berchtesgaden Hitler would visit his old comrade at Hintersee. Now here's the link; Dori Weiss was Gerd Bartel's uncle. Herr Weiss and Gerd's mother were brother and sister. It was probably Heinrich Hoffmann's idea to take some photographs showing Hitler in the company of children and little Gerd and his cousin Anni, the daughter of Dori Weiss, became the subjects of a number of iconic propaganda images depicting the Führer interacting with children.

Gerhard Bartels was born in Bischofswiesen on 6 January 1932. His cousin, Anni Weiss was born on 5 July 1931. The majority of the photographs taken at Hintersee by Heinrich Hoffmann went on to be published as photographic postcards providing great propaganda value. The location for these photographed encounters between little Gerd, Anni and Hitler was around Hotel Post, the property owned by Anni's father, Dori Weiss. The Weiss family had lived at Hintersee for many years. Gerd's maternal grandfather, also called Dori Weiss came to Hintersee from Laufen; a town situated approximately 52 kilometres (32 miles) north of Salzburg. Laufen is on the German side of the German/Austrian border. Weiss already owned Hotel Post in 1900 when he bought Wörndlhof, a building and some land just a few hundred metres away from Hotel Post. Gerd's father, August Bartels came to Hintersee from the Münsterland soon after the First World War. August Bartels and Maria Weiss were married in 1929 and took over the running of Wörndlhof later that year. They soon set about expanding the estate renaming it 'Posthof'.

With dreams of owning their own business the ambitious young couple set about constructing 'Alpenhof' in 1937. Building work was completed by the end of the following year, 1938. Sheet metal shortages at the time meant the roof had to be finished with roofing felt rather than the usual galvanised tin or copper. The builders couldn't say when, or even if the required metal might arrive; but they had a roof. Obviously the roofing felt had a limited lifespan and it wasn't particularly well suited to Alpine weather conditions, as a result the felt deteriorated quite rapidly. One day, following a particularly bad hailstorm in 1941, Gerd's mother Maria was standing outside the property looking up at the roof when Dr Fritz Todt (1891–1942), then Reich Minister for Armament and Munitions walked by.

Todt owned the Altes Zollhaus (Old Customs House) on Hirschbichlstraße, less than a ten-minute walk from Alpenhof. As he was passing Dr Todt struck up a conversation with Gerd's mother. During the conversation Todt asked why the roof on what appeared to be a new building was in such a poor state. Gerd's mother explained how the shortage of metal left the builders with no option but to use roofing felt. The conversation ended, Dr Todt took his leave and continued on his way. A couple of days later an unexpected delivery arrived in the form of a lorry carrying all the metal necessary to replace the tattered felt roof on Alpenhof; Fritz Todt had telephoned Berlin and used his connections to help out his neighbour.

Between 1933 and 1937 Adolf Hitler visited Hintersee often; he would come to have coffee with Gerd's grandmother, Rosina Weiss, and his Uncle Dori. These visits finally came to an end with the outbreak of the Second World War. In October 1939 as the Polish campaign came to an end a number of *Gebirgstruppen* (Mountain Troops) were billeted at Alpenhof. These troops were there until May 1940. Gerd recalls how in 1941, as a result of allied bombing of German cities, they received a number of evacuated children through the *Kinderlandverschickung;* KLV (Child Land Dispatch). These children were mainly from Hamburg. The Hamburg docks were bombed many times by the Allies. These KLV children loved Hintersee: so much so that many of them came back after the war. Even as adults some of them were still returning until as recently as 2015.

As was the case with the majority of German boys Gerhard Bartels joined the *Deutsches Jungvolk* (German Young People). Young Gerd was very interested in flying and hoped one day to be a pilot in the Luftwaffe. He attended the German Gymnasium School in Riga in Latvia from 1942 until 1944. August Bartels, Gerd's father, was working in Latvia as a regional farmer. He was in charge of the food supply for all of northern Latvia.

The Riga Ghetto had been established in 1941. Gerd remembers that the perimeter consisted of a three-metre high security fence. While it was forbidden, he can still remember exchanging 50-gram bread stamps for 50 Pfennigs per stamp with the ghetto inmates. 'We felt sorry for the poor people', he recalls. He remembers on one occasion he used the money to go to the circus. The ghetto closed in 1943. It was said that the remaining inmates had been resettled. There were a number of military hospitals in Riga where wounded German soldiers were treated. As members of the Hitler Youth the boys often sang for the soldiers in the hospitals.

The Bartels family fled Riga in June 1944 in the face of advancing Soviet forces when the Russians invaded the country for a second time. The family tried to send some of their belongings to Gotenhafen by ship; unfortunately the ship carrying their belongings was attacked and sunk by a Russian submarine. Most of Gerd's classmates escaped to the small island of Süderoog, one of the Halligen islands off the west coast of Schleswig-Holstein where lessons resumed for a short while. With the situation rapidly deteriorating the family decided to return home; they returned to Berchtesgaden making most of the journey by train. Having returned to Hintersee, Gerd, now twelve years old, went back to school in the summer of 1944. (The independent state of Latvia was invaded by Soviet forces on 17 June 1940. This first Russian occupation ended when German forces marched into Riga on 1 July 1941. In July 1944 Russian forces again invaded Latvia as the Germans were driven back. Fighting between German and Russian troops in western Latvia continued until the last day of the war.)

Gerd recalls how he was at school in nearby Bad Reichenhall on the day the RAF bombed the Obersalzberg on 25 April 1945. Bad Reichenhall was also targeted that day killing over 200 civilians. Gerd remembers how as the air raid sirens began to wail that the teachers led the children down into the cellars beneath the school, the Karlsgymnasium on Salzburger Strasse. He recalls that as children they'd come to see air raids as fun as this brought about an end to their lessons and nothing ever happened; the warnings were usually due to a sighting of enemy aircraft flying high above the town *en route* to other targets.

That day, Wednesday 25 April would be different; that day Bad Reichenhall was targeted. Gerd remembers sitting in the cellar with dust falling all around as the building shook to the shock waves of exploding bombs and how the little girls cried for their mothers. As they emerged from the cellar they could see that the roof of the school had been badly damaged. The school caretaker's wife brought the children in and made pancakes for everyone before they were sent home. Gerd recalls how he and the other boys were thinking, 'Great, no more school!' In addition to the number of deaths the bombing caused a lot of damage in Bad Reichenhall. However the two large army barracks situated on the outskirts of the town were undamaged.

(For the Allies, these bombing raids on the Obersalzberg and Bad Reichenhall on Wednesday 25 April 1945 were the last major air raids of the Second World War. Some 359 Avro Lancaster bombers and 16 De Havilland Mosquitos attacked the Obersalzberg that morning dropping over 1230 tons of bombs on the complex. Despite the deployment of the smoke-generating equipment and the fact that the buildings were well camouflaged only a few buildings emerged unscathed, many were badly damaged while a smaller number were completely destroyed. The nearby town of Berchtesgaden itself was untouched.

Reichsmarshal Hermann Göring, his wife Emmy and their little daughter Edda were on the Obersalzberg that morning, as was Martin Bormann's wife Gerda and her nine children. Having taken refuge in the underground bunker systems constructed beneath their respective homes all of the abovementioned survived the air raid. There were over 3000 people on the mountainside that day; this included the regular staff employed at the various residences and administration workers together with SS, RSD (RSD; *Reichsicherheitsdienst* – Reich Security Service) and the best part of some 3000 labourers. Most of these people made it into the vast underground tunnel and bunker system to survive the air raid. Considering the intensity of the bombing that morning it is surprising that only eleven people died. Other sources state that only six people were killed. Much of the underground tunnel/bunker system beneath the Obersalzberg survives. Indeed it was so well constructed that even the 5433-kg (12000-lb) 'Tallboy' deep-penetration bombs specifically designed to penetrate and destroy underground facilities failed to have any real impact.

In addition to the usual anti-aircraft gun positions, part of the air-defence system for the area had included the installation of smoke-generating equipment. This was to be used in the event of an air raid and would 'cloud' the entire valley in an effort to hide intended ground targets from view. The smoke-generating equipment had been activated earlier that morning when the Obersalzberg had been bombed, this left a strong vinegar-like smell and fog everywhere.

Having been released from school Gerd and a friend, a boy named Ritter, an evacuee from Munich who was living at Hintersee began making their way home. In these circumstances the boys faced a long walk; it was 18 kilometres (11 miles) to Hintersee. Bad Reichenhall had been transformed; it was now a place of death and destruction.

Fires were raging everywhere: buildings had been destroyed and many were still burning. There was rubble everywhere. Thinking a second attack might occur the boys made their way quickly out of the town.

They were walking along the road by the Saalachsee when a passing military vehicle, a Kübelwagen with two soldiers stopped and offered them a lift. The men brought the boys as far as Jettenberg where they got out. As they continued along the Deutsche Alpenstraße towards Hintersee they got another lift, this time with a soldier on a motorcycle with sidecar. He brought them as far as Hindenburglinde. Getting out of the sidecar they thanked the soldier and continued the rest of the way on foot.

In April 1945 the Red Army were pushing hard towards the centre of Berlin. Despite desperate efforts the beleaguered and vastly outnumbered defending German forces were conceding ground on a daily, and in some cases an hourly basis. Soon after his 56th birthday celebrations in his Berlin bunker, and knowing the end was approaching, Hitler took the decision to release a number of staff and send them south towards Berchtesgaden. To that end three Junkers Ju52 aircraft left Berlin and flew south carrying a number of people who, since January that year had spent most of their time within the confines of the Reich Chancellery bunker. One of these aircraft crashed in Sachsen; there were no survivors. The other two aircraft landed at Ainring near Bad Reichenhall from where the passengers made their way to the Obersalzberg. One of those on board was Albert Bormann, Martin Bormann's brother. Other accounts state these two aircraft landed in Munich.

The Obersalzberg complex was bombed on 25 April 1945. The following day, Thursday 26 April, Albert Bormann ordered that Alpenhof be taken over. This effectively led to Alpenhof becoming a last unofficial headquarters of the Third Reich when the property was commandeered and occupied by evacuees from the Obersalzberg, many of whom had only recently arrived from Berlin on the aforementioned Junkers Ju52s.

Amongst those accommodated at Alpenhof were:

Dr Hugo Blaschke (1881–1959), Hitler's personal dentist.

Gruppenführer Albert Bormann (1902–1989), Chief of Main Office I, Personal Matters of the Führer in the Private Chancellery of the Führer and Hitler's NSKK Adjutant. Bormann brought his wife and new-born child.

Erna Dönitz, sister-in-law of Grand-Admiral Karl Dönitz (1891–1980). Just days before he committed suicide, Adolf Hitler named Karl Dönitz his successor. Erna was married to the Admiral's elder brother, Friedrich.

SA-*Obergruppenführer* Paul Giesler (1895–1945), *Gauleiter* of Munich and Minister-President of Bavaria. Giesler brought his wife and mother.

SS-*Obersturmbannführer* Erich Kempka (1910–1975), Hitler's personal chauffeur. Kempka brought Hitler's Mercedes to Hintersee. Kempka's ex-wife was also there.

SS-*Obersturmbannführer* Heinz Linge (1913–1980), Hitler's valet from 1935– 1945. Linge brought his wife and family.

Konteradmiral Karl-Jesko von Puttkamer (1900–1981). Von Puttkamer, Hitler's Naval Adjutant brought his wife, his children and his mother.

SS-*Obergruppenführer* Julius Schaub (1898–1967). Schaub, Hitler's Personal Adjutant arrived with his partner, Hilde Marzelewski.

Christa Schroeder (1908–1984) one of Hitler's longest-serving private secretaries.

Eugen Bühler, Hitler's gardener on the Obersalzberg came with his son. The vegetables Bühler grew on the Obersalzberg were shipped to Berlin and other places including Hitler's various headquarters as part of the Führer's diet.

Others included Dr Rohkamm and a female cook named Ruloff. Dr Rohkamm had been an assistant of Dr Hugo Blaschke, Hitler's personal dentist.

In total some twenty-five to thirty people, amongst them a number of high-ranking SS officers arrived at Alpenhof and many of these brought their families.

Erna Dönitz would continue to live at Alpenhof for another two years where she helped around the house and did office work. Frau Dönitz is buried in Ramsau.

Gerd remembers some ten vehicles carrying both people and supplies arriving from the Obersalzberg. The supplies they brought included coffee beans, crisp-bread, oatmeal, boxes of marzipan, nougat, tinned meat, bottles of cognac and Heidsieck champagne; luxury items, things that ordinary people couldn't get at the time. The SS guarded the supplies. Those recently arrived lived very well; many of the men drank too much which meant they were intoxicated a lot of the time.

Gerd still remembers seeing a high-ranking SS officer sitting at a table in Alpenhof, he was just sitting there. Suddenly an SS soldier entered the room, the soldier hurried over to the officer and standing before him he said, *'Der Führer ist Todt!'* ('The Führer is dead!'). As the news spread many of the ladies began crying; the men began drinking cognac. Provisions were running low when on 8 May news came telling the occupants that American troops were making their way towards Hintersee. In an attempt to evade the Americans many of the men left Hintersee to disappear into the surrounding countryside while others slipped across the border into neighbouring Austria. The women and children remained at Alpenhof to await the arrival of the Americans.

The arrival of these recent 'evacuees' from the Obersalzberg meant the Bartels family had to relocate and take up residence in the 'Posthof' (today the Wörndlhof) the adjacent property. Fortunately the new arrivals had brought substantial supplies with them. Eugen Bühler, Hitler's Obersalzberg gardener, brought lots of seeds and seed plants with him. On 10 May Herr Bühler said, 'The war is over boys; now let us work!' Herr Bühler proceeded to plant a large vegetable garden that he and his son, also called Eugen and young Gerd tended all summer. Using an ox to pull the plough they spent an entire day ploughing before planting. Then they erected a high fence around the garden to prevent deer in the area from destroying the crops.

Gerd and young Eugen Bühler discovered one of Hitler's fabulous Mercedes cars hidden in the barn behind Alpenhof. Kempka, Hitler's chauffeur had brought the vehicle from the Obersalzberg. On checking the boot of the vehicle the boys found boxes of sugar cubes and bottles of French champagne and cognac that Kempka had placed there. The two boys climbed into the car and proceeded to eat sugar cubes and consume alcohol to a point where they were both sick. Despite the car being well hidden under hay in the barn the Americans discovered it following a tip-off from a couple of Polish POWs. The car disappeared soon after; it eventually reappeared in the United States.

Prior to the arrival of the Americans the situation had been extremely tense. Gerd recalls,

With everything that was happening it looked like the remaining German forces in the area were planning a last battle. From the end of Hirschbichlstraße and up to the Bindalm the whole area was full of military vehicles and all kinds of weapons. A field hospital had been set up in a large tent there. We had a look inside the tent and found boxes of morphine ampoules. We took a few boxes of the ampoules and gave them to Dr Schindler at the local hospital; he was very grateful, he was completely out of morphine. The anticipated final battle did not take place.

My friend Hans Gimmelsberger and I took a cart and went to the Klausbach Valley to look for food and weapons and things. I found three Luger P08 pistols, an MG42 machine-gun and an MP40 submachine-gun. Unfortunately I had to hand them in after the Americans arrived, they placed a ban on the possession of all weapons; it was announced that anyone who failed to comply risked a death penalty. At the beginning of May 1945 we had a small number of Ukrainian 'Vlasov' soldiers staying in our barn. These men from the Ukraine had fought with the Germans against the Soviets. They were taken prisoner by the Americans and handed over to the Russians. The Russians were just across the border in Austria. Denounced by the Soviets as 'collaborators and traitors' these unfortunate men, having been subjected to rough treatment at the hands of their captors, were eventually executed close to Salzburg. My Aunt Anni, my Uncle Dori's widow was then running Hotel Post; she hid one of these Vlasov soldiers, a man called Nicolai. He worked for her and he ran a 'black market' on the side.

The Americans were the first allied troops to reach Hintersee; French soldiers arrived soon after. The French only stayed for two or three days, just long enough for them to do their looting! The Americans on the other hand showed much greater discipline and behaved correctly. The Americans spent the entire summer at Hintersee. Men from the 101st Airborne Division came and went in groups to spend two weeks vacation in the area. The Yanks had their own cook; he made over a hundred pancakes for breakfast every day for the troops. Gerd recalls how the Americans had things like maple syrup and peanut butter to put on the pancakes. Gerd told me, 'We'd never seen peanut butter before, but we liked it!' If one of the soldiers managed to shoot a mountain goat they used the meat to make hamburgers. The cook would make large batches of hot chocolate and occasionally he allowed Gerd and Eugen to fill a couple of cans with it. Eugen Bühler and his son stayed at Hintersee until September 1945 when they returned to their home in Stuttgart.

Gert continued,

In the middle of May 1945 we acquired a pregnant Haflinger mare from the Obersalzberg, Martin Bormann had been breeding Haflinger horses at the Gutshof, his mountain farm on the Obersalzberg. The mare had a piece of shrapnel, a bomb splinter in her neck. We cared for her and nursed her back to health. She gave birth to a healthy foal. Eventually we had four horses; I remember riding our stallion on the Obersalzberg, up where the golf course is today. I spent a lot of time up there looking for pieces of shrapnel and things.

Even at the end of June 1945 there were still a few former SS soldiers hiding out on the Hochkalter, the mountain area on the opposite side of the lake, directly opposite Bartels Alpenhof. It was said they killed an American soldier who was out hunting chamois. Time passed and eventually life returned to normal at Hintersee. In 1946 some thirty asylum-seekers from Czechoslovakia arrived at Hintersee; these people were taken in and lived at Alpenhof for about two years. These were ethnic Germans from the Sudetenland, a German speaking area of Czechoslovakia. As the Second World War ended these ethnic Germans had been driven out of the country. Many of these Sudeten Germans found work in agriculture and forestry in the area and were soon integrated into the community.

(The Sudetenland was a part of Bohemia bordering Germany and home to some three million ethnic Germans. The region had been awarded to Czechoslovakia in 1919 under the Treaty of Saint-Germain-en-Laye that was drawn up between the Allies and Austria after the First World War. Konrad Henlein, the leader of the pro-German *Sudetendeutsche Partei* (SdP) founded in 1933 received considerable financial support from Nazi Germany. Continued agitation and claims of the mistreatment of ethnic Germans at the hands of the Czech population would see Henlein and his party demand autonomy for the Sudetenland in 1938. The growing tension in the Sudetenland played right into Hitler's hands. The Führer took full advantage of the escalating crisis as he entered into the negotiations that ended in the Munich Agreement in September 1938.)

By 1949 most of the Americans had left Hintersee and the Bartels family could think about renovating Alpenhof and about a return to welcoming tourists back to the area. In 1950 Gerd started training as a pastry chef in Cologne. In 1960 he met Inge Lüx. Inge, from Augsburg, had come to work at Alpenhof. Gerd and Inge were married on 18 March 1961. Inge was a trained cook and her work helped tremendously in re-establishing the family business at Hintersee. Their first son Günter was born in 1961, their second son Gerd was born in 1963. Both boys are trained cooks and, following one and a half year's military service, both worked in the kitchen at Alpenhof.

Gerd junior now runs the kitchen in Alpenhof with the help of his wife Victoria, also a trained cook. They have a son Christoph. Having completed his apprenticeship as a cook Christoph joined the business in 2017. Gerd junior and Victoria have won a number of international ski racing competitions run specifically for members of the catering business. (Sadly, Victoria passed away in 2021.) In 1972 the family bought a house in the

Zauberwald just outside Ramsau that they planned to renovate. In 1983 Gerd's eldest son Günter took over the property. Günter runs the 'Wirtshaus im Zauberwald' as a restaurant where he also provides accommodation. Günter married in 1995, he has three children, two boys and a girl.

Gerd's younger brother Wolfgang, born on 14 July 1940, was a keen skier. He was a member of the United Team of Germany that competed in the 1964 Winter Olympics in Innsbruck where he won a bronze medal in the downhill event. Wolfgang and his wife Margit began running Wörndlhof next door to Alpenhof in 1967. Wolfgang passed away aged 67 in February 2007. His widow Margit and her son, also called Wolfgang continue to run Wörndlhof.

Gerd's sister Marianne was born in 1936, she worked in the family business until 1960 when she and her husband Walter emigrated, they moved to Brazil. When Walter died, aged just 37, Marianne returned with her three children. Marianne now lives in Rosenheim near Munich where she runs a wine bar.

Gerd Bartels would go on to run the business established by his parents; this is his story. The majority of the postcards used in this book are original Third Reich period produced images. Finally I must thank my friend Gerd for putting his trust in me and for all his help and co-operation in putting his story together.

While visiting Hintersee in December 2022 Gert proudly showed me two large framed documents in his possession. They were the original German Army discharge documents of both his father August and his uncle, Dori Weiss. These impressive documents give the men's names, dates and places of birth, when they joined the German Army, where they served and the awards they earned during the First World War. Both men served through the entire period of the conflict and took part in many of the major battles on the western front. In addition to winning a number of other awards both men earned the Iron Cross (Second Class) and the Military Service medal with Crown and Swords.

While Gerd's story is quite unique and particularly interesting I felt it was necessary to expand on the subject and to include other areas of historical significance in an effort to provide a more complete picture and a greater understanding of the events that shaped Gerd's early life. We must understand that were it not for Hitler's love of this region and his being acquainted with Gerd's uncle, notwithstanding the importance the area achieved through the Third Reich period, Gerd Bartels would never have been photographed with Hitler in the first instance.

To appreciate Gerd's story we must first understand the importance of this region to Adolf Hitler and by extension the Nazi Party. Hitler's association with the area covers a period of more that twenty years, firstly during the early years of his political ambitions, then through the Third Reich period and, it could be argued, to the present day. By including these aforementioned 'other areas' I hope this aim may be achieved.

James Wilson
April 2023

Nazi Propaganda

I t's probably fair to say that the Nazi Party displayed an unequalled mastery of propaganda even long before they came to power in Germany in January 1933. Everything they had, everything they were, was harnessed and put to use to influence the people and bring them into the Nazi fold. The bold colours of their flags and banners, the symbolism, the uniforms, the torch-lit night-time processions snaking their way through the streets, the cleverly crafted rousing speeches delivering messages of hope composed in a way that deliberately targeted the hopes and fears of the common man. Nothing was left to chance, nothing was random, everything, but everything was premeditated and delivered with ruthless efficiency.

For his own part Hitler fully understood the function and value of well-directed and precise propaganda. He knew how the repetition of simple themes, slogans and hard-hitting imagery could influence the masses. In the first part of his book *Mein Kampf* (My Struggle) Hitler states;

> All propaganda must be presented in a popular form and must fix its intellectual level so as not to be above the heads of the least intellectual of those to whom it is directed. Thus its purely intellectual level will have to be that of the lowest mental common denominator among the public it is desired to reach.
>
> When there is question of bringing a whole nation within the circle of its influence, as happens in the case of war propaganda, then too much attention cannot be paid to the necessity of avoiding a high level, which presupposes a relatively high degree of intelligence among the public.

He goes on:

> The art of propaganda consists precisely in being able to awaken the imagination of the public through an appeal to their feelings, in finding the appropriate psychological form that will arrest the attention and appeal to the hearts of the national masses.

This short excerpt clearly shows Hitler's incredible insight regarding the value and use of propaganda, and he would be proved right when in later years the Nazi Party would show what could be achieved through their mastery and application of its use to invade all aspects of public, and to a great extent, private life.

Adolf Hitler was the first politician in the world to use aircraft in his electioneering campaigns. He would be seen and heard at rallies in towns or cities two, perhaps three times in a single day. His opponents on the other hand, those old 'dyed-in-the-wool' politicians, men whose families had been in politics for generations had absolutely no idea what they were up against and even less idea of how to deal with it. A fear of the expansion of communism, rampant unemployment, an economy in ruins, an overriding hatred for the despised Versailles Treaty imposed on a defeated nation, degradation and general apathy would all play into the hands of Adolf Hitler and the *Nationalsozialistische Deutsche Arbeiterpartei* (NSDAP; National Socialist German Workers' Party). In *Mein Kampf* Hitler refers to the Party as the National Socialist German Labour Party.

Adolf Hitler was appointed German Chancellor on 30 January 1933 and it wasn't long before the Party moved to acquire control over all forms of communication. Control of communication was seen as key to both gaining control over the politically undecided amongst the population and in maintaining control and perhaps more importantly the continued loyalty of those who already supported the Party.

Eventually the Party would control the press, radio, film and later television. Everything that the public would see, hear or read would come under the control of Dr Joseph Goebbels, Hitler's brilliant and totally devoted Minister for Public Enlightenment and Propaganda. Imagery in all its forms invaded everyday life, there was no escaping it. From posters of Hitler, to flags and Nazi eagles adorning public buildings, from loudspeakers installed outside radio shops to relay the Führer's speeches to photographs of the Nazi leadership, and postcards, thousands upon thousands of postcards. All these things came together to create a visual spectacular at the annual *Reichsparteitage* (National Rally Days) held in the city of Nuremberg every September. These massive rallies had but one aim, to impress the onlookers and to further cement the relationship between the Party and the people. Those attending these events witnessed military bands leading huge formations of SA, SS and other party organisations through the streets of the city. They saw Hitler and other members of the Nazi hierarchy watch these march-pasts as the uniformed masses made their way through the Adolf-Hitler-Platz in the centre of the old city while numerous events played out on the newly constructed rally grounds on the outskirts of Nuremberg.

As for postcards, well who sends postcards anymore? However we must remember that in the days before mobile phones, digital cameras, tablets and all the other electronic devices we now use on a daily basis and simply take for granted, in those days very few people even owned a camera. In those days if someone was travelling and wanted to show someone back home something of an area they had visited, a postcard was the most popular and cheapest way of doing this. For the greater part of the twentieth century postcards were an affordable way of sending both a photograph and a message to friends or family from another location, perhaps somewhere far away. Thus postcards were immensely popular and were produced in great numbers.

Heinrich Hoffmann, Hitler's personal photographer, was a truly great photographer: one of the best of his generation. Hoffmann took over two million photographs of the Führer, a staggering number by any estimate. Many of these photographs appeared in postcard form to depict Hitler in incalculable situations. Postcards showing Hitler in Berlin, attending official functions, meeting foreign leaders, meeting the people, attending rallies, in the area of Berchtesgaden, on the Obersalzberg, and as the following pages will show, at nearby Hintersee. These postcards, available on every street corner, played their part in the continuing programme for the winning of hearts and minds in presenting Hitler as an approachable, friendly, home-loving, caring leader, a man who was fond of children. After all, what modern self-respecting politician doesn't recognise the importance and value of being photographed in the company of children, and yet, in those days, this was unheard of: a politician being photographed with children!

Today such things are considered perfectly normal, but we must remember that it was the Nazis who invented many of today's electioneering methods; they set the standards by which many, if not all politicians run their campaigns today. The Nazis were ahead of their time in conceiving ways of reaching and influencing the masses with previously unseen, innovative methods and the use of deliberately targeted imagery. Imagery that stirred the emotions: emotions ranging from sympathy to rage, from satisfaction to desire, from despair to bliss and everything in between. In many ways this relentless bombardment of the senses and the Party's early successes in dealing with many of the social problems facing Germany at the time would see huge numbers of the population come to lend their support to the new regime.

Prior to the outbreak of the Second World War on 1 September 1939 it has to be said that in the eyes of the average German Adolf Hitler and the Nazi Party had achieved remarkable success in a number of areas. A disgruntled and fragmented nation had been reunited. Many of the German regions lost after the First World War had been regained through political means and plebiscite, including the annexation of Austria, the Führer's homeland. A terrifying, crushing inherited unemployment situation had been addressed and turned around. Hitler had reintroduced conscription and rearmament. The Führer had successfully, and as it appeared impartially presided over both the summer and winter Olympics held in Germany in 1936. A massive programme of public works had improved people's everyday lives. In short, Adolf Hitler had restored national pride together with a sense of identity and well-being.

The Nazis' use of potent imagery convinced many that Germany's return to greatness lay in the hands of one man, Adolf Hitler. For the most part Nazi propaganda succeeded in convincing people to place their trust in Hitler; that the journey they were setting out on was one that had to be made together, hand in hand with their Führer. The cult of personality, the unshakable belief in the ability of one man and his vision for his people became a constant, unavoidable presence in peoples' everyday lives.

Unless otherwise stated the following images are all period postcards that have been reproduced in their original black and white format. Finally, it should be pointed out that with regard to the captions, any text appearing in **'bold'** *is a direct translation of the original German caption printed on that particular postcard, whether the caption appears on the front or on the reverse of the image. All captions are numbered to allow cross-referencing with photographers' and publishers' details in the appendix.*

Johann Dietrich Eckart

D ietrich Eckart was born in Neumarkt in der Oberpfalz, a town southeast of Nuremberg in the Upper Palatinate region of Bavaria on 23 March 1868. His father, Georg Christian Eckart, a Protestant, was the royal notary; as a result the Eckart family enjoyed a comfortable lifestyle. When his mother, Anna, died of influenza in 1878 the then ten-year-old Dietrich was devastated. On completing his education Dietrich Eckart moved to Munich where, in 1891, he began studying medicine. He gave up his studies later that same year.

When his father died in 1895 Eckart received a large inheritance. By this time Dietrich Eckart was already a heavy drinker and addicted to morphine. In 1899 he moved to Berlin where he attempted, rather unsuccessfully, to become a dramatist, journalist and poet. However, on 12 December 1904 his first play 'Family Fathers' premiered in the Regensburg City Theatre. Nonetheless his efforts to become a dramatist continued to prove frustrating.

Eckart's fortunes improved dramatically when, in 1910, he invested 5000 Marks in Die Neu Aeroplan-Baugesellschaft, an aircraft factory established by his friend Karl Guido Bomhard and his partner, Josef Sablatnig. This shrewd investment made Eckart a lot of money.

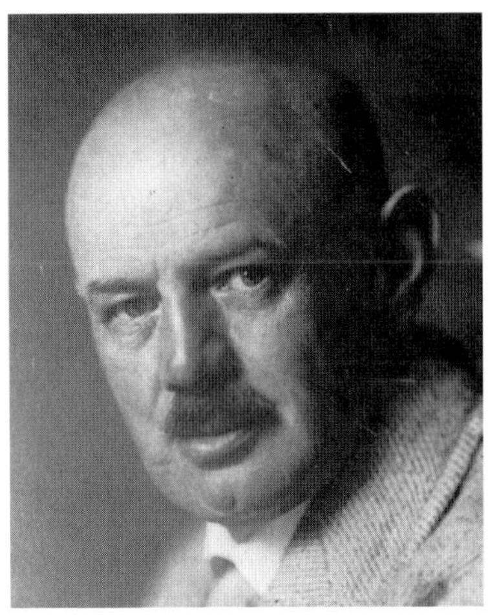

Johann 'Dietrich' Eckart.

Already an anti-Semite, on returning to Munich in 1913 Eckart soon made contact with and joined the Thule Society. In 1914 Eckart finally finished work on his adaptation/translation of Peer Gynt, which premiered, at the express request of Kaiser Wilhelm II on 18 February 1914. On 30 January 1915 Eckart attended the premier of *Heinrich der Hohenstaufe*, a dramatic work he'd written at the request of the Kaiser to celebrate the marriage of his only daughter, Princess Viktoria Luise.

At the end of 1918 Eckart, with the help of funds provided by the Thule Society, established *Auf gut Deutsch* (In Plain German), a weekly newspaper that he edited and published. The paper attacked the Weimar Republic, the Versailles Treaty and portrayed the Jews as responsible for Germany's defeat in the war. It was around this time that Eckart coined the phrase, '*Deutschland Erwache*' (Germany Awake). This phrase would become popular with the emerging *Deutscher Arbeiterpartei* (DAP; German Workers' Party) later the *Nationalsozialistische Deutscher Arbeiterpartei* (NSDAP; National Socialist German Workers' Party), later referred to as the Nazi Party. It was while Hitler was giving his first speech at a meeting of the DAP in August 1919 that Adolf Hitler met Dietrich Eckart. In early August 1921 Eckart became editor-in-chief of the *Völkischer Beobachter* (Nationalist Observer) by that time recognised as the official Nazi Party newspaper.

By 1921 both Eckart and Hitler had apartments on Munich's Thierschstraße. Eckart spoke at the Nazi Party's first major rally, the 'Germany Awake' themed rally held in Munich in January 1923. He accompanied Hitler as the Führer spoke to groups at different venues during the rally. Dietrich Eckart was replaced as editor of the *Völkischer Beobachter* in March 1923. Eckart's appointed successor was Alfred Rosenberg (1893–1945) a Nazi idealist and theorist.

Knowing that he was wanted for questioning by the police and that a warrant had been issued for his arrest regarding insulting comments he'd made about President Friedrich Ebert, Eckart was spirited away to Berchtesgaden and the Obersalzberg by Christian Weber (1883–1945) an early Nazi Party official and later SS-*Brigadeführer* (Major-General). Using the alias Dr Hoffmann, Eckart stayed in Pension Moritz on the Obersalzberg where he successfully evaded the authorities. It was Eckart's presence on the Obersalzberg that brought Hitler to the region for the first time in April 1923. This first visit to the area made a deep impression on Hitler, so much so that his relationship with Berchtesgaden and the Obersalzberg would continue until his death on 20 April 1945.

Eckart was offered accommodation in the Göllhäusl at Hinterbrand above Berchtesgaden by its owner, Baroness Claire von Abegg, a supporter of Hitler. In mid-October 1923 Eckart returned to Munich where, on 15 November he was arrested as he made his way to his office at the *Völkischer Beobachter*. While he was accused of having taken part in the Beer-Hall *Putsch,* Eckart denied any involvement in the *Putsch* of 9 November. Despite his denials Eckart ended up in Landsberg Prison with Hitler and the other Nazi conspirators. However Eckart's health was deteriorating, he had a heart condition, and following a plea for clemency he was released on 20 December 1923.

With his health failing Dietrich Eckart returned to Berchtesgaden and his rented room in the Sonnblickhäus'l on Locksteinstrasse. He died there on 26 December 1923. The funeral, under police guard, took place on 31 December with Eckart being laid to rest in Berchtesgaden's *Alter Friedhof* (Old Cemetery). Some fifty people from Munich, Hallein and Salzburg attended the funeral.

Hitler was determined to honour his old friend and early mentor Dietrich Eckart, the man with whom he'd shared and shaped many of his political and racial ideas. The future Führer and German Chancellor dedicated the second volume of his book *Mein Kampf* (My Struggle) to Eckart. The second volume concludes with the following paragraph where Hitler begins by paying homage to the sixteen Nazi comrades who'd died during the Munich Beer-Hall *Putsch* (Revolt) on 9 November 1923.

Hitler writes:

I have dedicated the first volume of this book to our eighteen fallen heroes. Here at the end of this second volume let me again bring those to the memory of the adherents and champions of our ideals, as heroes who, in the full consciousness of what they were doing, sacrificed their lives for us all. We must never fail to recall those names in order to encourage the weak and wavering among us when duty calls, that duty which they fulfilled with absolute faith, even to its extreme consequences. Together with those, and as one of the best of all, I should like to mention the name of a man who devoted his life to reawakening his and our people, through his writing and his ideas and finally through positive action. I mean: Dietrich Eckart.

In the above excerpt, Hitler refers to 'our eighteen fallen heroes.' Sixteen of these are the comrades who died in Munich while taking part in the Beer-Hall *Putsch* on 9 November 1923, they were:

Allfarth, Felix, Merchant, born 5 July 1901
Bauriedl, Andreas, Hat Maker, born 4 May 1879
Casella, Theodor, Bank Official, born 8 August 1900
Ehrlich, Wilhelm, Bank Official, born 19 August 1894
Faust Martin, Bank Official, born 27 January 1901
Hechenberger, Anton, Locksmith, born 28 September 1902
Körner, Oskar, Merchant, born 4 January 1875
Kuhn, Karl, Head Waiter, born 26 July 1897
Laforce, Karl, Student of Engineering, born 28 October 1904
Neubauer, Kurt, Waiter, born 27 March 1899
Pape, Klaus von, Merchant, born 16 August 1904
Pfordten, Theodor von der, Councillor to the Provincial Court, born 14 May 1873
Rickmers, Johann, retired Cavalry Captain, born 7 May 1881
Scheubner-Richter, Maximilian Erwin von, Engineer, born 9 January 1884
Stransky, Lorenz Ritter von, Dr of Engineering, born 14 March 1899
Wolf, Wilhelm, Merchant, born 19 October 1898

As to the remaining two, one of these is Dietrich Eckart; the other is almost certainly Albert Leo Schlageter (12 August 1894 to 26 May 1923). Schlageter, a Nazi supporter,

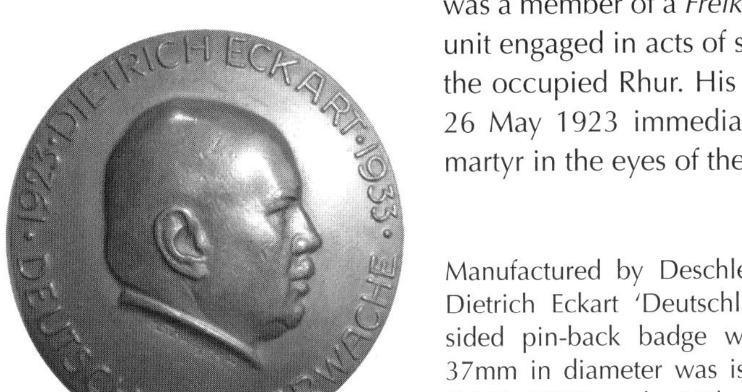

was a member of a *Freikorps* (Free Corps) paramilitary unit engaged in acts of sabotage against the French in the occupied Rhur. His execution by firing squad on 26 May 1923 immediately turned Schlageter into a martyr in the eyes of the Nazis.

Manufactured by Deschler & Söhn, München, this rare Dietrich Eckart 'Deutschland Erwache' die-cast, double-sided pin-back badge with a bronze finish measuring 37mm in diameter was issued in remembrance of Eckart (1868–1923) on the 10th anniversary of his death in 1933. (*Author's collection*)

Photographs of Hotel Post and Hintersee

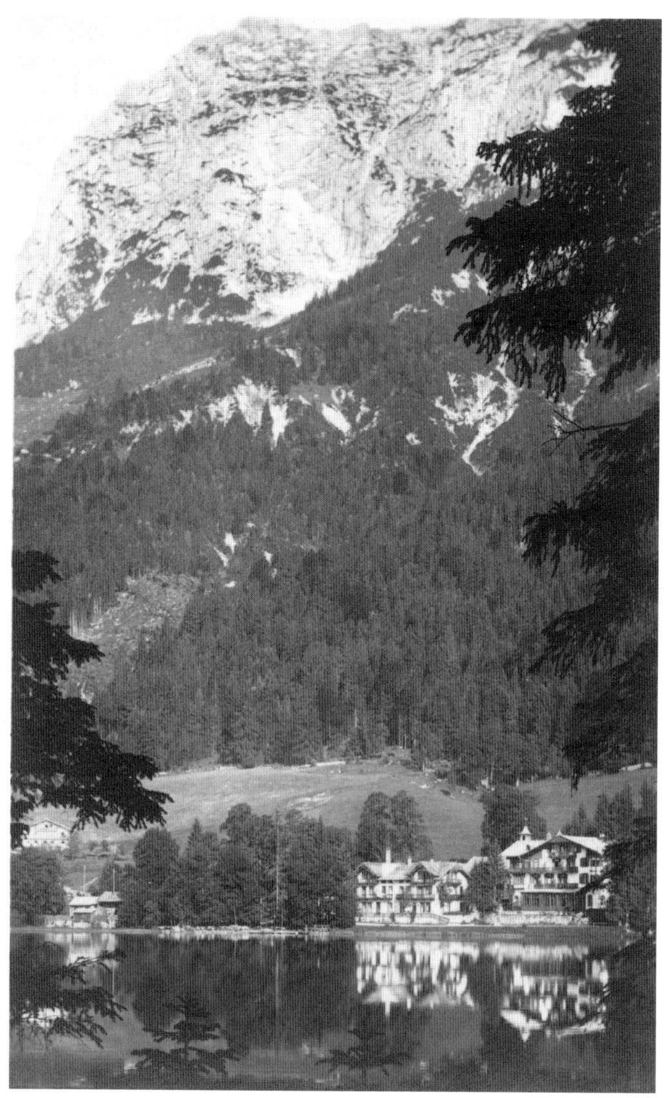

1. Hotel Post and Gemsbock Hintersee near Berchtesgaden.
Elegant summer and winter stay. Owner J. R. Weiss.
Regardless of the season this region certainly offers much in the way of outstanding natural beauty.
Here the rugged and majestic Reiteralpe rise high above the lake.

2. Hintersee, Hotel Post.

Hotel Post with its fabulous lakeside position and a backdrop of rich pastureland and thick Alpine forest. It was in the grounds of Hotel Post that Heinrich Hoffmann, Hitler's personal photographer, took a series of photographs of the Führer in the company of Gerd Bartels and his cousin Anni Weiss in the 1930s.

Looking at the hotel we might think we are looking at two separate buildings, and we would be right in that assumption. Hotel Post stands on the left; the building on the right, while standing very close to Hotel Post was a separate enterprise, this was Hotel Gemsbock.

In the wake of the First World War Germany experienced an unprecedented period of hyperinflation. The value of the German Mark collapsed totally and to a point where it wasn't worth the price of the paper it was printed on. It was during this period, in November 1923, that Gerd's maternal grandfather Isidor Weiss bought the Gemsbock for three bread rolls, yes, three bread rolls! The two buildings were then connected to create an enlarged Hotel Post.

Hintersee is an area of outstanding natural beauty and sits on the edge of the Berchtesgaden National Park. The National Park was established in 1978.

This postcard was sent to an address in Passau on 3 August 1949. Passau is a town approximately 160 km (98 miles) northeast of Hintersee.

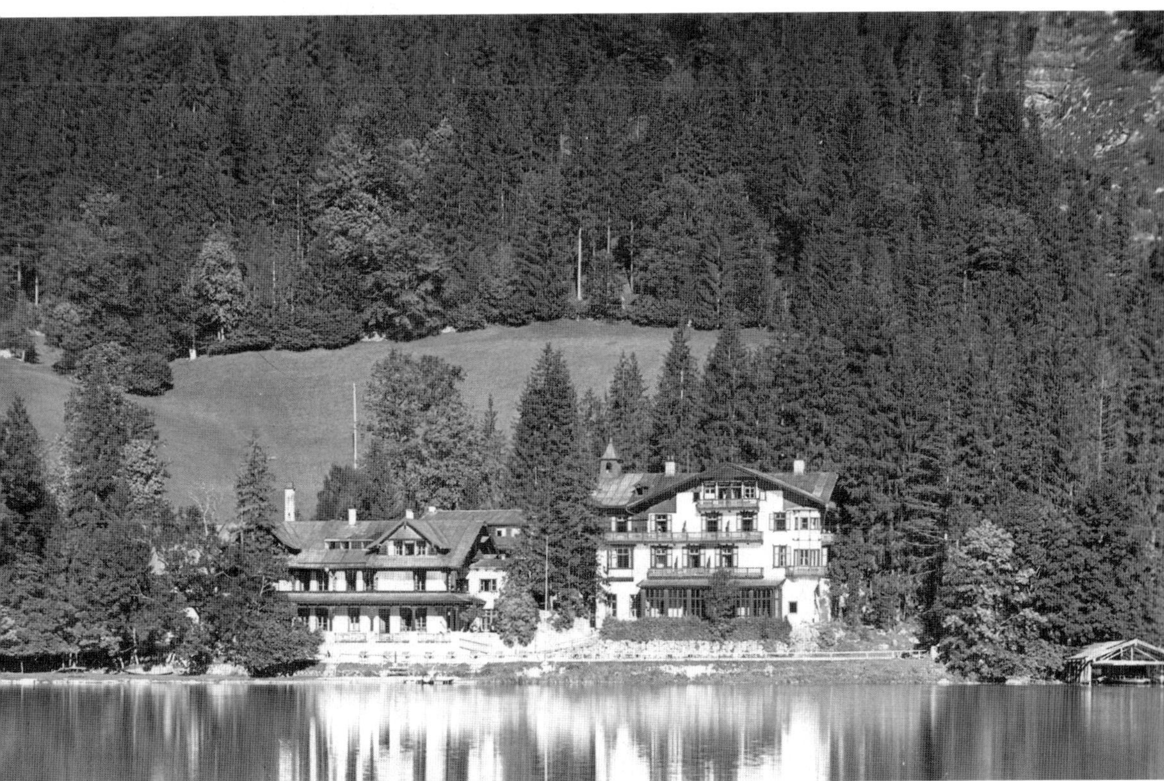

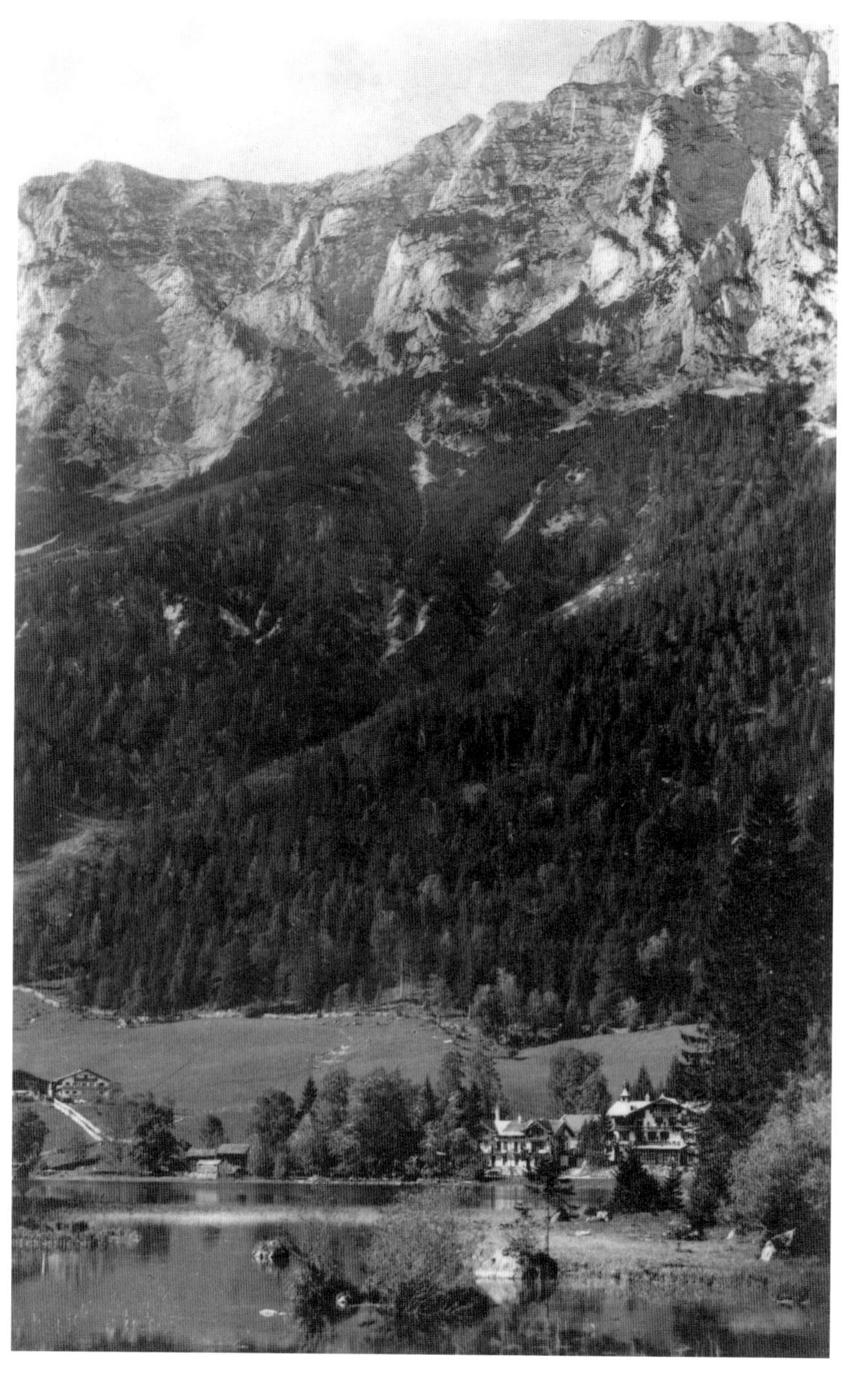

3. Berchtesgaden, Hintersee, 800m.
Hotel Post and Gemsbock with Reiteraple.
The imposing Reiteralpe provide the magnificent backdrop in this particular image.

24

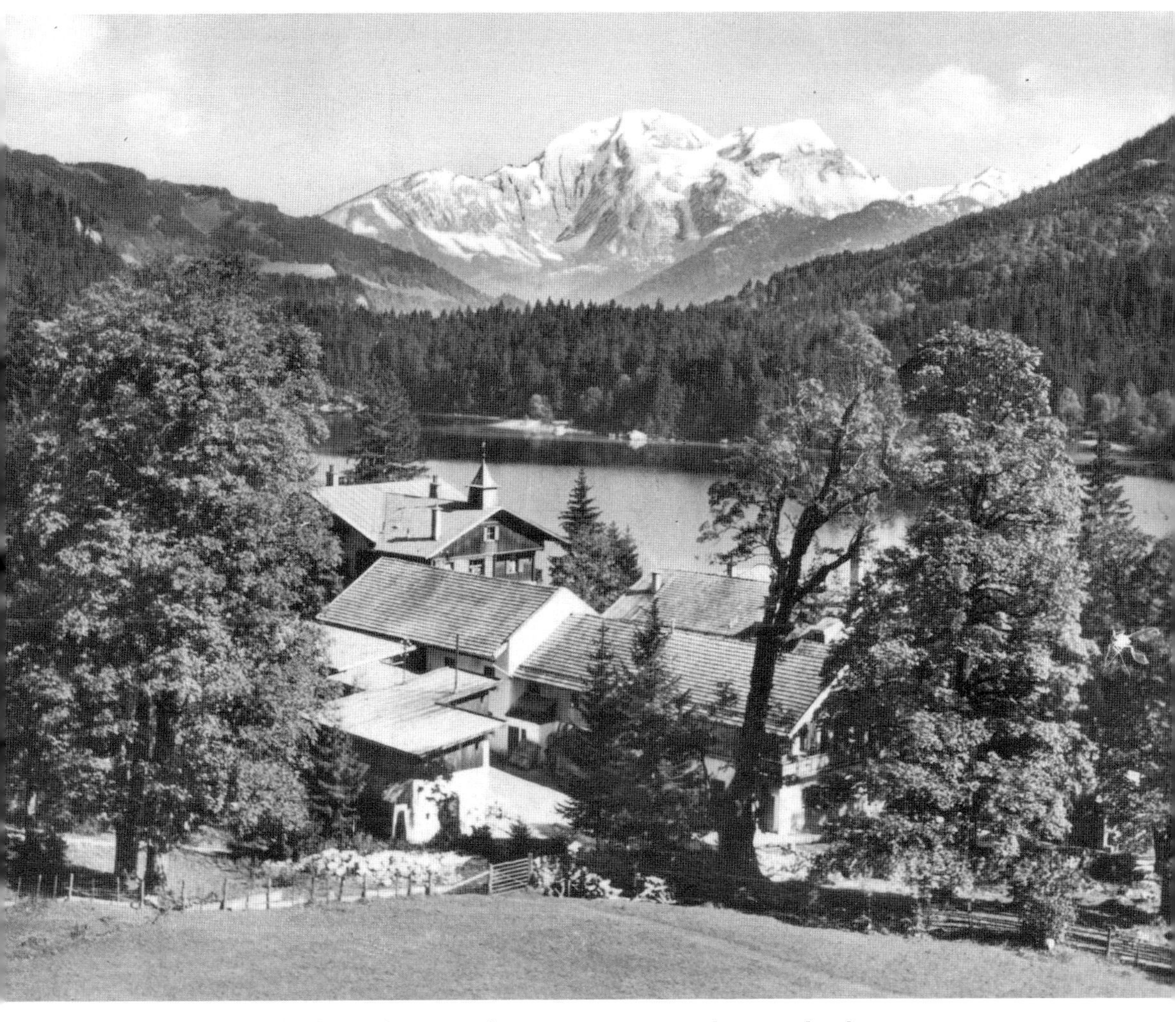

4. Berchtesgadener Land. Hotel Post at Hintersee. 800 metres above sea level.
Photographed from a point a little way up the hillside behind Hotel Post and looking northwest across the lake towards the nearby village of Ramsau with the Göll and Brett in the background.

We walked across the frozen Hintersee when we stayed with the Bartels family at Alpenhof for Christmas 2007. That Christmas Eve my wife and I accompanied Gerd when he went to visit the graves of his parents in the churchyard in nearby Ramsau.

Gerd went to light the candles on the Christmas tree that was already in place on the plot. I found this a moving experience and felt honoured to have been invited to join him on something so personal.

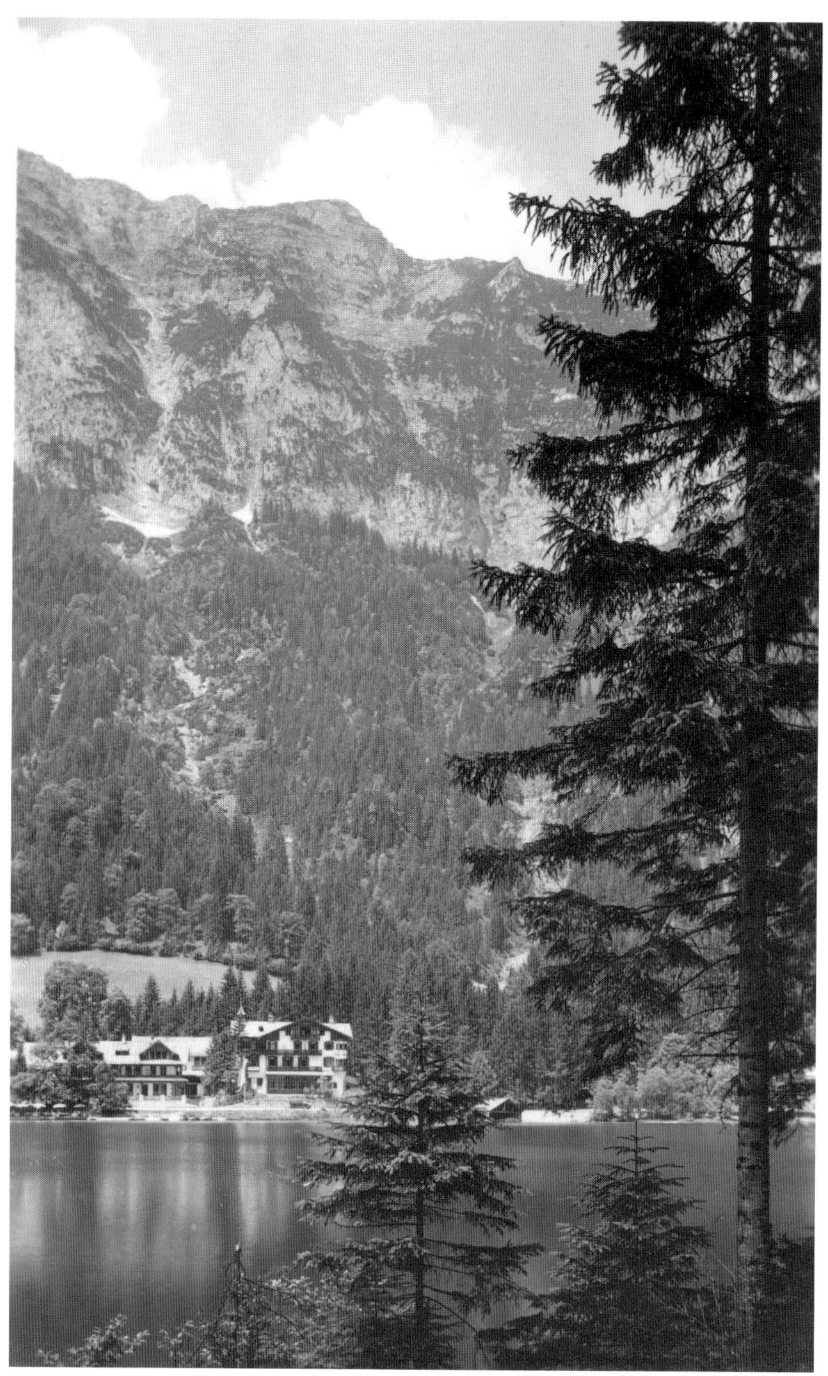

5. Hintersee Hotel Post.
Looking back across the lake towards the southwest and Hotel Post. While not actually posted, this postcard bears the handwritten date of 15 October 1930 on the reverse.

6. Hotel Post, Berchtesgaden-Hintersee. (800m above sea level). Tel. Ramsau 40.
The dining-room with a view of Hintersee, Hohen Göll and Brett.
Period photographs showing the interior of Hotel Post are rare. This postcard shows the dining room in Hotel Post as Adolf Hitler would have known it during the 1930s and it was here that Hitler occasionally dined during his visits to Hintersee. The large windows afforded wonderful views across the lake and to the mountains beyond.

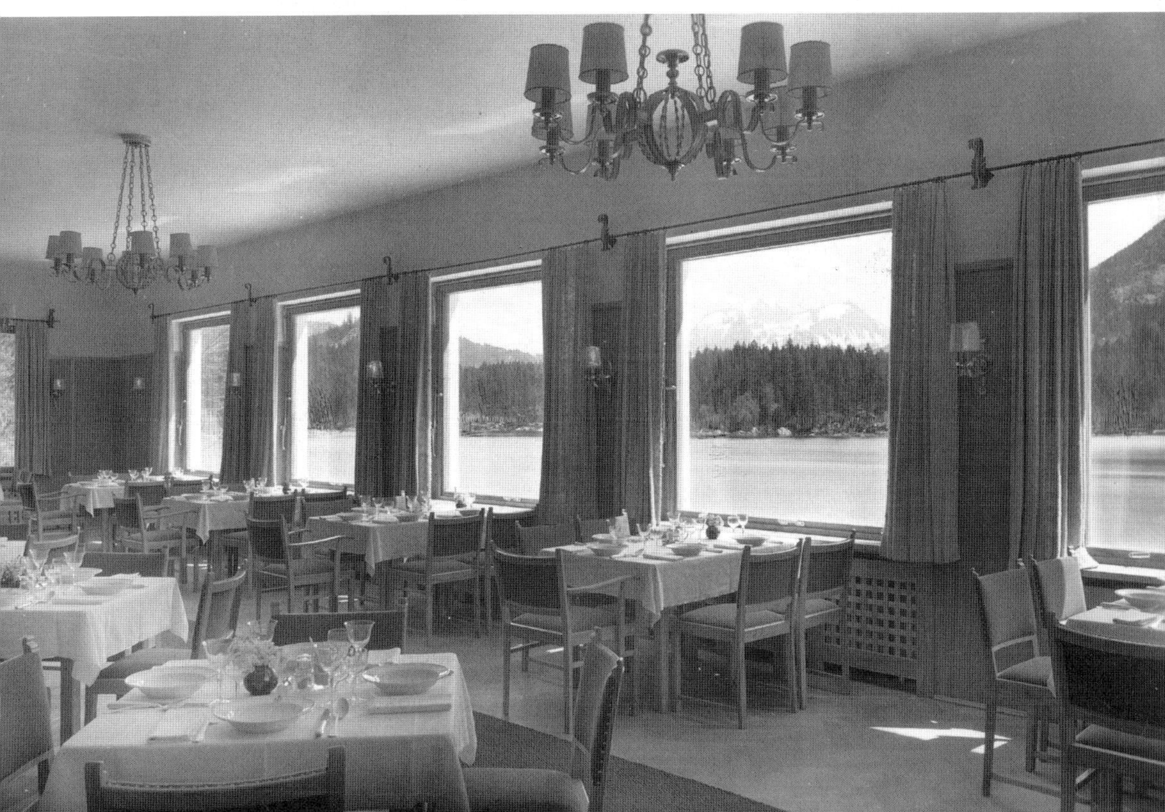

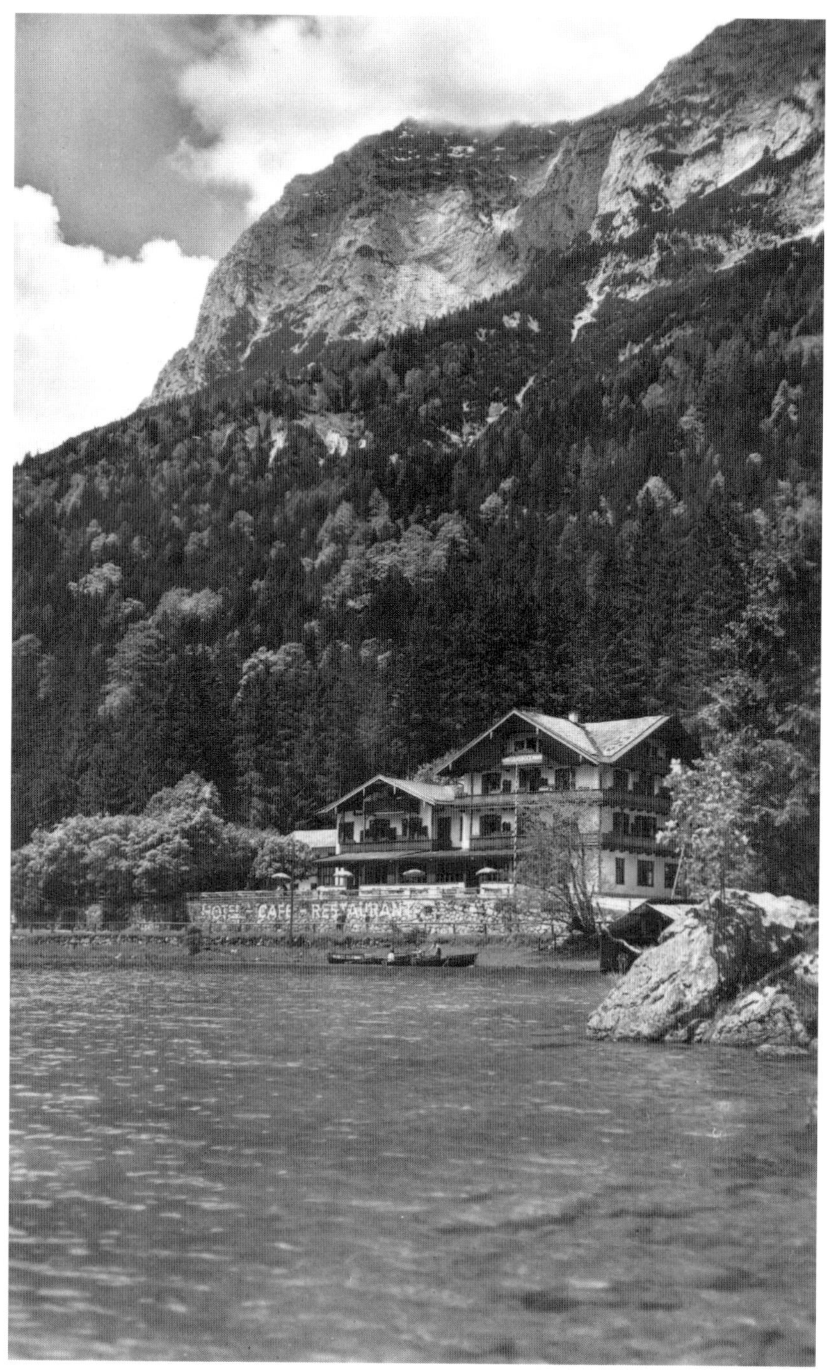

7. Hotel Gemsbock at the Hintersee.
A handwritten date on the reverse reads: 25.09.1940. Just two days later, on 27 September 1940 the 'Tripartite Pack', a military alliance between Germany, Italy and Japan was signed in Berlin.

8. Hotel Post at the Hintersee near Berchtesgaden.
A fine view of Hotel Post photographed from the lake. On looking at postcard number 21 on page 43 showing Hitler, his sister Paula and Hermann Göring on a visit to Hintersee, it is in the area on the left hand side in this photograph where they are observed walking.

Here we can see the wall by the roadside with the pillars that support the wooden railings, this wall and these railings are also present in image number 21. This postcard bears a Hintersee-Berchtesgaden postmark and a date of 25 May 1928. It was sent to an address in Lichterfelde in southwest Berlin.

Interestingly, the old Prussian military cadet training school, the Lichterfelde Kaserne at Lichterfelde West was taken over by the Nazis in 1933 to become the training school then later the headquarters of Hitler's personal bodyguard regiment the Leibstandarte-SS 'Adolf Hitler' (also known as the LSSAH).

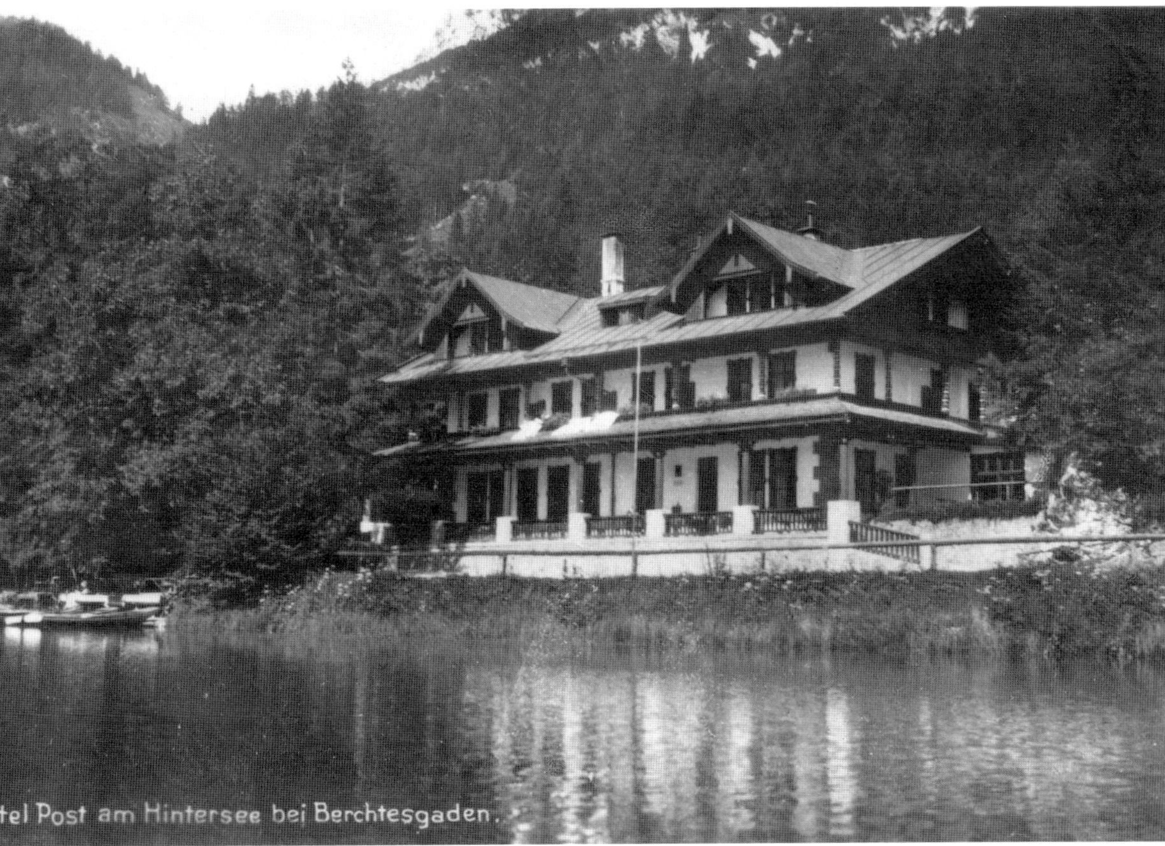

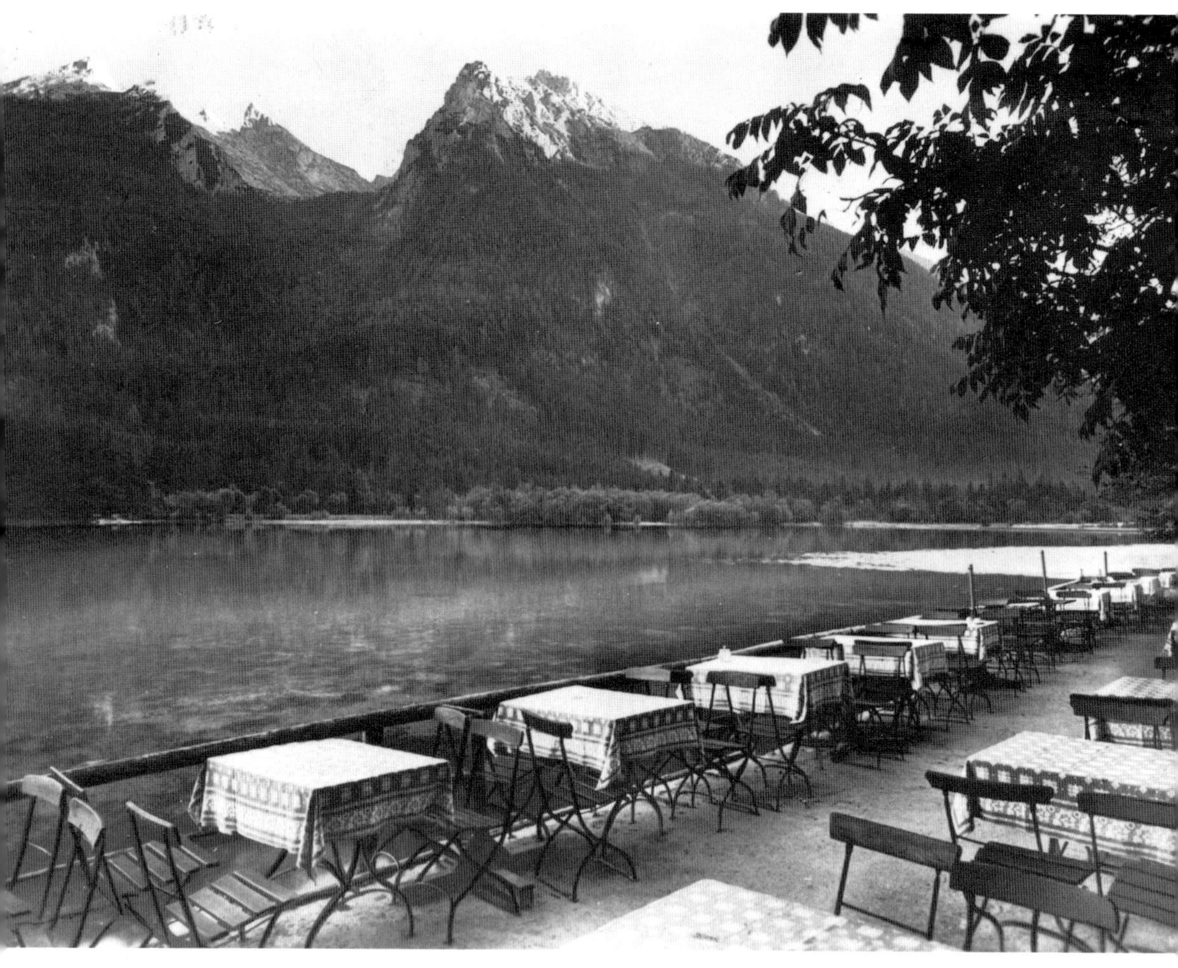

9. Hotel Post Hintersee (Terrace).
Reverse reads: **Hintersee 'Hotel Post' 800 metres above sea level.**
With views across the lake towards the Hochkalter standing at 2607 metres (8553 feet) this period postcard shows the terrace in front of Hotel Post. This is how the terrace would have appeared to Adolf Hitler on his visits during the summer months. Given the harsh winters experienced in the area the terrace would have been clear of tables and chairs through the winter months.

Bearing a Hintersee-Berchtesgaden postmark dated 3 June 1935 this postcard made it way to an address in Schwangau, a small town in the Allgäu region southwest of Munich and close to the Austrian border.

10. Hintersee with Hohen Göll 2519m and the Ramsau Valley.
Reverse reads: **Hintersee 'Hotel Post' 800m above sea level.**
This photograph has been taken from a position high up on the Reiteralpe behind the hotel. The photographer, having put in some considerable effort, has been rewarded with a beautiful shot of the lake looking towards Ramsau. The impressive Hohen Göll can be seen in the background.

Today Hintersee is a popular destination with tourists visiting the Berchtesgaden area. Back in the nineteenth century, a time when Hintersee would have been considered a fairly remote place, it was a favourite destination for many artists who came to capture the natural beauty of the area on canvas.

There's a public car park close to Alpenhof that leads to a delightful pathway, this path follows the shoreline around the lake. Information boards placed at specific points along the path provide background information on these aforementioned artists and shows examples of the work they produced having set up their easels and painting at the same spot.

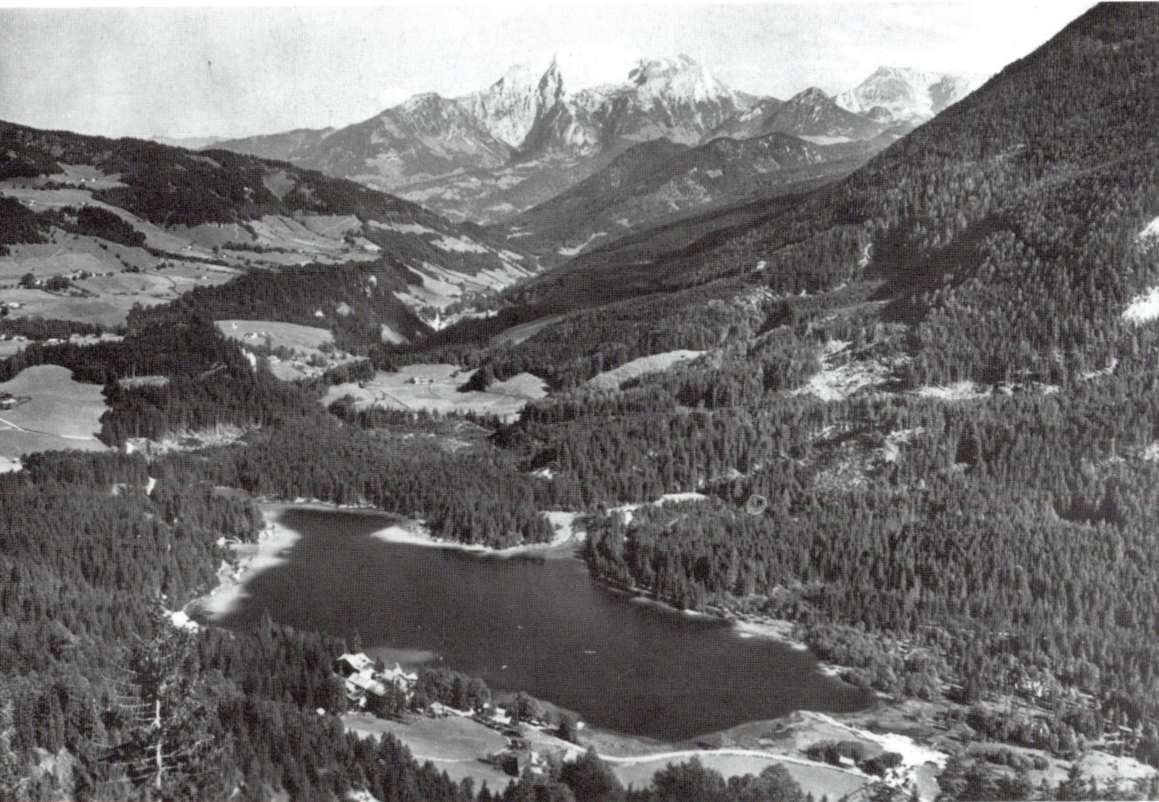

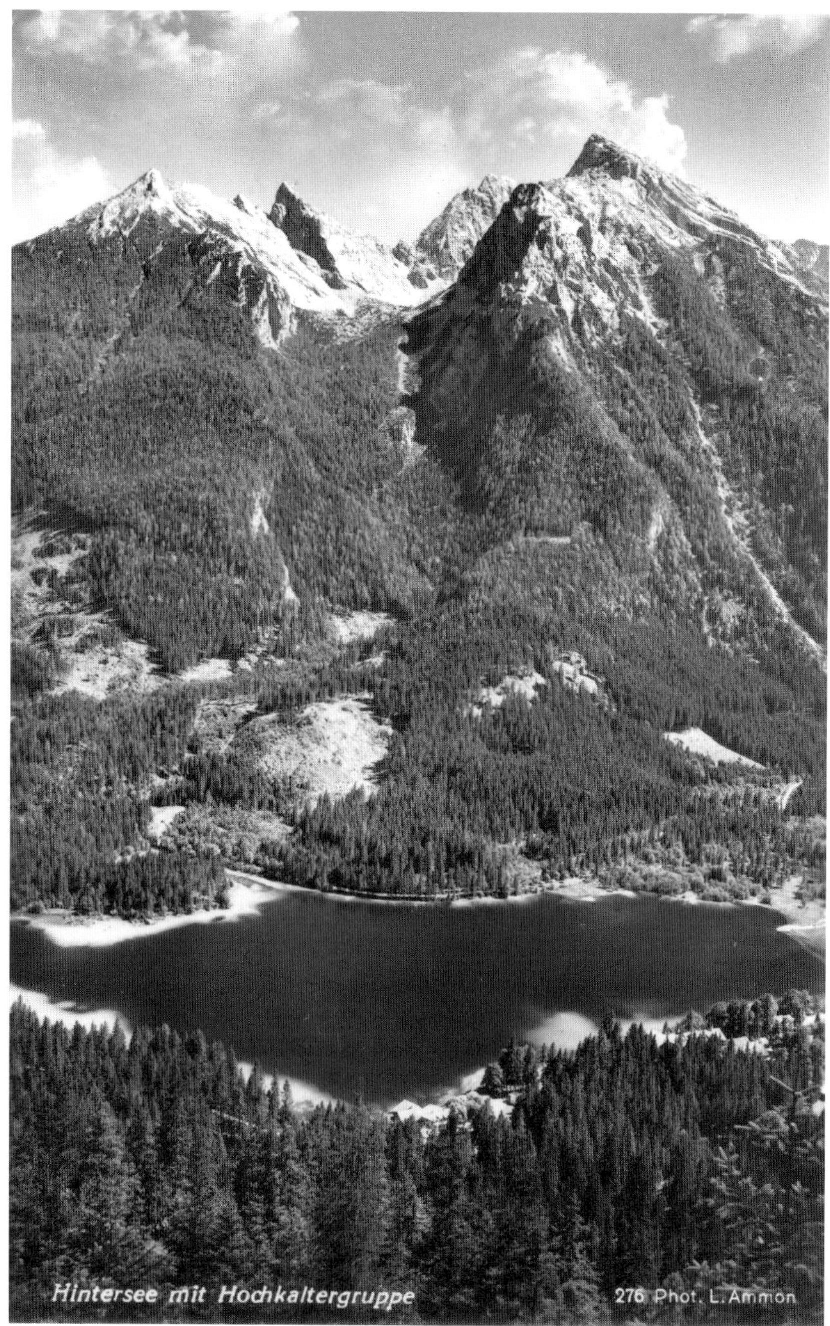

11. Hintersee with the Hochkalter group.
This postcard shows Hotel Post right on the edge of the lake in the lower foreground. Here the magnificent Hochkalter provides the impressive backdrop. A small number of former SS soldiers were still hiding out on the Hochkalter in June 1945.

12. Hintersee Hotel Post (800 metres above sea level) Tel. Ramsau 40.
Large lakeside terrace / Cosy residence / 70 beds / Central heating / Hot and cold water / Garages / Parking lot.
A resort adapted to summer and winter sports.
Given that the caption begins with the words, 'Hintersee Hotel Post' we could be forgiven for asking where the hotel is to be found in this photograph. In fact the hotel cannot be seen. The photographer is looking in the direction of Hintersee and Hotel Post from a point on the Deutsche Alpenstraße and close to the Taubensee, a long way from the hotel.

The mountain range we see is the Rieteralpe. The Hintersee, barely visible, sits between the tree in the centre of the image and the tree to the left. The lake appears as a small strip of white in an almost central position between these trees. Despite the somewhat inaccurate caption this photograph certainly delivers on beautiful scenery.

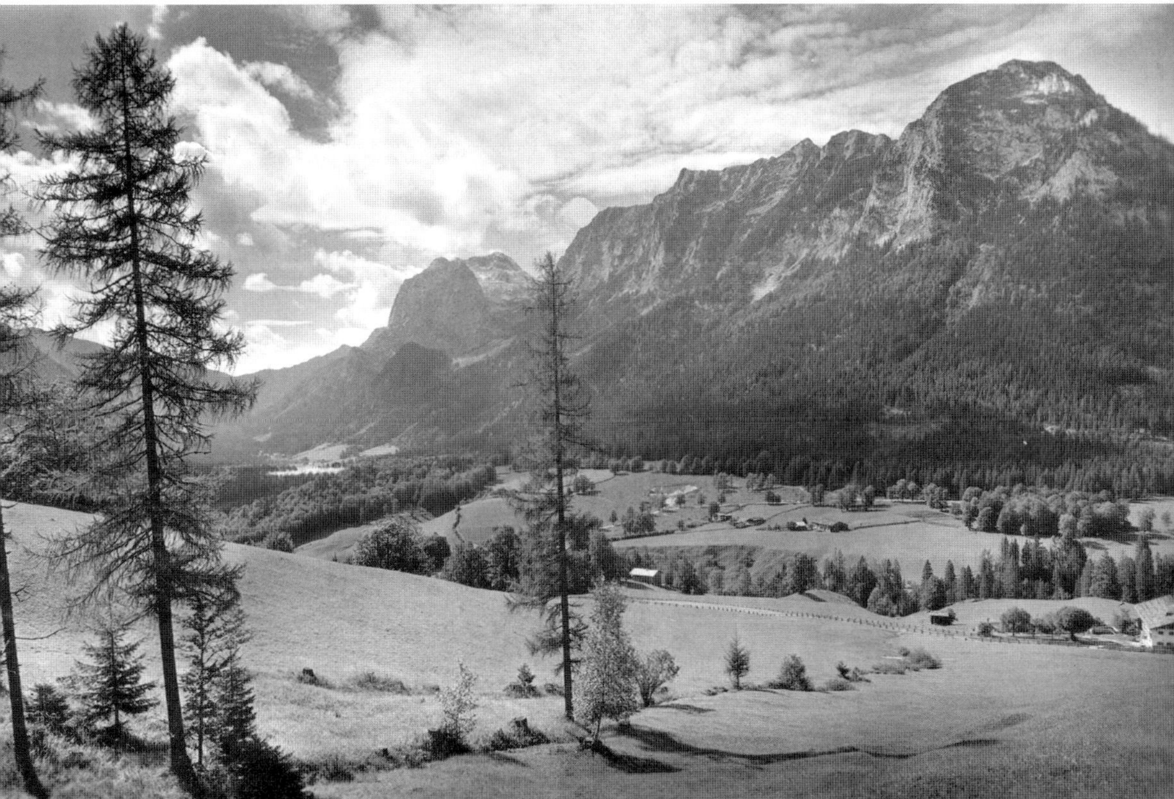

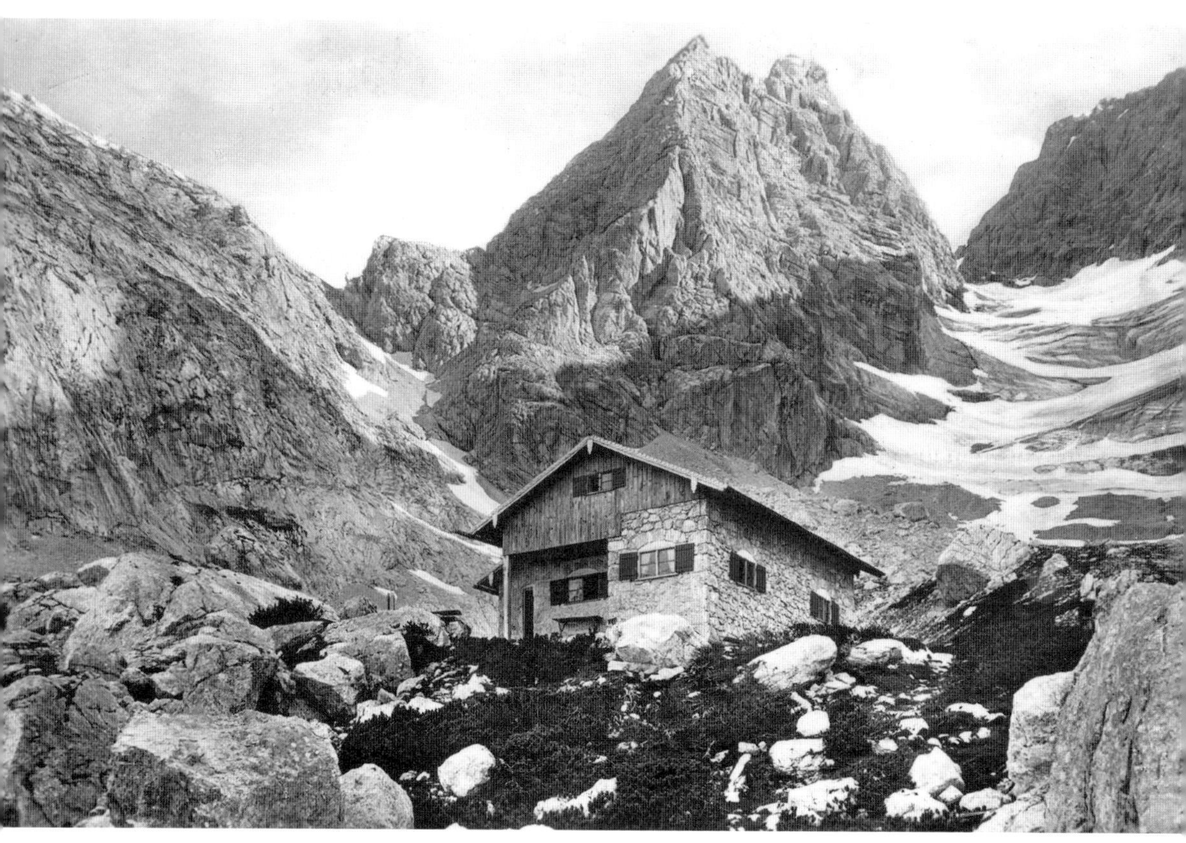

13. Blaueishütte 1756m on the Hochkalter.

This, the original Blaueishütte was located high on the Hochkalter opposite Alpenhof. Gerd Bartels remembers making his way to the Blaueishütte at the end of the Second World War and finding food supplies in the building. In 1955 an avalanche on the Hochkalter completely destroyed the building seen here. Rising to a height of 2607 metres (8553 feet) the Hochkalter are amongst the highest peaks in the Berchtesgaden Alps.

The reverse of this particular postcard bears a large hand-applied rubber stamp reading: *Blaueishütte 1750m Sektion Hochland Deutsch- u. Oesterr. Alpen-Verein* (Blaueishütte 1750m Highland Section German and Austrian Alpine Club). It was posted on 15 October 1934 to an address in Oberpfaltz, a city situated southeast of Nuremberg.

34

Hotel Post — Guest Book

The guest book from Hotel Post reads like a 'who's who' of the Nazi leadership. The following information is taken from copies of pages of the guest book given to me by Gerd Bartels. Through the early part of the twentieth century visitors included Princes, Princesses, Dukes, Duchesses, Counts, Countesses, Prime Ministers and Diplomats.

As this book focuses chiefly on the Third Reich period I have selected only those prominent personalities associated with the regime and whose names appear as they were written in the guest book. The names have been placed in alphabetical order.

We should remember that the hotel may have received other high-ranking Nazi figures and that these individuals simply neglected to sign the visitor's book.

August Wilhelm, Prinz von Preußen

Böhme, SA-Sturmbannführer, Generalmajor

Brückner Wilhelm, Adjutant des Führers

Forst, Generalleutnant

Giesler Paul, Gauleiter

Goebbels Dr.

Göring Hermann

Heß Rudolf, Stellvertreter des Führers

Hitler Adolf

Hoffmann, Fotograf Hitlers

Krahmer, Generalleutnant

Lammers, Staatssekretär als Reichsminister

Lutze Victor, SA-Führer

Mackensen von, Generalfeldmarschall

Meissner, Staatssekretär, Chef der Reichskanzlei

Schacht Hjalmar

Selte Franz, Stahlhelmführer

Sonnemann Emmy, Schauspielerin (Frau Göring)

Todt Fritz, Reichsbauminister

Wagner Adolf, Gauleiter

Wilhelm Karl. kgl. Preuß. Generalleutnant

The Führer at Hintersee

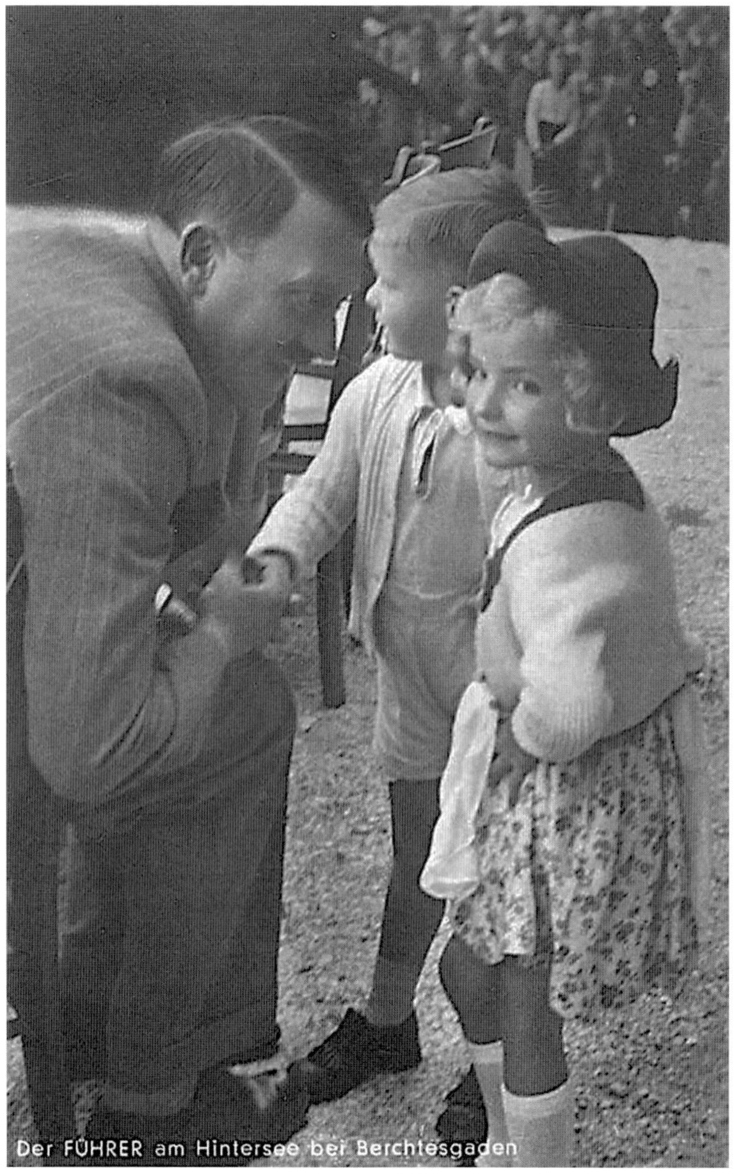

14. The Führer at Hintersee near Berchtesgaden.
This is one of the first and earliest postcard images showing little Gerd Bartels and his cousin Anni Weiss with Hitler. The location is close to Hotel Post. The large crowd of people observed in the upper right background are held back while the photograph is taken.

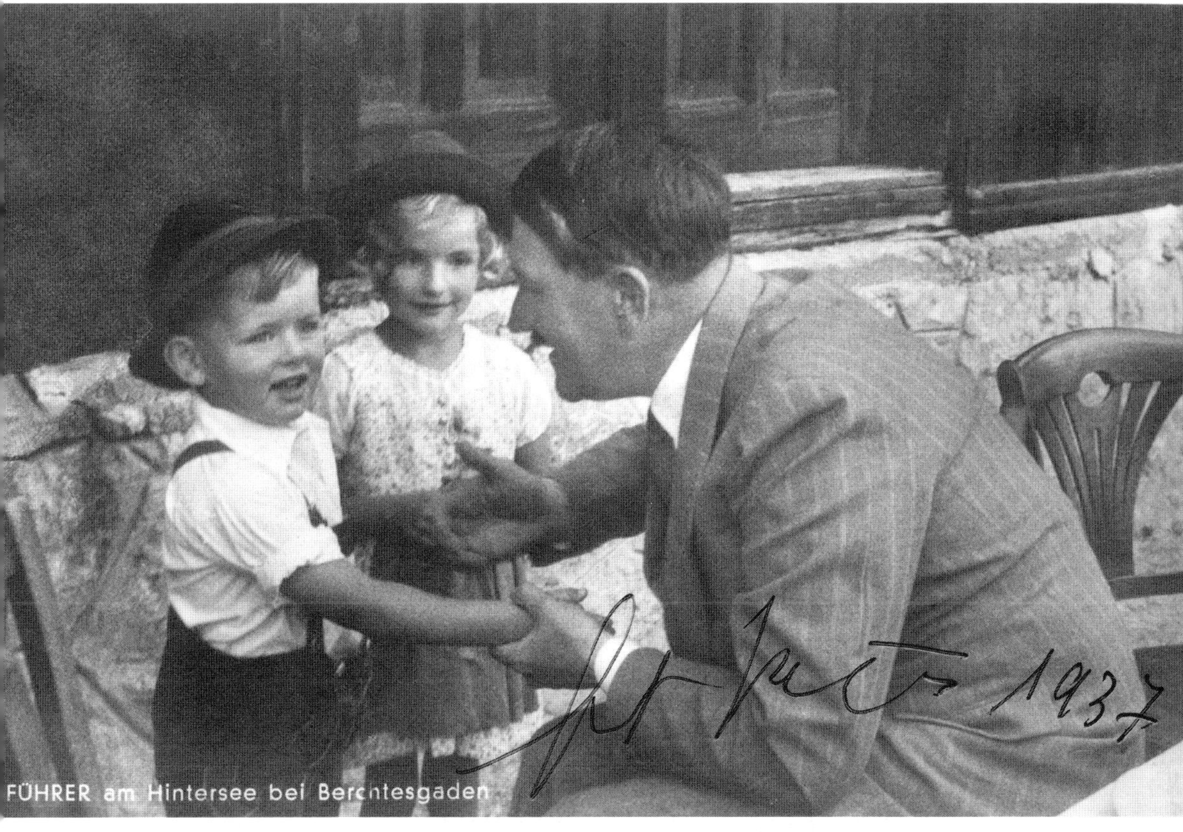

15. The Führer at Hintersee near Berchtesgaden.

Adolf Hitler pictured with Gerd Bartels and his cousin Anni Weiss during one of the Führer's visits to Hintersee. Heinrich Hoffman, Hitler's personal photographer certainly knew what it took to create a great propaganda photograph.

Numerous images of Hitler interacting with children were produced and circulated in postcard form to show how at ease the Führer was in the company of young people. Photographs such as these helped spread the idea that the Nazi Party was a party of family values.

Gerd told me how he came to know when these photographic sessions with Hitler were happening. On the morning in question he was subjected to a more thorough washing regime than was usual, or, as he got older, he was told he must wash properly. He was dressed in his best clothes and told he must remain clean. This meant no playing with the other children where he might get himself dirty. That was something he didn't like.

It was Hitler's connection with his former sergeant and Anni's father, Dori Weiss that brought the Führer to Hintersee. During these visits Hitler would meet Gerd's grandmother Rosina Weiss for coffee, on some of these occasions he dined in Hotel Post. Gerd Bartels has signed this postcard and written the year 1937, this being the year that this particular photograph was taken.

16. Our Führer with General Inspector Dr Todt at Hotel Post at Hintersee.

This superb Hoffmann image sees little Gerd Bartels and his cousin Anni Weiss pictured with Adolf Hitler and Dr Fritz Todt (extreme left) then Inspector General of the German Road and Highway System. As we know Dr Todt had a home at Hintersee. Todt had served through the First World War, first as an infantryman, then later as a flying observer. He joined the fledgling Nazi Party in January 1922. Fritz Todt would oversee the planning and construction of the German Autobahn system, the world's first motorway system. As head of Organization Todt he constructed the 'West Wall' defences along Germany's western border, then later, following the fall of France in 1940, his huge army of engineers and construction workers began the job of constructing the 'Atlantic Wall', an almost endless system of bunkers and gun emplacements along the French coast overlooking the English Channel.

Later as Reich Minister for Armament and Munitions, Fritz Todt proved himself able and very efficient. Todt and Hitler were on very friendly terms and got along well together. Fritz Todt was killed in an air accident on 8 February 1942 when the Heinkel He-111 he was travelling in crashed soon after leaving Hitler's eastern headquarters the *Wolfsschanze* (Wolf's Lair) near Rastenburg in East Prussia. Hitler gave the eulogy at his friend Fritz Todt's funeral on 12 February 1942. Todt was given a funeral with full military honours and was the first to receive the then newly created *Deutscher Orden der NSDAP* (German Order of the Nazi Party). This was the highest honour that could be bestowed on an individual for having performed the most important duties for state or party. Fritz Todt held the rank of General in the SA, the SS and the Luftwaffe. His grave can be found in Berlin's Invalidenfriedhof.

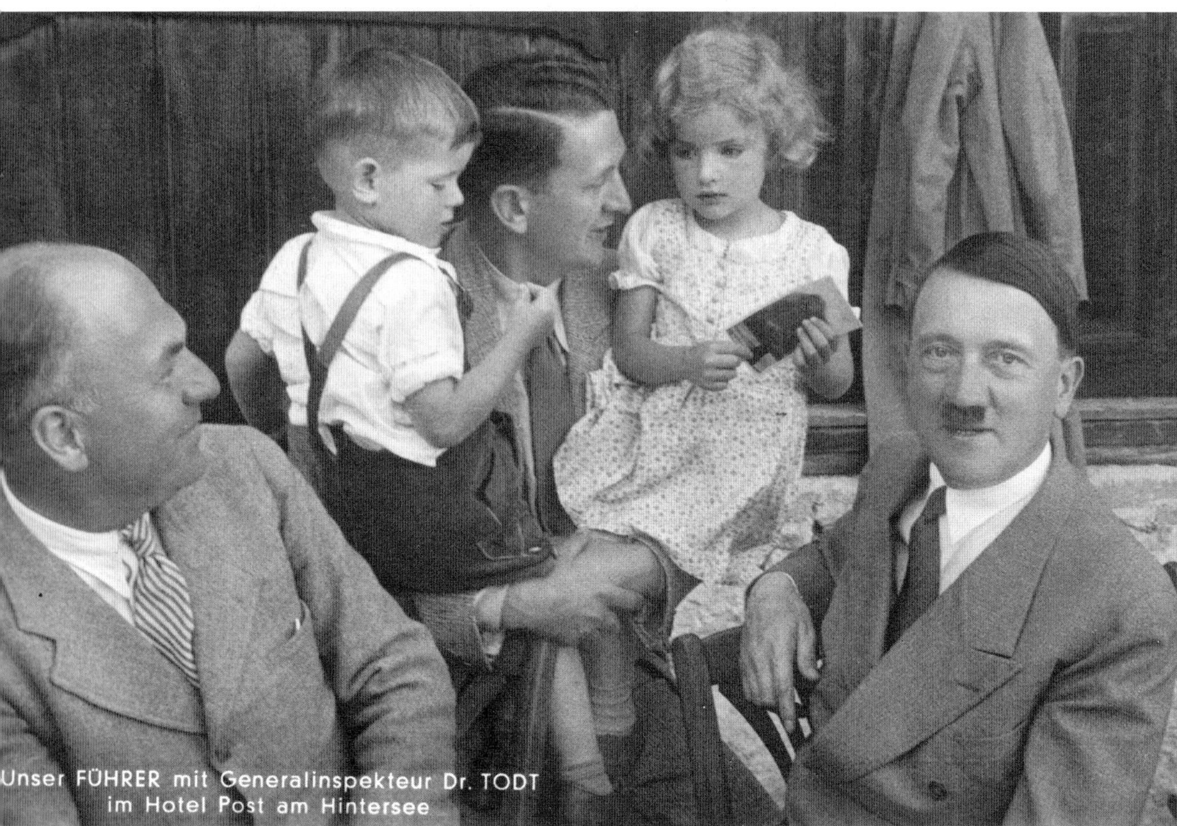

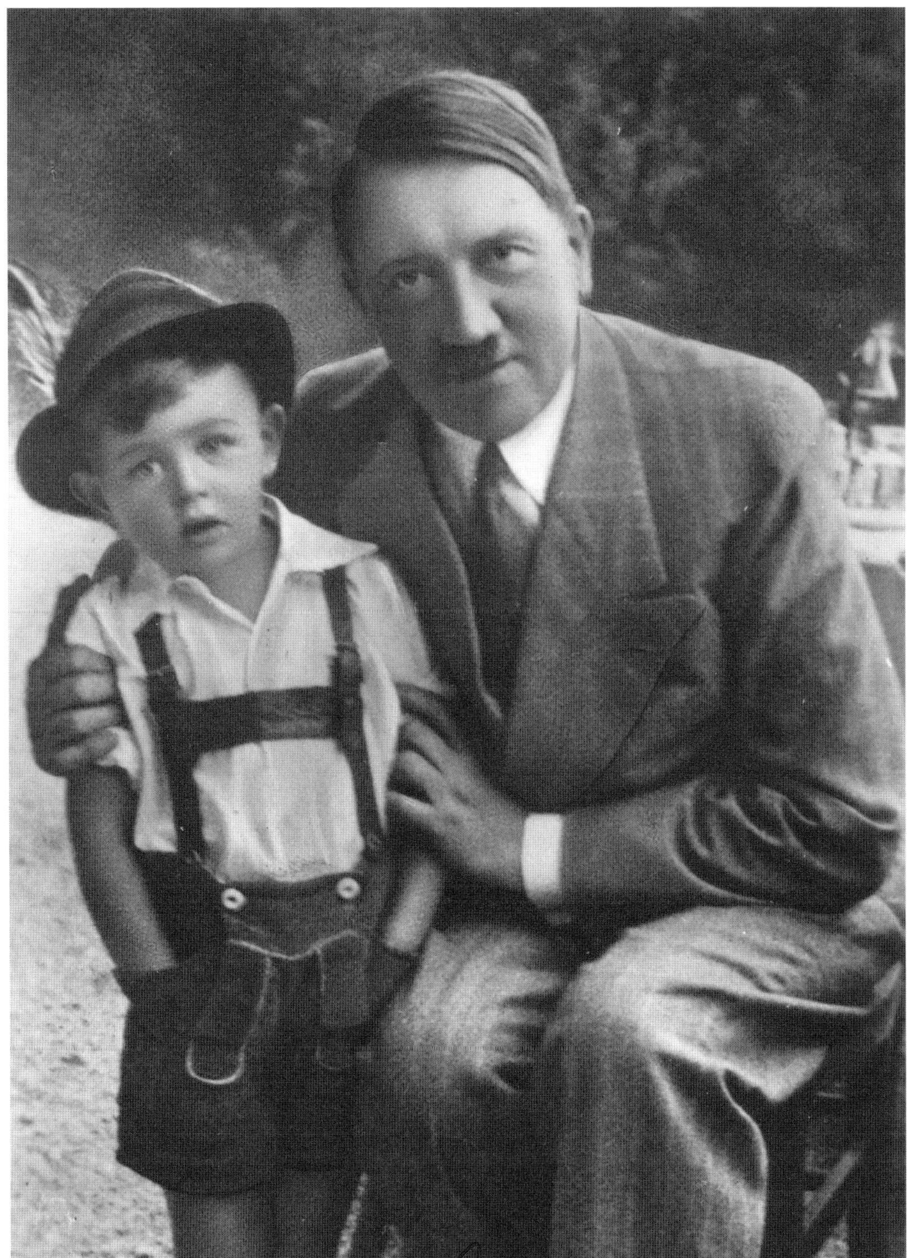

17. Uncaptioned.
This is undoubtedly the most commonly encountered and best-known image showing Gerd Bartels with Adolf Hitler. While little Gerd appears to be drawing away from Hitler there is a simple enough explanation: just out of view on the left was a table laden with cakes and pastries that Gerd's playmates were already enjoying. With his attention focused on the table and feeling left out Gerd was becoming impatient, all he wanted was to get stuck in before all the goodies disappeared.

18. The Führer at Hintersee near Berchtesgaden.
Yet another image portraying the Führer as a warm and caring father figure. As time passed many of the youth of Germany came to see Hitler as a kind of father figure. Many of these young people would join the *Hitlerjugend* (HJ; Hitler Youth, the male branch of the German youth movement) and the *Bund Deutscher Mädel* (BDM; League of German Girls, the female branch of the German youth movement) as they pledged their allegiance to the Führer and the Party.

Gerd Bartels still remembers how during one of these photographic sessions Hitler asked, 'So, what kind of cake do you like to eat?' Gerd replied 'Apple cake!' perhaps thinking a piece of apple cake was on its way. Sadly for little Gerd the cake never arrived.

As an adult Anni Weiss, Gerd's cousin, seen here, suffered from heart problems. She died in February 1981; she was just fifty years old. Anni is buried in Hamm on the outskirts of Dusseldorf.

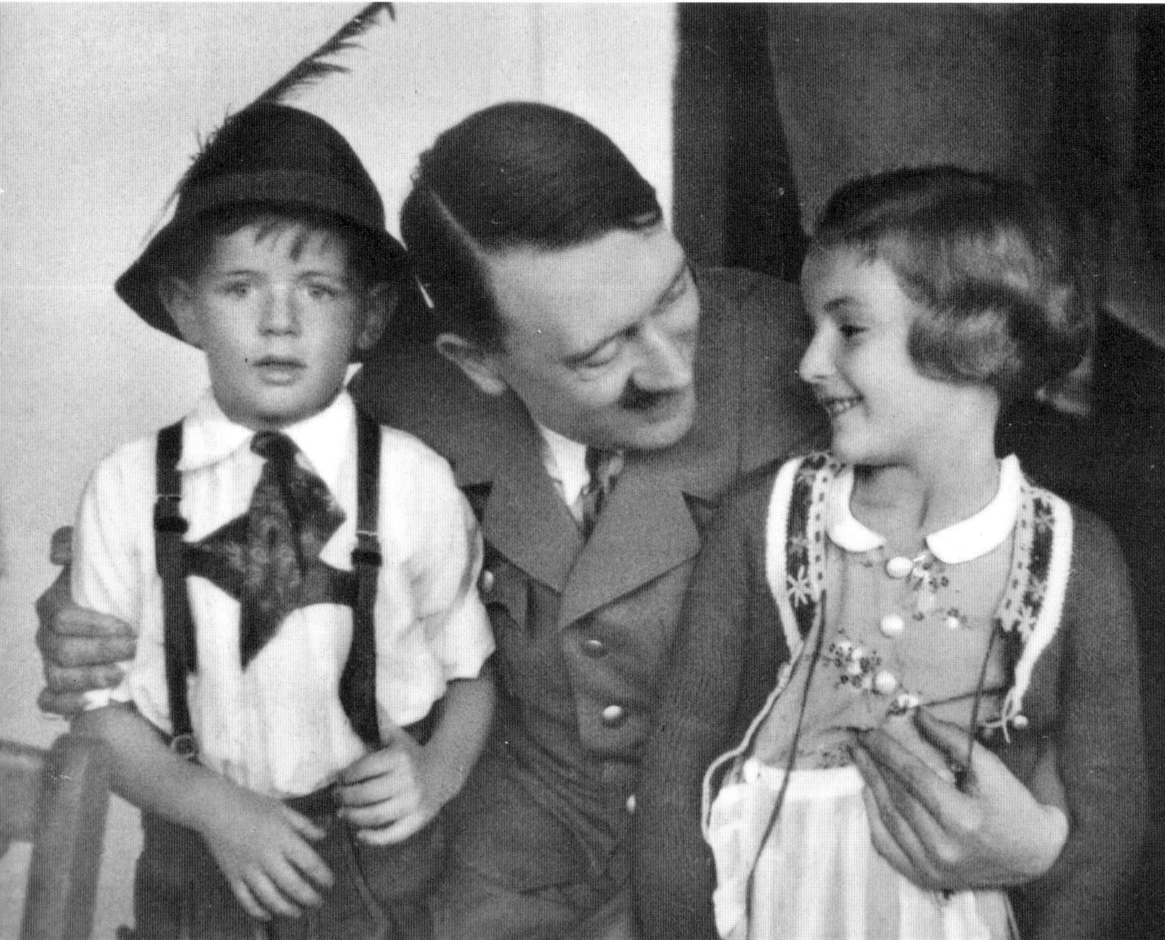

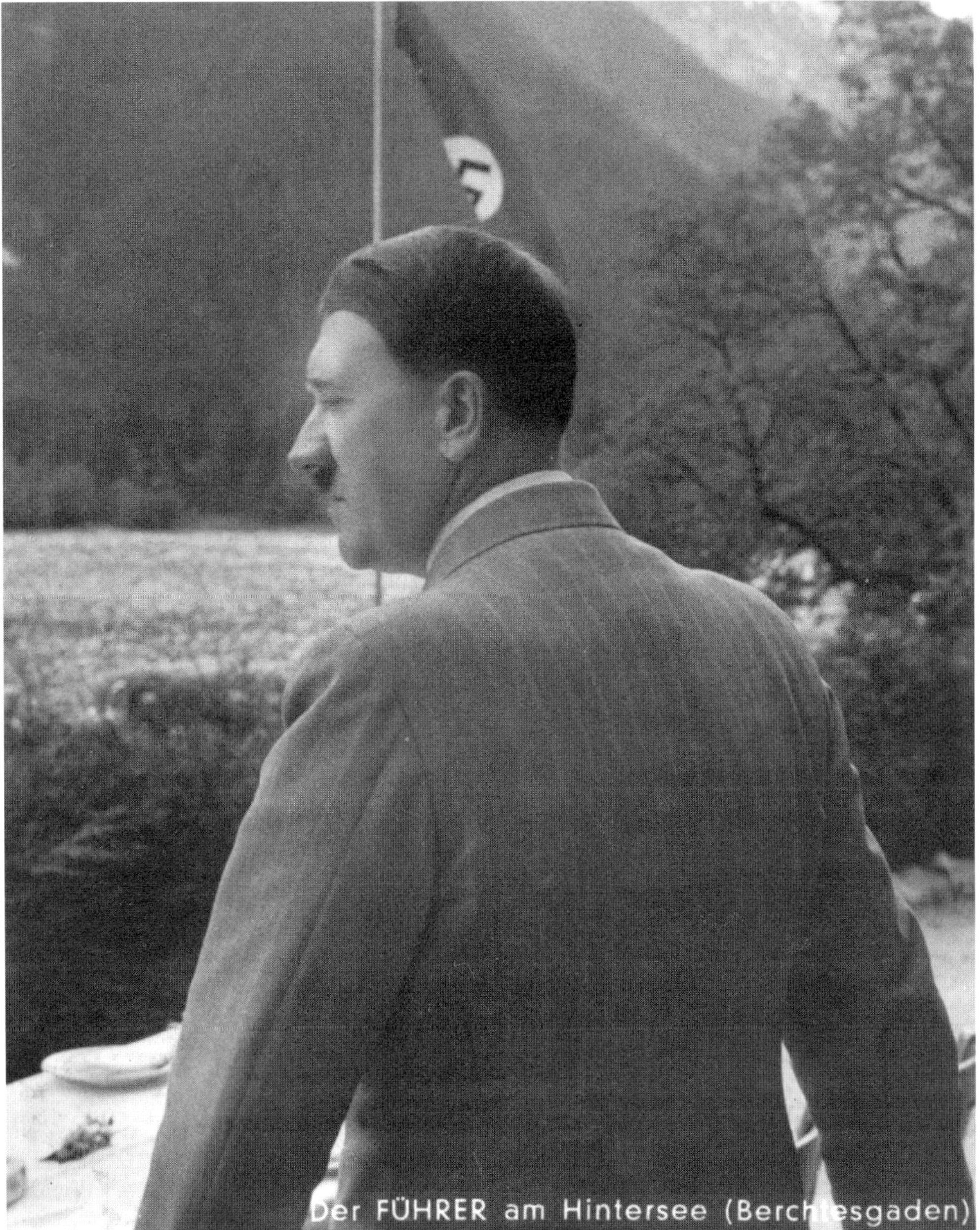

19. The Führer at Hintersee (Berchtesgaden).
Hitler, standing in front of the Seeklause, a restaurant located just along the road from Hotel Post, gazes out across the lake. The tables we see, located just a few metres from the water's edge, allowed uninterrupted views towards the imposing Hochkalter on the opposite side.

Posted in Berchtesgaden on 7 April 1936 this postcard made its way to an address in Munich, the 'spiritual capital' of the Nazi movement.

20. German youth greet the Führer.

Again the location for this photograph is Hotel Post at Hintersee. While Hitler engages the smallest of these four boys the other three lads patiently await their turn to speak with the Führer. It's difficult to describe the expressions on the faces of the three older boys; but in that moment it appears a mixture of awe, anticipation, and a respect bordering on worship. Images such as these had the desired affect on German youth, encouraging them to join the various youth movements.

The use of subtle and cleverly targeted propaganda would have the desired effect on the youth of Germany. Millions of young people, both male and female, became convinced and truly believed that Hitler was indeed their spiritual father.

Given that this photograph was taken in the mid 1930s it is entirely possible that the older boys pictured here went on to join the Wehrmacht and fight during the Second World War.

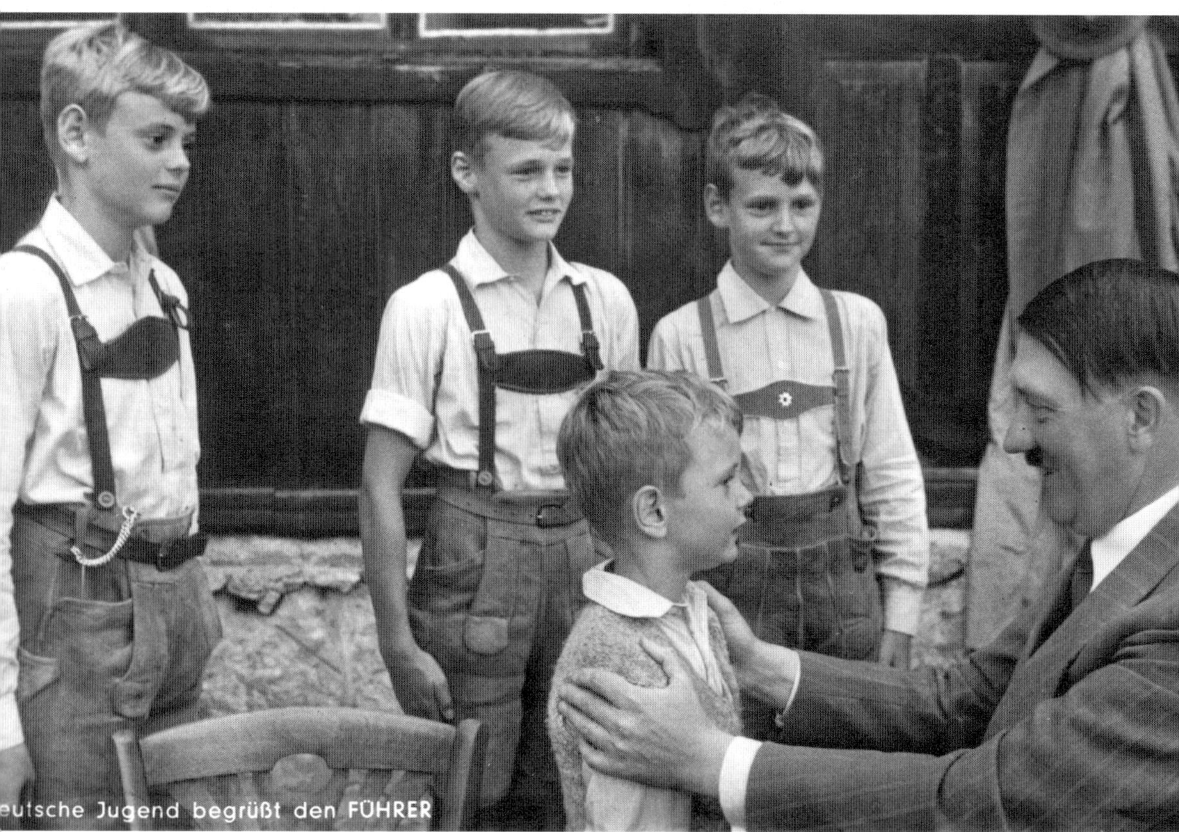

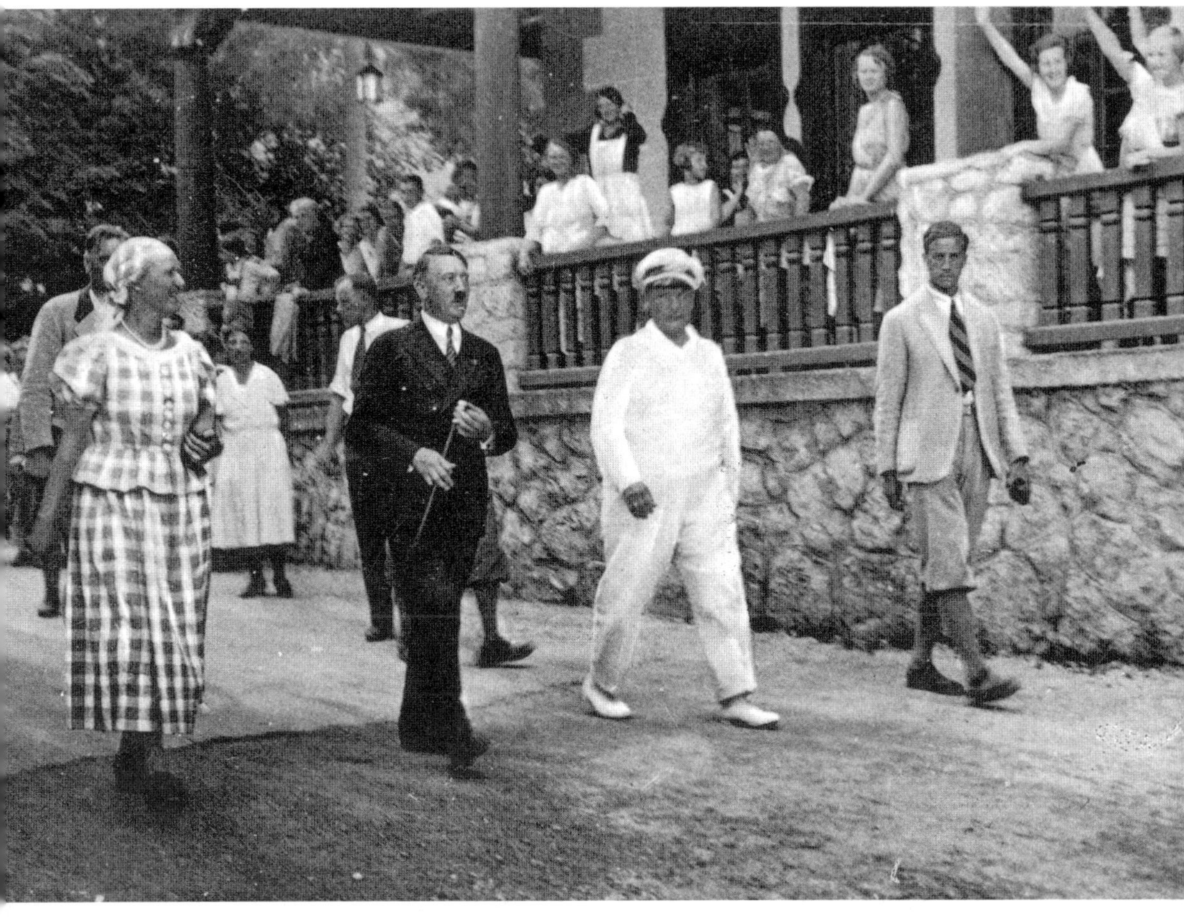

21. Our Führer at Hintersee with Göring, Brückner and his sister.

This extremely rare postcard image shows the Führer visiting Hintersee with Hermann Göring, Wilhelm Brückner, and Hitler's sister Paula. Crowds of people have gathered on the terrace of Hotel Post to salute and greet Hitler as he passes the building. It's been said that having achieved political success Hitler distanced himself from family members; this image instantly disproves any such notion.

Paula Hitler (1896–1960) was the Führer's youngest surviving full sibling. She would outlive her brother to die peacefully in Berchtesgaden in 1960. Hitler would invite his sister to Berchtesgaden once or twice a year. The Führer provided Paula with financial help and every Christmas she received a gift of 3000 Marks. After the Second World War Paula lived for a time at Vorderbrand, the very restaurant frequented by Hitler's mentor Dietrich Eckart. Hitler and Eckart met and dined at Vorderbrand on more than one occasion during the time of Hitler's first visit to the region in 1923. Paula Hitler is buried in Berchtesgaden's Bergfriedhof.

Hermann Göring (1893–1946) head of the German Luftwaffe was a close confidant of Hitler. Wilhelm Brückner (1884–1954) is the man partially obscured seen walking behind Paula Hitler. SA-*Obergruppenführer* Brückner was Hitler's chief adjutant from 1934 until 1940 when he joined the German Army. The man on the right is Dr Karl Brandt (1904–1948), Hitler's personal physician. There are two ladies standing on the balcony between Göring and Brandt; the shorter lady on the left is Gerd Bartels' grandmother, Rosina Weiss. Gerd's grandmother was not a fan of Hitler.

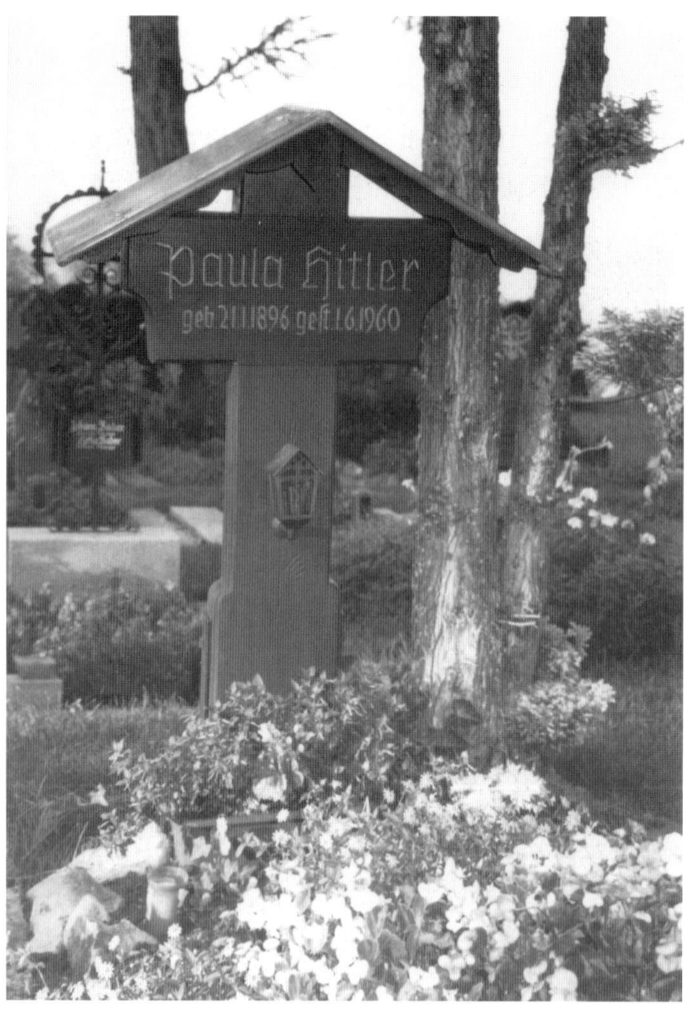

22. Paula Hitler's grave in the Bergfriedhof situated on Oberschönauer Straße on the outskirts of Berchtesgaden. As the photograph shows the grave is very well cared for. Planted flowers cover the grave and, as is the custom, someone leaves a lighted candle on the plot every evening. I took this photograph in early 2007.

Later that year a new plaque bearing a different name was placed over the marker we see here. This tells us that someone else owns the plot, perhaps friends of Paula who allowed her ashes to be buried here. The presence of the new nameplate makes it very difficult for those unfamiliar with the graveyard to find the plot. As the Second World War drew to a close, Paula, then living in Austria, was picked up by two SS men and brought to Berchtesgaden where she was installed in Hotel Berchtesgadener Hof. Soon after she found refuge with the Beer family who ran Vorderbrand. She was eventually arrested and questioned by US intelligence. Shortly after her release she returned to Vienna where during the 1920s and 30s she had worked as a housekeeper then later as a secretary.

Paula Hitler would use the family name Wolf (also spelled Wolff). She returned to Berchtesgaden in 1952 where she lived quietly, avoiding public interest as best she could for the remainder of her life. In his youth Hitler's nickname was Wolf; he also used the name in adulthood. It is said that it was at Hitler's request that Paula used the name in an effort to avoid unwelcome attention. The Führer provided Paula with financial support for much of her life and continued to do so until his death. Paula Hitler had no interest in politics and was never a member of the Nazi Party.

23. The Führer at Hintersee (Berchtesgaden).

A pensive Hitler occupies at a table on the terrace of the Seeklause. Just a short walk along the shore from Hotel Post, the Seeklause was another restaurant the Führer visited when at the Hintersee. The man opposite is Dr Otto Dietrich (1897–1952) a friend and confidante of Hitler.

Dietrich won the Iron Cross 1st Class for bravery during the First World War. Having joined the Nazi Party in 1929 Dietrich joined the SS in late December 1932. He held the rank of SS-*Obergruppenführer* (Lieutenant General).

In November 1937 Dietrich was appointed Press Chief of the Reich and State Secretary to the Propaganda Ministry. He was at Rastenburg, East Prussia (the Wolf's Lair), Hitler's eastern headquarters on 20 July 1944 when the attempt was made on Hitler's life; in fact it was Dietrich who telephoned Berlin to inform Dr Joseph Goebbels that Hitler had survived the attack when a bomb planted by *Oberst* (Colonel) Claus von Stauffenberg (1907–1945) had exploded in the briefing room in the Rastenburg compound.

Der FÜHRER am Hintersee (Berchtesgaden)

Barrels marked 'Nebelsäure' (fog acid) were stored east of the Seeklause at Hintersee. The Obersalzberg had been 'fogged' using a chemically generated mist since 1944, soon after the first observed approaches of allied aircraft in the area. The fogging system had been set up in a way so as to take advantage of thermals and wind direction. Nebelsäure was a 50/50 mix of Chlorosulfonic Acid and Sulphur Trioxide.

This artificially created fog would climb out of the valley to reach the height of the Obersalzberg to cloud the entire mountain complex in an effort to hide ground targets from allied bombers. Hintersee was just one of a number of sites around the Berchtesgaden valley for the positioning and storing of the chemicals needed for these fog generating operations.

24. Our Führer in Hotel Post at Hintersee with war comrades.

This particularly interesting image shows Hitler meeting former comrades from the First World War during another a visit to Hintersee. The man pictured in the middle is Dori Weiss. Weiss was Hitler's sergeant for a time during the First World War. The two men obviously got along and Hitler resumed contact with his former sergeant around the time he came to Berchtesgaden to meet with Dietrich Eckart. Hitler often dined at the hotel owned by Dori Weiss during these visits.

Adolf Hitler served through the entire period of the First World War where he proved a brave and able soldier. He took part in more than forty battles and was often right in the thick of it. Hitler won the *Eisernes Kreuz* (Iron Cross) both First and Second Class. He received the Iron Cross (Second Class) in 1914 and was awarded the Iron Cross (First Class) on 4 August 1918.

In 1916 Hitler was awarded the *Verwundetenabzeichen* (Wound Badge) in black after he was wounded in the thigh by a piece of shrapnel. For a time Hitler served as a 'regimental message-runner' carrying messages between headquarters and the front line; this was considered a particularly dangerous job. Hitler never rose above the rank of *Gefreiter* (Lance-Corporal), it has been said that he refused to be considered for promotion. His experiences during the First World War transformed Hitler's character; he would emerge from the conflict with much stronger views on nationalism and patriotism. Hitler, like many, believed the German Army had been 'stabbed in the back' in 1918 and in the Jews' role in Germany's defeat.

This postcard was posted on 18 August 1936 to an address in Unterstein, an area northeast of Berchtesgaden, close to Marktschellenberg.

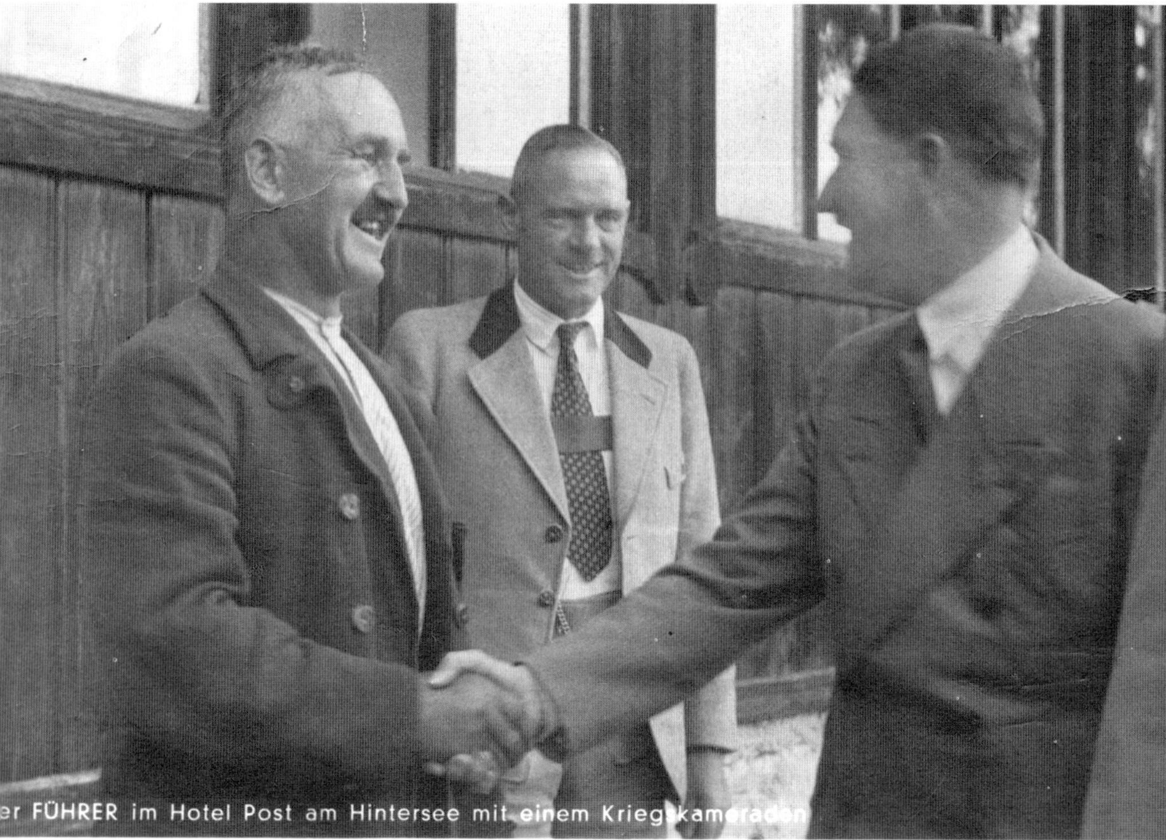

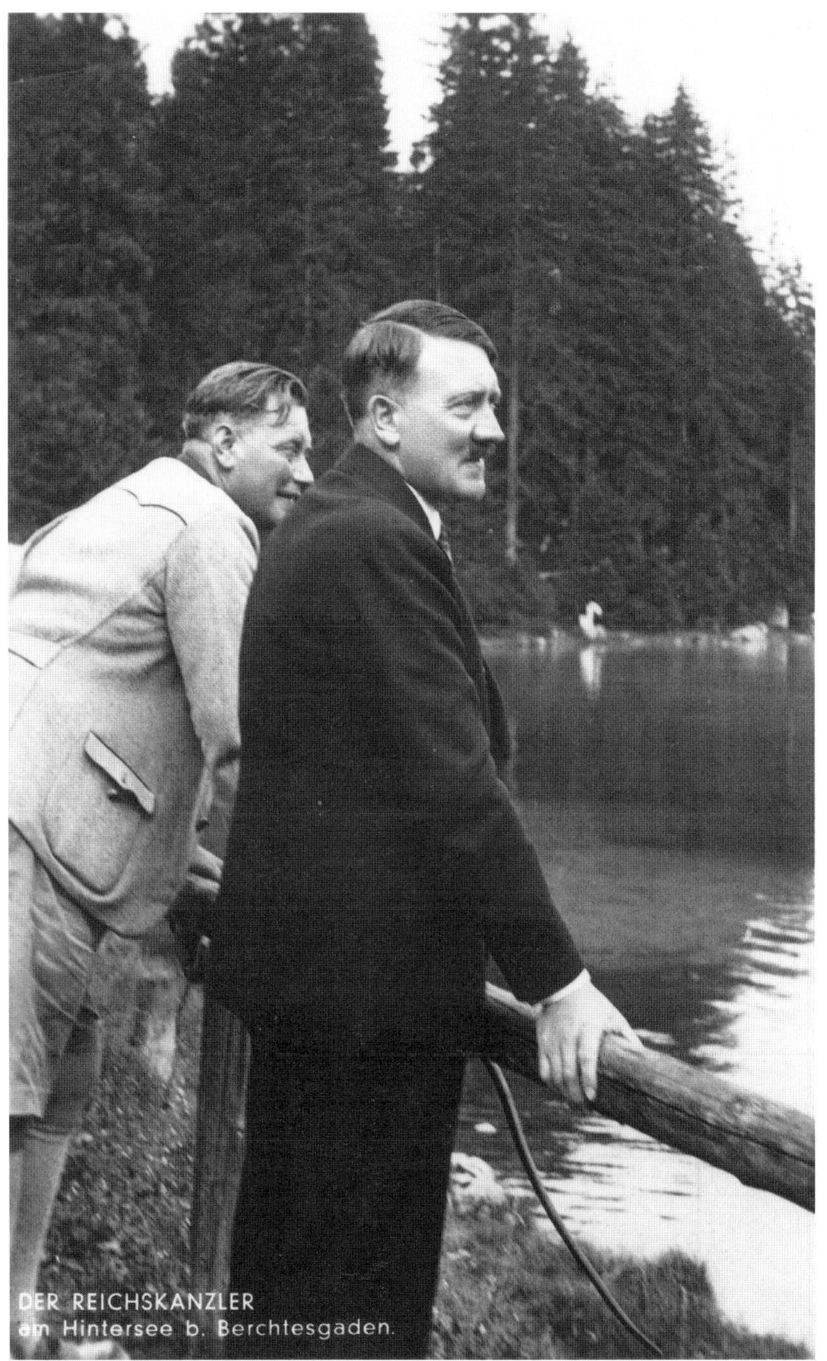

25. The Reich's Chancellor at Hintersee near Berchtesgaden.
Standing beside the lake in front of the Seeklause, Hitler and his adjutant Brückner pause to admire the view towards the Hochkalter.

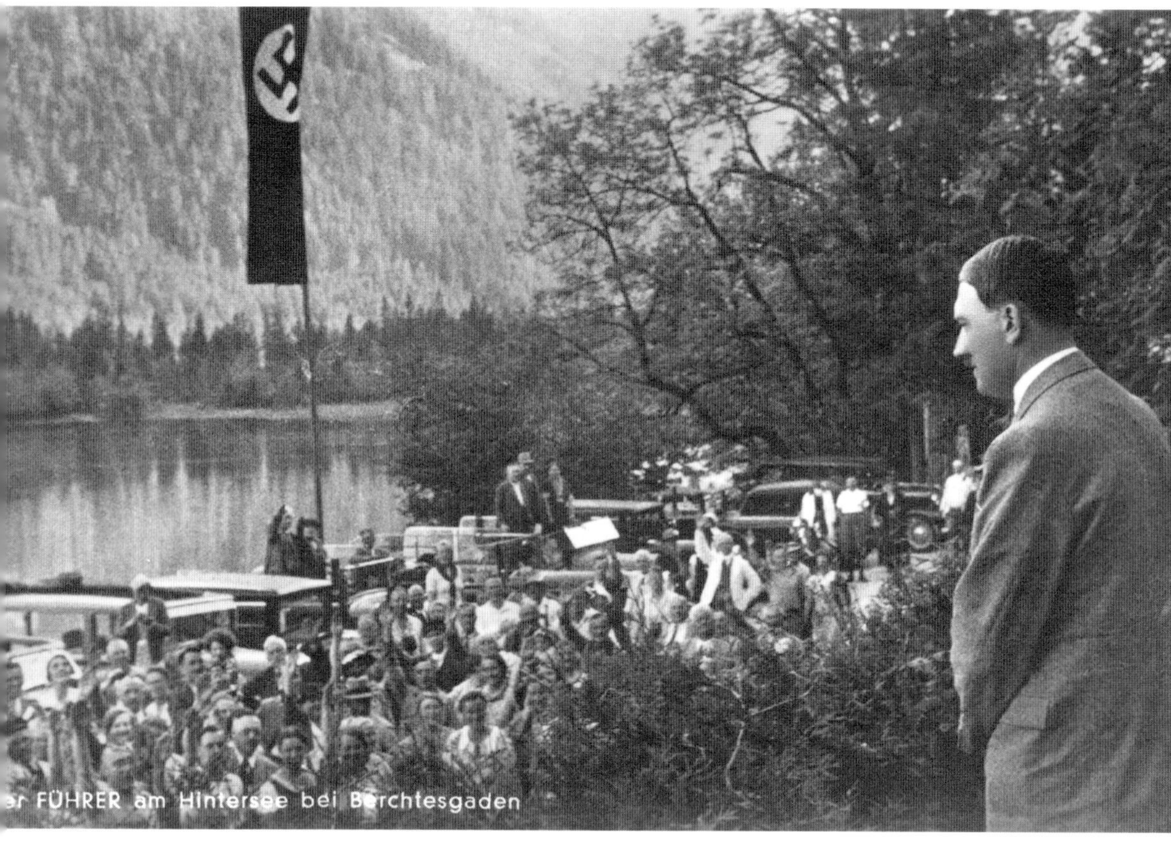

26. The Führer at Hintersee near Berchtesgaden.

As word of Hitler's presence at Hintersee spreads people in the area make their way to the lake in the hope of seeing their Führer. Hitler steps out onto the road in front of the hotel to an enthusiastic reception. A number of people in the lower left foreground can been seen giving the Nazi salute.

This scene was repeated wherever Hitler went; such was his popularity during the mid 1930s. Both Hitler and his personal photographer, Heinrich Hoffmann, became extremely wealthy thanks to the image rights attached to the use of each and every image of the Führer. During the course of their association it is estimated that Hoffmann took as many as two million photographs of Hitler. Their work together would help make Hitler the world's first 'political superstar'.

In the war of propaganda even the simple postcard had become an important weapon in the Nazi arsenal, another means of influence. Postcards were cheap to produce; they were available at newspaper stands, shops, party offices, public transport hubs and many other outlets. Produced in unimaginable numbers, postcards were a means of promoting and maintaining the popularity of the Party leadership and in keeping the Party and its message at the forefront of people's imagination.

While the purchaser has placed a 3 Pfennig 'Hitler Head' stamp on this postcard they have, for some unknown reason, not written anything on it and it remains unused.

The story of Ida Sahra Meister

Gerd tells the story of a Jewish lady who lived at Hintersee; she was the only Jew living in the Berchtesgaden region. In 1906 Ludwig Meister, a wealthy court chamber musician built a holiday home, the Seehäusl, in the northwest corner of the Kainzerfeld at Hintersee. The house, located higher up on the hillside behind Alpenhof is still there today. Meister was not a Jew, but his wife, Ida Sahra Meister, *née* Maier, was Jewish. Prior to the outbreak of the First World War the couple spent most of the year in their home at Hintersee. Ida Meister, an accomplished painter, spent much of her time

27. Hintersee with Reiteralpe.
Seehäusl, the Meister home at Hintersee can be seen highlighted near the centre of the image. A little lower on the right by the lakeside stands Hotel Post. This postcard was posted in Berchtesgaden on 14 July 1937 to an address in the Harlaching area of Munich. As Bartels Alpenhof was not constructed until 1938 it does not appear in this photograph, however the arrow seen to the left of the Meister home shows where Alpenhof would be built.

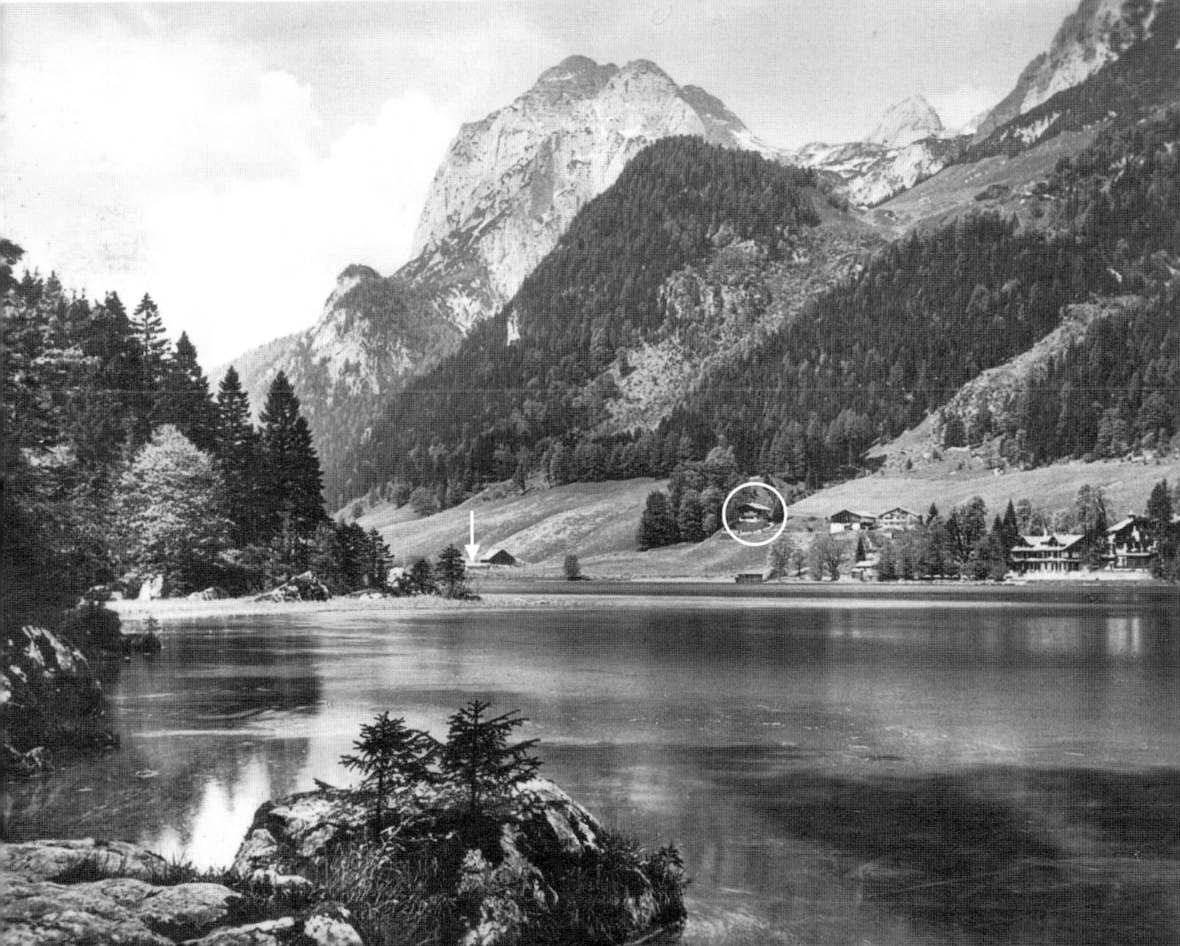

producing landscapes of the surrounding area while her husband gave music lessons to local students.

In the second half of the First World War it was the smaller households that suffered most. Tenant farmers and those with smallholdings suffered considerable food shortages. During these particularly hard times, Ida Meister, through her contacts in Ramsau, managed to order and acquire basic foodstuffs and seeds that she distributed amongst the local people. How she managed to do this despite the strict official controls in place at the time remains unknown. Ida Meister's thoughtfulness and generosity through these difficult times made her extremely popular and she was highly respected by the local population.

During the Nazi period, but particularly towards the end of the 1930s, things became increasingly difficult for Frau Meister. Dr Fritz Todt (1891–1942) initially Inspector General for German Roads, then later Reich Minister for Armament and Munitions had a home at Hintersee. Todt had built the German Autobahn, the world's first motorway system. He had built the *Deutsche Alpenstraße* (German Alpine Road; undoubtedly one of the most beautiful Alpine roads in Europe running from the Bodensee in the east to the Königssee in the west, a distance of some 515 kilometres (320 miles). He had overseen the construction of the German Westwall defences (the Siegfried Line) and had built all of Hitler's wartime headquarters. Despite having a good relationship with the Todt family who also spent considerable time at Hintersee the continued persecution of the Jews meant Frau Meister's position became more and more precarious. (Given the number of times that Hitler visited Hintersee through the 1930s it seems more than a little strange that Ida Meister's existence was unknown to him, or to some of those who accompanied him.)

However, the local residents, including those in nearby Ramsau remembered Frau Meister's kindness during the latter years of the First World War and remained silent. The road from Berchtesgaden to Hintersee passed through the long valley and the village of Ramsau, this meant that any unrecognised vehicles travelling to Hintersee were quickly spotted, including any Gestapo vehicles. In the event that a suspicious vehicle was spotted word reached Hintersee in good time and Frau Meister was quickly assisted into hiding.

There were very few telephones in Ramsau at the time, probably less than ten, and yet the secret warning system set up by local people worked perfectly. Dori Weiss, the owner of Hotel Post and a comrade of Hitler from the First World War had the only telephone at Hintersee. Weiss, Gerd's uncle, and a neighbour of Ida Meister was obviously one of those involved in keeping the lady safe. Even the local mayor and Nazi Party member, Franz Moser, declared Ramsau free of Jews in two sworn affidavits. Most of those living in Ramsau knew of Frau Meister's whereabouts, but said nothing.

As a young lad and contemporary witness, Gerd Bartels can remember how the mayor and a local 'party-spinner' as he has been described came to Hintersee with the intention of confiscating Ida Meister's *Volksempfänger* (People's Radio). Gerd's father, August Bartels, himself a party member, confronted the men and following a lengthy conversation and much persuasion he convinced them to let the lady keep her radio. To clarify, there were Nazi Party members everywhere, but only a few of them, a dozen or so, were as fanatical as the one who accompanied the mayor on that occasion. If a local person, that is a party member who was employed elsewhere in the country returned home on vacation, things suddenly became particularly dangerous for Frau Meister, even more so should this person attempt to trace her whereabouts.

If these people reported their suspicions and offered possible locations as to Ida Meister's whereabouts the result was inevitably increased Gestapo visits. Despite the increased risks those protecting Frau Meister were always warned in advance and managed to hide the lady in stables, huts and hay-barns during the hours of darkness, sometimes changing location every hour. As the war progressed all the men fit for duty were drafted into the military, this left the wives with their children and grandparents at home to run the farms meaning Frau Meister's safety was chiefly in the hands of the womenfolk in the area.

If caught by the Gestapo the consequences would be dire, anyone involved would be sent to Dachau concentration camp. Those involved in protecting Frau Meister were very courageous. Ida Meister survived the Second World War and continued to live in the area until her death in 1971 aged 94. She spent the last year of her life in the *Altenheim und Pflegeheim* (Retirement Home and Nursing Home) at Insula near Bischofswiesen. Ida Meister is buried in Freilassing.

Ramsau

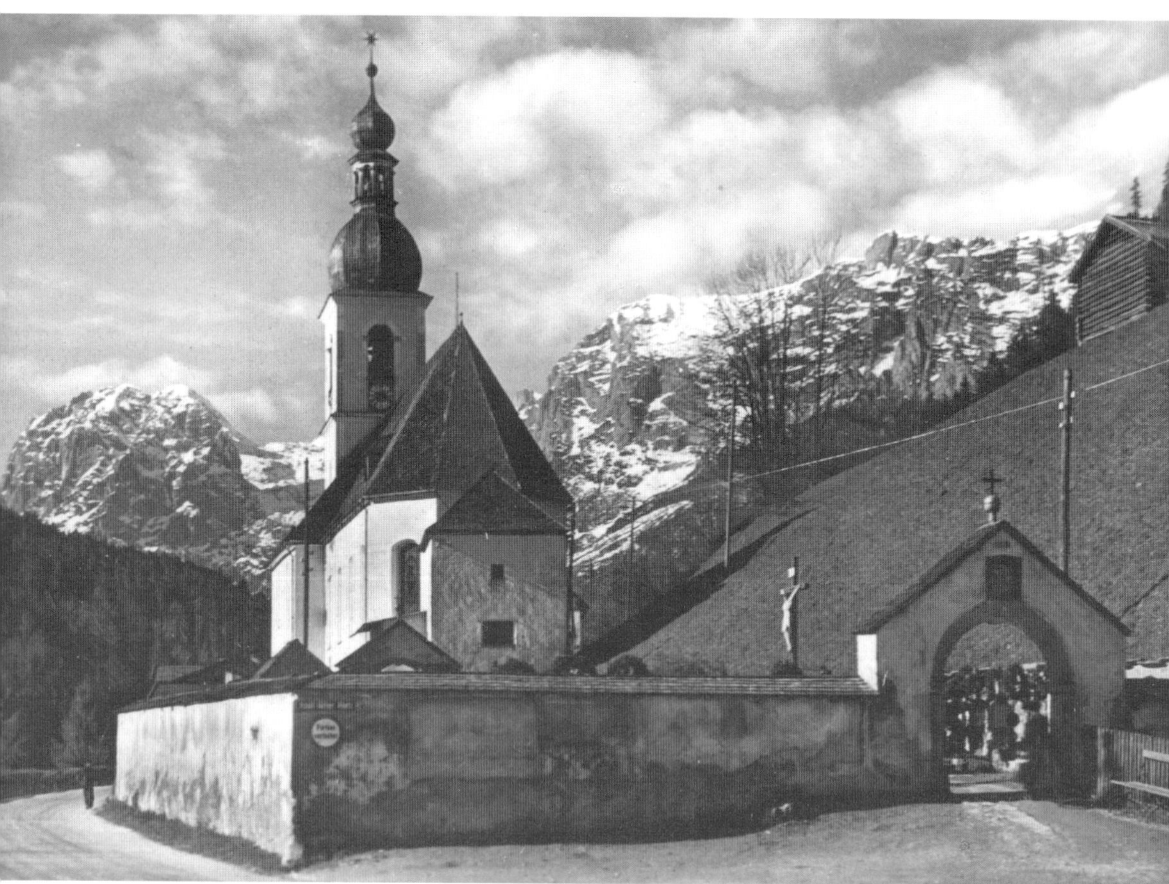

28. Ramsau church with the Reiteralpe.

This period postcard shows the parish church of St. Sebastian in Ramsau near Hintersee. Dori Weiss, Hitler's former sergeant is buried in this small churchyard. On entering the graveyard through the arched gateway his grave can be found on the left hand side.

My wife and I accompanied Gerd Bartels to this churchyard on Christmas Eve 2007 when he went to visit the grave of his parents and to light the candles on the Christmas tree that had been placed on the plot. Ramsau is a pretty village lying about halfway between Berchtesgaden and Hintersee.

Posted in 1942 this postcard was sent to a soldier stationed in the *Adolf Hitler Kaserne* (Adolf Hitler Barracks) located on Gebirgsjägerstrasse in Strub, just outside Berchtesgaden. Construction of the barracks began in September 1937. The 2nd Battalion *Gebirgsjägerregiment* (Mountain Rifle Regiment) 100 moved into the completed complex on 11 November 1938. The barracks, while having been extended in more recent years, still stands today.

29. The beautiful and picturesque little church of St. Sebastian in Ramsau is instantly recognisable for it is famous the world over. The image appears on everything from postcards and chocolate-box covers to jigsaw puzzles. It is probably one of the most photographed and painted Alpine churches anywhere. I took this photograph in 2019 and was surprised not to find the usual hordes of tourists fighting for an opportunity to capture the same scene; it was unusually quiet.

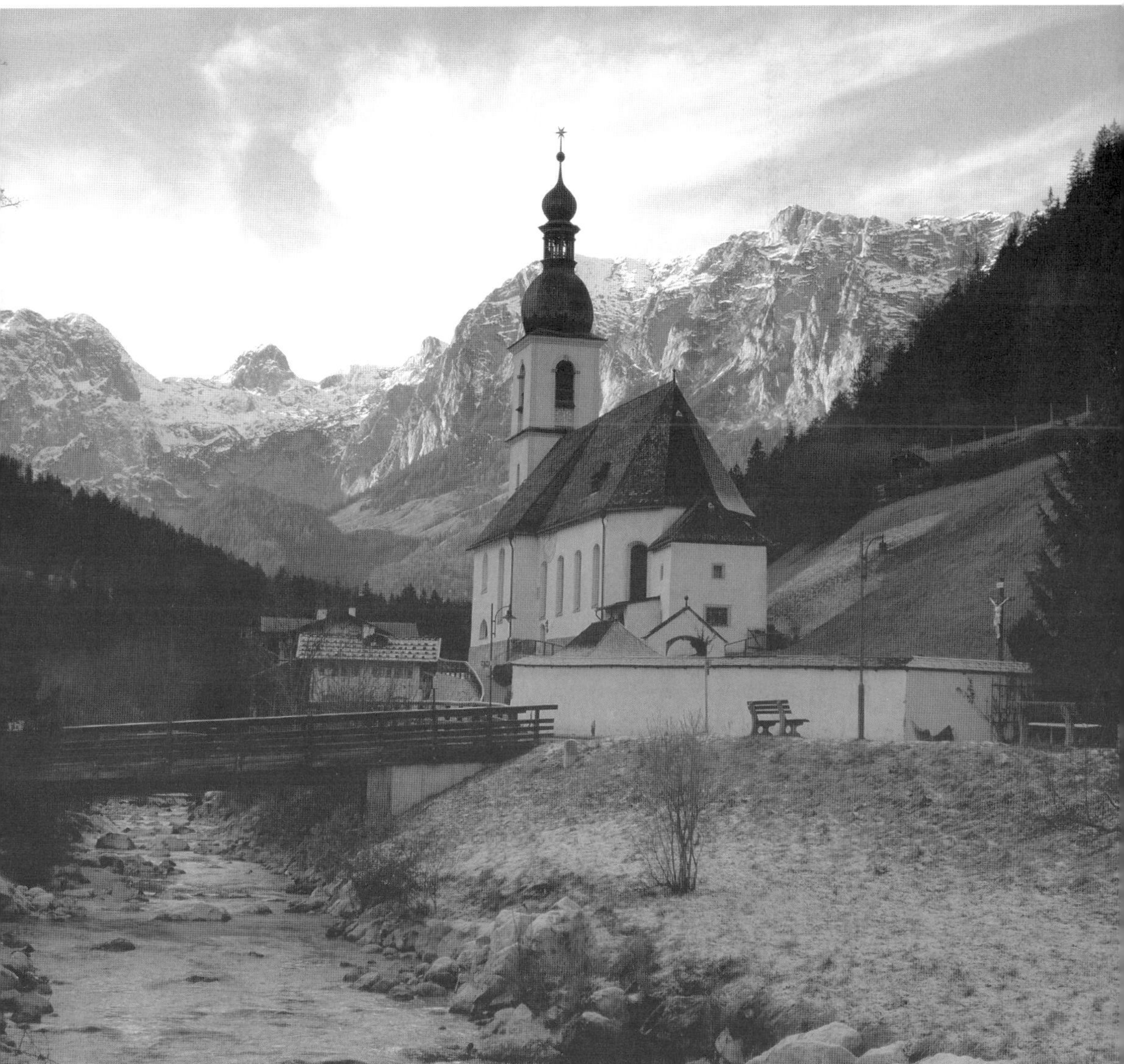

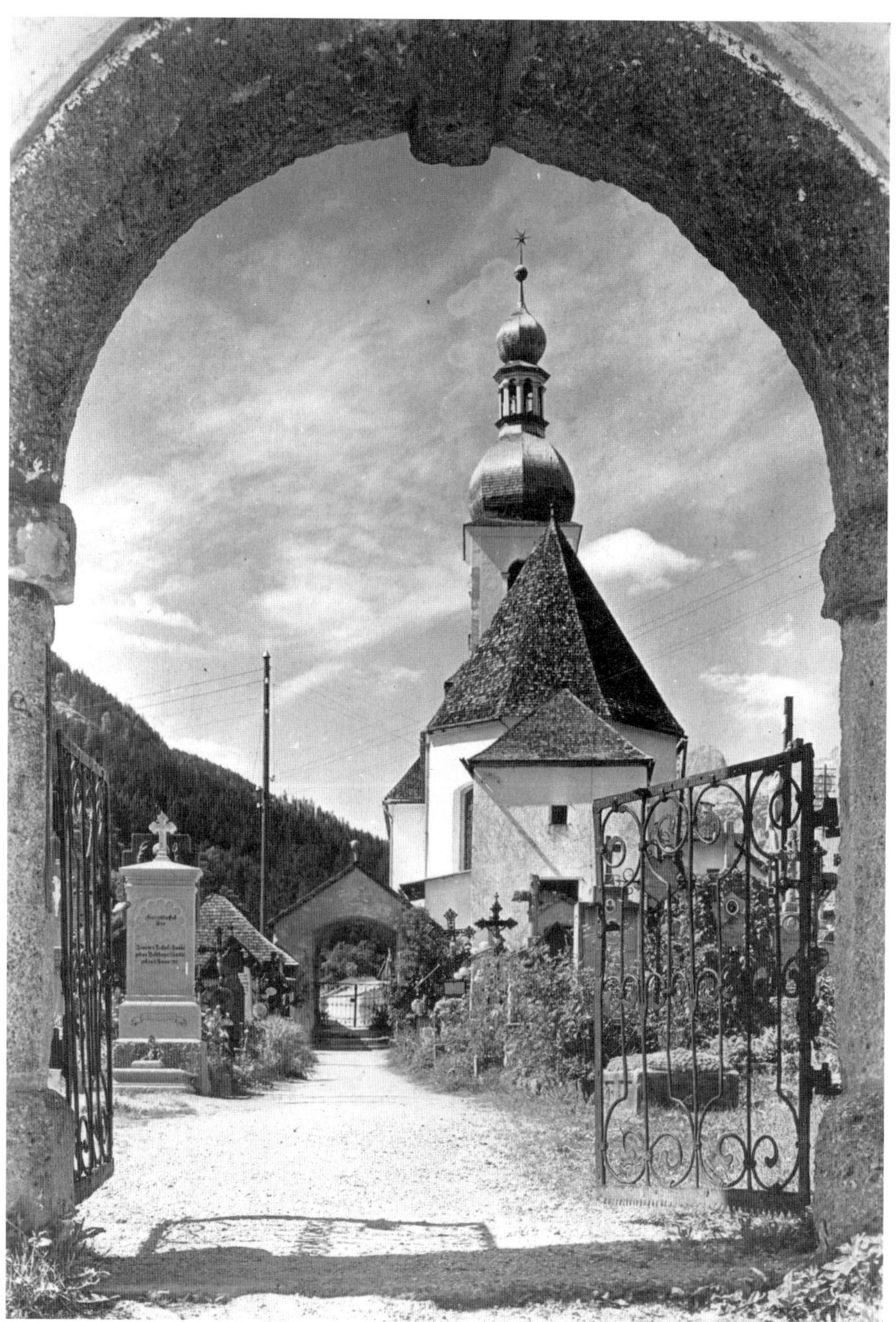

30. Ramsau village church.
Looking through the arched gateway into the cemetery with the famous church in the background.
The grave of Dori Weiss can be found in the third row on the left inside the gate. This postcard bears
a Berchtesgaden postmark dated 30 July 1936.

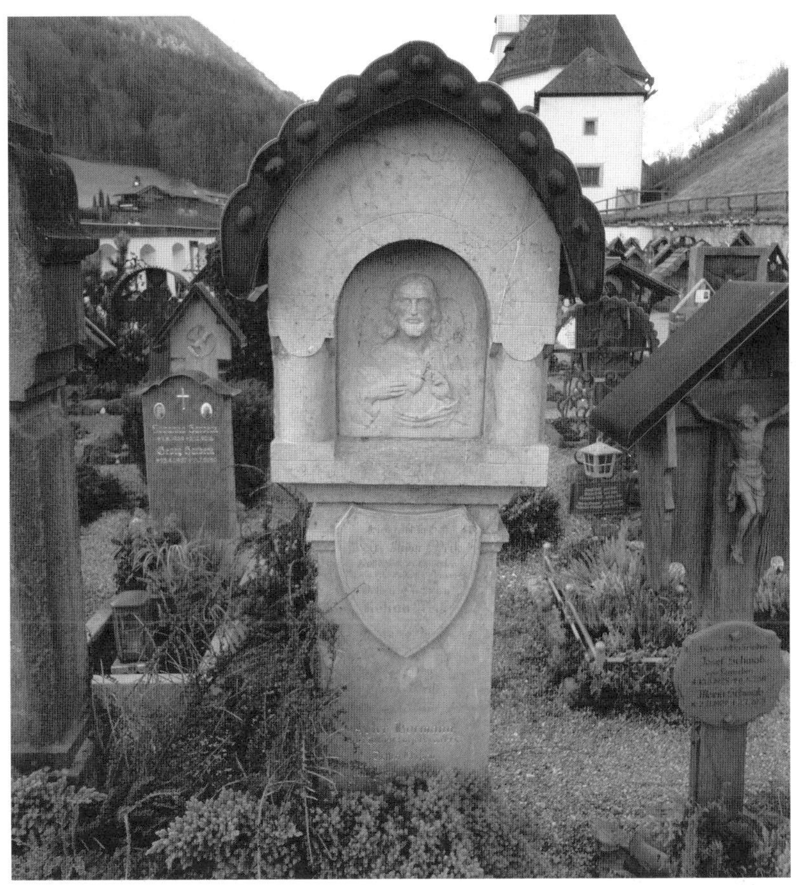

31. The Weiss family grave in the quiet and beautifully tended cemetery in Ramsau.

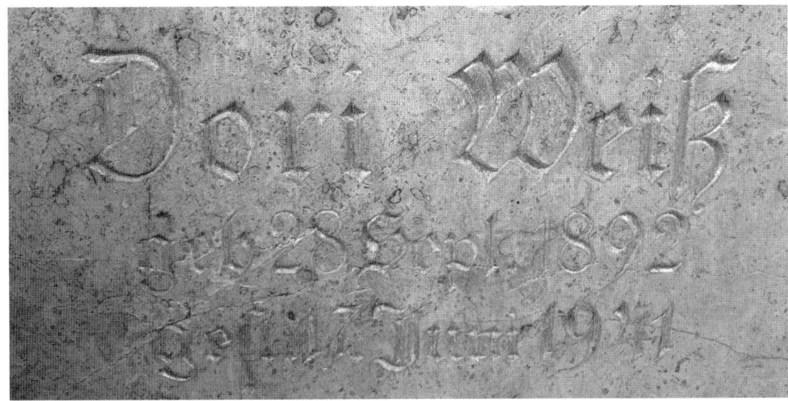

32. A close up of the inscription to Dori Weiss on the gravestone. While the gold on the lettering has faded the engraving remains legible. The wording reads: Dori Weiss, geb (born) 28 Sept 1892, gest (died) 17 Juni 1941.

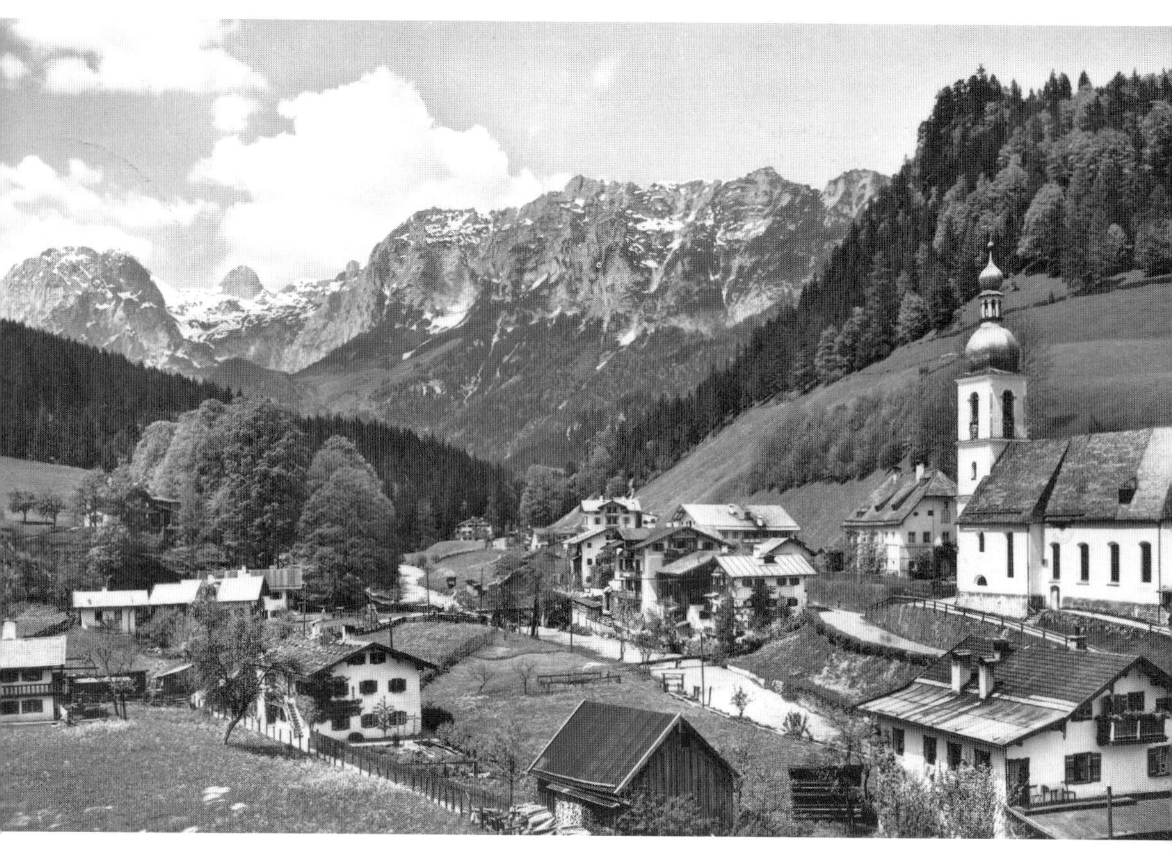

33. Ramsau with Reiteralpe.

This postcard shows the upper part of the village of Ramsau with the church of St. Sebastian on the right. Hintersee lies at the base of the Reiteralpe seen in the background. The lake is no more than a ten-minute drive from Ramsau. The hill on the right above the church, the Hochgartfeld, was to become one of the defence points where mountain troops and members of the *Volkssturm* dug out a series of trenches in March and April 1945. Today this area is part of the cemetery.

Bearing a Ramsau postmark, this postcard was posted on 5 June 1936 to an address in Töging am Inn, a town in Upper Bavaria approximately 84 kilometres (52 miles) east of Munich.

34. Haus Zauberwald Ramsau Obb.

This period photograph taken in the 1930s shows what was then known as 'Haus Zauberwald.' This is the house that the Bartels family purchased back in 1972. Today it is known as the 'Wirtshaus im Zauberwald', a guesthouse and restaurant owned and run by Gerd's eldest son, Günter Bartels.

The Zauberwald (Magic Forest) is an area of outstanding natural beauty. Using the Wirtshaus as a starting point a forest trail following the Ramsauer Ache (the river) leads through the forest and takes you all the way to Hintersee. Covering a distance of roughly 2 kilometres (1.5 miles) it takes around thirty and forty minutes to complete this enchanting walk.

As the war progressed Haus Zauberwald became a KLV camp (KLV; *Kinderlandverschickung* – Child Land Dispatch). These were places where children were sent for short periods to escape the Allied bombing of German cities. Boys and girls were separated; Haus Zauberwald became a boy's camp. The *Hitlerjugend* (HJ; Hitler Youth) were involved in running the KLV organisation. The KLV evacuated between 2.5 and 3 million German children during the Second World War.

This postcard was posted in Ramsau on 31 March 1932 to an address in Berlin. Earlier that month, on 13 March 1932 during the presidential elections held in a climate of increasing economic uncertainty and growing social unrest, Hitler and the Nazi Party achieved 13.7 million votes.

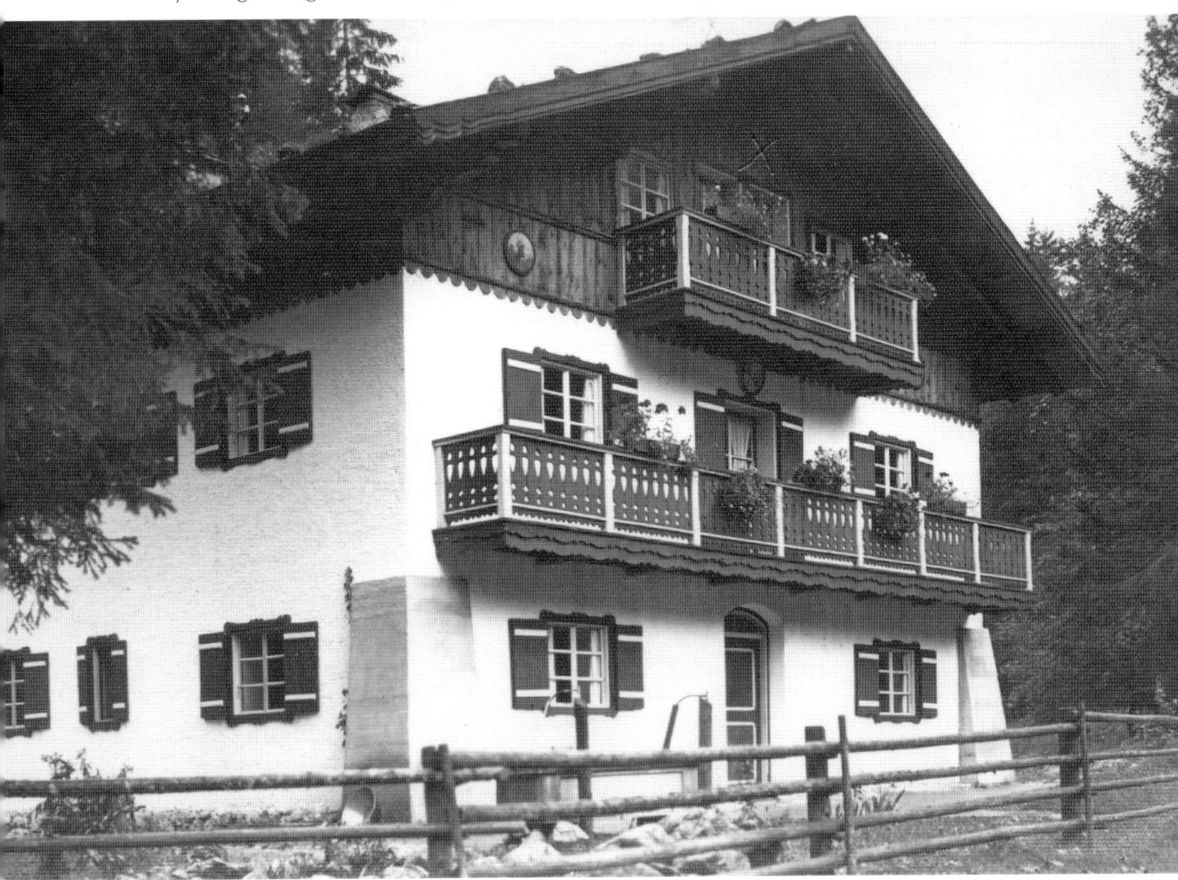

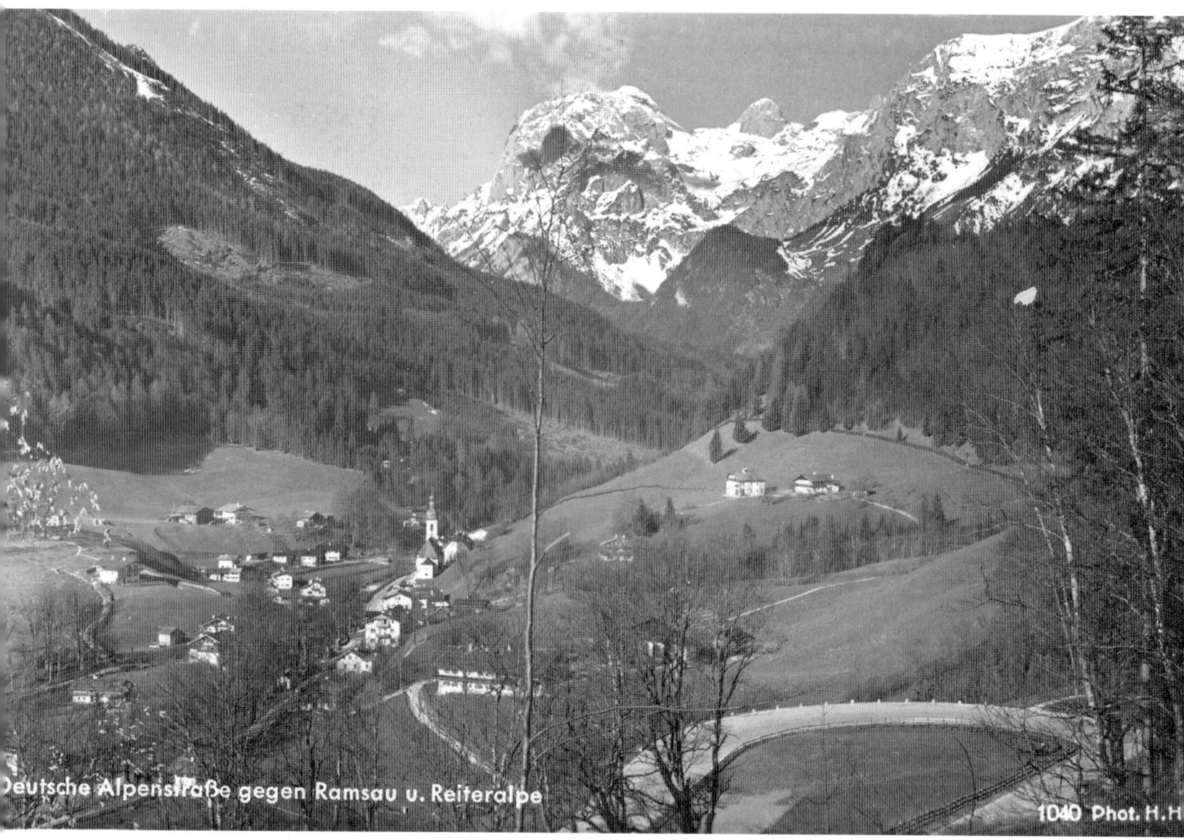

35. German Alpine Road towards Ramsau and Reiteralpe.

In the foreground we see just one of the many hairpin bends to be found on Dr Fritz Todt's Alpine road. Here we look down from the Alpine road towards the village of Ramsau with its famous church of St. Sebastian clearly visible. Hintersee lies at the opposite end of the Ramsau valley close to the Reiteralpe seen in the background.

This postcard was posted in Berchtesgaden on 9 October 1941 to an address in Bad Tölz. Bad Tölz lies approximately 38 kilometres (30 miles) south of Munich. In 1934 an SS-*Junkerschule* (SS Officer Training School) was established on the outskirts of Bad Tölz. Alois Degano, the architect responsible for so many Third Reich buildings also designed the Bad Tölz SS complex.

Many men who went on to make names for themselves on the battlefields of Europe passed through the Bad Tölz training school, men like:

SS-*Brigadeführer* (Brigadier-General) Fritz Witt (1908–44).

SS-*Brigadeführer* (Brigadier-General) Kurt 'Panzer' Meyer (1910–64).

SS-*Hauptsturmführer* (Captain) Michael Wittmann (1914–44).

SS-*Obersturmbannführer* (Lieutenant-Colonel) Joachim 'Jochen' Peiper (1915–76).

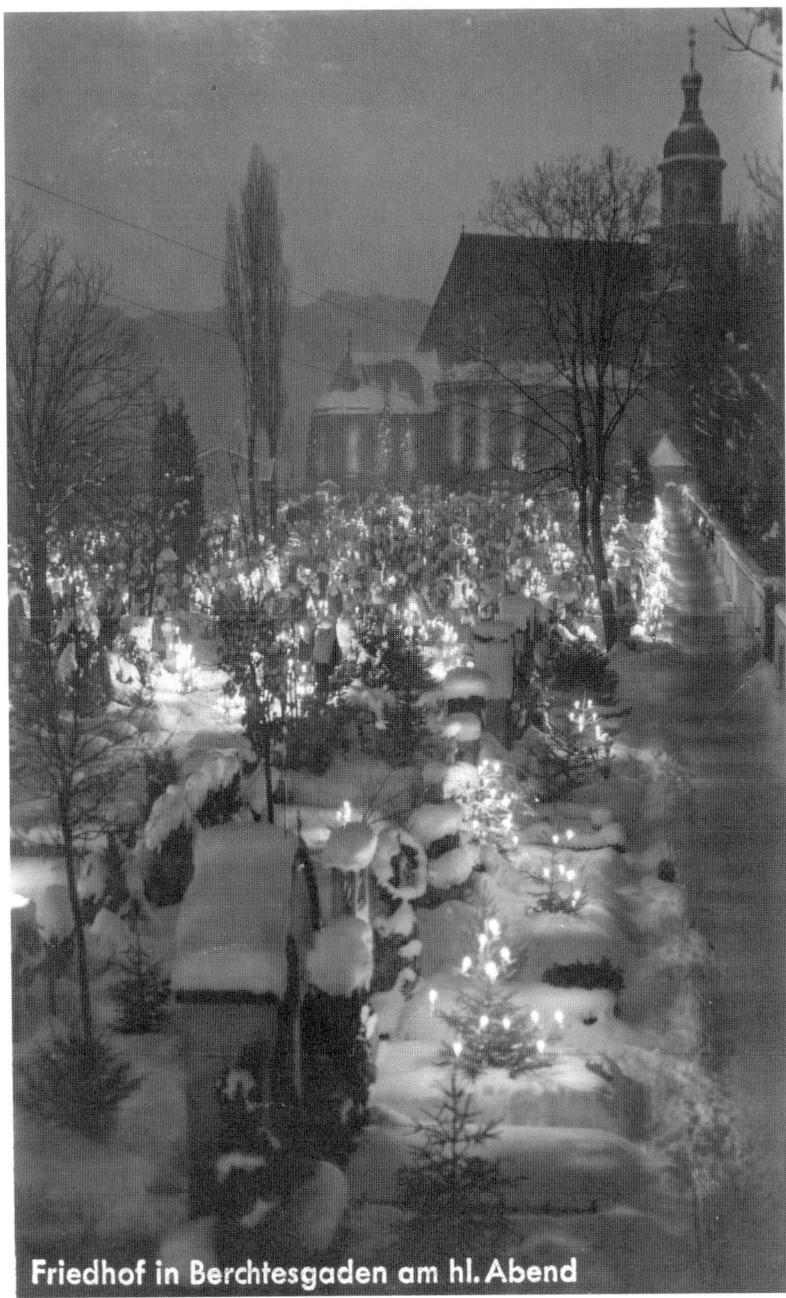

36. Churchyard in Berchtesgaden on Christmas Eve.

The sight of Christmas trees with lighted candles is spectacular and moving. While this is not Ramsau but Berchtesgaden, the scene observed is similar in many respects. Dietrich Eckart's grave is located in the row in the foreground. A handwritten date on the reverse reads: 24 December 1925. Eckart had died two years earlier on 26 December 1923.

𝕬lpenhof

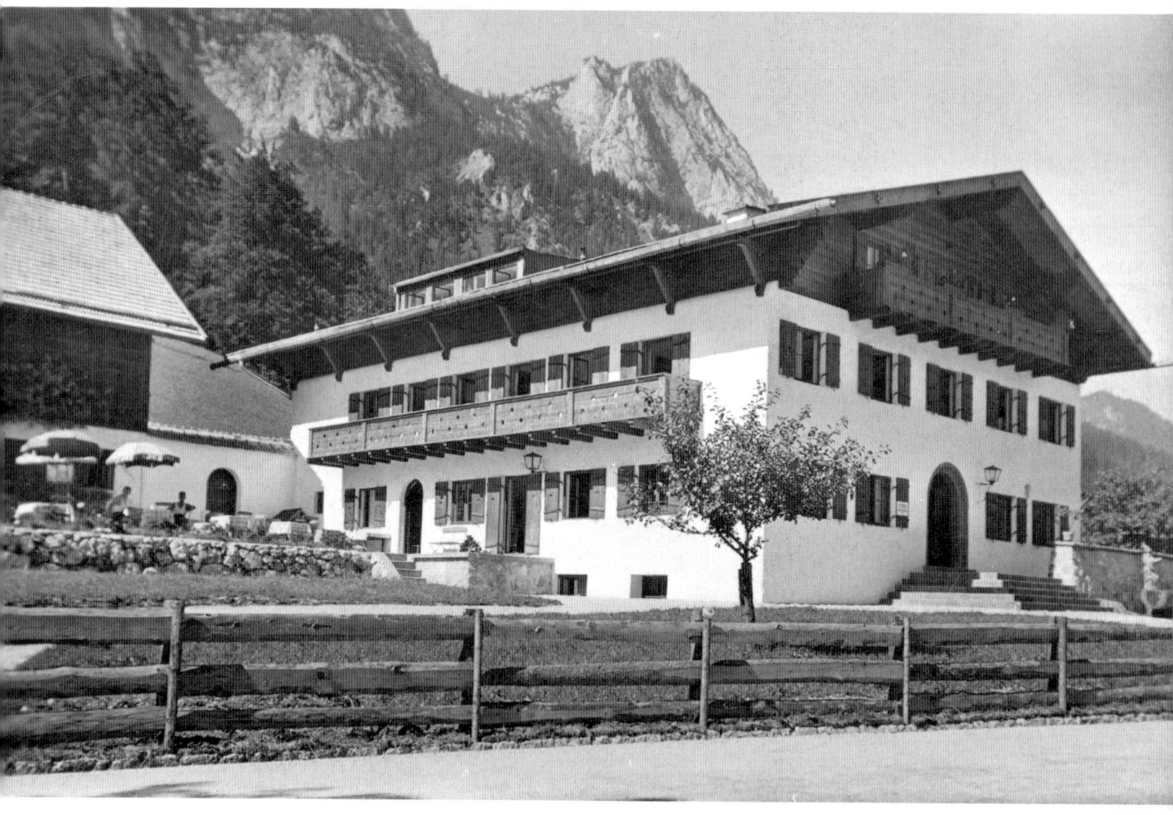

37. Alpine Boarding House Bartels. Hintersee 820 metres above sea level.
As the construction of Alpenhof came to an end in late 1938 this postcard shows the building soon after opening. The terrace on the left is laid out with tables and sun umbrellas and would have provided wonderful views across the lake and to the Hochkalter beyond.

It was in the barn on the left behind the terrace that Gerd Bartels and Eugen Bühler found Hitler's hidden Mercedes, and where, having discovered bottles of alcohol in the boot of the vehicle they proceeded to get drunk to a point where they were both sick.

Posted in Ramsau on 17 July 1940 this postcard made its way to an address in Henndorf, a village 20 kilometres (12.5 miles) north of Salzburg just across the border in nearby Austria. Austria had become part of the Reich a little over two years earlier when over 99 per cent of the Austrian population had voted in favour of unification in a plebiscite held on Sunday, 10 April 1938. Needless to say Hitler was delighted when his homeland joined the German Reich with such obvious enthusiasm.

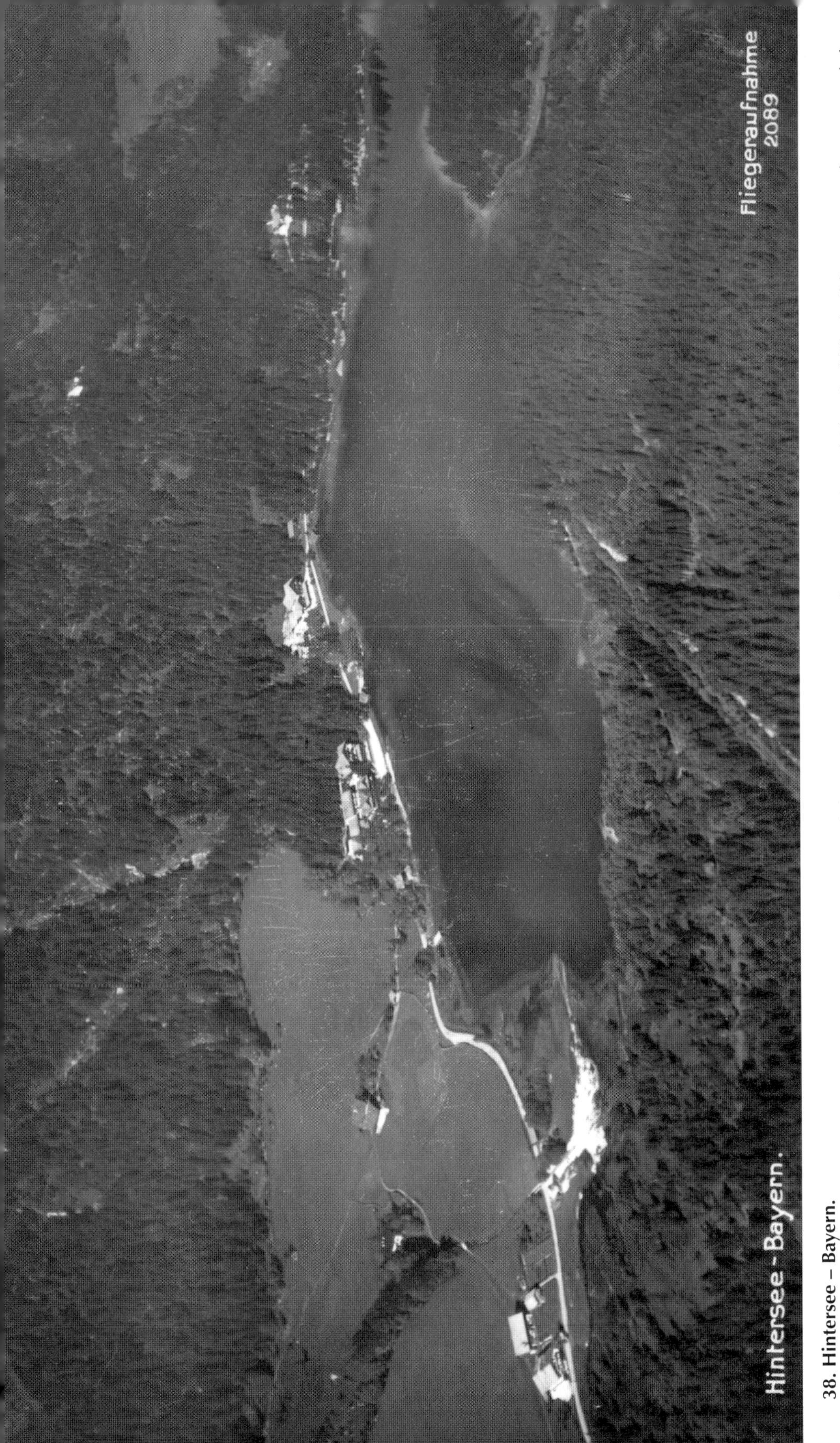

38. Hintersee – Bayern.

Posted on 7 August 1936 to an address close to Salzburg this postcard shows Hintersee prior to the construction of Alpenhof. The building seen on the extreme left is Wörndlhof; the construction of Alpenhof did not begin until 1937. Gerd's maternal grandfather Dori Weiss bought Wörndlhof around 1900. The building in the centre of the image is Hotel Post; further right is the Seeklause. Prior to building Alpenhof Gerd's mother and father worked in Hotel Post.

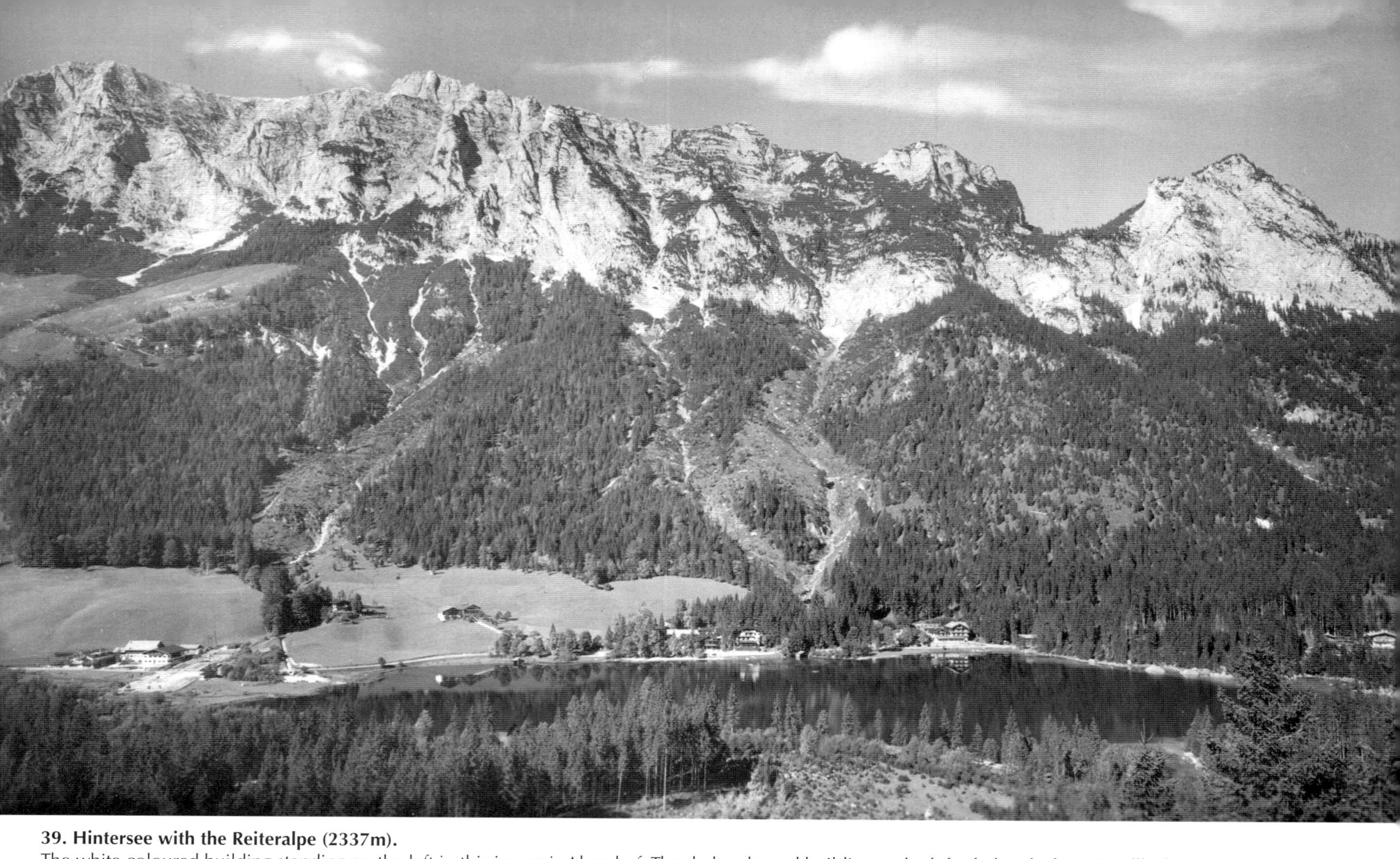

39. Hintersee with the Reiteralpe (2337m).
The white coloured building standing on the left in this image is Alpenhof. The dark coloured building to the left of Alpenhof is Wörndlhof as seen in the previous image number 38. This photograph shows the close proximity between the two buildings. While this photograph would have been taken sometime earlier, perhaps years earlier, this particular postcard was posted on 5 September 1952.

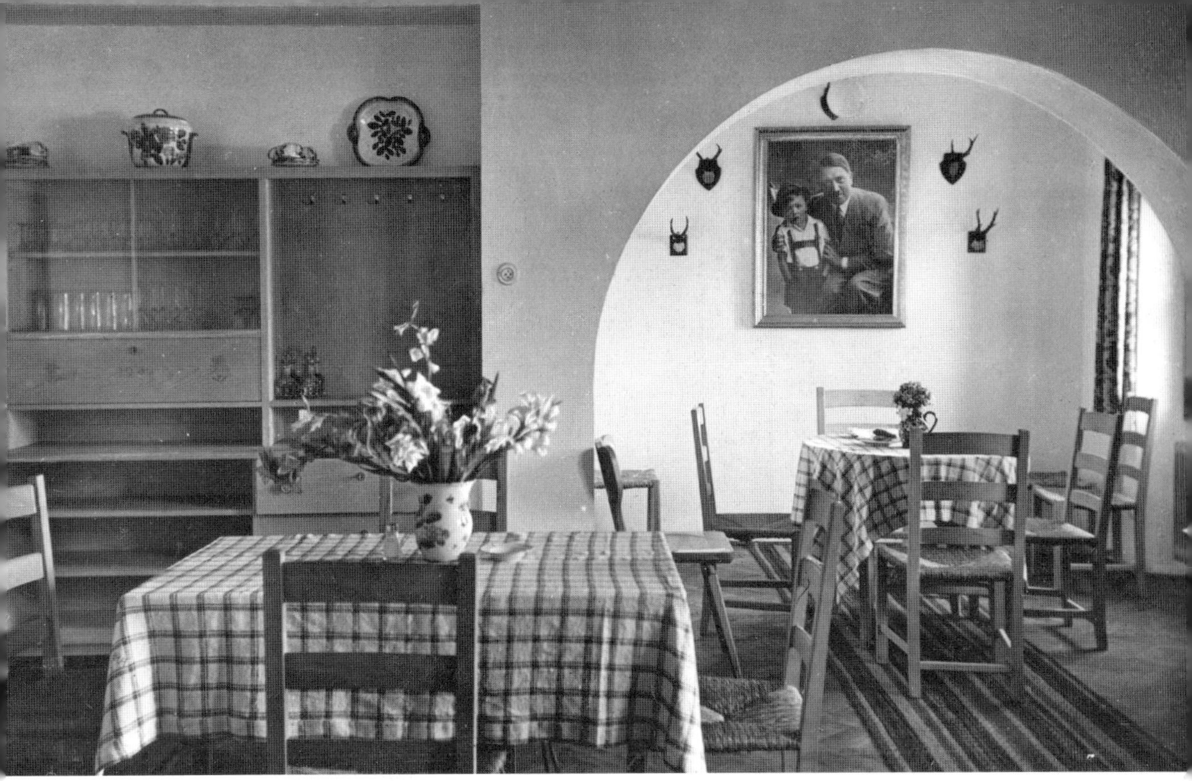

40. Alpine Boarding House Bartels. Hintersee 820 metres above sea level.
This period postcard shows a section of the restaurant in Bartel's Alpenhof as it appeared when photographed in 1939. Looking into the additional dining area in the background we see a large picture of Adolf Hitler and young Gerd Bartels hanging on the wall. This is the same image as observed in postcard number 17 on page 39. The practice of hanging pictures and wall plaques showing images of the Führer in German homes was not unusual; indeed it was common practice at the time, particularly during the early years of Hitler's immense public popularity.

41. Many buildings constructed during the Third Reich period incorporated the symbolism of the regime and this was expressed in many ways. As Alpenhof was constructed between 1936 and 1938, one might argue the high point of the regime, it would have been considered perfectly normal to include examples of this symbolism. In this instance that symbolism takes the form of a woodcarving.

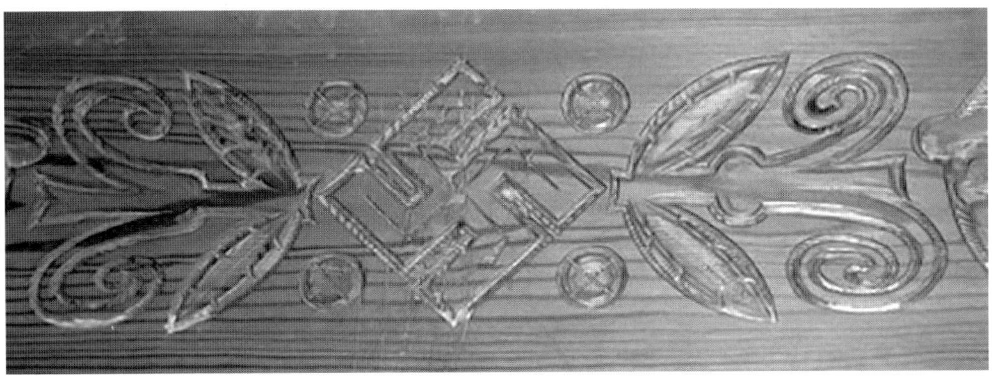

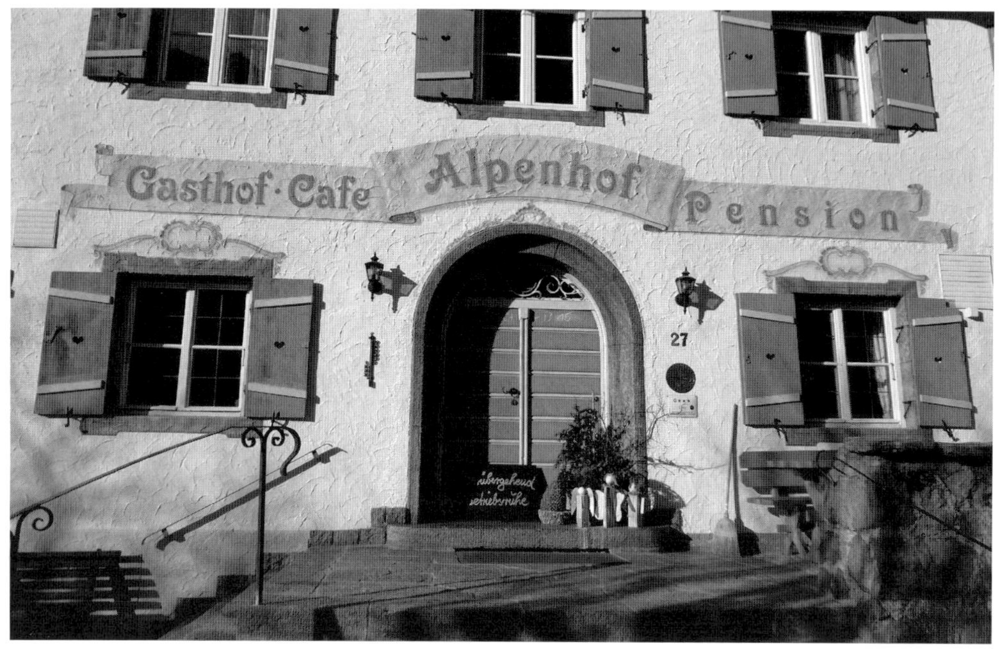

42. The main entrance to Alpenhof as photographed in 2019.

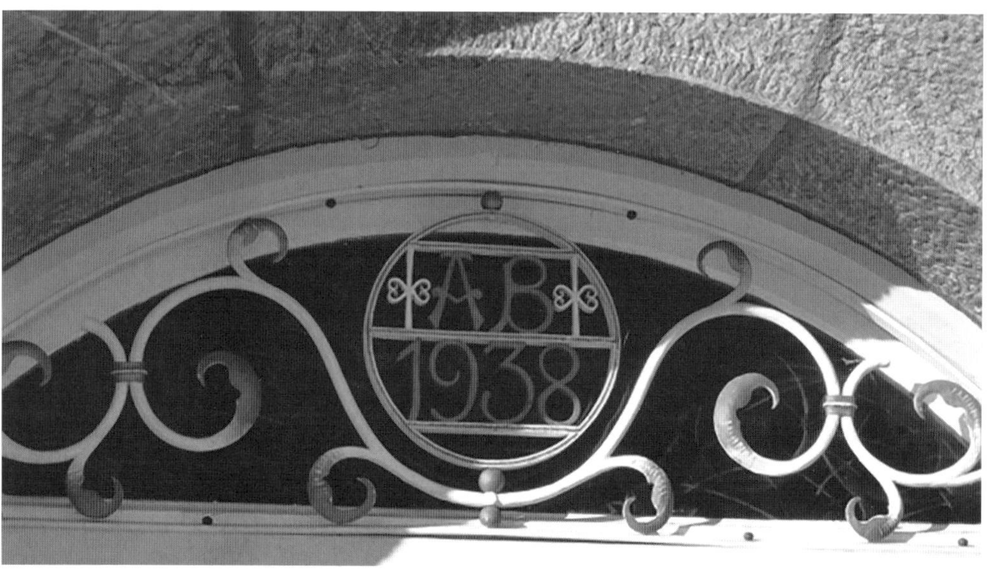

43. The wrought ironwork above the door shows the letters 'AB' remembering Gerd's father August Bartels and the year Alpenhof was completed 1938.

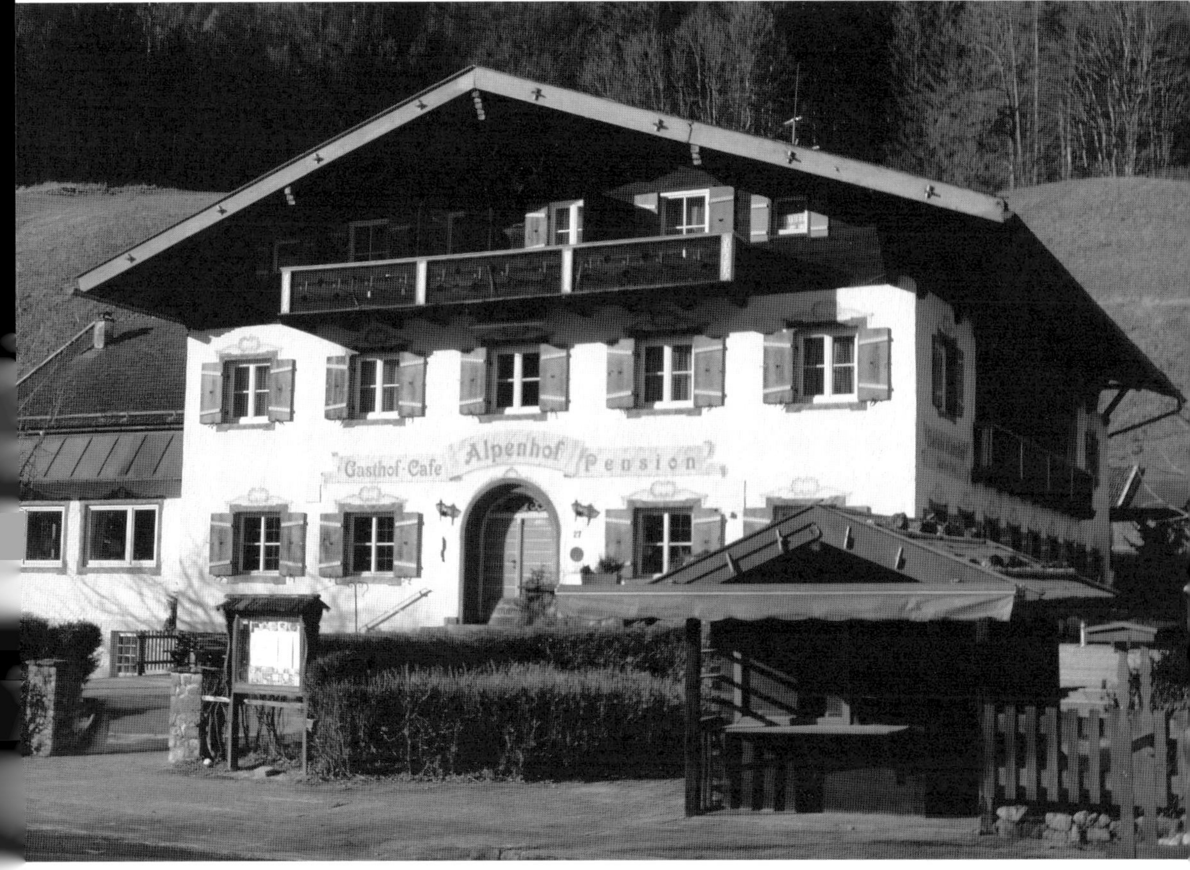

44. Bartels Alpenhof as photographed in 2019. I've spent many happy hours in this building chatting to Gerd Bartels. While giving private history buff tours I've brought small groups of between two and eight people to Hintersee where we've had lunch at Alpenhof. On many such occasions I managed to persuade Gerd to come and join us. The guests sat enthralled as Gerd recounted his life as a small boy in the area and answered their many questions.

This is where the evacuees from the Obersalzberg assembled on 26 April 1945, the day after the bombing of the mountainside. *Nationalsozialistisches Kraftfahrer Korps* (NSKK; National Socialist Motor Corps) *Gruppenführer* (*Generalleutnant* – Lieutenant General) Albert Bormann commandeered Alpenhof and Hotel Post to accommodate the evacuees. Bormann was Hitler's NSKK Adjutant from 1938 to 1945. A branch of the Nazi Party, the NSKK was responsible for overseeing the initial training of all German Army drivers. The NSKK was one of the smaller Nazi organisations. *General der Gebirgstruppe* (General of Mountain Troops) August Winter, Chief of Alpine Troops in Berchtesgaden informed Bormann of Hitler's death on 1 May 1945.

The Bormann brothers, Albert and Martin were not on good terms; indeed they barely spoke to each other. They had no personal contact and kept any official contact to a minimum. Albert had married in 1933. Martin Bormann did not approve of Albert's wife, Ilse, *née* Hillmann, a Hungarian; as a non-Aryan she was totally unsuitable. Martin Bormann would not even refer to Albert by name, dismissively referring to him as 'the man who holds the Führer's coat'. The brothers would remain estranged.

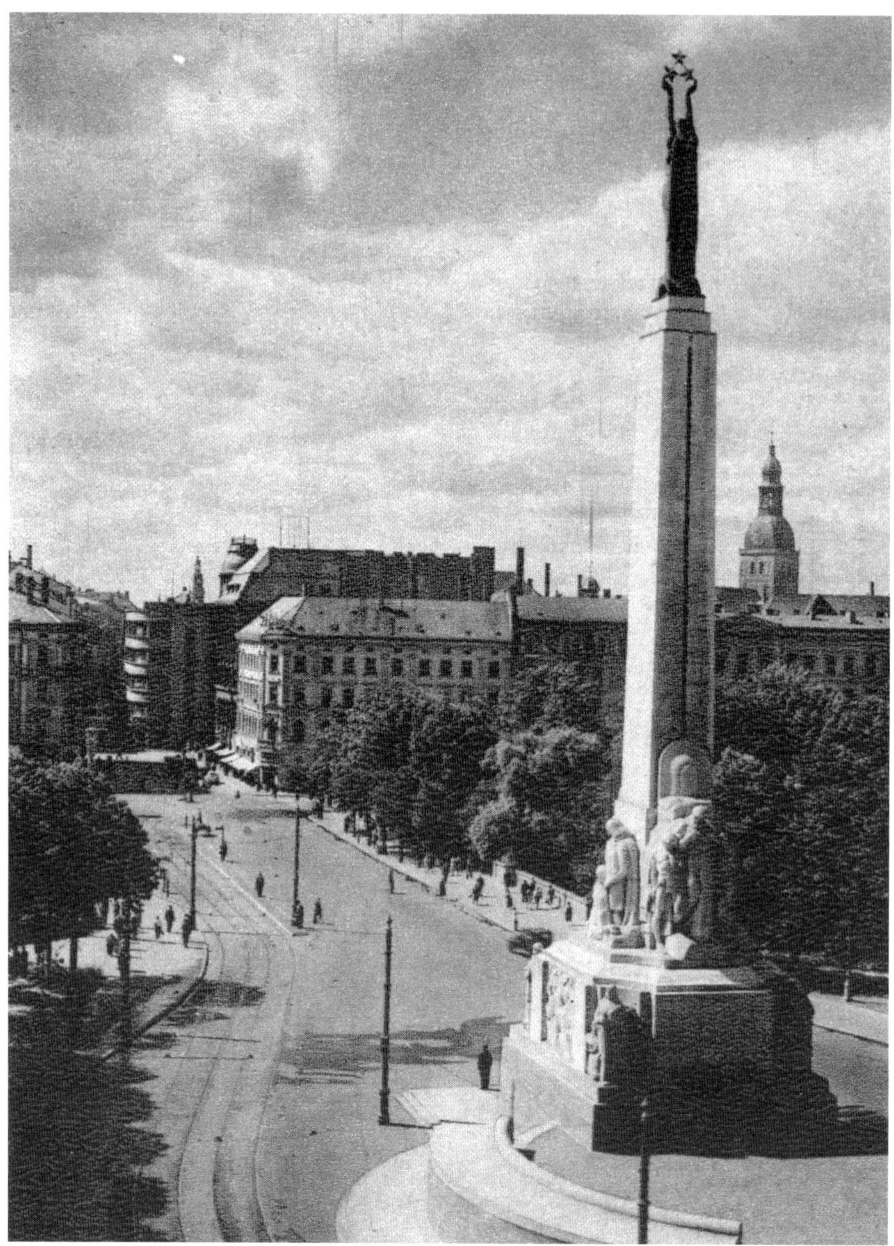

45. Riga – View of the Adolf-Hitler-Strasse.
This postcard shows the 'Freedom Monument' located on the Adolf-Hitler-Strasse in central Riga. Designed by Karlis Zale, the monument was unveiled on 18 November 1935 as a memorial to those who'd died fighting in the Latvian War of Independence (1918–1920). While his father was employed in Latvia as a regional farmer, young Gerd Bartels attended the German Gymnasium School in Riga from 1942 to 1944. The school, which stood off to the left, is just out of sight in this photo. The Bartels family fled Riga in June 1944 to return to Hintersee.

46. Riga. Market Square with the House of the Black Heads.

A view of central Riga showing the Market Square in the old town, as we can see Riga was clearly a city with a lot of history and a great architectural heritage. The horse-drawn carriages seen on the right are a common sight in many cities today offering visitors a more leisurely way of seeing the main sights in the city.

The 'House of the Black Heads' on the right was built in 1334 as a venue for meetings and banquets held by the various public organisations based in the city. The Soviet Union attacked Latvia on 15 June 1940; by 17 June the take-over of the small Baltic state of Latvia was complete. During the early stages of 'Operation Barbarossa', the German invasion of the Soviet Union beginning 22 June 1941 Riga, then in Russian hands, was bombed by the Germans on 28 June 1941.

As a result many of Riga's historic buildings, including the House of the Black Heads were destroyed. Latvia was under German occupation between 1941 and 1944 when the Germans were forced to evacuate the city as Soviet forces advanced on Riga once more. The House of the Black Heads was rebuilt between 1996 and 1999.

During the time Gerd Bartels spent in Riga between 1942 and 1944 the city would have borne the scars of shelling and bombing inflicted upon it by both German and Russian forces. On looking at this photograph Gerd told me there was an area in one of the buildings in the centre of the picture where he and other boys in the Hitler Youth helped sort *Feldpost* (Field Post) letters and packets.

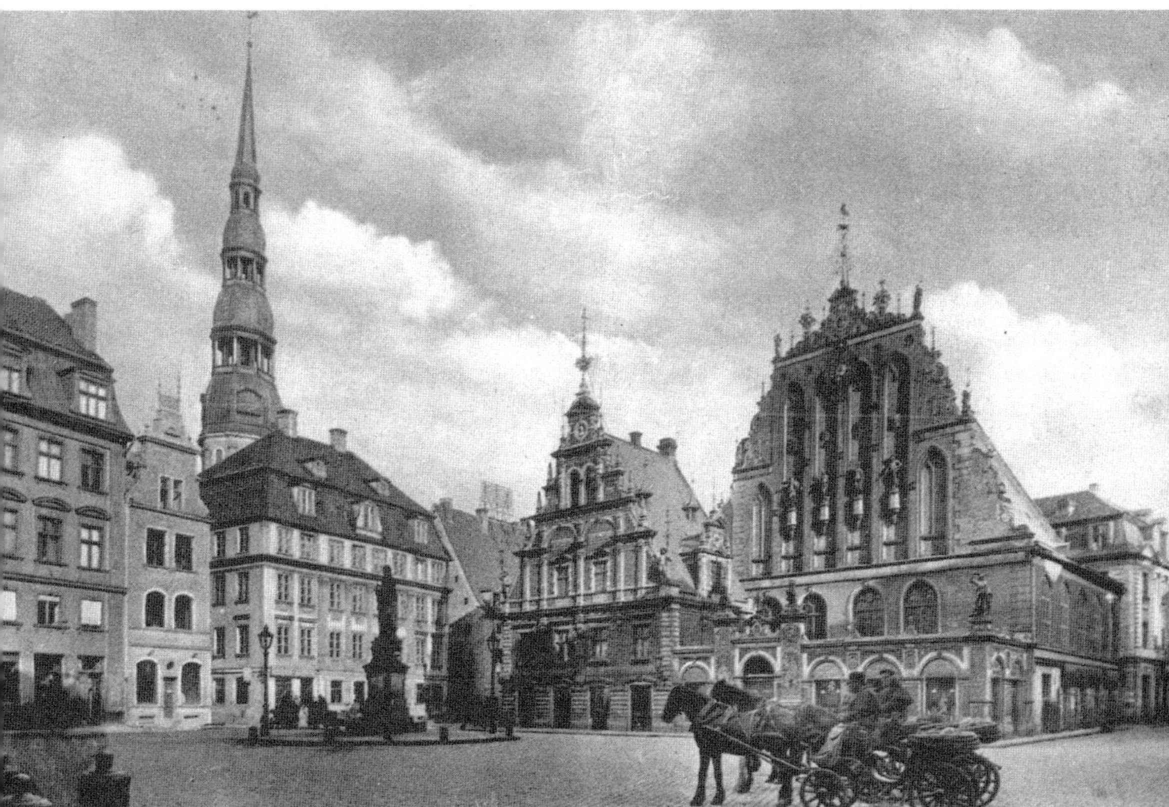

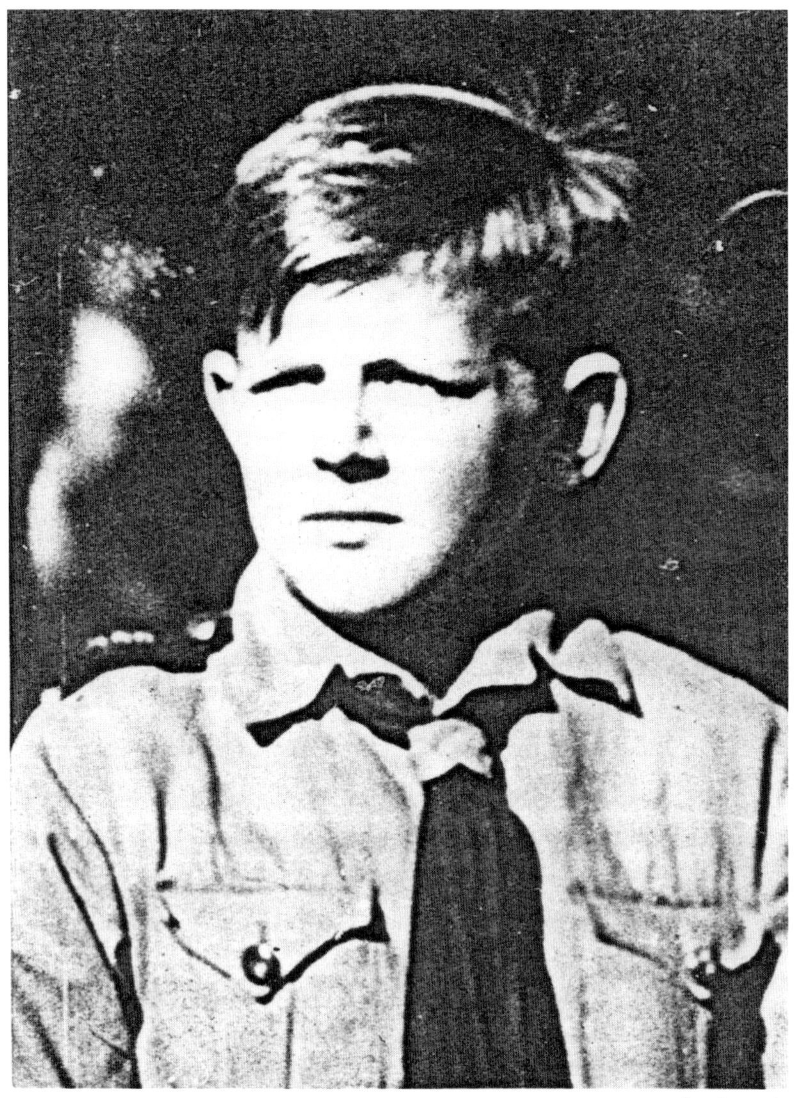

(Courtesy Gerhard Bartels)

47. Gerhard Bartels in DJ (DJ; *Deutsches Jungvolk* – German Young People) uniform. This photograph was taken in Riga in 1943 during the period when Gerd's father was employed as a regional farmer in Latvia. As Soviet forces advanced towards the city the Bartels family left Riga in June 1944 and returned to Hintersee.

A law passed on 25 March 1939 made it mandatory for all German youth aged ten to eighteen years to join the relevant youth organisation. This law applied to both boys and girls.

Boys aged ten to fourteen joined the *Deutsches Jungvolk*, boys aged fourteen to eighteen the HJ (HJ; *Hitlerjugend* – Hitler Youth). On leaving the Hitler Youth the young man entered military service. Girls aged ten to fourteen joined the *Jungmädelbund* – Young Girls' League, girls aged fourteen to eighteen the BDM (BDM; *Bund Deutscher Mädel* – League of German Girls). This photograph of Gerd Bartels appeared in a period magazine; Gerd does not have the original photograph.

Hitler's Mercedes 770K

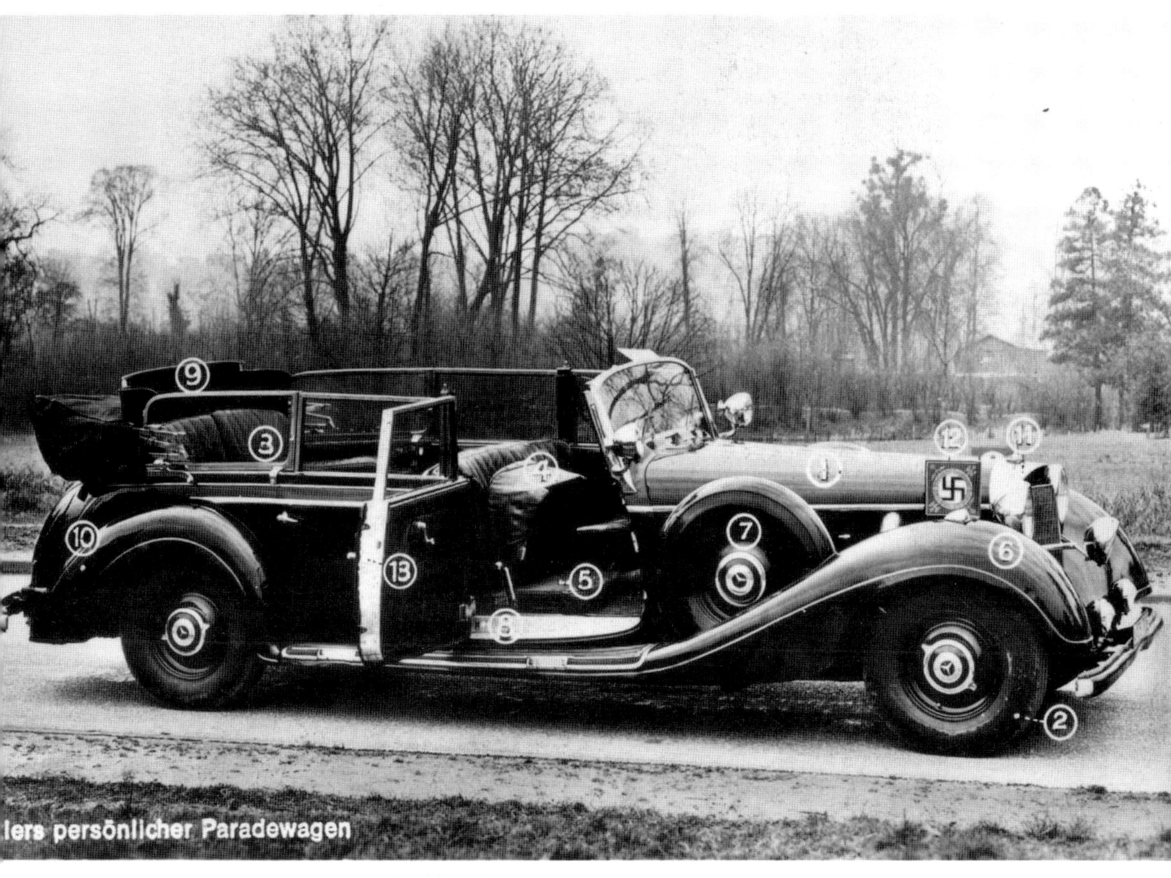

48. Hitler's Personal Parade Car.

In 1938 the prestigious German car manufacturer Daimler-Benz introduced the 770K their most luxurious car at the Paris Motor Show. When the model was adopted as Hitler's personal parade car the designers went to considerable lengths in their efforts to incorporate the required protection into the construction of the Führer's cars. However, it has to be said that Hitler's habit of standing up in the vehicle whilst being driven slowly through towns and cities would have provided any would-be assassin with an opportunity offering a good chance of success. The Führer survived some forty attempts on his life between 1932 and 1944. Having survived so many attempts on his life Hitler eventually came to believe that he was protected by providence in his great mission.

Obviously Hitler had more than one Mercedes car at his disposal. Vehicles were garaged and available for the Führer's use in most major cities, these included Berlin, Munich, Nuremberg, and of course at his Alpine retreat up on the Obersalzberg. It was a car like the one pictured that Gerd Bartels and Eugen Bühler discovered hidden in the barn at the back of Alpenhof within days of the arrival of those who had fled the Obersalzberg following the bombing of the area on 25 April 1945. A number of these vehicles found their way to the United States and into private collections after the Second World War.

The following information appears on the reverse of postcard number 48.
The numbers 1 to 13 relate to the numbers seen on the photo of Hitler's Mercedes.

HITLER'S PERSONAL PARADE CAR

Manufactured in 1942.

Weight empty: 4,780 kg/10,538 lbs./4.7 tons.

1. 400 HP engine/approx. 7655cc engine.
2. 20 cell tyres.
3. 40mm bullet-proof windows.
4. Hitler's seat; raised 13cm higher.
5. Hitler's footrest; raised 13cm higher.
6. Aluminium parts to lighten the car.
7. Spare wheels, used to protect the engine.
8. Electro-magnetic circuit locking the doors.
9. Manganese-treated armour plating.
10. 300 litre/66 gallon gasoline tank.
11. Nickel-silver radiator.
12. Hitler's personal flag.
13. Overall 18mm armour plating.

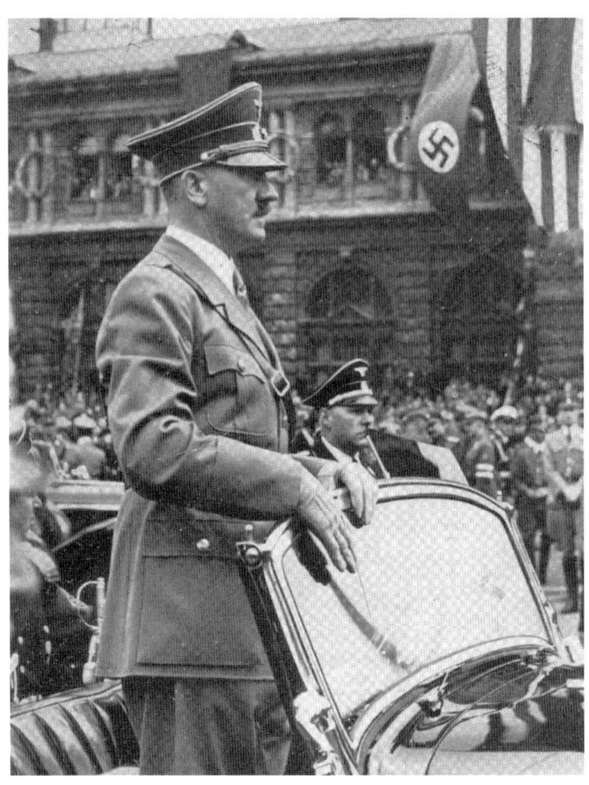

49. The arrival of the Führer at the Reichsparteitag.

Hitler is driven slowly through the streets of Nuremberg as he arrives in the city for the 1938 Reichsparteitag.

The Führer often stood up in his Mercedes cabriolet when being driven through crowded areas.

This apparently reckless act reduced the effectiveness of the vehicle's inbuilt protection leaving Hitler a target for any would-be assassin.

The 1938 Nazi Party Rally, *Der Parteitag Großdeutschland* (The Rally for Greater Germany) ran from 5 to 12 September that year.

This would be the last and the largest of the Nuremberg Rallies attracting over 700,000 Nazi Party members alone. Posted in Nuremberg on 7 September 1938 this card was sent to an address near Graz in Austria.

Hintersee, Obersalzberg, Berchtesgaden and the surrounding area

The importance of this region during the Third Reich period should never be underestimated. This area would become the Nazi southern headquarters, a place second only to Berlin in terms of importance. With that in mind it is hardly surprising that so much construction took place in and around the area during that time.

This included the Obersalzberg complex that sprang up close to Hitler's Berghof (see postcard number 59, page 81). Martin Bormann (1900–1945) Hitler's private secretary had a home overlooking the Berghof, while Hermann Göring (1893–1946) had a home located not far from the Bormann house. Albert Speer (1905–1981) Hitler's architect, later Reich Minister for Armaments and Munitions had a home, Waltenbergerheim, a little way down the mountain. Speer's home overlooked Bormann's mountainside farm, the 'Gutshof', most of which can still be seen.

Down in the valley a new train station was constructed in Berchtesgaden, and a new hotel, Hotel Berchtesgadener Hof; a Reich Chancellery and a state of the art hospital, the Dietrich Eckart Hospital in nearby Stanggaß; a youth hostel, the Adolf Hitler Youth Hostel, and a large military barracks, the Adolf Hitler Barracks at Strub just outside Berchtesgaden. There was a small airport at Ainring near Bad Reichenhall and two further large military barracks in the Karlstein area of Bad Reichenhall itself.

Back on the Obersalzberg housing was built to accommodate the required staff and maintenance personnel. These included the buildings at Hintereck, the closest to the central complex. Hermann Göring's adjutancy, also located at Hintereck provided accommodation for General Karl Heinrich Bodenschatz (1890–1979), his staff, and their families. A second settlement at Klaushöhe housed SS officers and their families. Klaushöhe was a short distance from the central complex.

The third and the largest settlement at Buchenhöhe was the furthest away from the main area. For the most part these three areas of accommodation, Hintereck, Klaushöhe and Buchenhöhe survived the intense bombing of the area on 25 April 1945. The largest and most complete of these facilities remaining is the Buchenhöhe settlement.

Somewhat miraculously Göring's adjutancy was one of the few buildings to survive the air raid completely unscathed. The former adjutancy along with the other buildings at Hintereck together with those at Klaushöhe and Buchenhöhe are now state owned and provide rented accommodation for local people.

While a good number of the buildings constructed during the Third Reich period, or those already existing that were put to use by the regime have been removed, many have survived and can still be seen today. That said, some of these constructions lie hidden in the forested areas of the Obersalzberg and many of these are now in a poor structural state and difficult to locate.

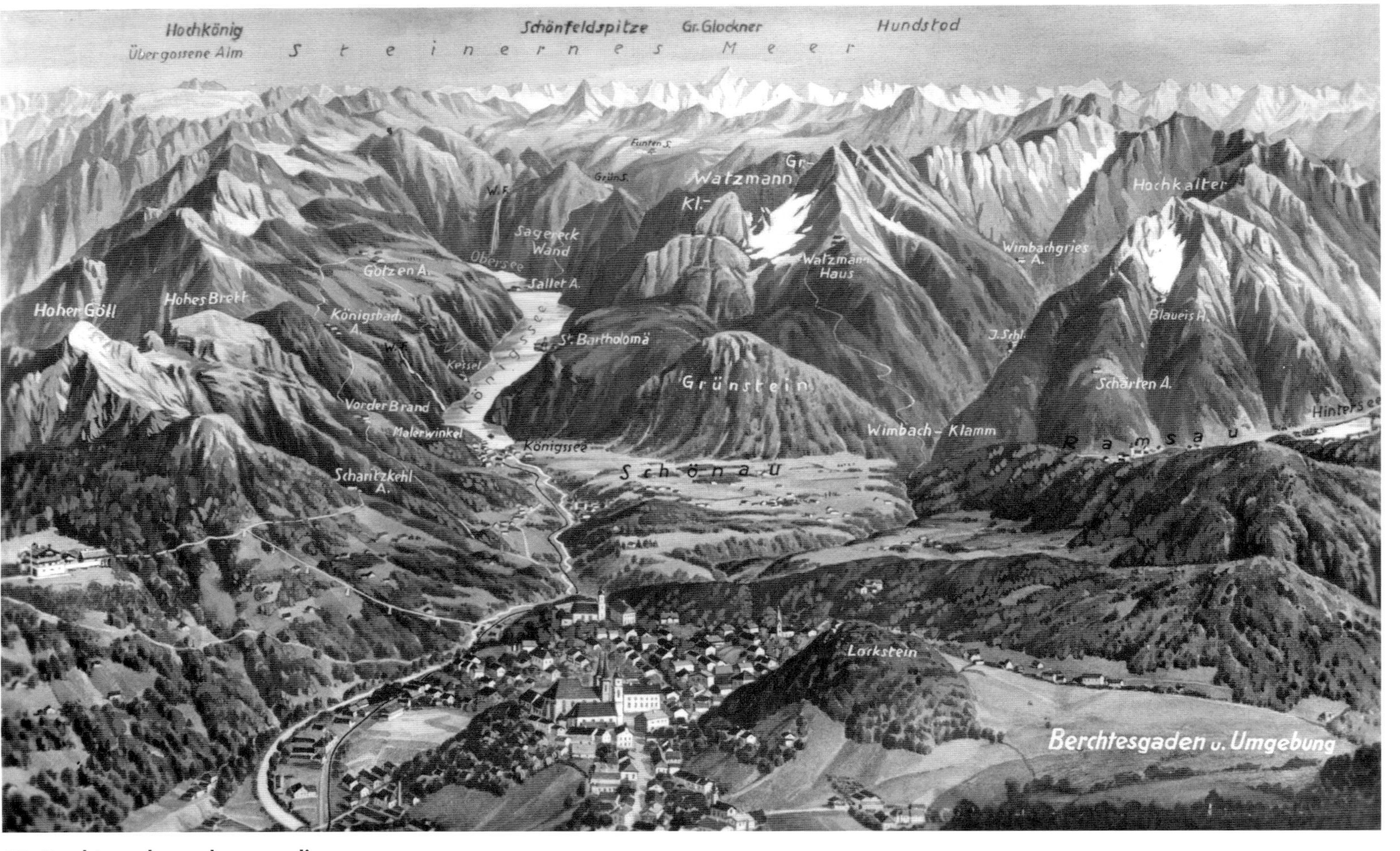

50. Berchtesgaden and surroundings.

This particular postcard shows the town of Berchtesgaden and other areas mentioned on these pages. On the extreme left of the image the house seen on the mountainside is Haus Wachenfeld; this is prior to the 1936/37 building work. On completion, the result of this building work was the much enlarged and better-known Berghof. The lake seen towards the centre of the image is the Königssee. The names Ramsau and Hintersee are printed in black on the right-hand side. While it has not been posted the reverse bears a hand-applied rubber stamp reading 'Hotel Post Hintersee' informing us that the postcard was purchased there.

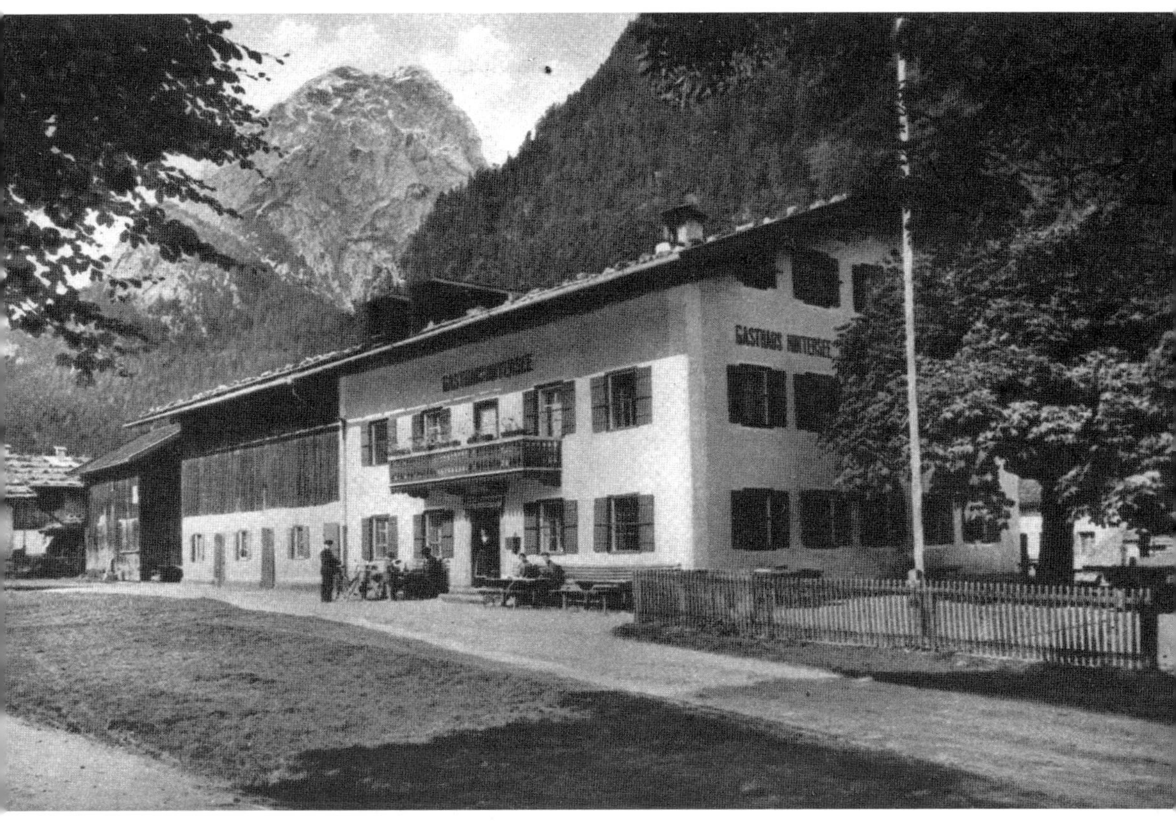

51. Auzinger's Restaurant Hintersee.
Opposite the Royal Hunting Lodge. Good home cooking. Superior beverages.
Guest rooms. Car garages. Telephone number 3 Hintersee. Owner S Hillebrand.
Whilst still open today, Auzinger's restaurant located on Hirschbichlstraße was close to the Altes Zollhaus (Old Customs House) owned by Dr Fritz Todt.

In the final days of the Second World War, *Generalleutnant* (Major-General) Rudolf Koch-Erpach (1886–1971) then acting Commander 1st Army stayed in Gasthaus Auzinger prior to his being captured. On 24 June 1940 following the battle for France and while commanding the 8th Infantry Division, Koch-Erpach was awarded the Knight's Cross of the Iron Cross.

In late 1944 with a deteriorating war situation and the ever-increasing risk of anticipated air raids in the area, men from the *Reichsarbeitsdienst* (RAD: Reich Labour Service) came to Hintersee and built three large wooden barracks in the Klausbachtal near the Ofental, about halfway between Hintersee and Hirschbichl. (The Klausbachtal is reached by continuing along the road past Gasthaus Auzinger). These large huts were used to store essential goods brought from the extensive supplies stored on the Obersalzberg. Subsequently these huts were guarded to prevent looting.

There were rumours doing the rounds suggesting that a last defence, a final battle would take place in Ramsau and Hintersee. These supplies would be absolutely essential if the military units in the region were to make a last stand. By early 1945 the Wehrmacht had an incredible amount of equipment stored in Ramsau, with machine-gun emplacements and anti-aircraft positions already in place.

52. The Altes Zollhaus, this is the former home of Dr Fritz Todt at Hintersee as photographed in 2022. On visiting Hintersee in December 2022 I was surprised to find that the line of high evergreen trees that previously hid the house from view had been cut down. Period postcards of the property are extremely rare and to get a photograph like this up until recently would have been impossible.

To date I have only seen one period postcard showing the Todt house at Hintersee. That image shows the property from the same angle. At that time a wooden fence sat on top of the low stone wall seen in the lower foreground. A flagpole flying the Nazi flag was located in a similar position to the tree seen on the left but closer to the house and behind the now removed fence. Apart from these small changes the property is virtually unchanged since the days when Fritz Todt lived here.

On learning of the difficulties Gerd's parents were experiencing in getting the necessary sheet metal for the roof of Alpenhof, Fritz Todt stepped in and used his influence to have the metal delivered quickly despite a nationwide shortage at the time. The Hintersee home of Dr Fritz Todt, former Reich Minister for Armament and Munitions was sold by his daughters in 1978.

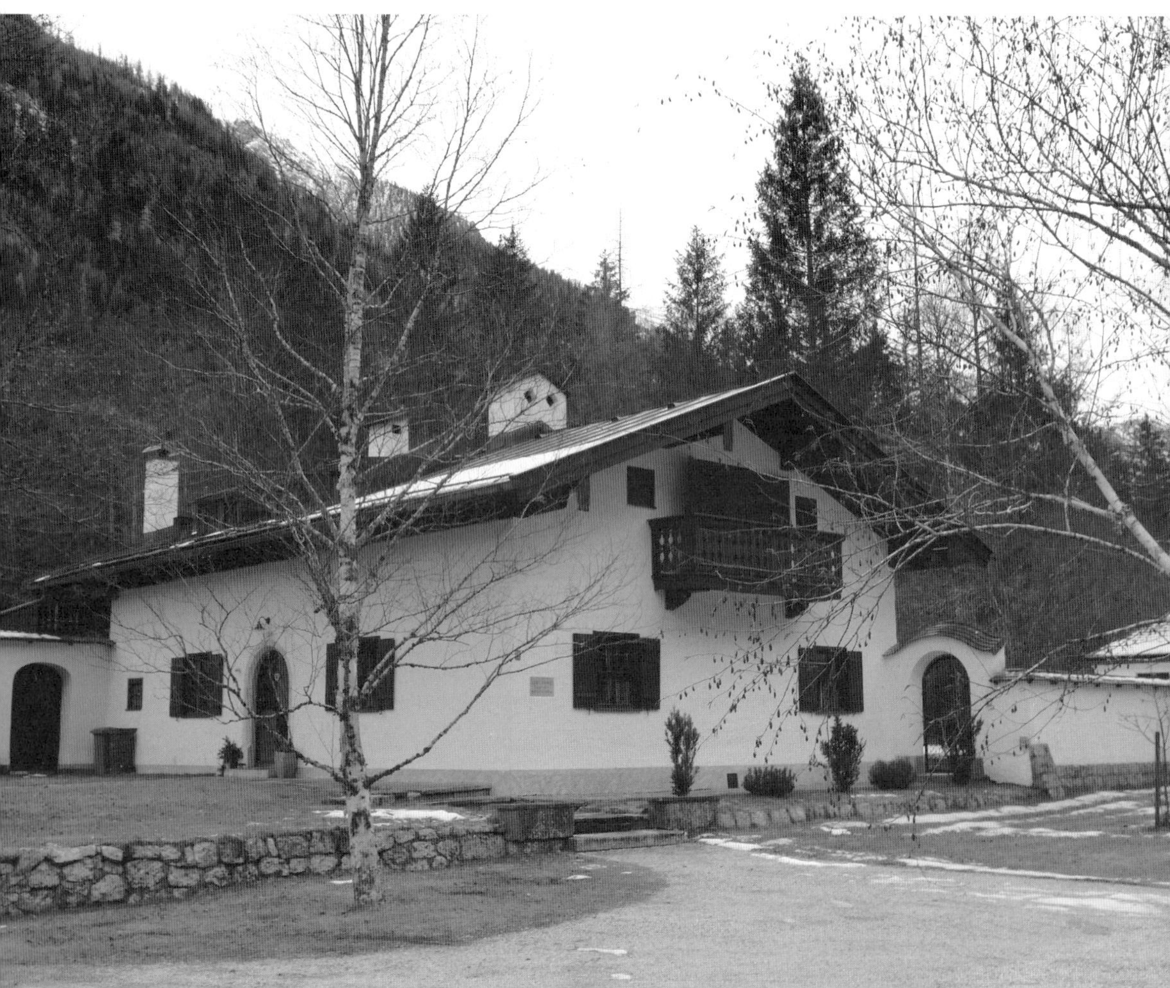

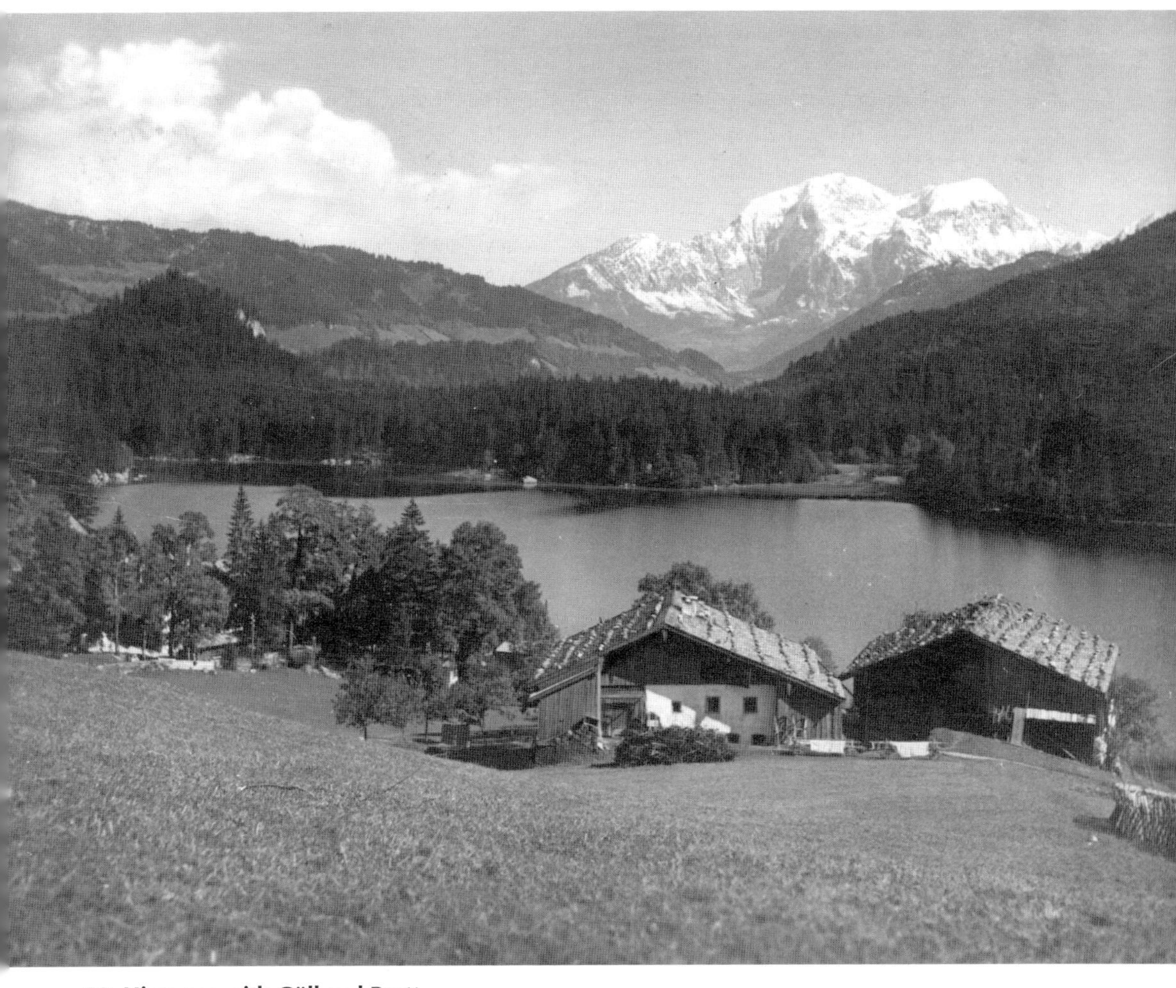

53. Hintersee with Göll and Brett.
The Berchtesgadener Land. At the Hintersee (800 metres above sea level).
This photo shows the Kainzierlhof located to the right and on the hill behind Alpenhof. Almost completely hidden amongst the trees the building on the left is Hotel Post. The Kainzierlhof was used to house refugees from Munich, people who'd fled the city to escape the bombing in the latter years of the Second World War.

The reverse bears a handwritten date of 12 September 1934. Less than a month later on 2 August 1934 and following the death of President Paul von Hindenburg, a law amalgamating the offices of President and Chancellor enabled Adolf Hitler to assume the title of *Führer und Reichkanzler* (Leader and Chancellor of the Reich).

Furthermore Hitler became commander-in-chief of the Wehrmacht (Combined Armed Forces). Thereafter all members of the armed forces were required to swear an oath of personal allegiance to Hitler.

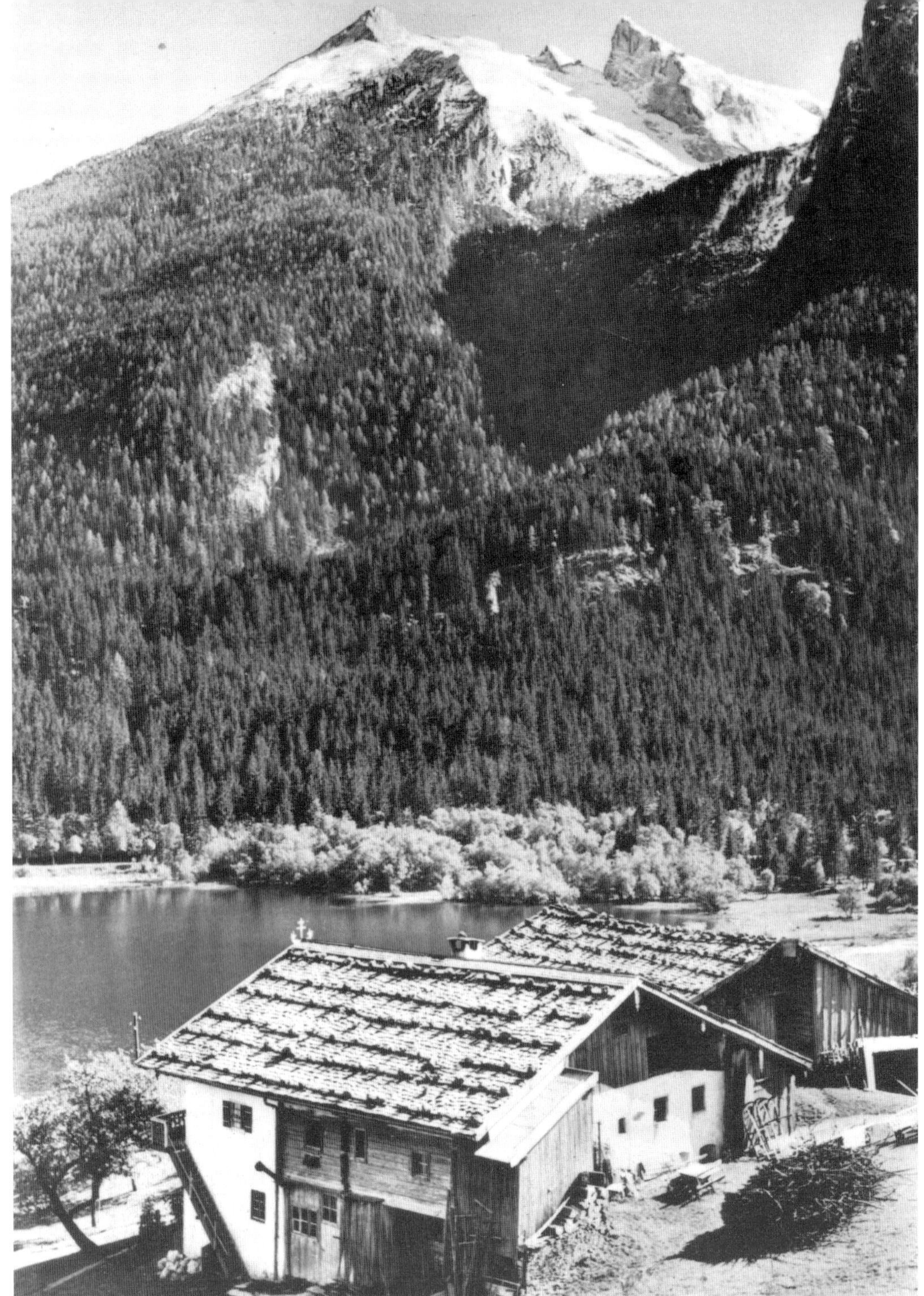

54. At the Hintersee.
The Kainzierlhof photographed looking towards the Hochkalter. This card was posted in Berchtesgaden on 8 September 1937 to an address in Rostock. The previous day Hitler had declared an end to the much-hated Versailles Treaty.

55. Dietrich Eckart Hut 1118m.

Dietrich Eckart, Hitler's friend and mentor was a founding member of the *Deutscher Arbeiterpartei* (DAP; German Workers' Party). Eckart, alongside Anton Drexler, Gottfried Feder and Karl Harrer had founded the DAP in Munich in January 1919. The *Deutscher Arbeiterpartei* were the forerunners of the *Nationalsozialistische Deutscher Arbeiterpartei* (NSDAP; National Socialist German Workers' Party).

Eckart lived in this property, the Göllhaüsl (later known as the Dietrich-Eckart-Haus) at Hinterbrand for a time in 1923 while he was in hiding. Aware that a warrant had been issued for his arrest following derogatory remarks in an article he'd written about the then President of the Weimar Republic, Friedrich Ebert, Eckart fled Munich to take refuge on the Obersalzberg under the assumed name Dr Hoffmann.

If there was one person who influenced Adolf Hitler during the early years of his political career it was undoubtedly Dietrich Eckart. It was while he was living in the Sonnblickhäusl on Berchtesgaden's Locksteinstr, later renamed the Dietrich Eckartstr, that Eckart died of a heart attack on 26 December 1923. He is buried in the town's *Alter Friedhof* (Old Cemetery).

Adolf Hitler never forgot Eckart, this man with whom he'd shared a strong personal bond. During the Third Reich period many town squares, streets, schools, sports stadiums, theatres and recreational facilities were named in honour of Eckart.

When a new hospital built at Stanggaß just outside Berchtesgaden was officially opened on 13 June 1942 it was named the Dietrich Eckart *Krankenhaus* (Hospital) in honour of the Führer's old friend. While the hospital is no longer in use, the complex remains standing. This postcard was posted on 9 July 1941 to an address in Neuburg an der Donau, a town west of Ingolstadt.

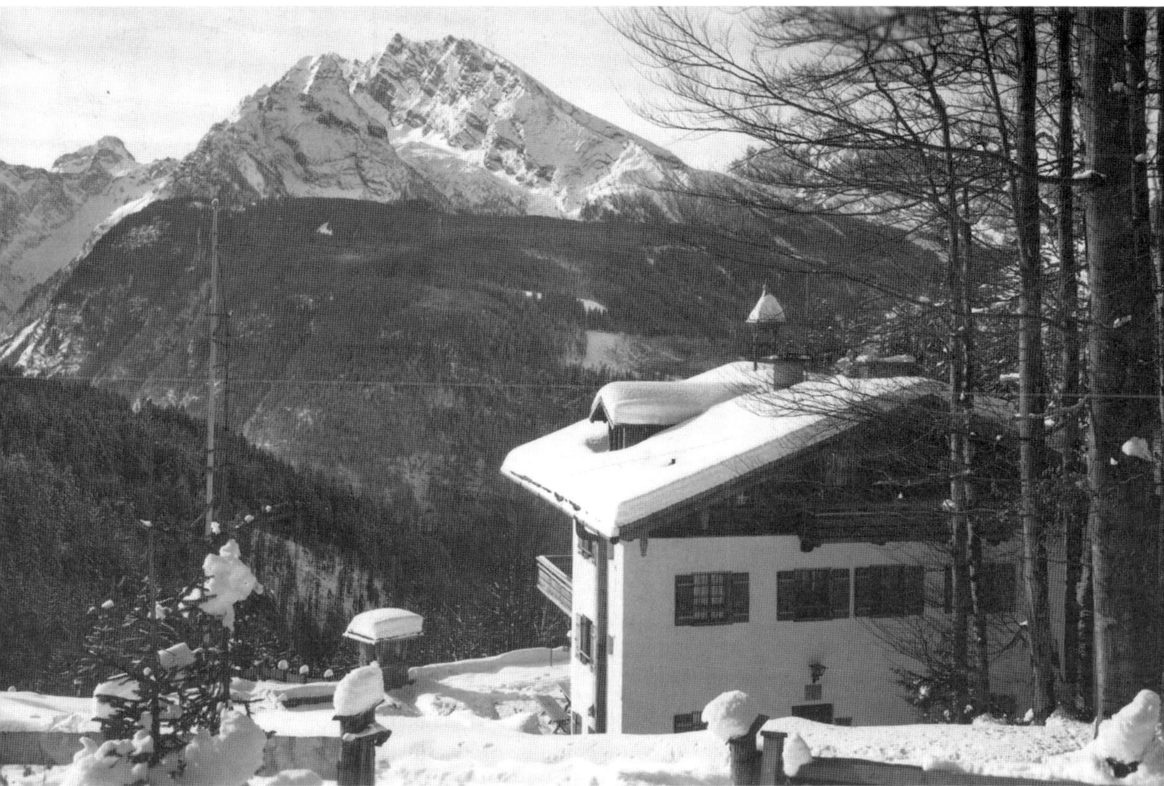

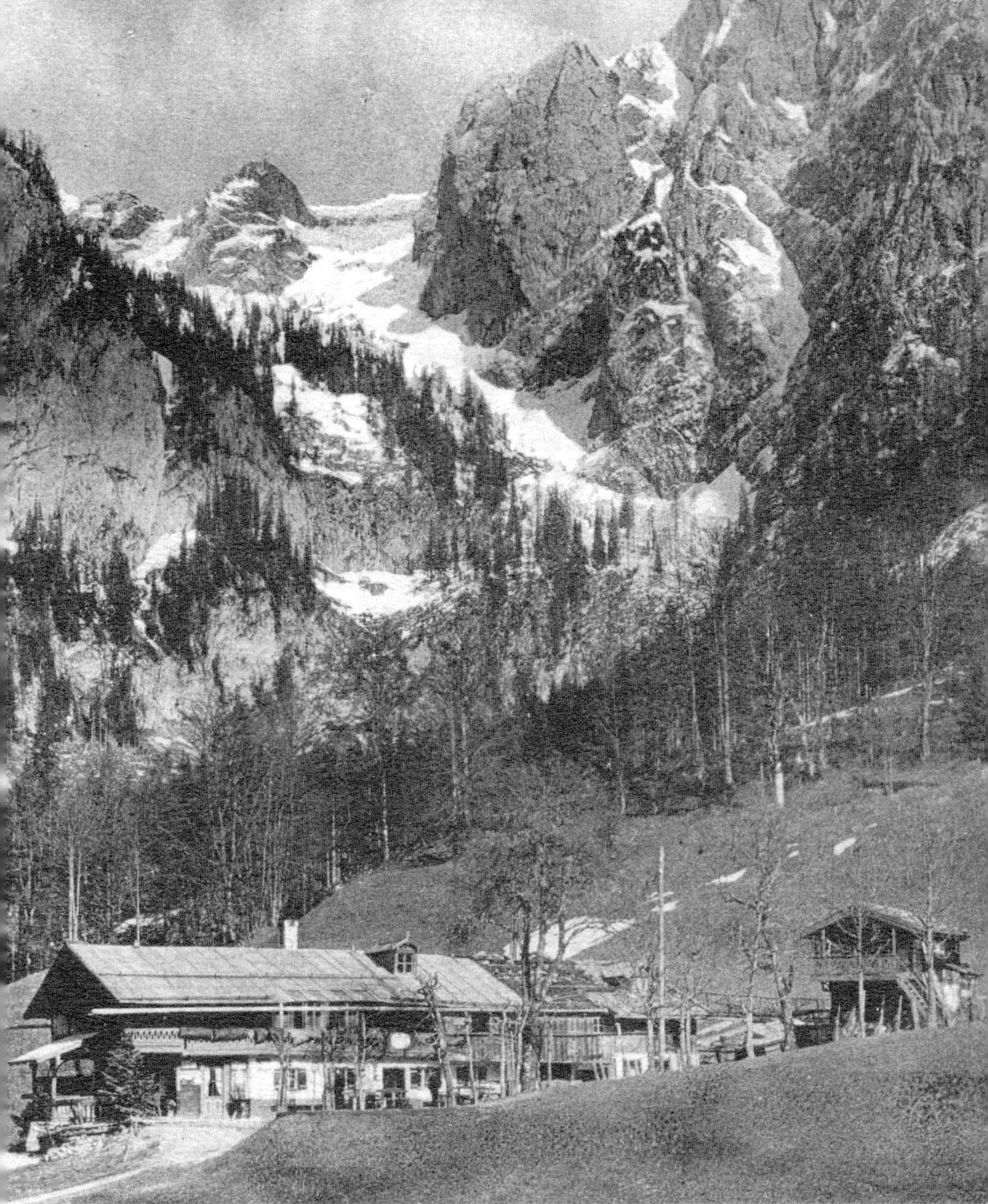

56. Vorderbrand near Berchtesgaden 1060m.
It was here at Vorderbrand close to the Dietrich-Eckart-Haus (the Göllhaüsl) at Hinterbrand that Eckart and Hitler met and dined during the period of Hitler's first visit to the area in April 1923 and also here that Hitler's sister Paula found refuge in 1945 when the Beer family took her in. Vorderbrand with its fabulous views towards Berchtesgaden and the Untersberg remains a popular venue.

57. Alpine Inn Vorderbrand (1067m) towards Untersberg.

The superb view across the Berchtesgaden valley looking towards the Untersberg massif as seen from Vorderbrand. Hitler's old friend Dietrich Eckart was well known at Vorderbrand; Eckart often dined at Vorderbrand located just a short walk from Hinterbrand where he stayed for a time during the period when he was in hiding and using the alias Dr Hoffmann. Occasionally Adolf Hitler accompanied Eckart on his visits to the nearby inn. Eckart and Hitler also visited Pension Moritz and Hotel zum Türken together. During this 'hiding-out' period on the Obersalzberg Dietrich Eckart also stayed in the Brüggenlehen, a farm again located in the Vorderbrand area.

The imposing Untersberg observed in the background straddles the German/Austrian border. In 1961 the Untersbergbahn (cable-car) opened to transport passengers to the summit at 1320 metres (4330 feet). Adolf Hitler had a fantastic view of the Untersberg from the Berghof, his Alpine retreat on the nearby Obersalzberg.

Bearing a hand-applied rubber stamp reading; *'Alpenwirtschaft Vorderbrand bei Berchtesgaden 1070m'*, this postcard was sent *'Feldpost'* (Military Post) from Berchtesgaden on 12 September 1940 to an address in nearby Bad Reichenhall. Less than a week before, on 7 September 1940, the Luftwaffe began its concentrated air attacks and bombing campaign against London and other strategic British cities.

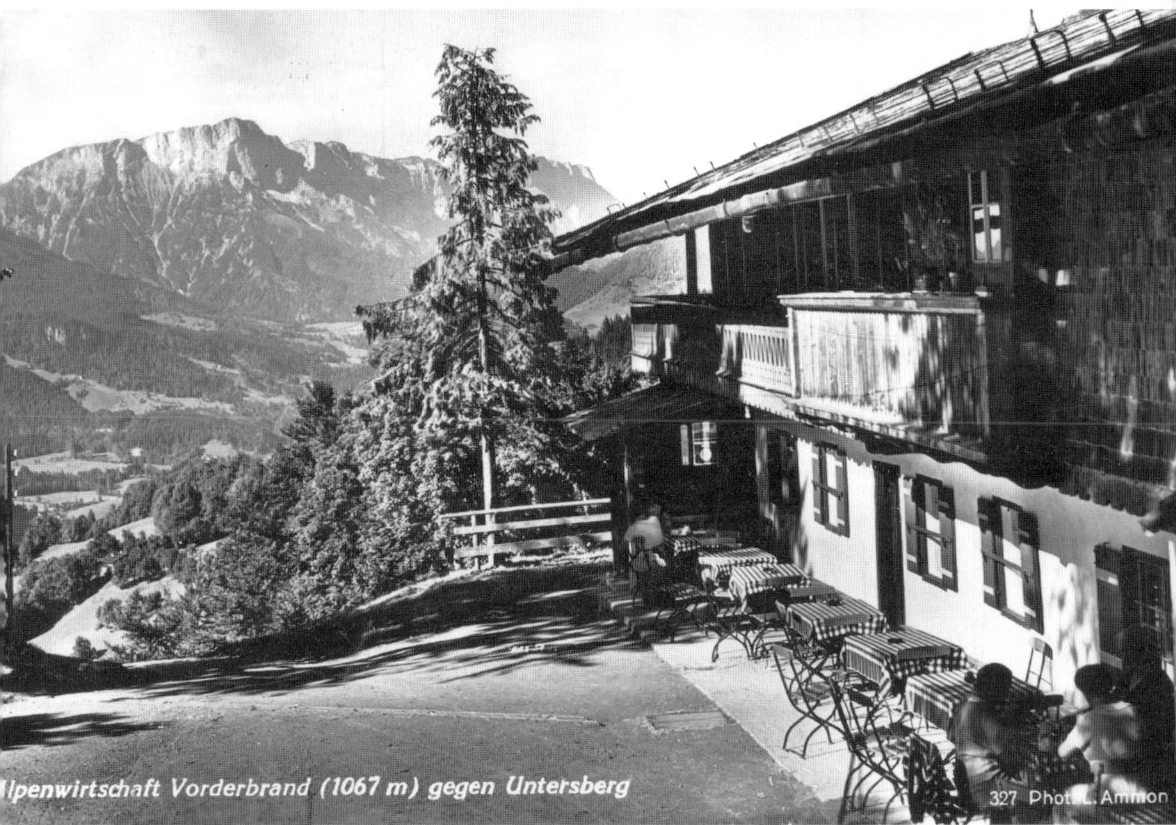

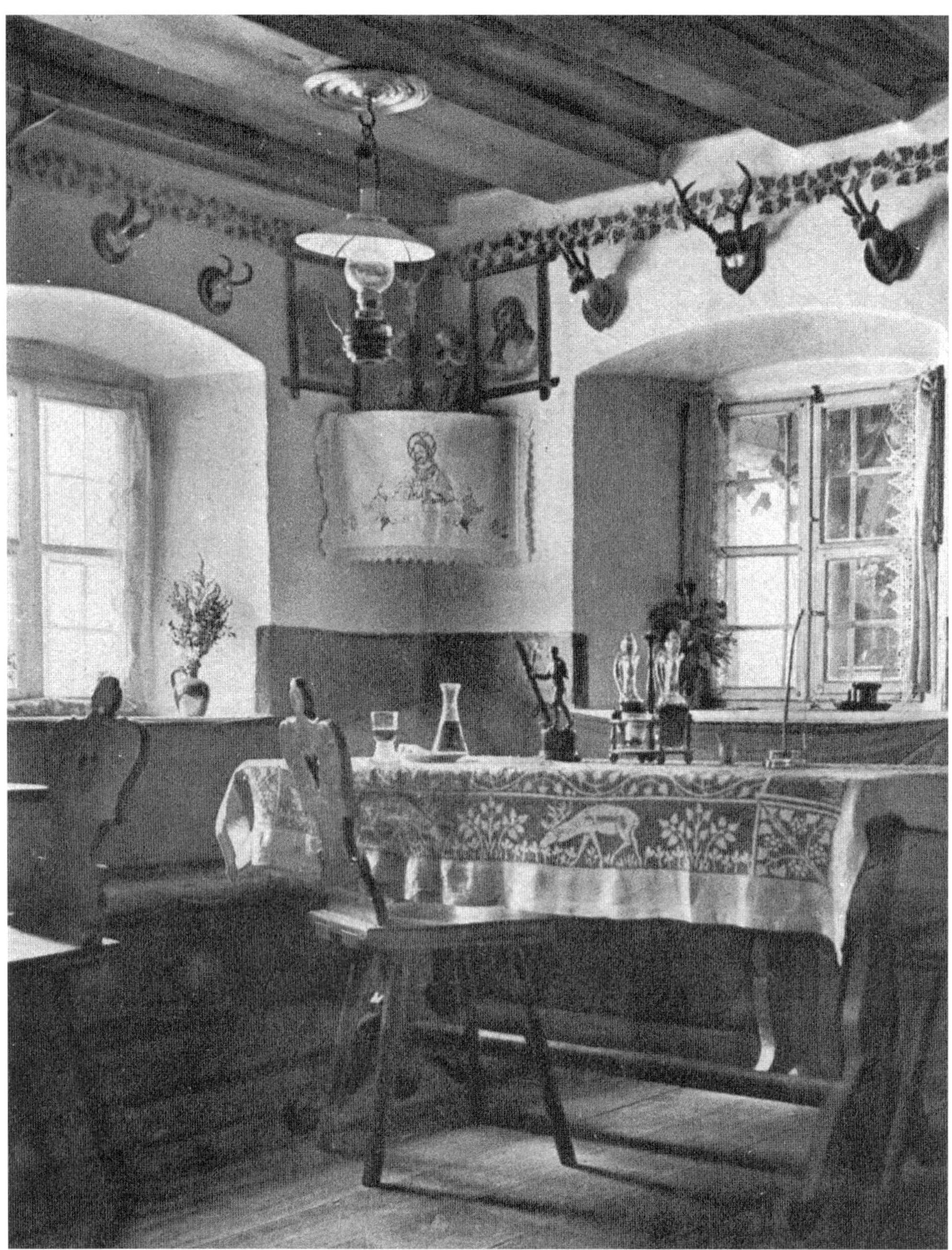

58. Vorderbrand near Berchtesgaden. Guest room.

This photograph dating from the early 1920s shows the smaller dining room, sometimes referred to as the Dietrich-Eckart-Zimmer at Vorderbrand. Eckart used this corner table when he visited the mountain inn. When accompanied by Hitler this is where both men sat and dined. While the furniture seen here has been replaced the room and this corner remain instantly recognizable today.

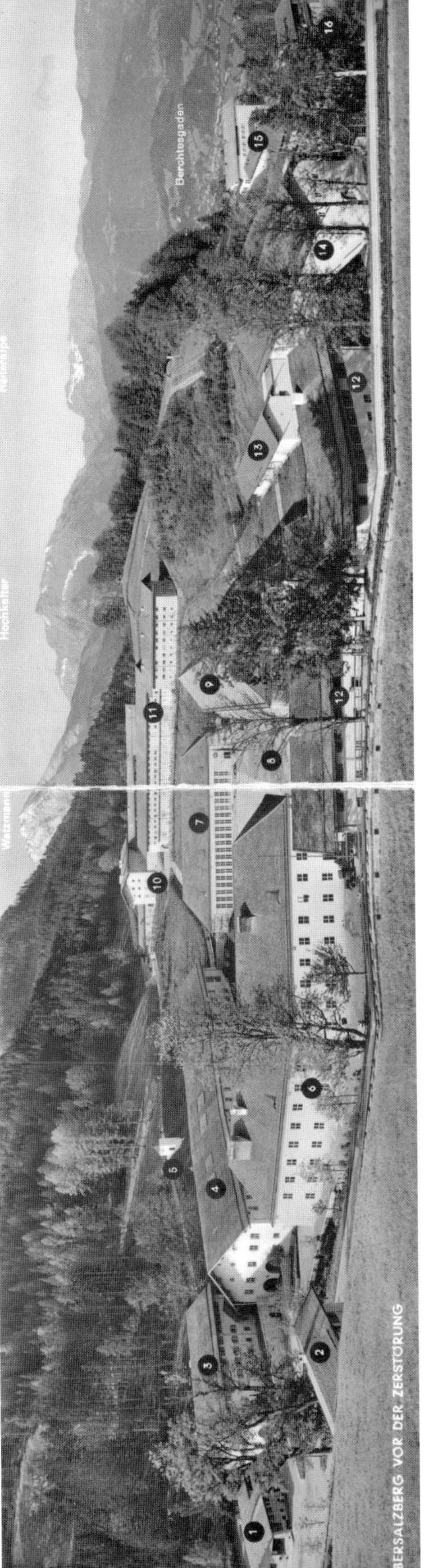

59. Obersalzberg before the destruction.
This double width, folding postcard shows the main Obersalzberg complex at the height of its development and prior to the bombing of the area on 25 April 1945.

The numbered buildings in the photograph are provided with accompanying text to indicate each building's function.
1. Post office in the prohibited area. **2.** Gardening ground with greenhouses and nursery. **3.** Chauffeur's living quarters. **4.** Large garage. **5.** Gatehouse to prohibited area. **6.** Barracks, economics building and kitchens. **7.** Barracks and drill hall of the bodyguard. **8.** Parade ground with underground shooting range. **9.** Barracks and living quarters. **10.** Hotel Platterhof. **11.** Hotel Platterhof staff living quarters. **12.** Obersalzberg administration building. **13.** Model house for architectural planning. **14.** Kindergarten. **15.** Berghof. **16.** Reich Security Service (RSD) and Gestapo (Hotel zum Türken).

60. Haus Wachenfeld home of Reich's Chancellor Adolf Hitler Berchtesgaden-Obersalzberg.
Using his own personal funds Hitler initiated the purchase of Haus Wachenfeld in September 1932; the purchase was completed in June 1933. Hitler bought the house for 40,000 Gold Marks. The vast sales of his book *Mein Kampf* had made Hitler a wealthy man.

This postcard shows the property following a number of renovations. These include the small additional single-storey room seen to the left of the main door and the garage with the terrace and balcony above.

The Führer spent considerable time on the Obersalzberg, initially here in Haus Wachenfeld, then following the major renovations through 1935/36 after which time the residence was generally referred to as the Berghof. That said, it is not unusual to find postcards with captions referring to the property as Berghof Wachenfeld after the 1935/36 renovations.

The arrival of the railway in Berchtesgaden in 1888 really opened the area to tourism. The arrival of the Reich Chancellor in 1933 provided yet another reason for thousands to flock to the area.

This postcard was posted in 1935 to an address in Salzwedel, a town northeast of Hannover.

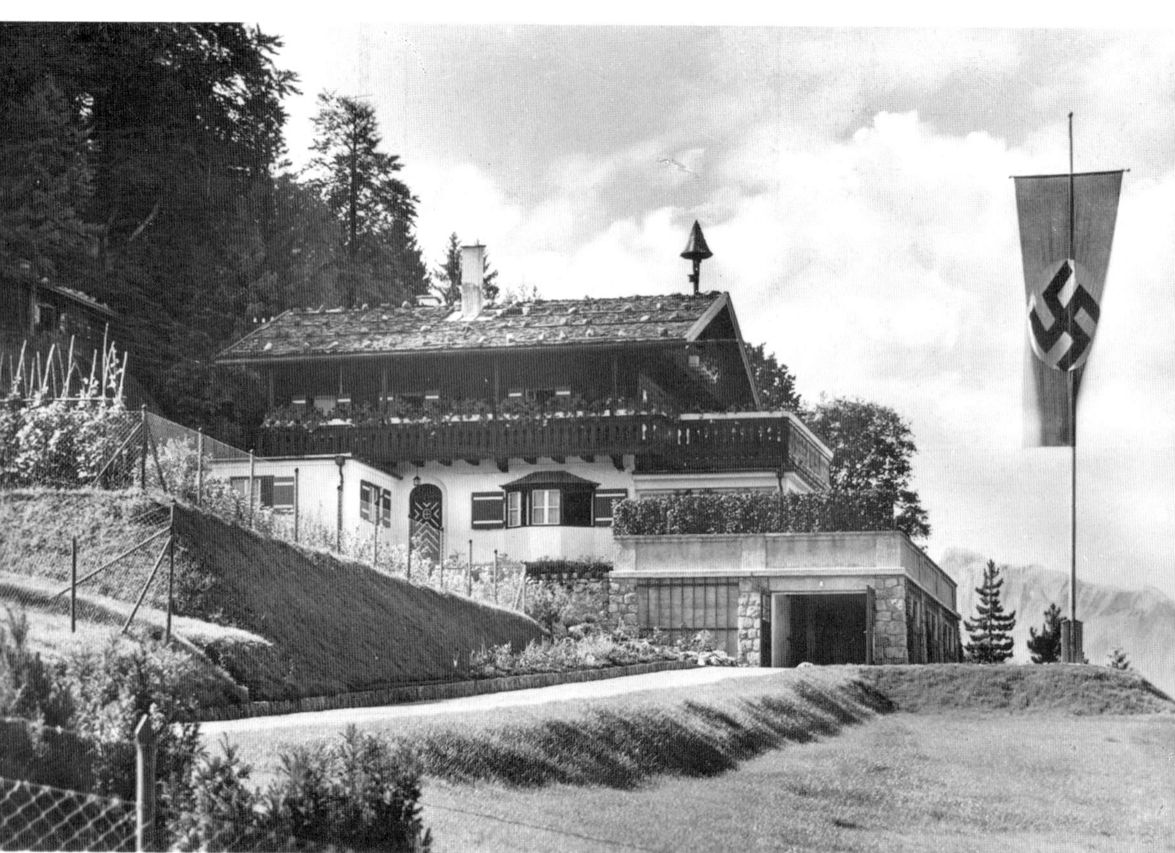

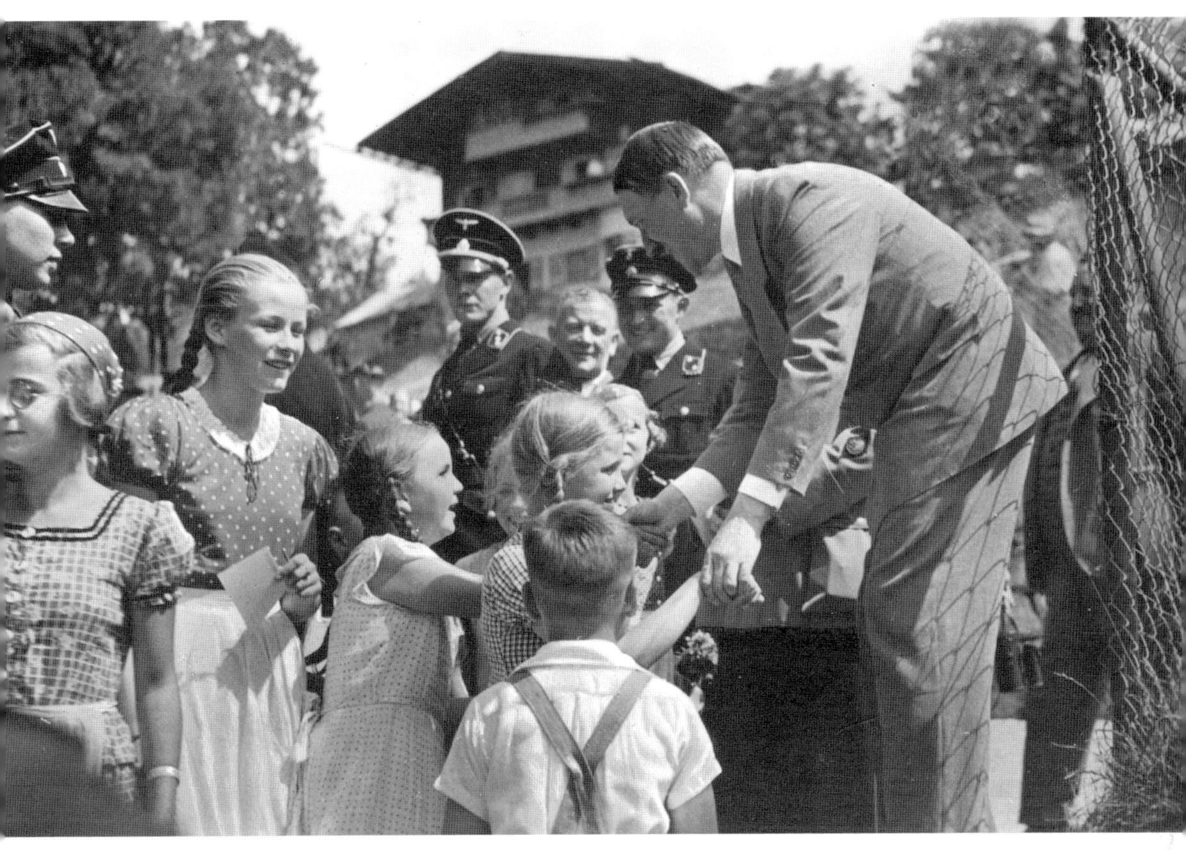

61. We all want to give the Führer our hand.
Hitler, standing on the low perimeter wall by the roadside at the end of the drive to Haus Wachenfeld greets a group of children. These young people are part of the daily procession on the road below the house. The building in the background is Hotel zum Türken. Ever-watchful black-uniformed SS-men mingle with the crowd.

It's interesting to note that Hitler gave something of an impromptu speech to local people gathered in Hotel zum Türken on Saturday, 28 April 1923, just days after celebrating his 34th birthday on 20 April. Hitler had gone to the hotel with his friend Dietrich Eckart who was then 'hiding out' in the area. This was Hitler's first speech on the Obersalzberg.

At that point in time the future Führer could not have known that he would rent the small Alpine chalet within sight of the hotel in October 1928, or how Haus Wachenfeld and this mountain would come to play a pivotal role in both his personal and political life, and in world events. This postcard was posted in Berchtesgaden on 10 September 1935.

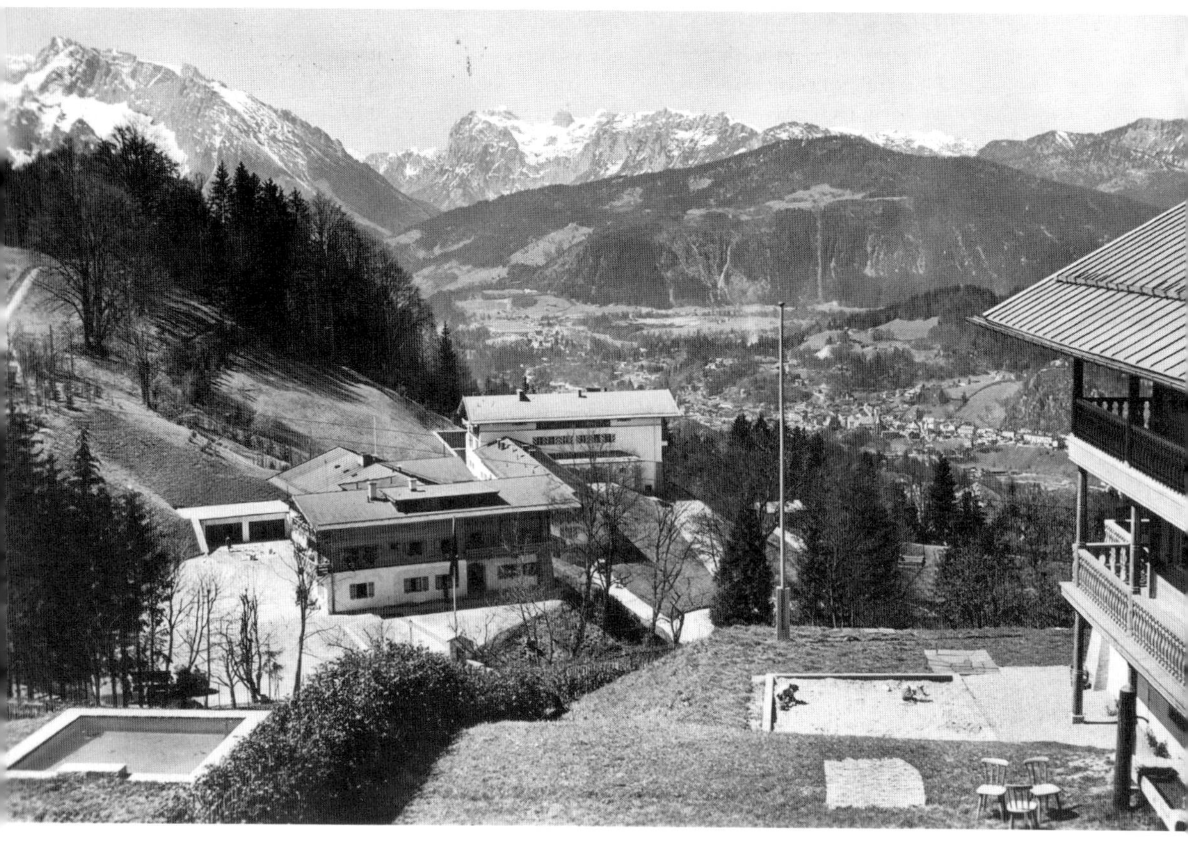

62. Obersalzberg: view of the Berghof and Berchtesgaden.

The building on the right was Martin Bormann's Obersalzberg home. As we can see Bormann's house overlooked both Hotel zum Türken and Hitler's Berghof. In addition to providing fabulous mountain views Bormann's home allowed him to observe all the comings and goings to the Berghof.

This photograph also shows the proximity of Hotel zum Türken (the building to the left below Bormann's home) to Hitler's Berghof (the building furthest away in the centre of the image). Hotel zum Türken's position made it a perfect location for the RSD and Gestapo: as many as forty men were stationed in the former hotel.

The owner of Hotel zum Türken, Karl Schuster, was forced to sell the hotel to Martin Bormann; the sale was completed on 25 November 1933. The property was taken over and occupied by the *Reichsicherheitsdienst* (RSD; Reich Security Service) and Gestapo who were responsible for Hitler's personal safety when he was on the Obersalzberg.

The Schuster family were successful in reclaiming the property after the war. This was the only instance where the owner of a property confiscated by Bormann was returned to the original owner on the Obersalzberg. The bomb-damaged building was renovated and reopened in December 1950. Karl Schuster's great-granddaughter, Monika Scharfenberg-Betzien has sold Hotel zum Türken, the sale being completed in January 2021. The new owners wished to remain anonymous. The local newspaper, the *Berchtesgadener Anzeiger* described the buyers as 'a long-established local family of entrepreneurs'. The building has been 'moth-balled' by the new owners; what will become of it in the future remains unknown.

63. Berghof Obersalzberg.

Haus Wachenfeld, the rather humble Alpine chalet as observed in image number 60, would evolve to become the 'Berghof' following extensive renovations through 1935/36. Hitler's emotional attachment to the old house saw the old building cleverly integrated into the new and much larger residence.

Of particular interest is the large picture window in the conference room/great hall; it measured 9 x 3.6 metres (27 x 12 feet) and had a surface area of thirty-two square metres (344 square feet). This huge double-glazed window, consisting of ninety panes of glass could be lowered into a specially constructed shaft in the basement below. This provided spectacular uninterrupted views across the valley towards the Untersberg and the city of Salzburg in nearby Austria, the Führer's homeland. Here the mighty Hoher Göll standing at 2519 metres (8264 feet) dominates the background.

The whole mountainside would eventually become a closed off security zone with no less than three SS-manned checkpoints to be passed on the road up from Berchtesgaden to the Berghof itself. The only building of any significance from the period and the one that was the closest to Hitler's Berghof, Hotel zum Türken, is the only building to remain standing. The hotel's proximity to the Berghof made it a perfect base for the *Reichsicherheitsdienst* (RSD; Reich Security Service) and Gestapo who were responsible for Hitler's personal security when the Führer was residing on the Obersalzberg.

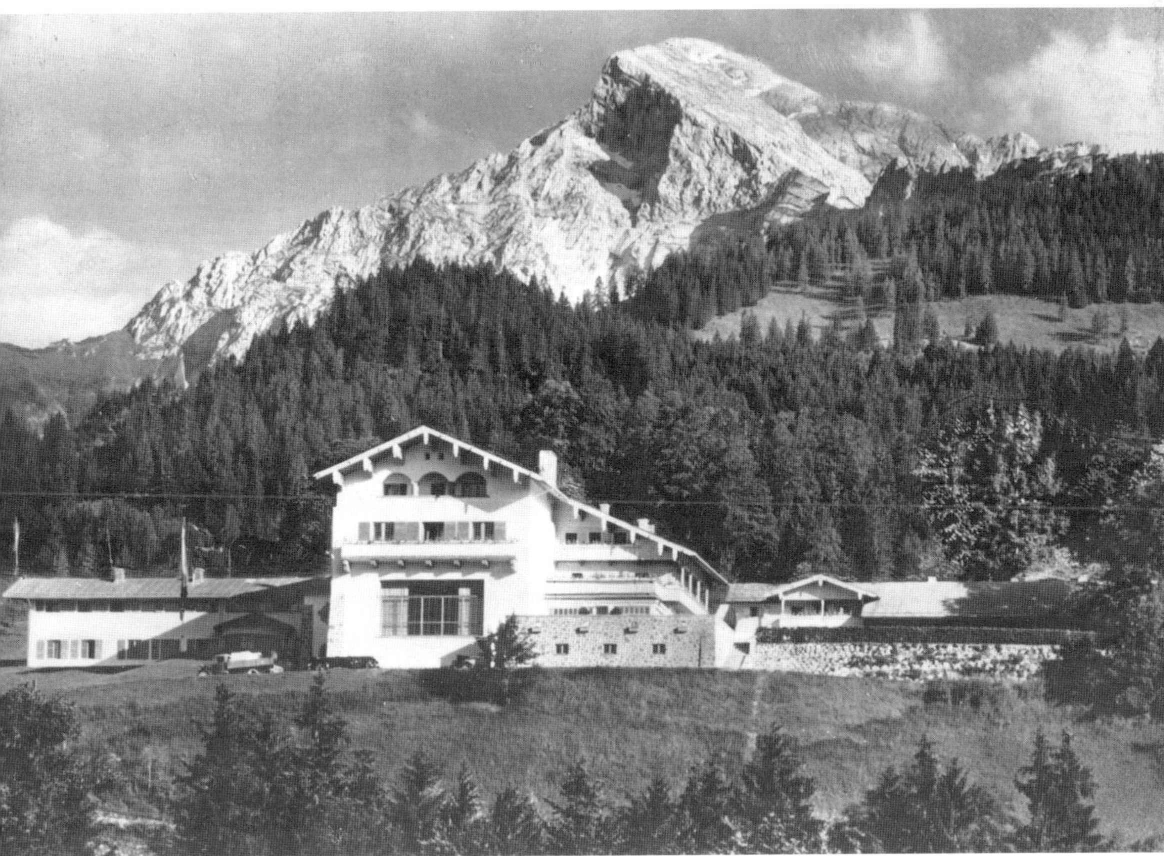

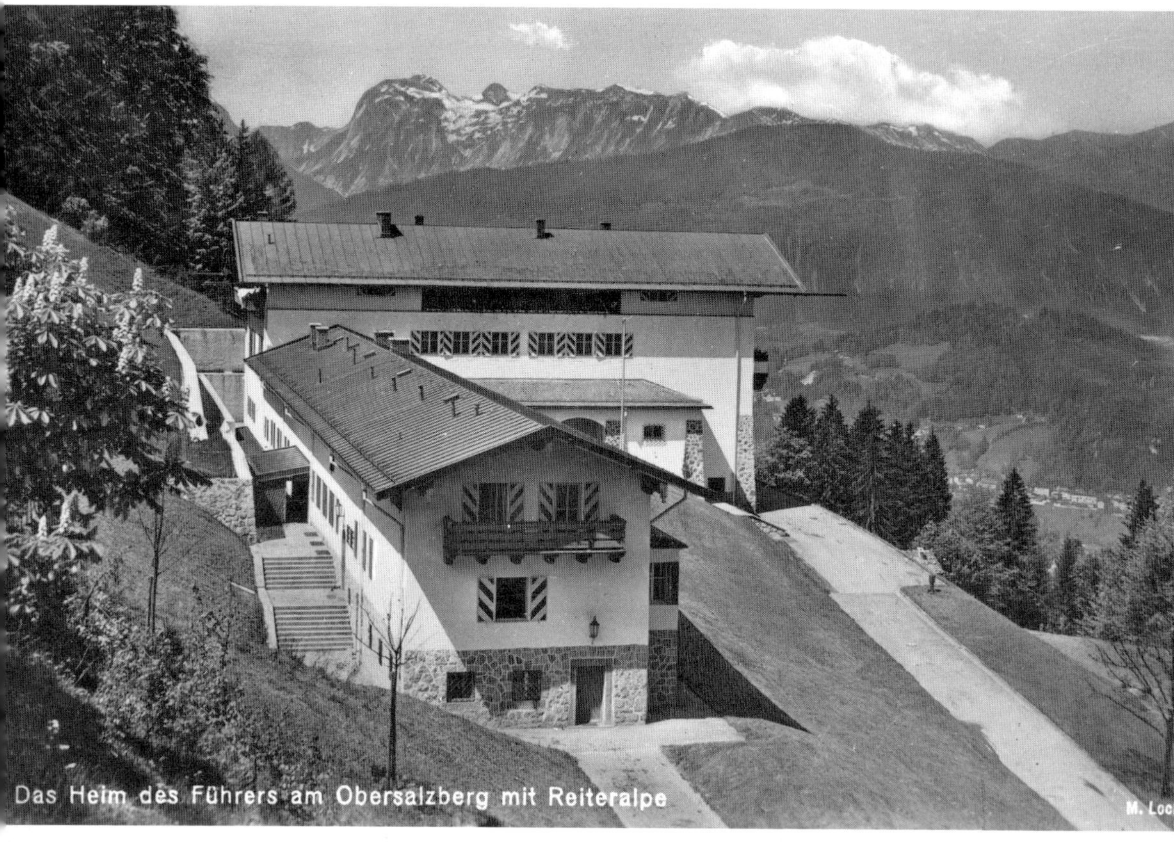

64. The home of the Führer on the Obersalzberg with Reiteralpe.

This image shows Hitler's Berghof on the Obersalzberg above Berchtesgaden following the final renovations. This is how the building would remain until the day of the Allied air raid on Wednesday 25 April 1945. The drive seen on the right hand side was the main drive leading to the flight of steps by which one entered the building. The drive seen in the centre of the image was a service road for deliveries to the Berghof.

It was here that many important political and military decisions were made. 'Operation Barbarossa', the planned invasion of the Soviet Union that began on 22 June 1941 would receive final approval here. Hitler described this area as his *Wahlheimat,* 'the homeland of his choice.' During the time of his Chancellorship Hitler spent two-thirds of that time on the Obersalzberg; more time here than anywhere else. This alone clearly indicates the importance of this area to Hitler on a personal level. The bomb-damaged remains of Adolf Hitler's Berghof were finally blown up on the afternoon of Wednesday, 30 April 1952.

Even today the Obersalzberg retains a number of lesser-known structures from the Third Reich period. Whilst not having been maintained through the intervening years most of these structures are now in a poor state, some dangerously so and unless familiar with the area they are difficult to locate.

65. The Berghof on the Obersalzberg.

This is one of very few postcards to show the Berghof and the Kehlsteinhaus (Eagle's Nest) in the same image. High on the right and at the top of the photograph we can see the Kehlsteinhaus perched on top of the Kehlstein Mountain.

Despite occasional circumstances where the Kehlsteinhaus and the Berghof have been presented, or have been perceived to be one and the same building this is clearly not the case. The Kehlsteinhaus was not designed nor was it intended to be lived in, the plans did not include bedrooms, and no one has ever spent a night in the building.

The Berghof itself stands at 1000 metres (3280 feet) above sea level while the Kehlsteinhaus stands at 1834 metres (6017 feet) a difference in elevation of 834 metres (2736 feet).

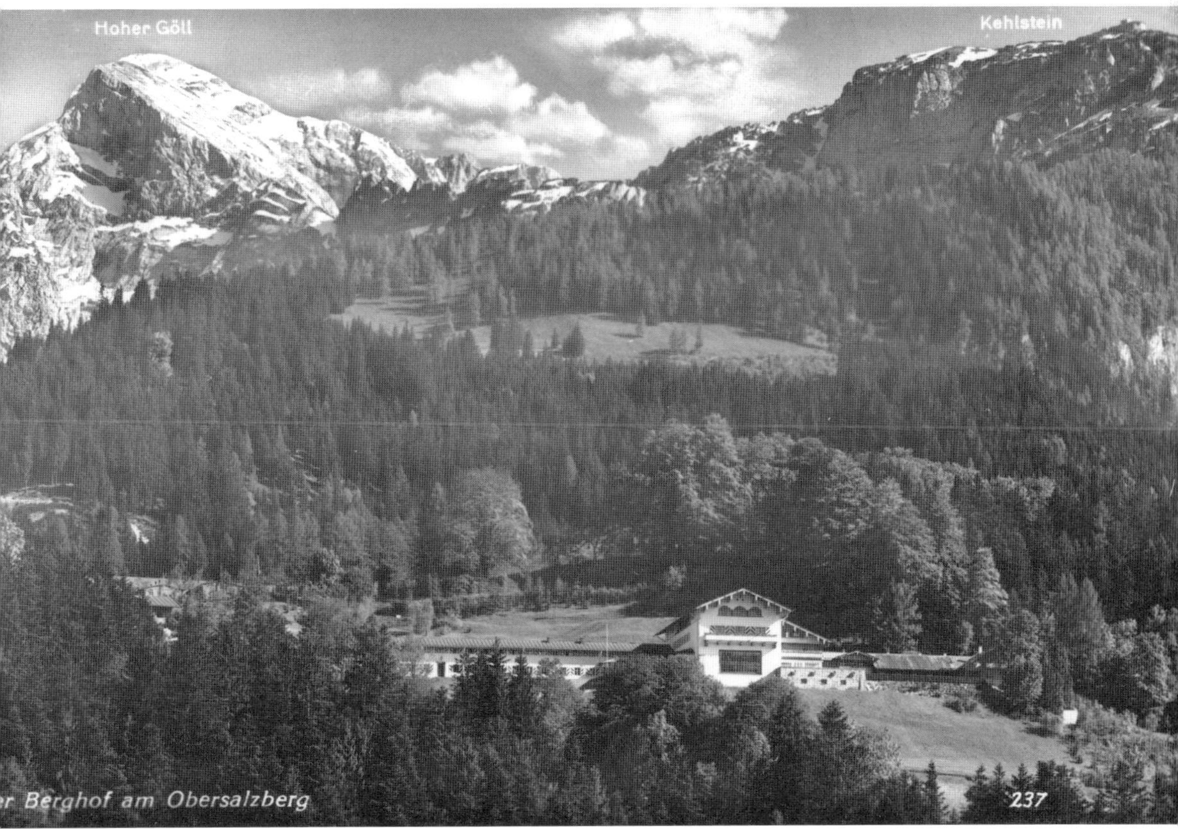

66. The Führer and Dr Goebbels at Berghof Wachenfeld.
This postcard shows Hitler and a small group walking down the drive towards the road; they may be setting out to walk to Mooslahnerkopf. Hitler made almost daily visits to the small teahouse located at Mooslahnerkopf below the Berghof when he was on the Obersalzberg.

Working left to right we see:

Professor Albert Speer (1905–1981), Speer was Hitler's favourite architect as well as a close friend and confidant. Following the death of Dr Fritz Todt on 8 February 1942, Albert Speer succeeded Todt as Reich Minister for Armament and Munitions, a position in which he was very successful.

Adolf Hitler (1889–1945), Nazi Party leader.

Dr Joseph Goebbels (1897–1945), Minister for Public Enlightenment and Propaganda.

The man next to Goebbels is unknown.

Dr Karl Brandt (1904–1948), Hitler's personal physician and a regular visitor on the Obersalzberg. Karl Brandt held the rank of SS-*Brigadeführer* (Brigadier-General) in the Waffen-SS and was a close friend of both Hitler and Speer. In August 1944 Brandt was appointed Reich Commissioner for Sanitation and Health.

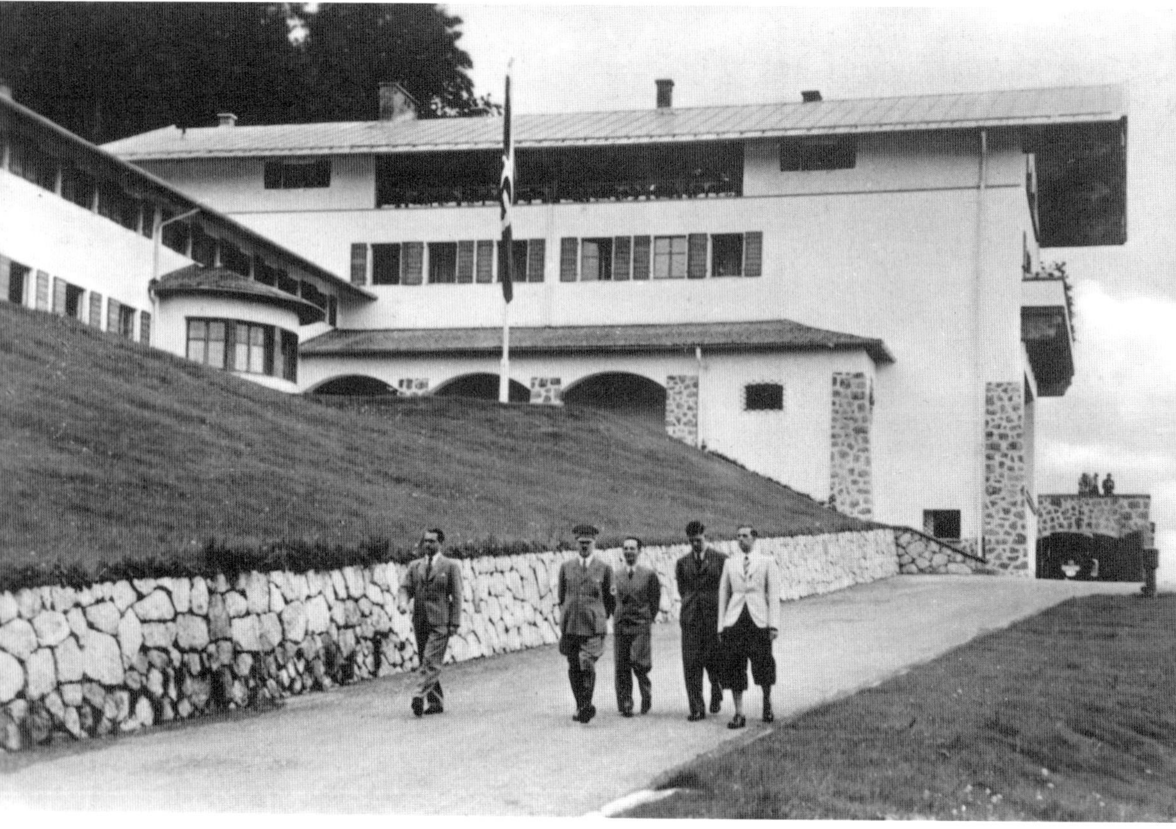

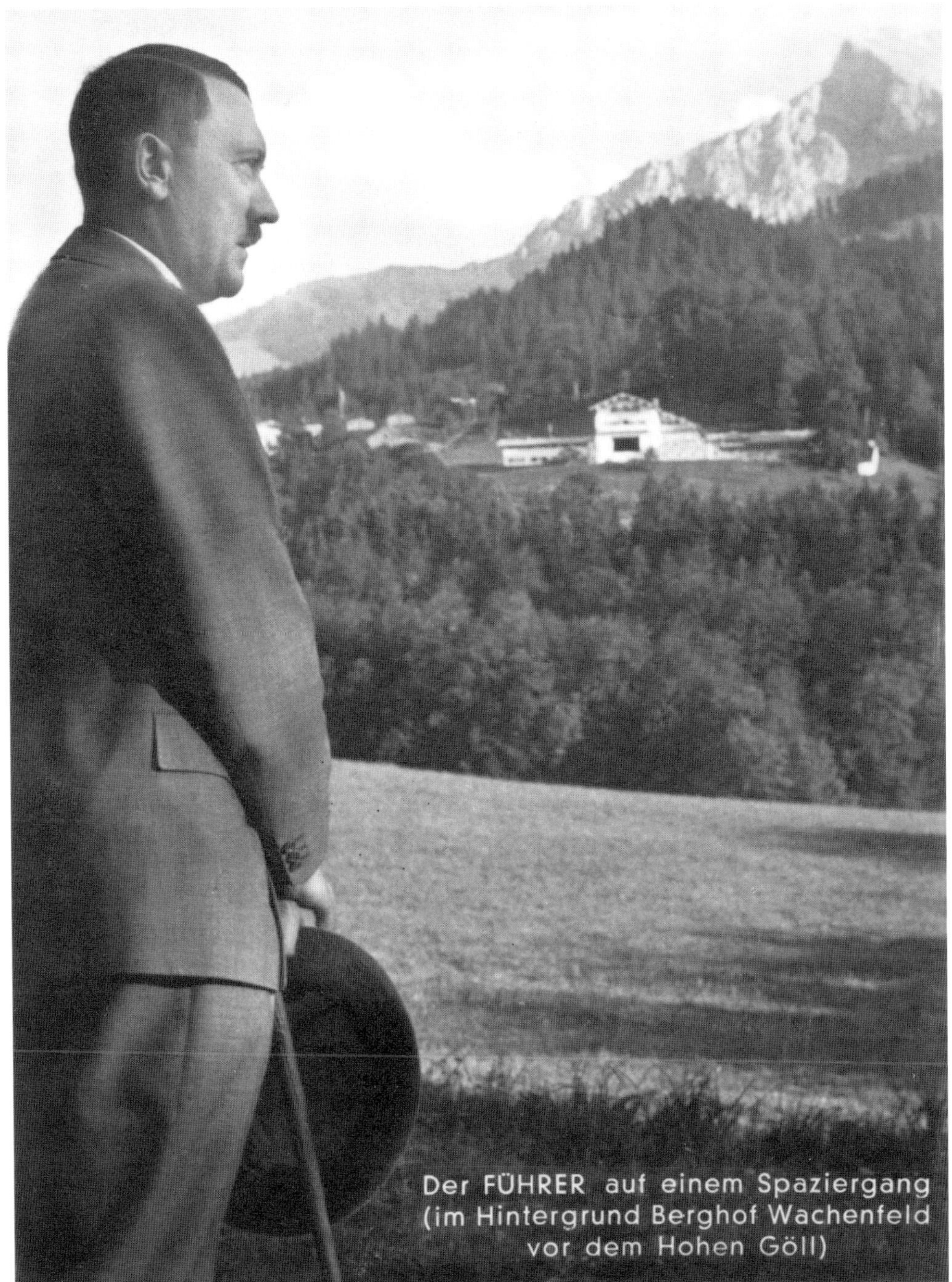

67. The Führer on a walk (In the background Berghof Wachenfeld in front of the Hohen Göll).
Hitler pauses to allow Hoffmann to take this photograph on what appears to be an outing to Mooslahnerkopf. The pasture seen in the foreground now forms part of the Obersalzberg golf course. Someone has addressed this postcard, written the date 6 September 1943 on the reverse; they have then written just one line and stopped there.

68. Reverse unmarked, source unknown.

Hitler's teahouse located at Mooslahnerkopf. Professor Roderick Fick (1886–1955), the man who designed almost all the buildings that were constructed on the Obersalzberg also designed Hitler's favourite teahouse at Mooslahnerkopf.

A very talented architect, Fick joined the Nazi Party in 1935. Martin Bormann commissioned Fick to provide the plans for the teahouse. Fick submitted the plans in 1936; incredibly building work was completed before the end of the following year. This project was yet another of Bormann's ideas as he strove to please the Führer and ingratiate himself. The building was partially constructed against the cliff behind it.

The circular room, the main reception room, was beautifully finished and accommodated a large round table and confortable armchairs. A long gold-framed mirror hung above the marble fireplace. A decorative clock sat on the mantelpiece.

The top of the mirror featured a type of wreath design with the letters 'AH' at its centre. A large chandelier hung above the central table; there were wall-mounted candelabras, each holding three candles. Heating had been installed beneath the marble floor. The rear of the building accommodated the kitchen, store-rooms and the usual facilities. Interestingly the four trees seen on the left in the foreground are still there.

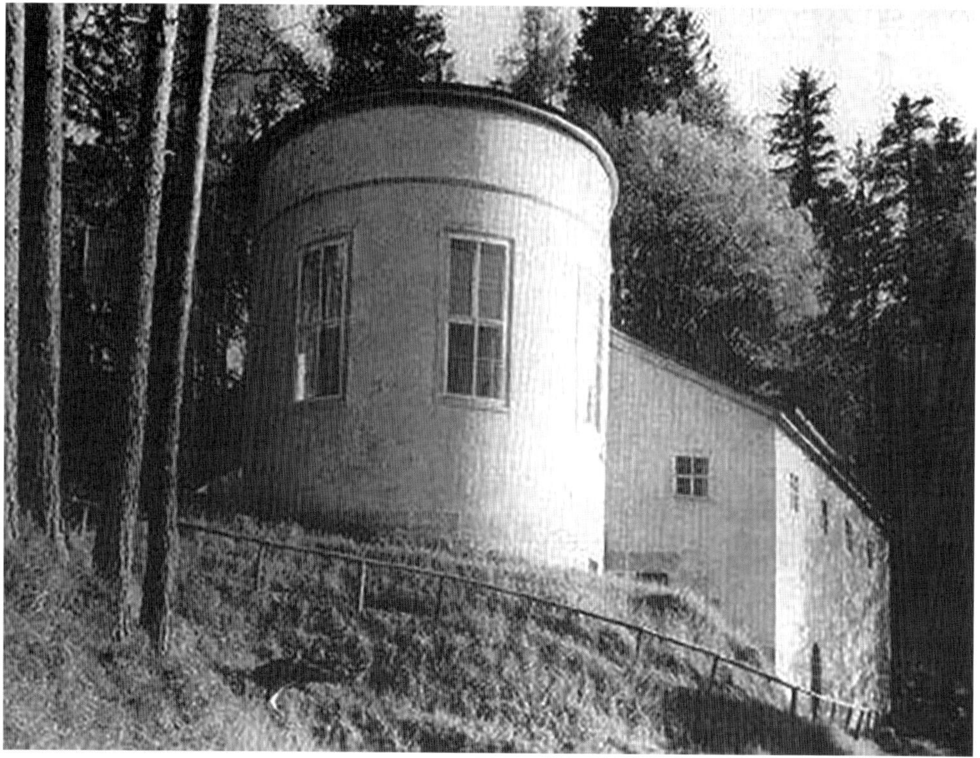

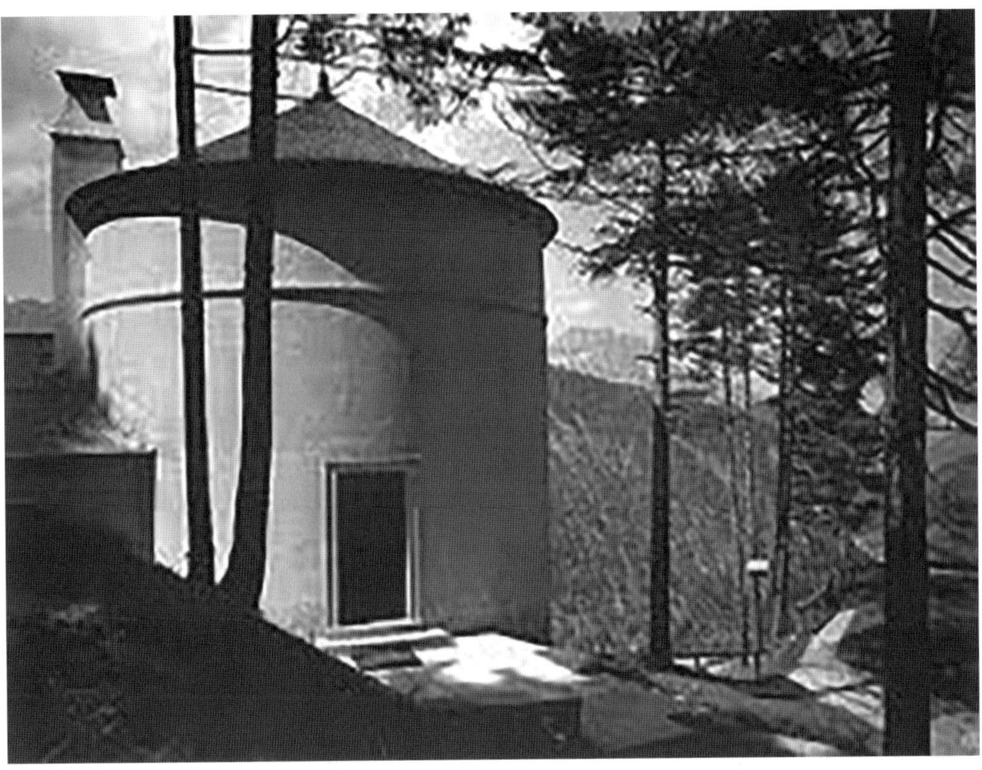

69. Reverse unmarked, source unknown.

This photograph shows the main entrance to the building. On the right of the photograph we can see the path leading to the famous overlook with views towards the Untersberg and, on a clear day, the castle in Salzburg is visible.

While the overlook remains unchanged there is little trace of the building itself today. As previously mentioned, having survived the bombing of the Obersalzberg in April 1945 the building was torn down in 1952 with the remaining ruins being cleared in 2007.

Hitler's daily walk from the Berghof down to Mooslahnerkopf would have taken a leisurely thirty minutes. Today it takes around forty-five to fifty minutes. This is due to the fact that one must now follow a route around the perimeter of the golf course.

The visits to this teahouse became part of the Führer's daily routine. Hitler liked to gaze out across the valley towards the city of Salzburg in nearby Austria, his homeland.

Once inside the teahouse Hitler could relax, enjoy tea and cake and chat with his guests; hot chocolate and apple cake were particular favourites. Here, in this small teahouse at Mooslahnerkopf the Führer could escape the pressures and daily grind of statesmanship for a short while.

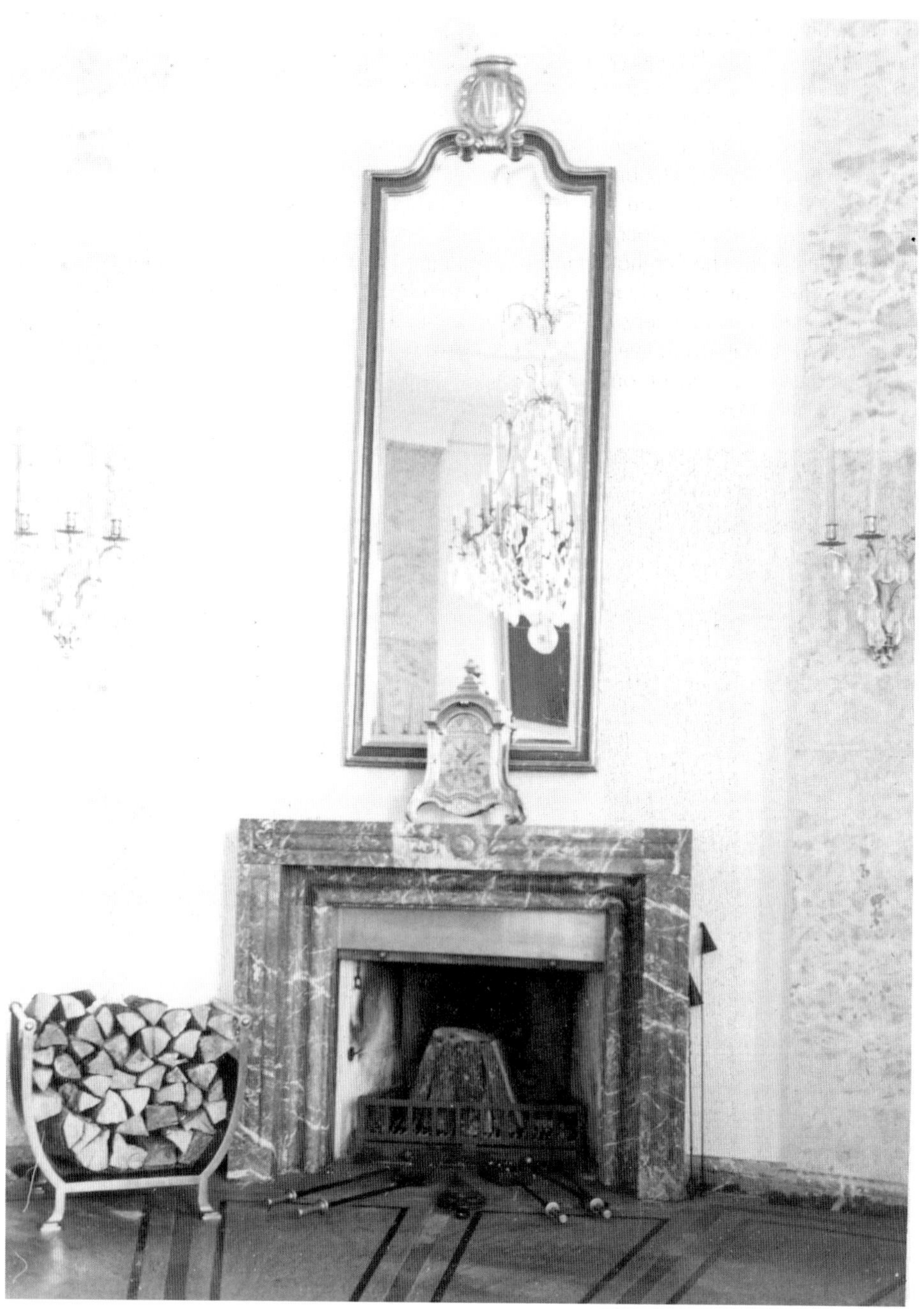

70. Reverse unmarked, source unknown.

The reception room at Hitler's Mooslahnerkopf teahouse with the long gold-framed mirror hanging above the Untersberg marble fireplace. The decorative clock occupies a central position on the mantelpiece. The central chandelier is reflected in the mirror while two of the candelabra can be seen on the outer edges of the photograph.

71. Reverse unmarked, source unknown.
Heinrich Hoffmann, the Führer's personal photographer and the man who introduced Hitler to Eva Braun relaxes in one of the comfortable chairs in the reception room. Another of the wall-mounted candelabra can be seen high on the left of the image.

Due to its position on the mountainside the Mooslahnerkopf teahouse survived the bombing of the area on 25 April 1945 unscathed. However, it would not survive the plundering of the Obersalzberg that took place on 1 May 1945. That Tuesday the people of Berchtesgaden and the surrounding area raided the Obersalzberg complex. They ransacked Albert Speer's home, Göring's home, Villa Bechstein, the Berghof, in fact any building standing or partially standing was targeted.

The people made off with any remaining food supplies. They removed fixtures and fittings from the buildings, including crockery, cutlery, pictures, carpets, and pieces of furniture. Everything that could be taken was removed. Even today there are many homes in and around Berchtesgaden that retain much of what was taken on the day. This left little for allied soldiers when they reached the Obersalzberg on 4 May.

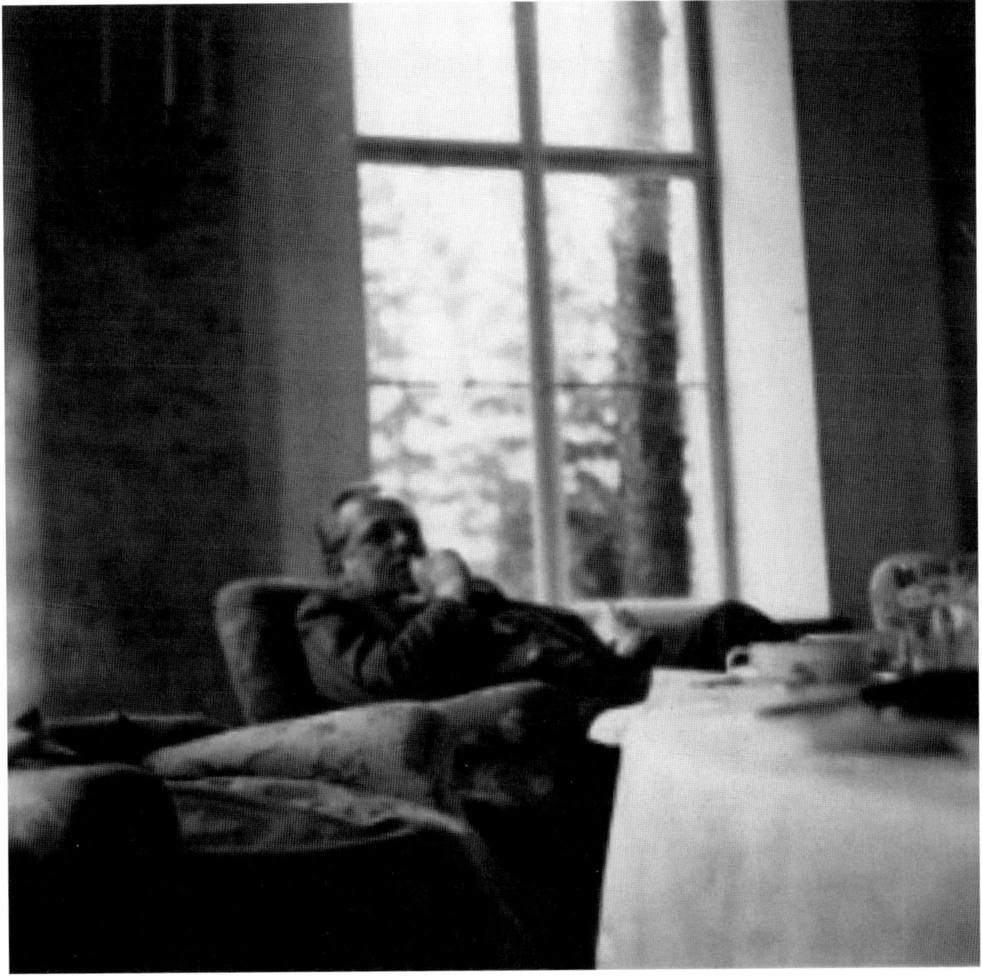

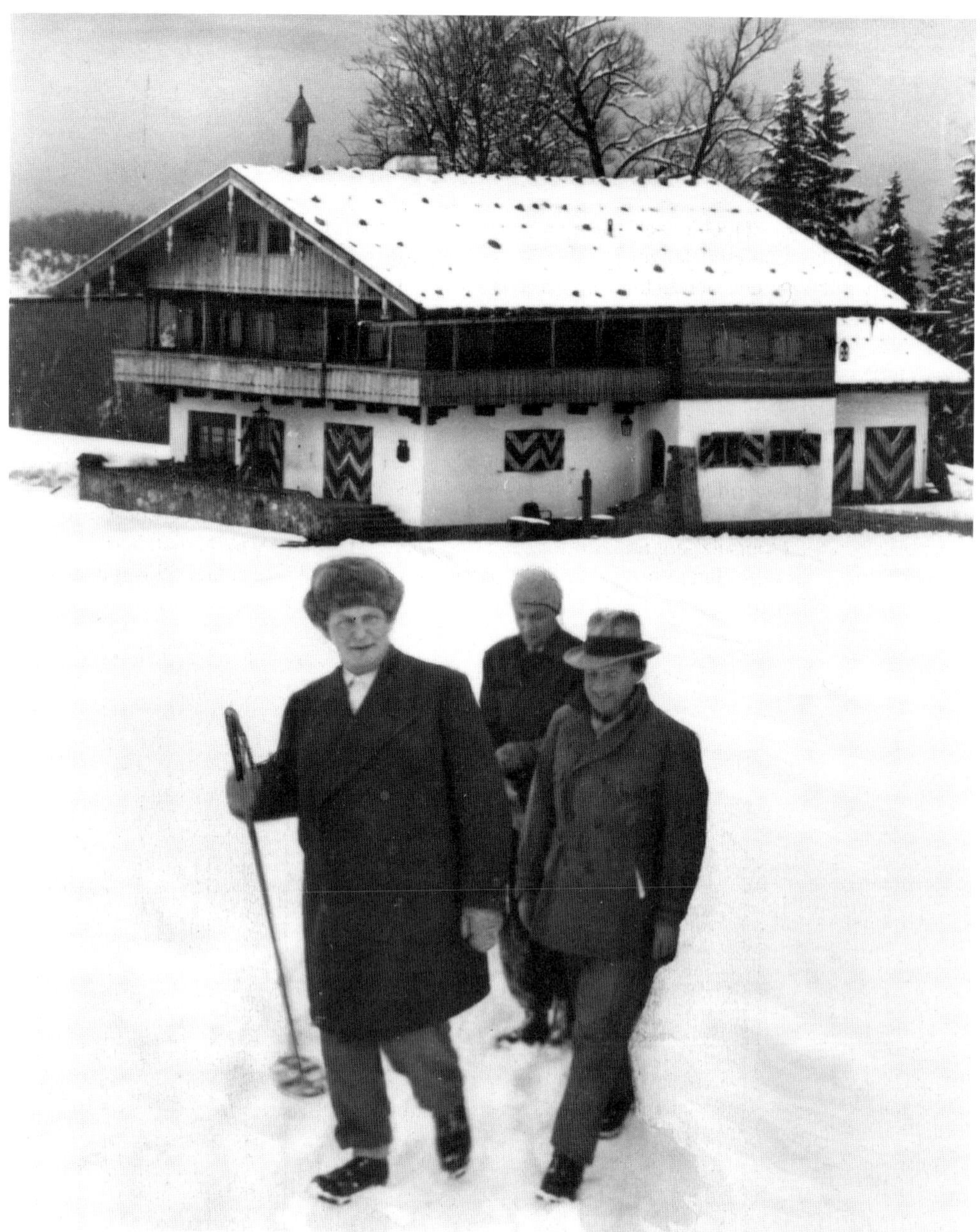

72. Prime Minister Hermann Göring in front of his home on the Obersalzberg.
This rare postcard shows Hermann Göring in front of his house on the Obersalzberg. The man next to Göring is Josef Zychski. Zychski and his wife Frieda, seen in the background, were Göring's housekeepers on the Obersalzberg from 1937 until 1945. While Hermann Göring and Martin Bormann, Hitler's private secretary, were neighbours on the mountain they did not get along; the two men disliked each other. Its fair to say that Bormann was generally unpopular, even those in the Nazi hierarchy disliked and avoided him.

73. Alpine restaurant 'Hochlenzer' towards Untersberg and Berchtesgaden.

Hitler often visited the Hochlenzer on the Obersalzberg. Its position on the mountainside affords the most incredible views across the valley and the town of Berchtesgaden below. During the years that he lived on the Obersalzberg and before coming to power Hitler visited the Hochlenzer often. The Führer could choose to be driven to the restaurant, or as was often the case he and a few of his inner circle could leave Haus Wachenfeld and walk the Carl-von-Linde-Weg through the forest to arrive at the restaurant.

Beginning close to where Hotel Platterhof once stood the Carl-von-Linde-Weg follows the same route today. It takes approximately forty-five minutes to stroll the forest path to reach the Hochlenzer where they still serve wonderful traditional Bavarian dishes today.

Looking carefully at this postcard we can see a Nazi flag in the lower left foreground. This card was posted on the Obersalzberg on 2 June 1936 to an address in Attersee in the Salzkammergut in Austria. Some two weeks later on 17 June 1936, Heinrich Himmler, *Reichsführer*-SS was appointed chief of German Police.

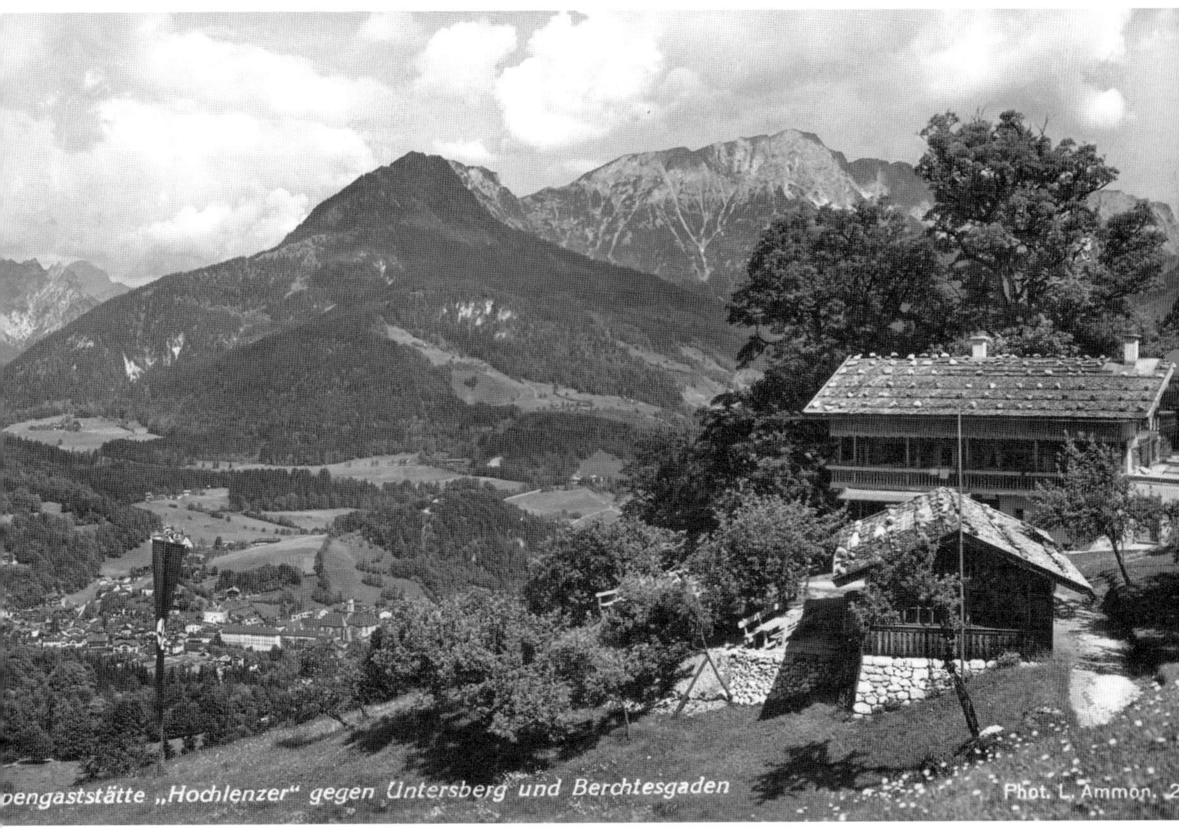

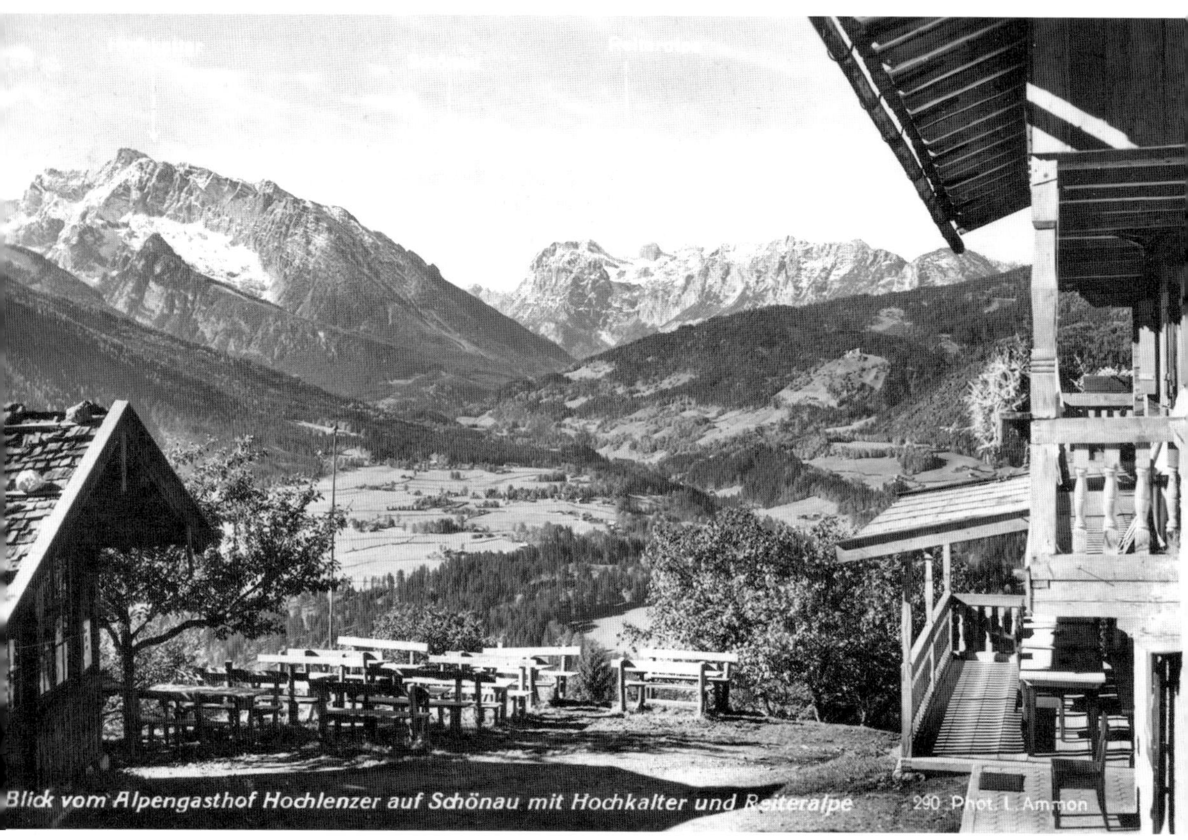

74. View from Alpine inn Hochlenzer to Schönau with Hochkalter and Reiteralpe.

In this instance the photographer has moved close to the main building and has focused his attention in the direction of Schönau just outside Berchtesgaden. The outside benches and tables have been placed to provide the best views across the valley. This is where Hitler and his walking companions would sit in good weather to take in the magnificent views of the Königssee, the Berchtesgaden valley and the mountains beyond.

The Hochlenzer has undergone a number of changes through the intervening years and the benches and tables seen here are long gone. Today a large terrace occupies the spot. Bearing a Berchtesgaden postmark this postcard was posted on 19 August 1940 to an address in Harlaching, a district in the southern part of Munich.

Just four days earlier, on 15 August 1940, SS-*Obersturmbannführer* (Lieutenant Colonel) Adolf Eichmann (1906–1962) presented his 'Madagascar Plan', a plan for the compulsory deportation of over four million Jews to the island of Madagascar. Having been considered but never implemented Eichmann's plan was finally shelved in 1942.

75. Our Reich Chancellor Hitler on a morning outing in his Berchtesgadener Land.
This interesting photograph shows Hitler sitting at one of the tables observed in the previous image, number 74. Moving left to right we see Adolf Hitler, seated beside Hitler is Sophie Stork (1903–1981) a Munich based artist and fiancée of Wilhelm Brückner. Stork, a friend of Eva Braun, joined the Nazi Party in 1931. She was a regular visitor at the Berghof. A talented artist, Stork painted a coffee service for Eva Braun and decorated a large ceramic-tile-covered Kachelofen in the Berghof lounge.

Next to Stork and with his back to the camera is her boyfriend and Hitler's chief adjutant, Wilhelm Brückner. Hitler was fond of Stork and was displeased with Brückner when in 1936 he broke off the engagement. Brückner was dismissed in 1940; his successor was SS-*Obergruppenführer* (Lieutenant General) Julius Schaub (1898–1967).

Opposite Sophie Stork is Heinrich Hoffmann (1885–1957), Hitler's personal photographer. Hoffmann had joined the Nazi Party in April 1920. He was a friend of Dietrich Eckart and was one of Hitler's intimates; the two men were close friends. It was Hoffmann who introduced Hitler to his studio assistant Eva Braun in October 1929. The camera we see on the table, probably a Leica, will belong to Hoffmann. On the extreme right the man with his back to camera is Dr Karl Brandt; Brandt has been discussed previously, see caption 66, page 88.

The relationship between Hitler and Hoffmann was undoubtedly one of the most important of the Third Reich period, their close collaboration established Hitler's public image and paved the way for some of the most imaginative, influential and successful propaganda imagery of the twentieth century.

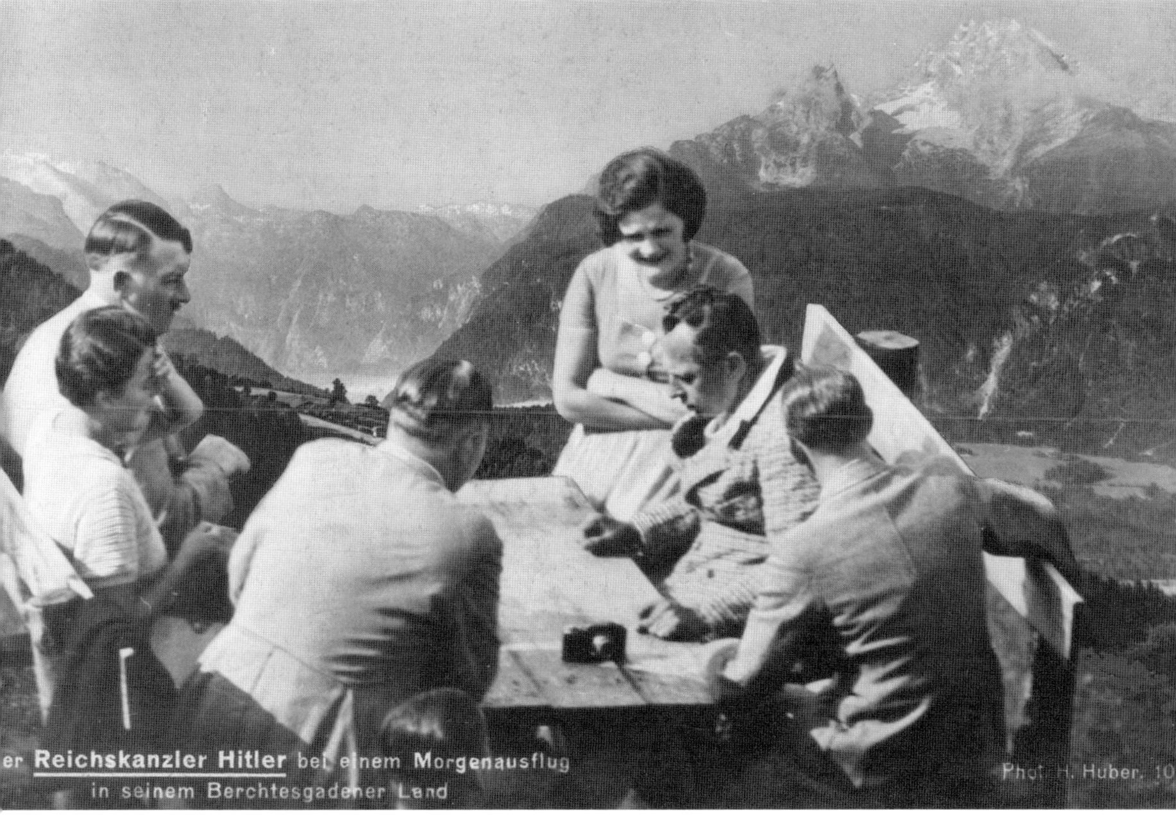

76. A child's view.

While there is no text on this postcard to indicate the location, there is good reason to presume that the photograph has been taken at the Hochlenzer. The lady seen seated between Hitler and the little boy is the same lady seen standing by the table in the previous postcard, number 75.

The Hochlenzer, owned and run by the Maltan family was a place Hitler visited many times. These visits began in the late 1920s and continued until the late 1930s. Other favourite walks for the Führer and members of the inner circle on the Obersalzberg were to Scharitzkehl and Vorderbrand, a place Hitler knew well from the early days when he had dined there with Dietrich Eckart.

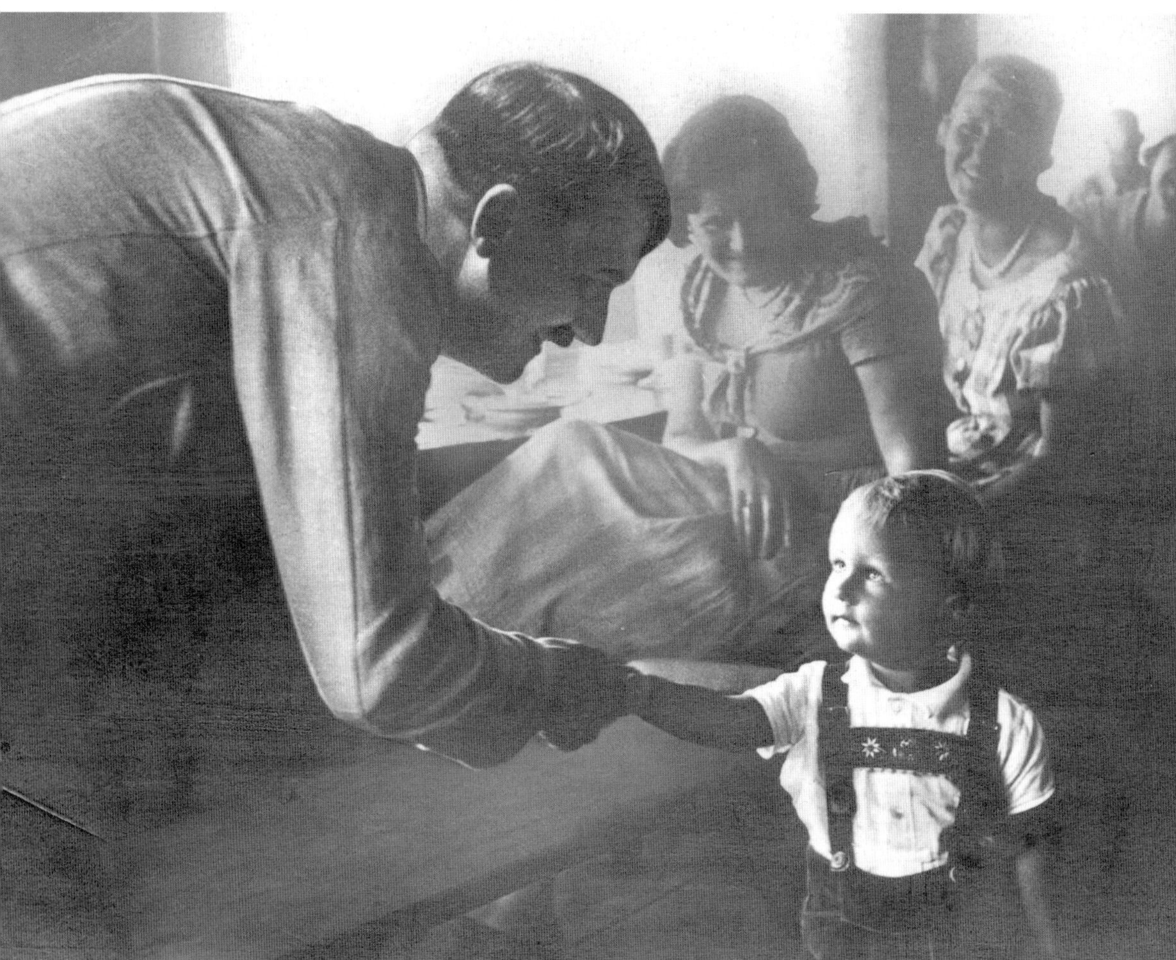

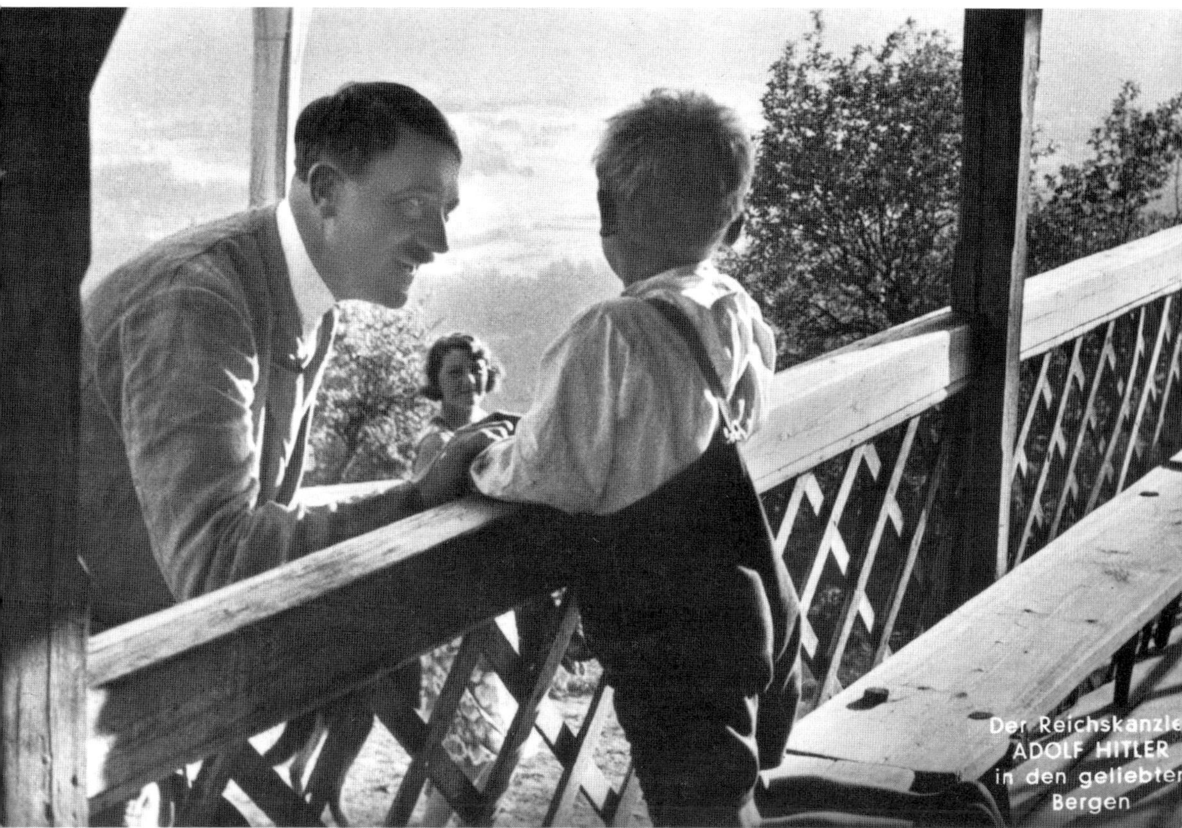

77. The Reich Chancellor Adolf Hitler in his beloved mountains.

While walking on the Obersalzberg Hitler stops to speak to this small boy. The location, while not confirmed, is again probably the Hochlenzer. The particularly interesting thing about this photograph is that the lady in the background is Hitler's niece, Geli Raubal (1908–1931), the daughter of Hitler's half-sister Angela who was his housekeeper at Haus Wachenfeld.

Using her uncle's Walther pistol, Geli committed suicide in Hitler's Munich apartment on the night of 17/18 September 1931 while the Führer was *en route* to Hamburg for a meeting with SA leaders.

Rumours that Hitler and Geli were having an affair led to much speculation about the circumstances of her death. It is presumed these rumours were exaggerated and spread by Hitler's political opponents. While proof of the alleged affair was never produced, Hitler remained inconsolable for many weeks following the tragedy. It has been said that while Hitler was very fond of Geli, he perhaps interfered a little too much in her life and sought to control both her movements and those with whom she associated.

While this photograph was obviously taken prior to Geli's untimely death in September 1931 it is interesting to note how the caption refers to Hitler as Reich Chancellor, a position he did not attain until 30 January 1933, some sixteen months later, meaning this postcard could not have been published before that time.

The image reflects happier times on the Obersalzberg and shows the young woman out walking with her uncle. Angela Maria 'Geli' Raubal is buried in Vienna's *Zentral Friedhof*.

78. The Führer at the Hochlenzer (Obersalzberg).

Hitler accompanied by Dr Otto Dietrich (on Hitler's right) and Wilhelm Brückner (extreme right) greets the owners, staff and members of the public outside the Hochlenzer. The enthusiasm on the faces of the people is clear for all to see while many in the group raise their arms in the unmistakeable Nazi salute.

The man seen standing between Hitler and Brückner and with his coat over his shoulder is Karl Wilhelm Krause (1911–2001). It was while serving in the German Navy that Krause, having been handpicked by Hitler, was asked to join the *Begleitkommando*-SS. Krause held the position of personal orderly and bodyguard to Hitler from August 1934 to September 1939. In 1940 Krause transferred to the 1st SS Panzer Division – *Leibstandarte-SS Adolf Hitler* and in December 1943 he joined the then recently formed 12th SS Panzer Division – *Hitlerjugend* where he rose to the rank of *Hauptsturmführer* (Captain).

The reverse bears a hand-applied rubber stamp reading: *'Alpenwirtschaft u. Caffee Hochlenzer 928 m hoch Salzberg'* (Mountain Inn and Coffee Hochlenzer 928 metres high Salzberg – the local abbreviation for Obersalzberg) the presence of this stamp tells us this postcard was purchased at the Hochlenzer.

The card was posted on the Obersalzberg on 17 May 1937 and sent to an address in Ebingen, a medium-sized town approximately 93 kilometres (58 miles) south of Stuttgart. Posted by a group of friends who talk about having visited the Hochlenzer, somewhat strangely, halfway through the message the writer has written the words 'Heil Hitler!' Just three days later, on 20 May 1937, Hitler gave a speech to construction workers on the Obersalzberg to mark the inauguration of a new cinema.

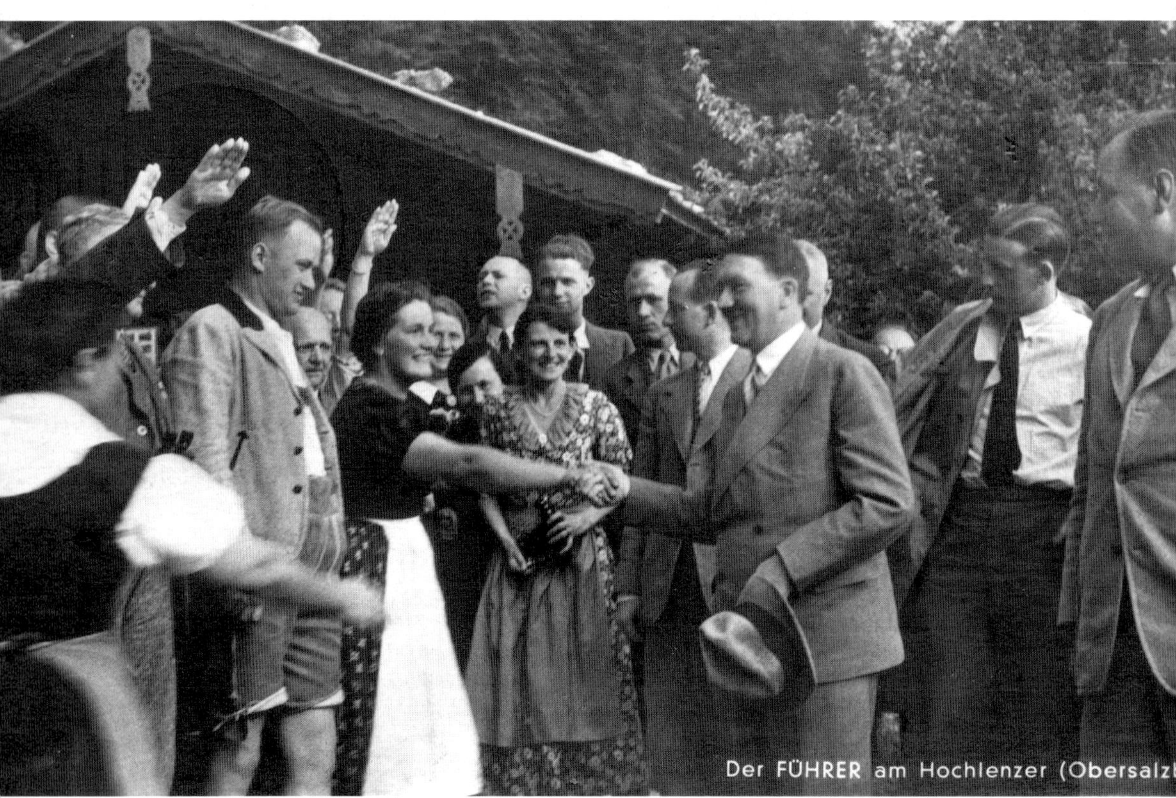

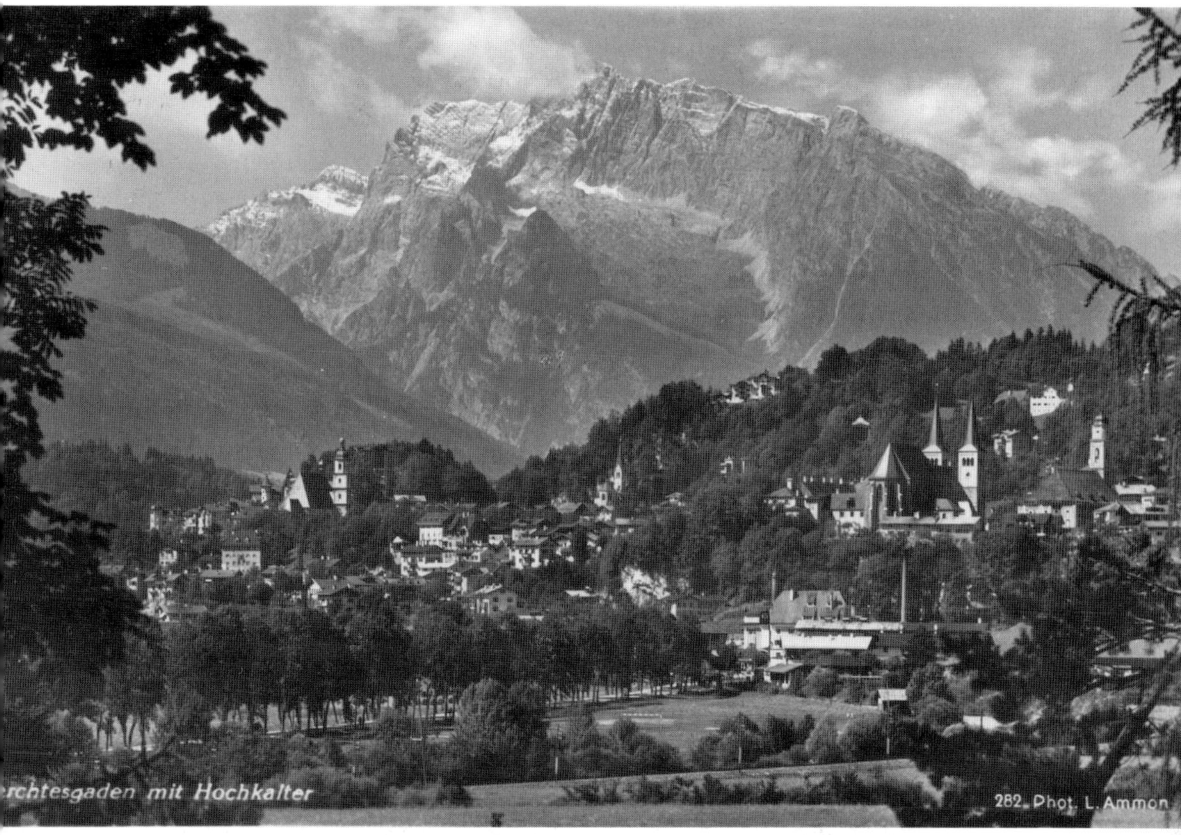

79. Berchtesgaden with Hochkalter.

This postcard shows the beautiful Alpine town of Berchtesgaden with the Hochkalter in the background. Ramsau and Hintersee lie on the other side of the Hochkalter range. It was on the Obersalzberg just outside Berchtesgaden that Adolf Hitler made his home, first in Haus Wachenfeld, then later, following renovation and extension after which time the building was generally known as the Berghof.

Hitler made many important decisions on the Obersalzberg. Operation Barbarossa, the invasion of the Soviet Union that began on 22 June 1941 was planned at the Berghof. It's said that Hitler came up with the name 'Barbarossa' as he gazed out of the large picture window in the Berghof's living room looking towards the Untersberg across the valley at a time when the mountain was bathed in the red glow of sunset.

Legend has it that the Untersberg is home to former emperors. While some state that the Emperor Karl der Große (Charles the Great also called Charlemagne) lives deep inside the mountain others say it is the Holy Roman Emperor Friedrich I (Friedrich Barbarossa).

The Untersberg is steeped in myth and legend. Stories tell of the mountain being home to many creatures, these include fairies, magicians, spirits and witches. It is reputedly a place inhabited by supernatural beings, a place where strange unexplained happenings occur and a place where supposedly time stands still. Posted in Berchtesgaden on 14 August 1941 this postcard made its way to an address in Oberschöneweide on the outskirts of Berlin.

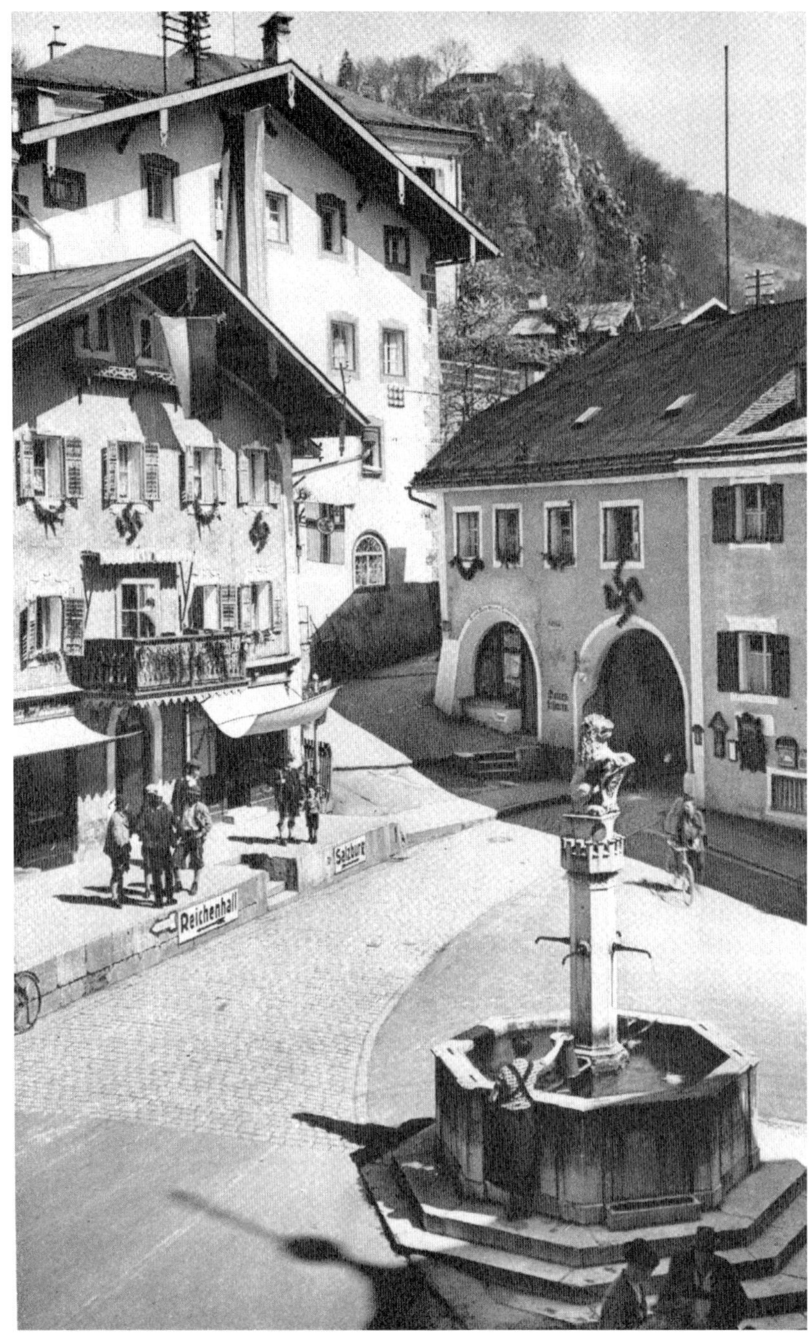

80. Market Square in Berchtesgaden.
Berchtesgaden is a charming Alpine market town with a long history. This postcard shows some of the buildings in the square displaying swastikas made from pine branches. The square remains virtually unchanged.

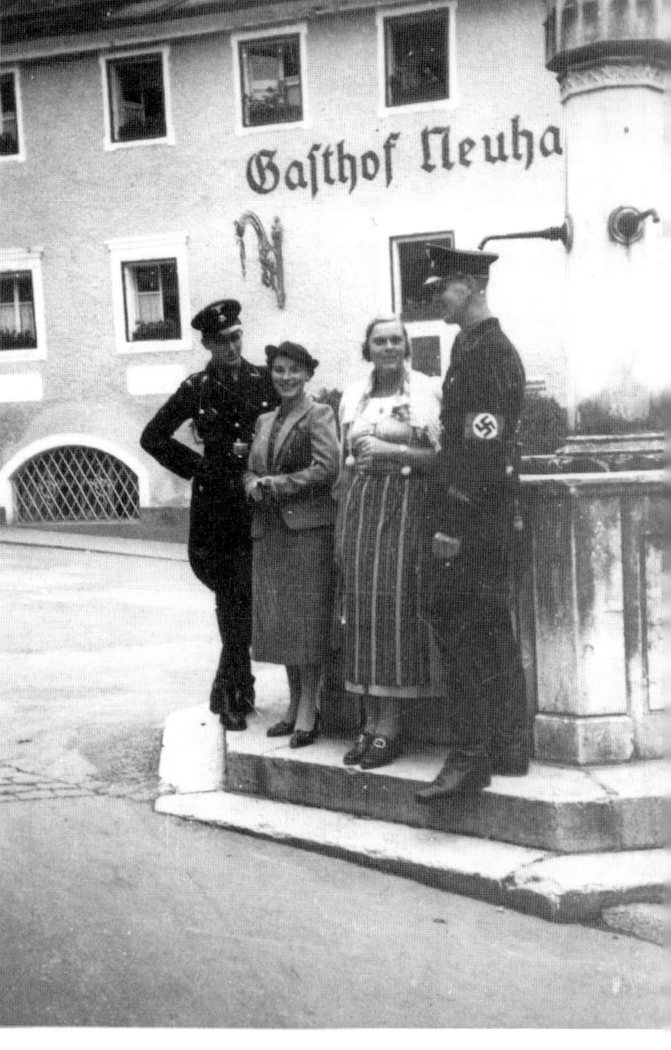

81. Reverse unmarked, source unknown.
This privately taken and almost certainly never before published photograph is both rare and unique. The photo shows two members of the *Allgemeine*-SS (General-SS) seen wearing their distinctive black uniforms. Hugo Boss was the man who designed the smart SS uniform.

The men are chatting to two local ladies. One of the ladies wears a smart two-piece suit while the other is seen wearing the traditional Bavarian *Tracht* (costume).

However, it is the content and location that makes this photograph so special; the group are standing by the *Marktbrunnen* (Market Fountain) located in the Marktplatz in the heart of Berchtesgaden. The building in the background, Gasthof Neuhaus, is one of the oldest inns in Berchtesgaden dating back to 1576. The market fountain where the group are standing also appears in the previous image number 80. The two men are members of the *Leibstandarte-SS Adolf Hitler*, (LSSAH) the premier SS division. While we can't read it, the cuff title on the sleeve of the man on the right identifies him as a member of the LSSAH. These men are probably members of Hitler's personal protection unit based on the nearby Obersalzberg seen spending their free time in the town.

Photographs showing members of the SS in Berchtesgaden are extremely rare. I was astonished when, on seeing this photograph, Gerd Bartels told me he knew the lady on the left; her name was Lotte. Gerd said that Lotte had moved to Pfaffenhofen an der Ilm, a town north of Munich and that she'd married a dentist.

A small amount of glue on the reverse tells us this photograph was once in an album. The photo is printed on Agfa-Lupex paper, one of the most popular at the time. It is entirely possible that this is the one and only print to have been produced from the negative. This photograph, alongside the postcard images on these pages must be viewed as singular moments in time that have been captured forever.

82. Berchtesgaden, Bayern – Market Square.

Looking back from Gasthof Neuhaus and up the Marktplatz towards Bier Adam. Further up the street and just to the right of the fountain we can see a large Nazi flag suspended above the street.

Posted in Berchtesgaden on 22 September 1938 this postcard made its way to Soltau in Hann, a large town situated about halfway between Hamburg and Hannover. What makes the address on the reverse interesting is the fact that the recipient lived in the Horst-Wessel-Straße in Soltau.

Horst Wessel (1907–1930) became a Nazi martyr. The son of a Lutheran minister, Wessel joined the Nazi Party in 1925. He was a *Sturmführer* (Assault Leader) in an SA (SA; *Sturmabteilung* – Storm Detachment) unit based in Berlin. Wessel was ambushed outside his apartment by Communists on 14 February 1930 and died of his injuries ten days later, on 24 February. Nazi propaganda declared Wessel a martyr; he would become a national hero in the fight against Marxism.

Wessel wrote the *'Horst-Wessel-Lied'* (Horst-Wessel-Song) also called *'Die Fahne hoch!'* (Raise the Flag High!). The song became a Nazi anthem and was adopted as a second national anthem alongside 'Deutschland über Alles' during the Third Reich period.

There was also a Horst Wessel Weg in Berchtesgaden (today the Zwingerstraße). For centuries it has been common practice to name streets and squares after major political and military figures. A section of Berchtesgaden's Maximilianstraße was once known as the Adolf Hitler Straße.

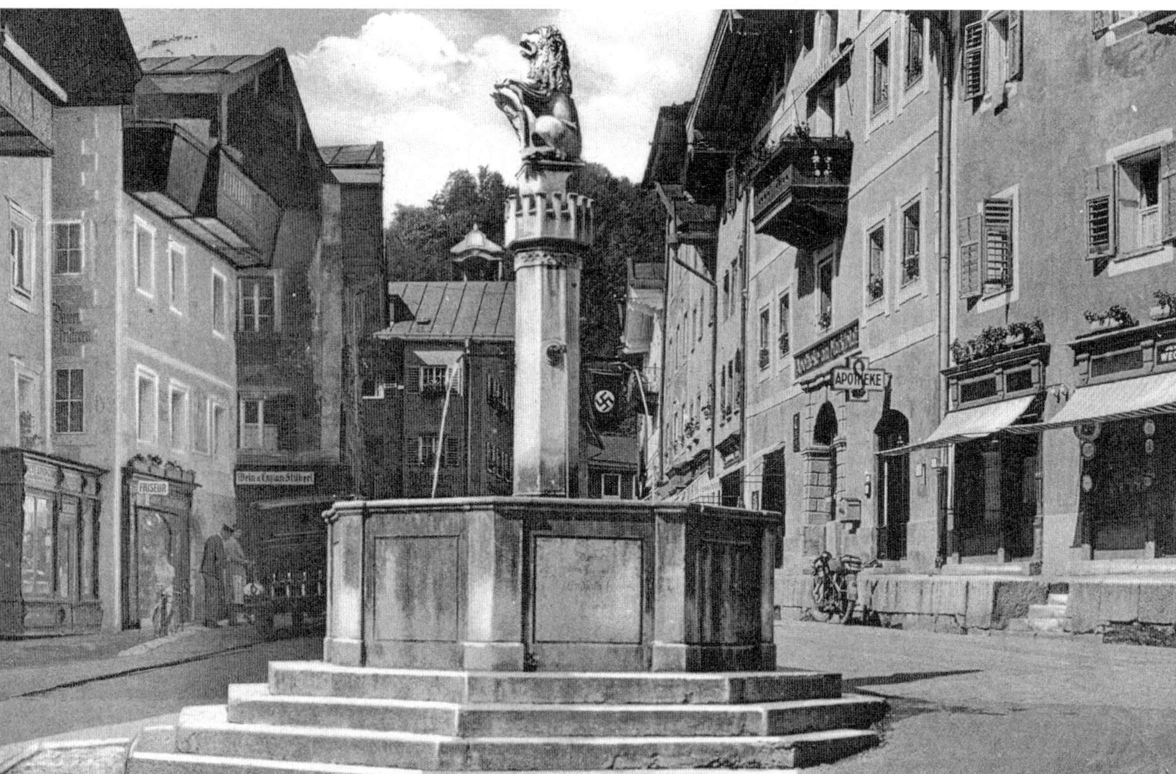

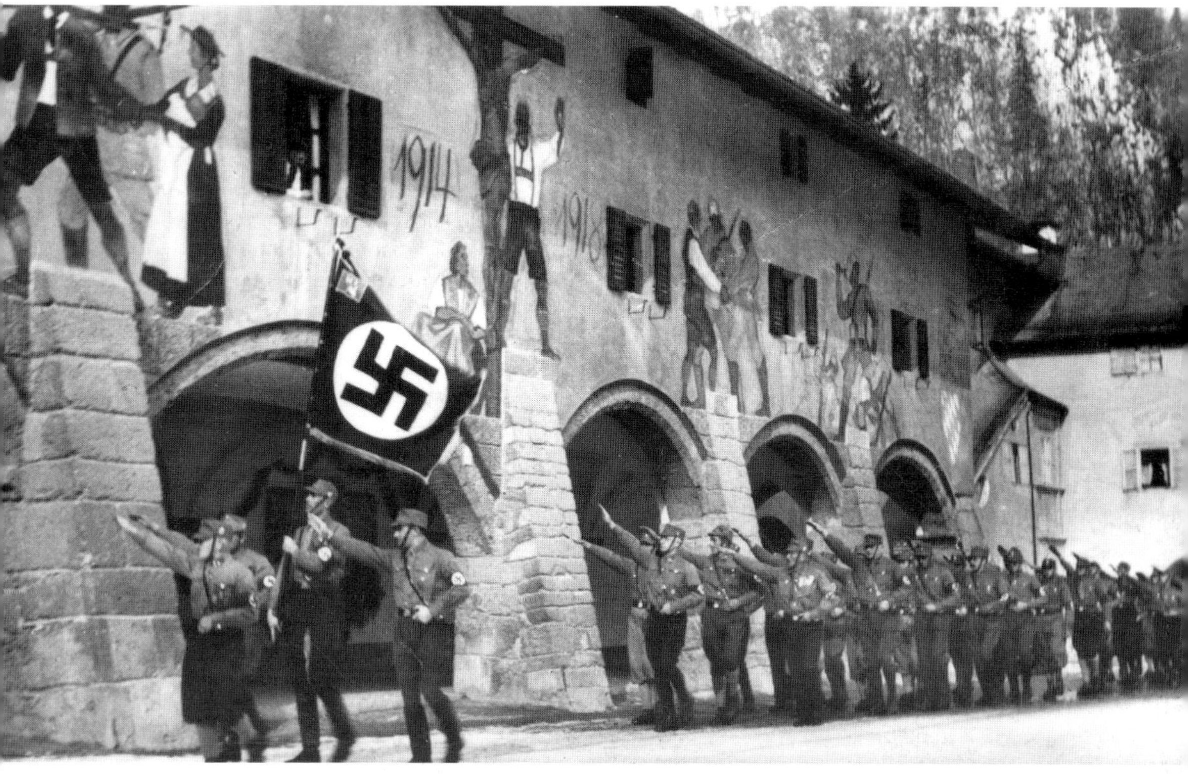

83. Berchtesgaden, heroes honoured at the war memorial.

This rare image shows a column of SA-men (SA; *Sturmabteilung* – Storm Detachment) often referred to as 'Brownshirts' marching through the Schloßplatz (Palace Square) in the centre of Berchtesgaden. As they pass the war memorial they give the distinctive Nazi salute. Painted in 1929 by Munich artist Josef Hengge (1890–1970) the mural on the wall above the arches depicts scenes relating to the First World War. A number of large marble plaques attached to the wall inside the arches record the names of those from the area who died in both World Wars.

This postcard was posted in Raeren in Belgium on 29 June 1933 to an address in Antwerp. Raeren sits in the eastern part of Belgium and close to the German border. The town is less than 10 kilometres (6.5 miles) from the German city of Aachen. This part of Belgium belonged to Germany but was ceded to Belgium after the First World War. It is an area where German remains the predominant language.

At first glance this would certainly appear a strange choice of image for a Belgian national to choose to post to a friend. However knowing that this part of Germany had become Belgian territory barely fifteen years earlier we must consider the idea that perhaps the sender identified more as German than Belgian. This was perhaps true of many living in the region. We must remember how during the Second World War many young men in this, the Walloon part of Belgium, volunteered for the SS and went on to form the 28th SS Freiwilligen-Panzergrenadier Division – *Wallonien*.

Towards the end of the Second World War the division was commanded by none other than SS-*Brigadeführer* (Brigadier-General) Leon Degrelle (1906–1994). Degrelle and the Division distinguished themselves in the many hard battles they fought against the Soviets on the Eastern Front. Hitler held Degrelle in high regard. He much admired the young Belgian's loyalty, his spirit and his great tenacity.

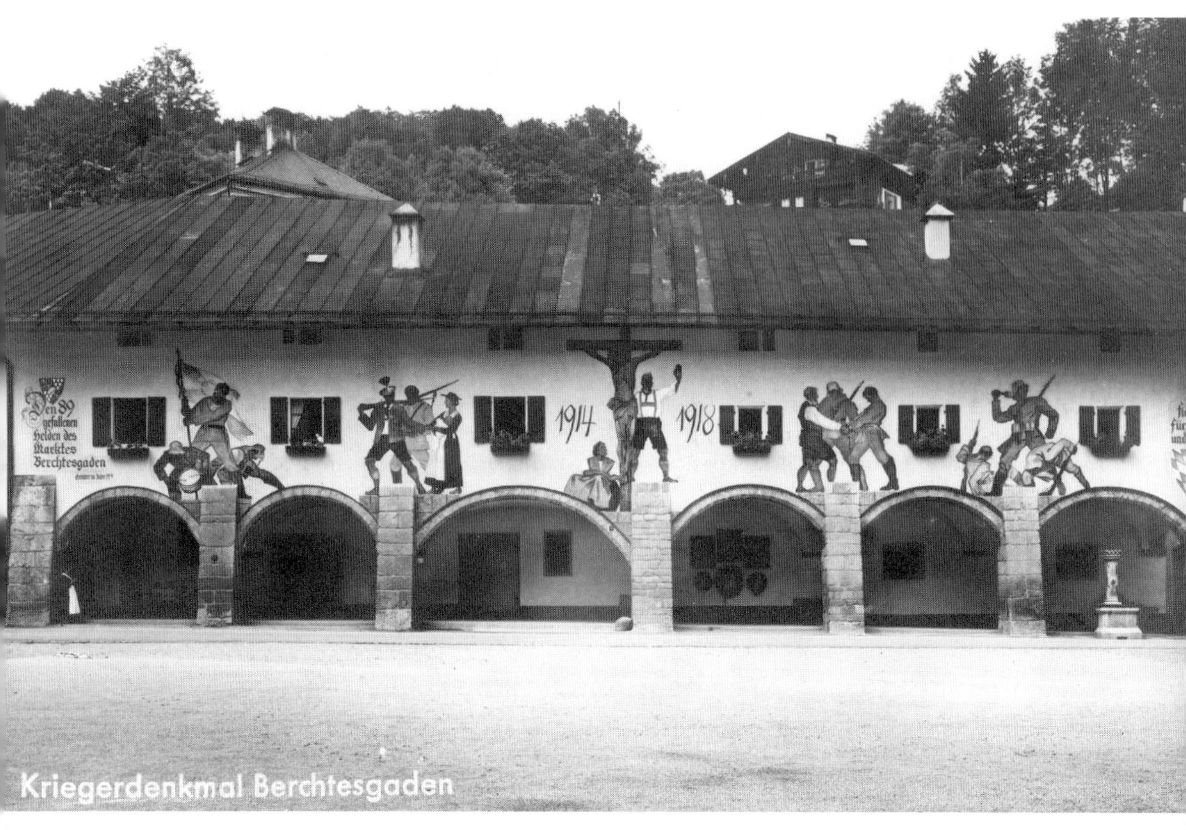

84. War memorial Berchtesgaden.

This postcard provides a full view of the mural painted by Josef Hengge. While impossible to read on the page, the wording on the left hand side of the memorial reads: *'Den 89 gefallen Helden des Marktes Berchtesgaden'* (The 89 fallen heroes of Marktes Berchtesgaden). Beneath this and in smaller lettering it reads: *'Erichtet im Jahre 1929'* (Erected in the year 1929). The wording on the right hand side reads: *'Sie fielen für Freiheit und Ehre des Vaterlandes'* (They fell for freedom and honour of the Fatherland).

The three marble plaques bearing the names of the fallen, with wreaths attached beneath them, can be seen on the wall through the third archway from the right. It was in this square in front of the war memorial that *Landrat* (District Commissioner) Karl Theodor Jacob surrendered the town to US forces on Friday, 4 May 1945. Following the end of the Second World War the years 1939 and 1945 were added to the mural. The memorial and its location, the Schloßplatz, are virtually unchanged since the time this photograph was taken in the 1930s.

85. Berchtesgaden, Maximilianstr. with Untersberg.

This photograph, taken from high up in the tower of the Franziskanerkloster, looks down on the Maximilianstraße and towards the town centre. During the Third Reich period the Maximilianstraße was known as the Adolf Hitler Straße.

The cemetery on the left, the *Alter Friedhof* (Old Cemetery) is where Dietrich Eckart, Hans-Heinrich Lammers and Professsor Ludwig Hohlwein are buried. Ludwig Hohlwein (1874–1949) was an artist best known for his poster designs. His early work involved designing posters for some of Germany's biggest companies.

Hohlwein joined the Nazi Party in 1933 and went on to design many of the striking posters that appeared during the period, including posters for the 1936 Olympic games. After the Second World War Hohlwein remained in the area. He maintained a small studio in Berchtesgaden until his death on 15 September 1949. This postcard bears a Berchtesgaden postmark dated 16 June 1929.

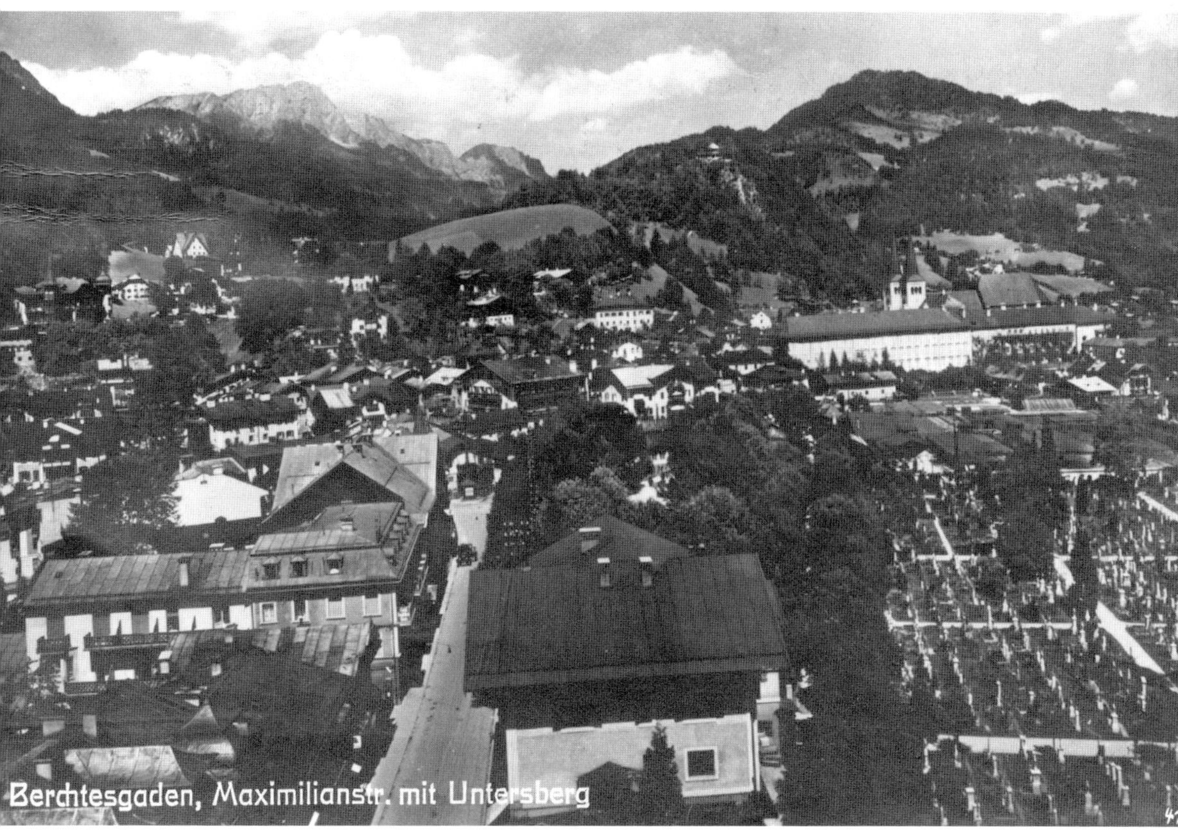

86. Sonnblickhäus'l
Anton Pfnür – Berchtesgaden, Dietrich Eckartstr. 17.

This is the house, the Sonnblickhäus'l on Locksteinstr where Dietrich Eckart died of a heart attack on 26 December 1923; he was fifty-five years old at the time. When the Nazi Party came to power in January 1933 the street was renamed Dietrich Eckartstr. in honour of Hitler's old friend. The name reverted to Locksteinstr. soon after the Second World War ended.

While Eckart was twenty-one years Hitler's senior the two men shared a genuine friendship. They shared similar political views and aims. Eckart introduced Hitler to Munich society and influential people who would later help fund Hitler's political ambitions. Hitler never forgot his old friend and mentor; when speaking of Eckart, Hitler would refer to him as 'Didi', a name used for Eckart by those who knew him best. It has been said that Hitler often had tears in his eyes when speaking of Eckart.

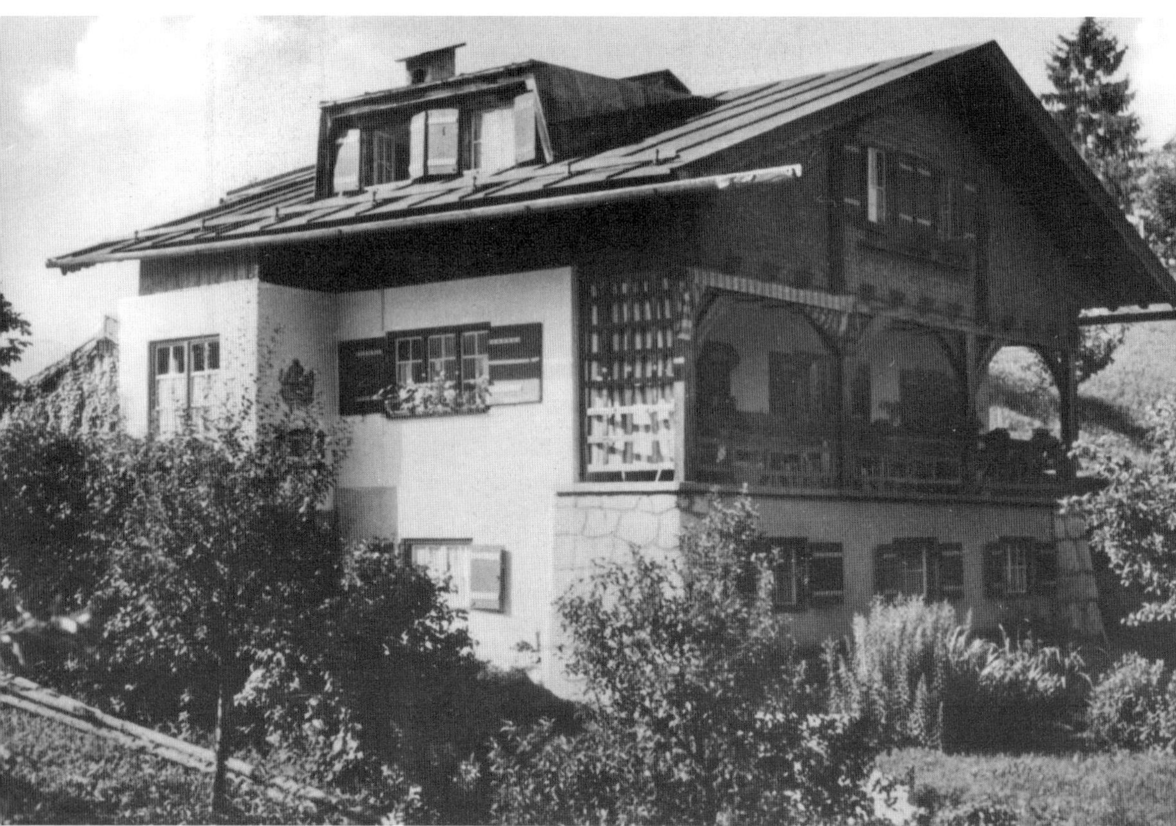

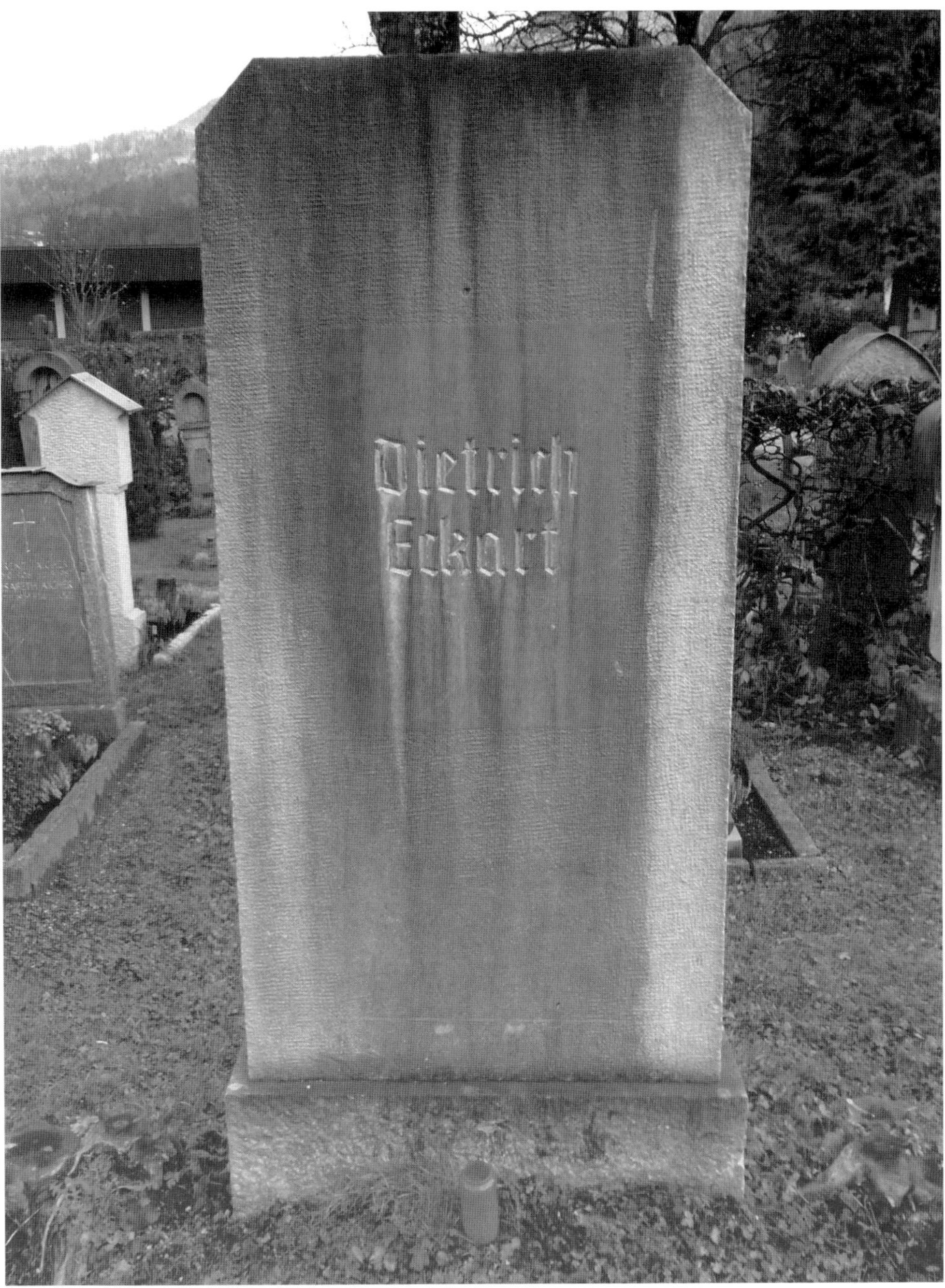

87. The grave of Dietrich Eckart as photographed in 2022. Until recently a tall evergreen stood either side of the gravestone. These have been cut down on the orders of the local authority. The stone we see today is not the original gravestone. It's interesting to note how people continue to place flowers and candles on the grave.

88. Railway Station Berchtesgaden.

The construction of Berchtesgaden's new train station began in 1937 and ended in 1940. The station is considerably larger than one might expect to find in a town the size of Berchtesgaden. Its scale reflected the status the area had achieved under the Nazis notwithstanding Hitler's continued presence in the area.

One end of the station was set aside for the Führer's personal use and that of visiting VIPs. This section cannot be seen in the photograph and stood to the right of the tower seen on the extreme right of this image. The station building is virtually unchanged, the original clock, flagpoles and lamps on the front of the building are all period and all remain in place. Part of the town of Berchtesgaden can be seen in the background behind the station.

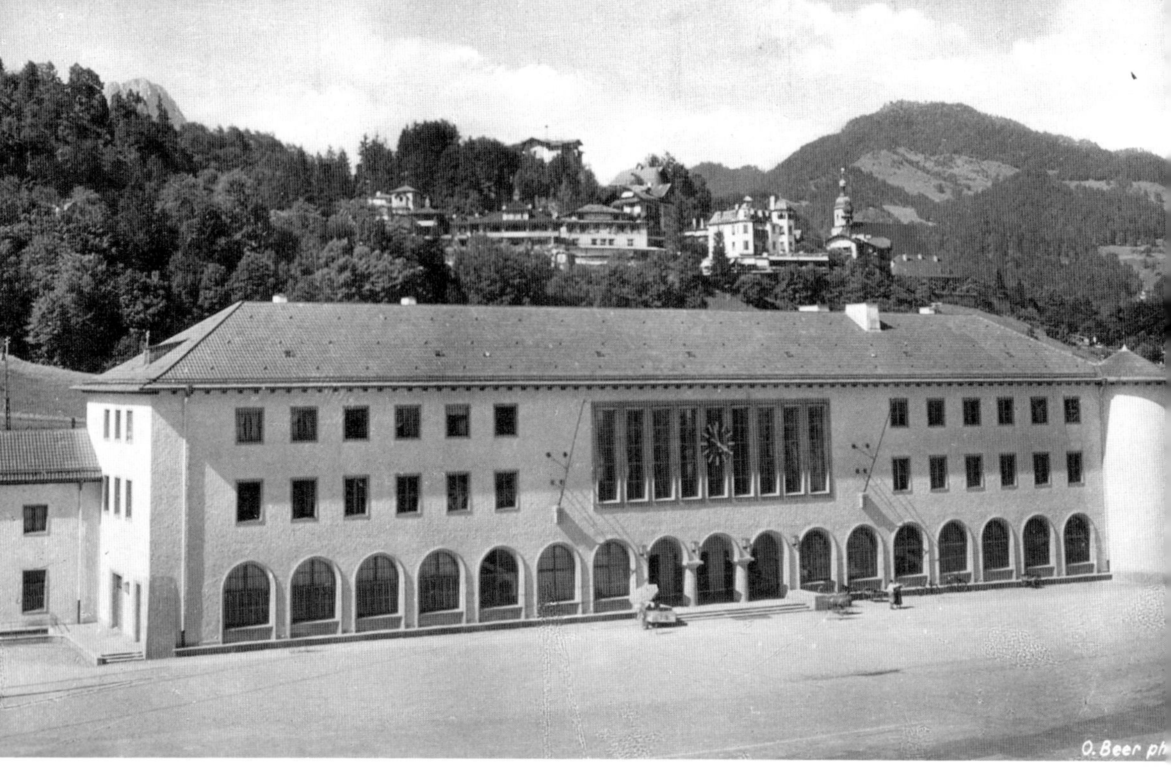

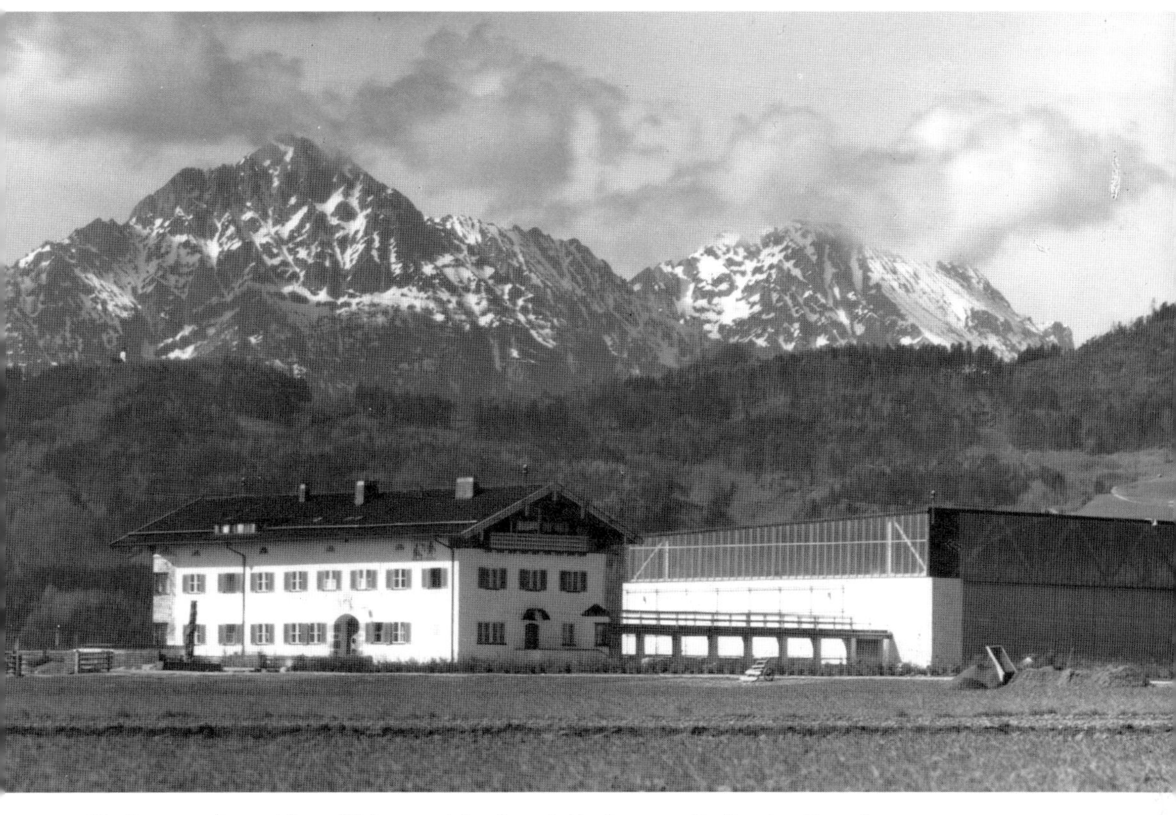

89. Germany's most beautiful mountain airport Ainring near Freilassing Bavaria.

It's said that Hitler personally explored the area to select Ainring as the site for the airport that would be constructed there. Following inauguration in October 1934 the airport proved extremely useful for those coming to see the Führer when he was at his Alpine retreat on the Obersalzberg. On arriving at Ainring visitors were then chauffeur driven the remaining 35 kilometres (22 miles) to the Berghof.

While capable of handling large passenger aircraft, Ainring's use steadily declined following the *Anschluss* with Austria in March 1938. After that time the larger airport at nearby Salzburg was increasingly used and to some extent replaced Ainring. Postcards of the airport at Ainring are rare; this example posted in Freilassing on 18 August 1935 made its way to an address in Berlin.

90. Reich's airport Bad Reichenhall-Berchtesgaden at Ainring.
In this instance the photographer has taken up a position close to the aircraft hanger seen on the right in the previous image, postcard number 89, to present the terminal building from the opposite side.

Posted *'Feldpost'* (Military Post) on 29 October 1939 to an address in Kärnten, Austria. The *Feldpost* system permitted free post for serving military personnel and their families throughout Germany. As the Second World War progressed the system was subject to regulation changes. As German forces had entered Poland just eight weeks earlier the Second World War had only just begun.

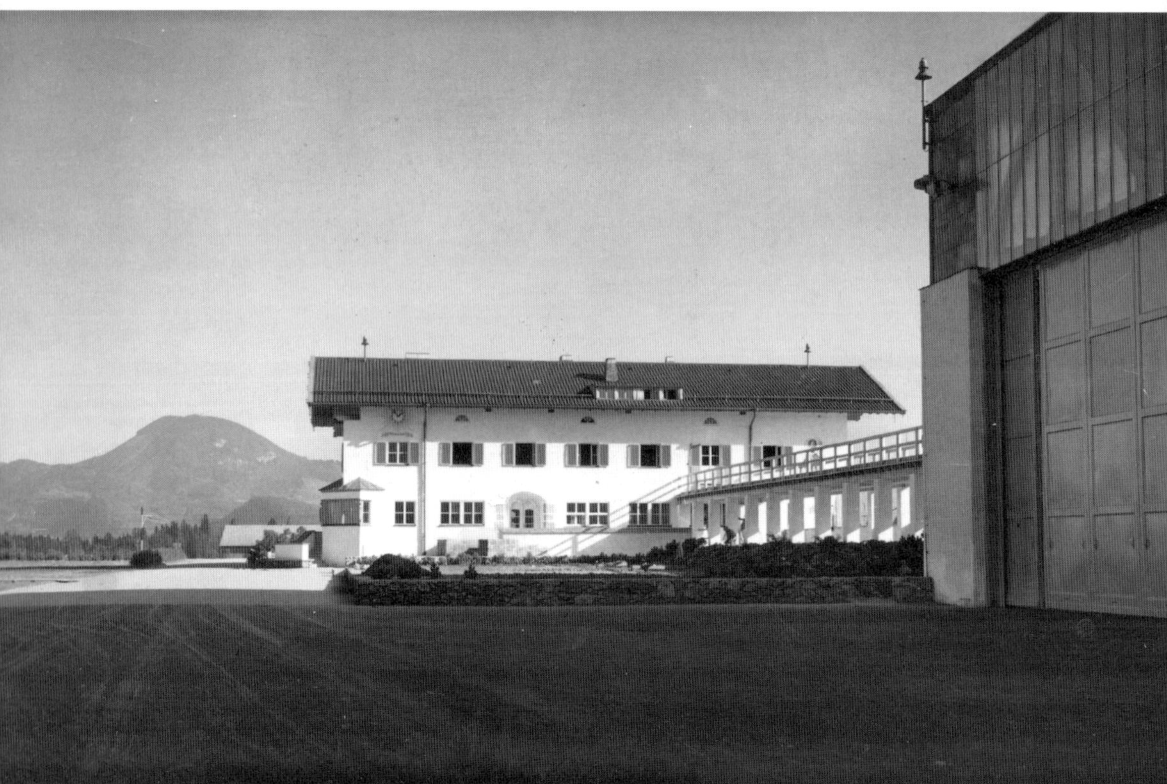

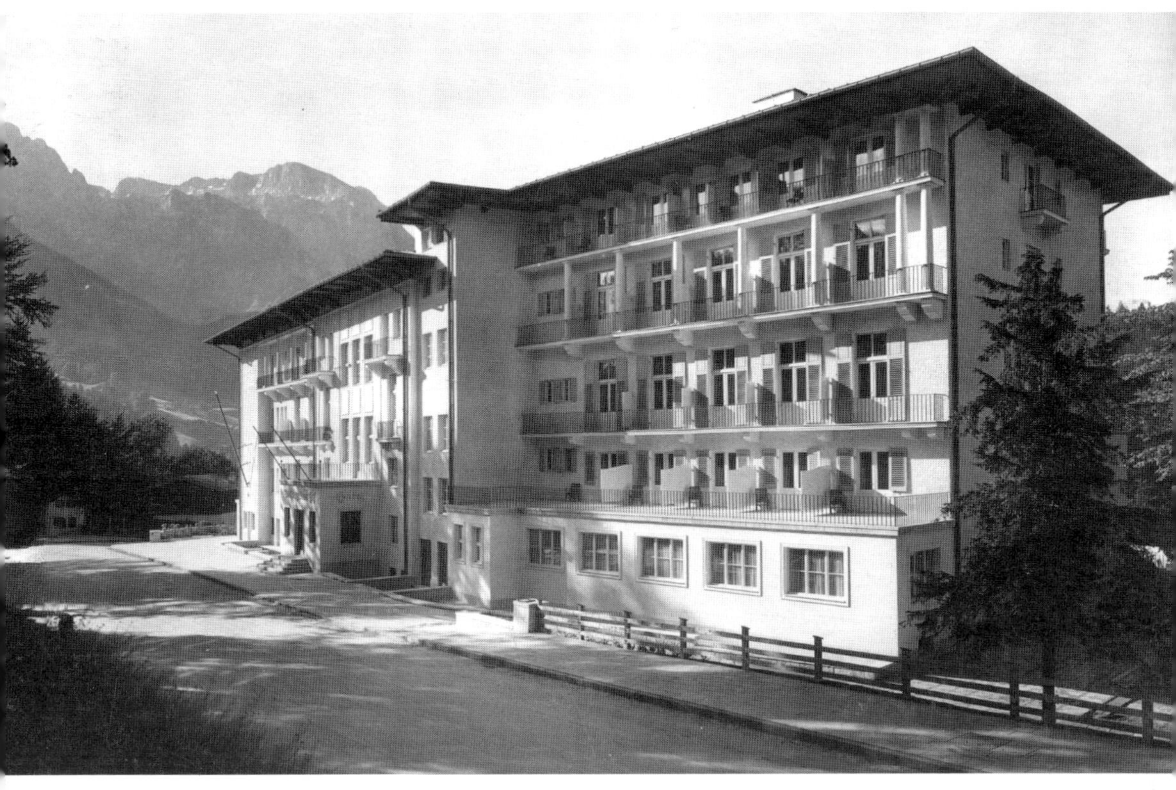

91. Hotel 'Berchtesgadener Hof' Berchtesgaden. View towards the street.
The Grand Hotel, also called the Grand Hotel Augusta Viktoria, after the wife of Kaiser Wilhelm II, opened in 1898. The Nazi Party bought the hotel in 1936 and following extensive renovation the hotel reopened as Hotel Berchtesgadener Hof. Gotthard Färber was the man charged with running the new hotel.

Numerous foreign dignitaries were accommodated at Hotel Berchtesgadener Hof when visiting the area to meet with Hitler. These included, the Duke (formerly King Edward VIII) and Duchess of Windsor, British Prime Minister Neville Chamberlain, and former British Prime Minister David Lloyd George. In addition many leading figures of the Third Reich stayed in the hotel, Albert Bormann (Martin Bormann's brother and head of Hitler's second Reich Chancellery in Berchtesgaden); Eva Braun, prior to her moving into the Berghof; Dr Joseph Goebbels, Reich Minister for Public Enlightenment and Propaganda; Heinrich Himmler, *Reichsführer*-SS; General Wilhelm Keitel, Commander in Chief of the German Army; Admiral Erich Raeder, Commander in Chief of the German Navy; Joachim von Ribbentrop, German Foreign Minister; General Erwin Rommel, Commander of the Africa Corps; SS-*Oberführer* (Brigadier General) Hermann Fegelein who later married Eva Braun's sister, Gretel, and Hitler's own sister Paula, who stayed there under the name Paula Wolf.

The hotel was taken over by the Americans after the Second World War ended and was once again used to accommodate visiting dignitaries before becoming one of many US Armed Forces Recreational Facilities. Hotel Berchtesgadener Hof closed with the departure of the Americans in 1995. The hotel stood empty until 2006 when it was demolished to make way for the new 'Haus der Berge'. The hotel was located on Hanielstr. on the outskirts of Berchtesgaden. Only a small part of the original complex remains standing today; these are the former garages and driver's accommodation block that stood behind the main hotel building on Gmundberg.

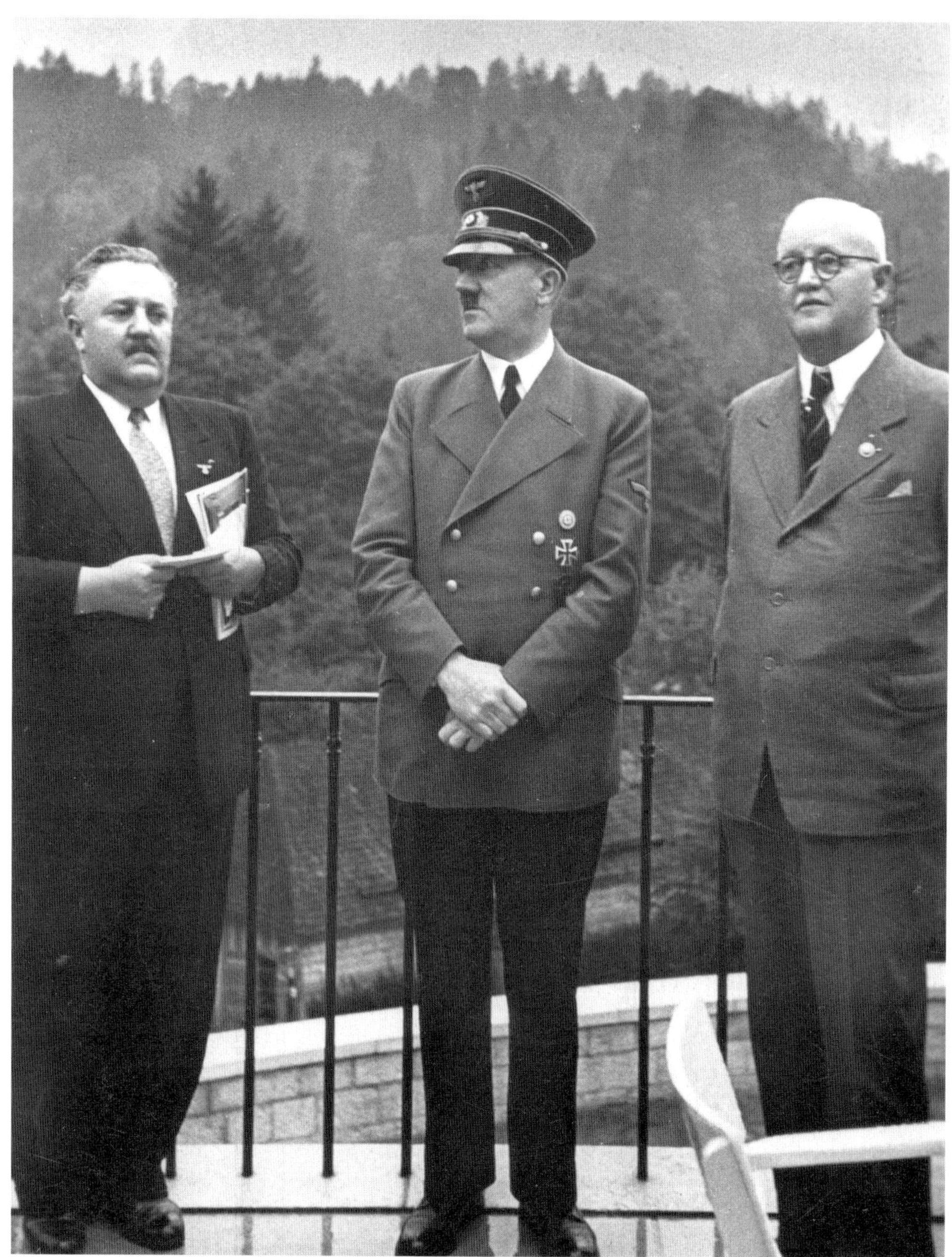

92. Uncaptioned.
Adolf Hitler pictured at Hotel Berchtesgadener Hof with Gotthard Färber (left) and Franz Xaver Schwarz (right). Färber was General Director of Hotel Berchtesgadener Hof. Schwarz, who was the Nazi Party treasurer, would stay in Villa Schön, the hotel annex. This rare postcard shows all three men standing on the large terrace.

93. Hotel 'Berchtesgadener Hof' Berchtesgaden – Large Reception Hall.

The hotel's spacious and tastefully furnished reception hall with its fine oak panelling. On the reverse someone has written; 'B'gaden 15 Sept 1942', they then placed a small 'X' on three of the chairs in the foreground to indicate the sitting positions of family members.

On entering the hotel at the time of demolition in 2006 it was clear that the demolition team were simply removing the panelling and other fittings with absolutely no thought of salvage or recycling. This may well have been on the instructions of the authorities being mindful of the building's history.

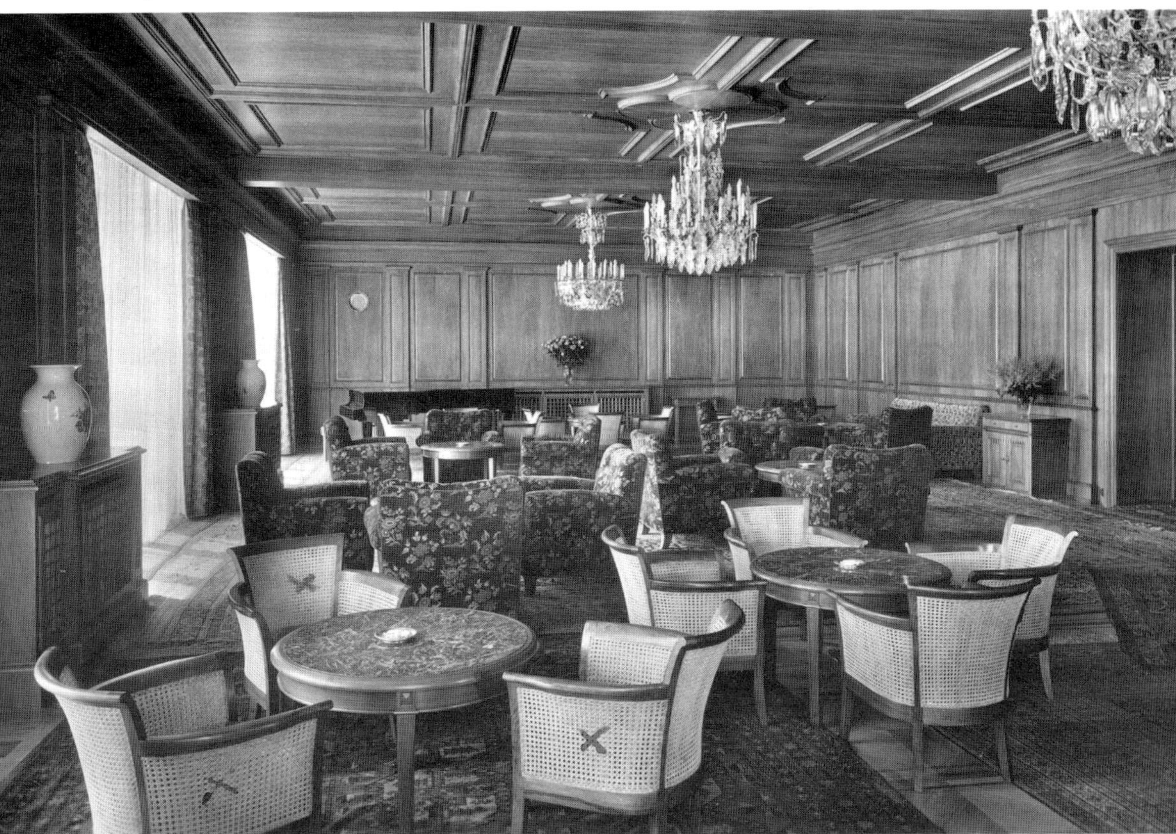

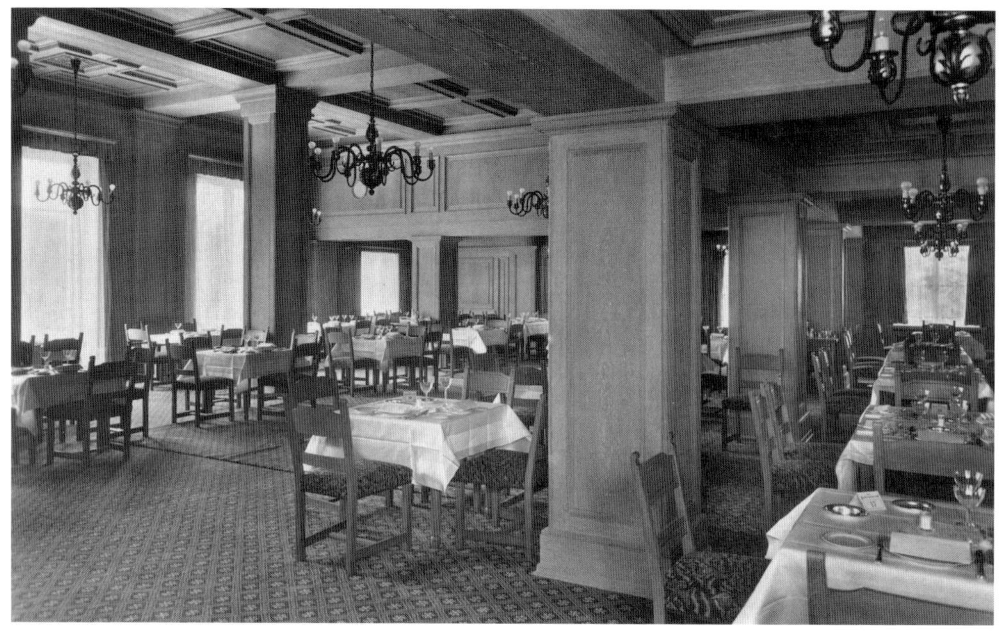

94. Hotel 'Berchtesgadener Hof' Berchtesgaden – Dining Room.
The hotel's dining room was bright and spacious.

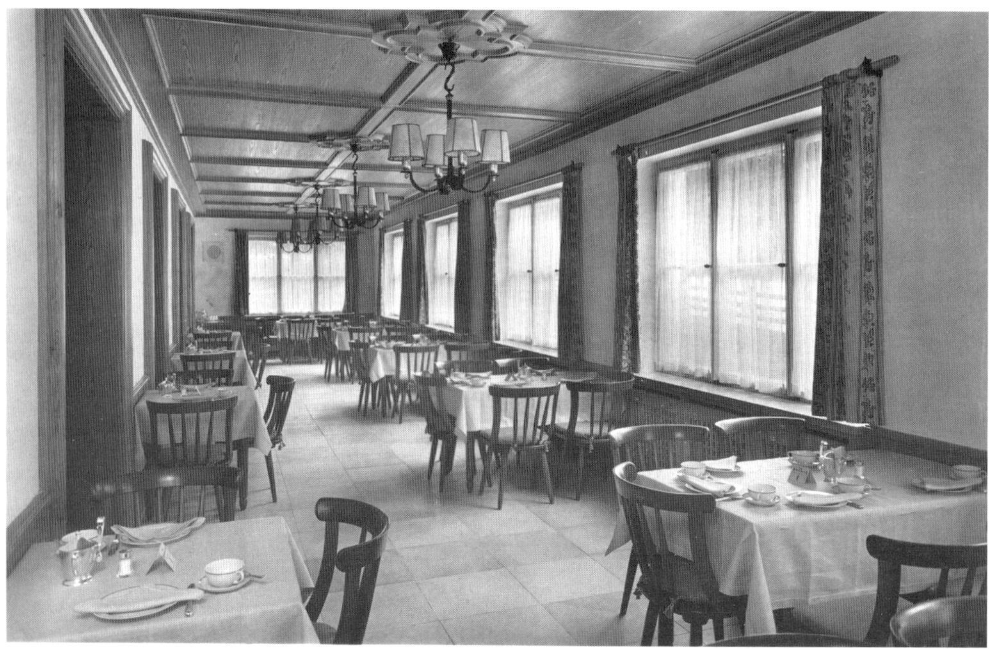

95. Hotel 'Berchtesgadener Hof' Berchtesgaden – Breakfast Room.
The breakfast room looked out on Hanielstrasse, the main street in front of the hotel.

96. Reich Chancellery with Watzmann and Hochkalter.

Located in Stanggaß just outside Berchtesgaden the Reich Chancellery was constructed through 1936/37. Alois Degano, the architect who had overseen the construction of both the Berghof and Hermann Göring's home on the Obersalzberg was again involved in the Reich Chancellery project. A number of large accommodation blocks for both Chancellery staff and security personnel were built close to the Chancellery and can be seen on the approach to the building. These former staff buildings are today state owned and now provide rented accommodation for local people.

Both *Generalfeldmarschall* (Field-Marshal) Wilhelm Keitel, Chief of the Supreme Command of the Armed Forces and *Generaloberst* (Colonel-General) Alfred Jodl, Chief of the Operations Staff of the High Command of the Armed Forces had private homes located within the complex and close to the Chancellery building. The Jodl house was demolished in 2006.

The Reich Chancellery, the accommodation blocks and Keitel's former home survive. The large marble eagle seen above the main entrance remains in place while the swastika within the wreath held in its talons has been removed. The former Reich Chancellery building is now privately owned.

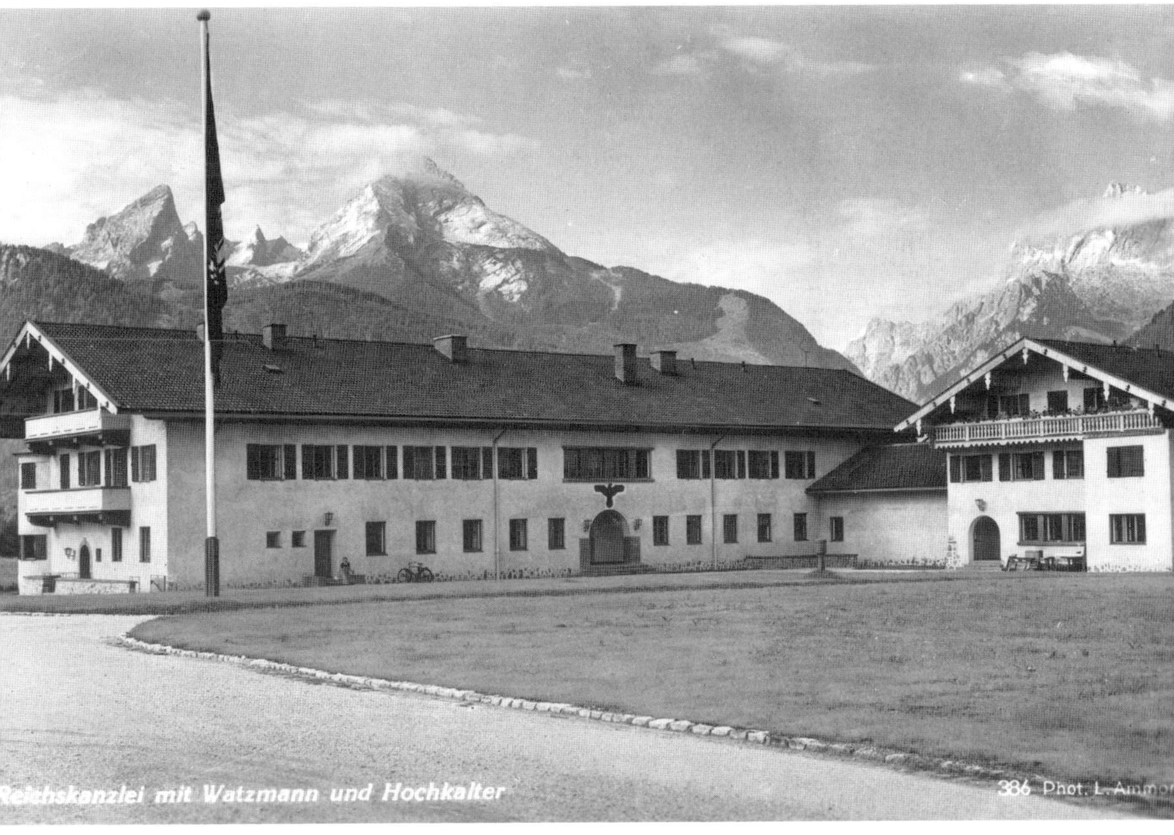

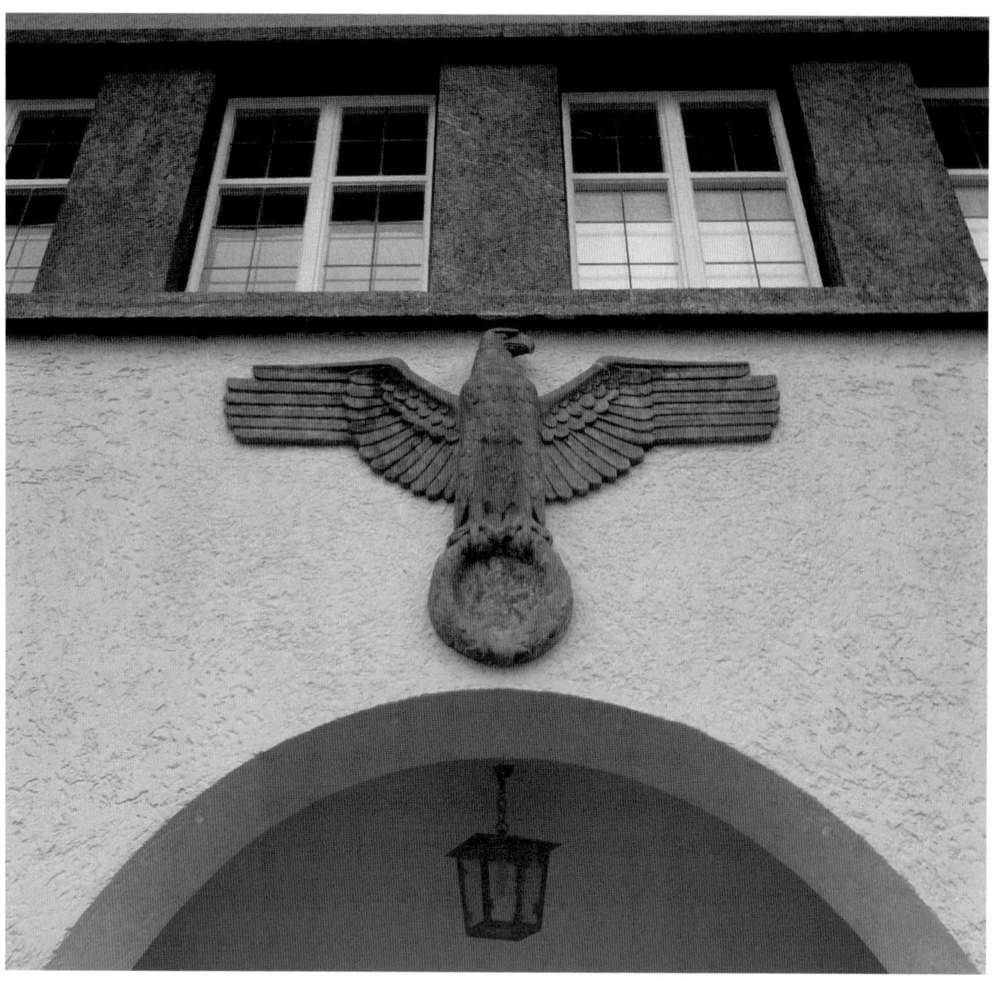

97. This photograph taken in 2022 shows the detail in the finely carved Untersberg marble eagle still in place above the main entrance to the former Reich Chancellery. As we can see the swastika has been removed from within the wreath held in the eagle's talons.

98. Reich Chancellery in Berchtesgaden.

This photograph shows the Reich Chancellery building from the opposite side. The Chancellery operated mainly as a diplomatic centre. Reich Minister and Head of the Reich Chancellery, Dr Hans-Heinrich Lammers (1879–1962) spent considerable time here. Albert Bormann (1902–1989) who from 1938 to 1945 was *Chef, Hauptamt I, Leiter der Privatkanzlei des Führers in Führerkanzlei* (Chief of Main Office I, Personal Matters of the Führer in the Private Chancellery of the Führer) also spent time at Hitler's second Reich Chancellery in Berchtesgaden.

As such, Albert Bormann, Martin Bormann's brother handled much of Hitler's private correspondence. The relationship between the Bormann brothers was not a good one; on the contrary, they barely spoke to each other. Albert Bormann was nothing like his brother; Albert has been described as decent, honest and trustworthy.

At the end of March 1945 Dr Lammers moved into the Reich Chancellery service building. Following the bombing of the Obersalzberg on 25 April he and his wife Elfriede left the Reich Chancellery and moved to Ramsau where they took up residence in the old forestry office building. Hans-Heinrich Lammers was captured and taken prisoner by the Americans. His wife Elfriede committed suicide on 8 May 1945; she was fifty-one years old. Just two days later, on 10 May 1945, their daughter Ilse also committed suicide; she was twenty-six years old.

Following trial at Nuremberg, Hans-Heinrich Lammers was sentenced to twenty years imprisonment, later reduced to ten years; he was released in 1952. Lammers died on 4 January 1962. He was buried with his wife and daughter in Berchtesgaden's *Alter Friedhof,* the same cemetery as Dietrich Eckart.

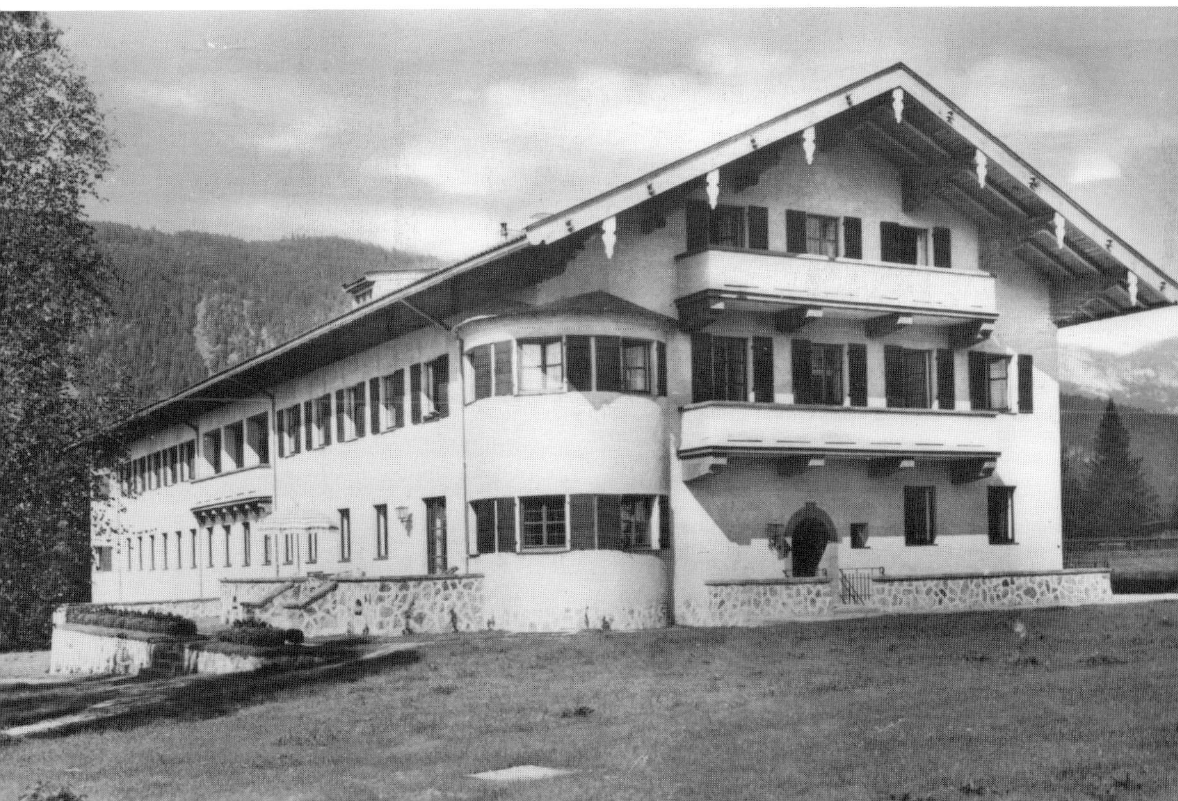

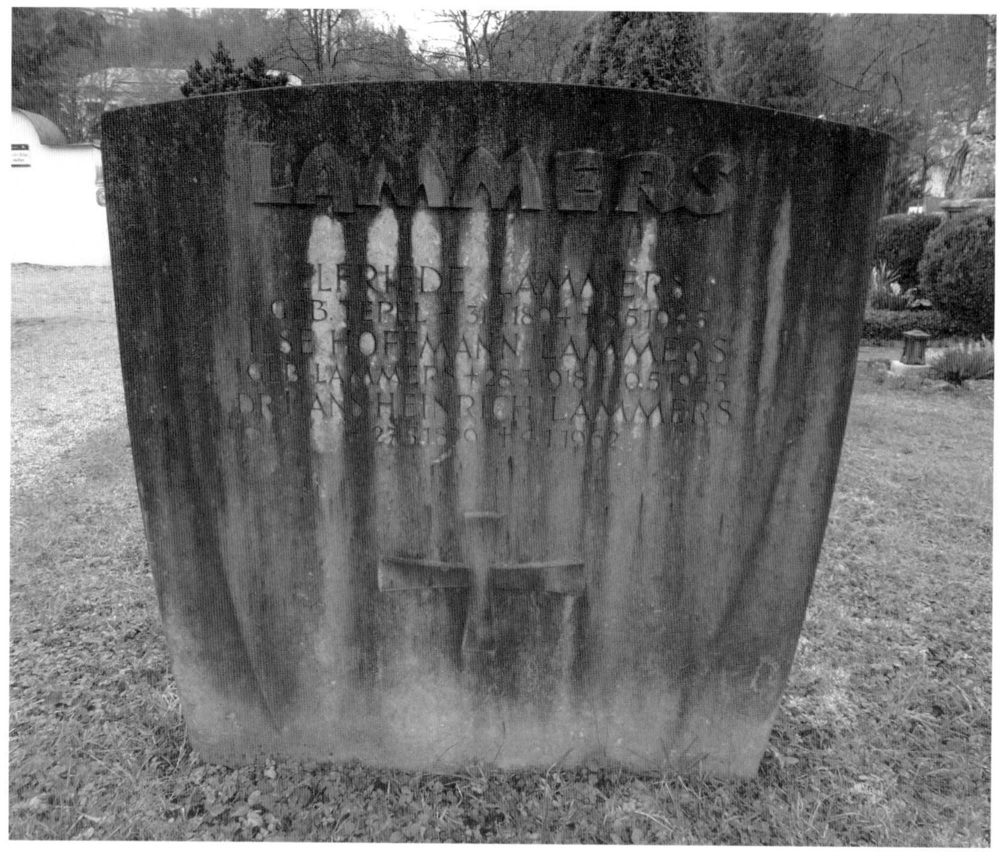

99. The final resting place of Dr Hans-Heinrich Lammers, his wife, and their daughter in Berchtesgaden's *Alter Friedhof*. The engraving on the stone reads:

LAMMERS
ELFRIEDE LAMMERS
GEB. TEPEL ✝ 31.1.1894 ✝ 8.5.1945
ILSE HOFFMANN-LAMMERS
GEB. LAMMERS ✝ 28.5.1918 ✝ 10.5.1945
DR HANS-HEINRICH LAMMERS
✝ 27.5.1879 ✝ 4.1.1962

As Reich Minister and Head of the Reich Chancellery Dr Lammers was an important figure in the Nazi hierarchy; Lammers and his family spent considerable time in and around Berchtesgaden.

100. Uncaptioned.

As already stated, Adolf Hitler never forgot his old friend Dietrich Eckart. This postcard shows the main entrance to the Dietrich Eckart *Krankenhaus* (Hospital) in Stanggaß. The hospital is not far from the already discussed Reich Chancellery complex. The foundation stone was laid on 6 May 1938 with the completed hospital being officially opened by Hitler's old friend, Adolf Wagner, Bavarian Interior Minister on 13 June 1942.

Reichsmarschall Hermann Göring, Commander in Chief of the Luftwaffe retained a private room in the hospital. Situated on the top floor, Göring's room looked towards the Watzmann. Standing at 2713 metres (9000 feet) the Watzmann is the second highest mountain in the Berchtesgaden Alps.

At the time of opening the Dietrich Eckart Hospital was ultra-modern, all rooms were private with many having their own private facilities. However within weeks of opening the complex was turned over to become a military hospital treating wounded German soldiers. The sign attached to the gatehouse on the right reads: *Reserve-Lazarett Berchtesgaden Dietrich Eckart Krankenhaus* (Reserve Military Hospital Berchtesgaden Dietrich Eckart Hospital).

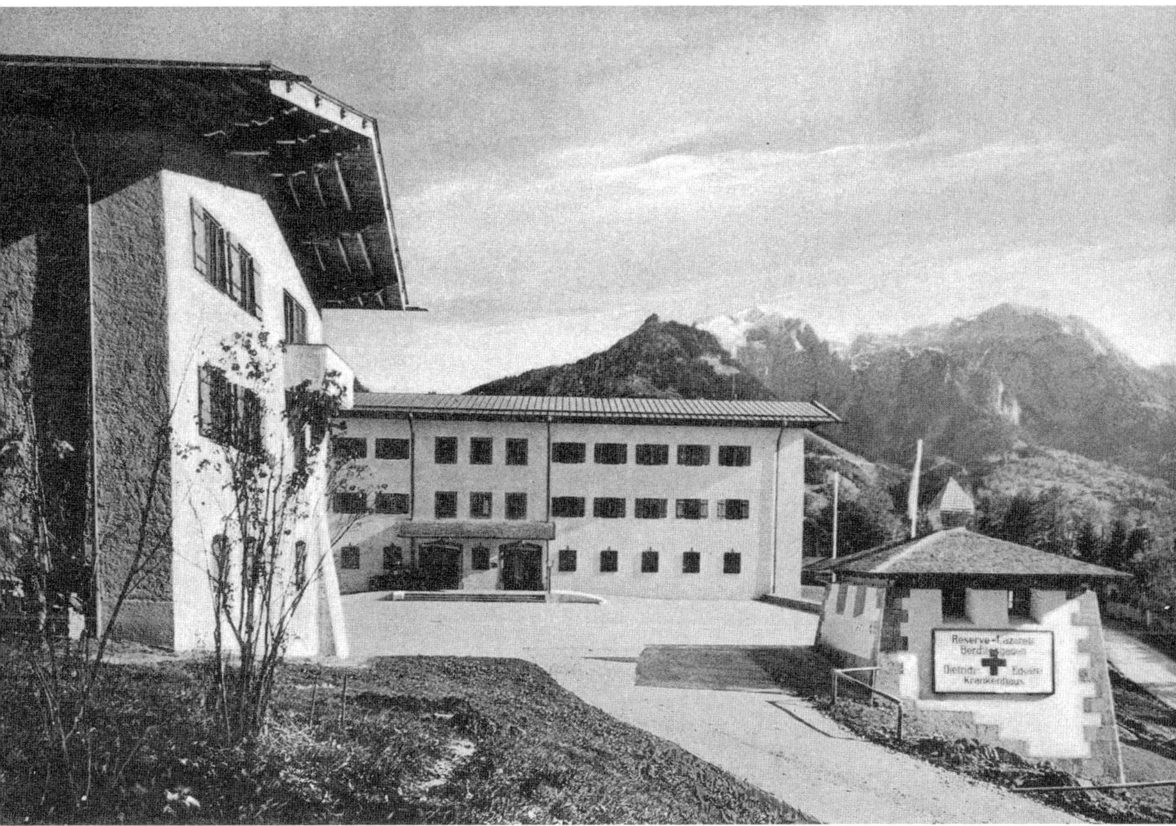

101. Uncaptioned.

The hospital complex covered a large area. After the Second World War the Dietrich Eckart Hospital became the local district hospital being renamed 'Klinik in der Stanggaß' Berchtesgaden. The hospital finally closed in late 1996, and although it remains standing, the complex is now quite dilapidated. The interior has been subject to looting and vandalism resulting in the usual damage and graffiti. What will become of the former Dietrich Eckart Hospital is unknown; there were rumours in 2015 that the complex had been purchased with plans for conversion into a hotel and spa.

In July 2022 it was announced that the Lucerne-based company, Unique Hotels and Resorts AG were involved in proposing plans that would see the former hospital complex demolished. The site would then undergo redevelopment to build what they describe as an 'Alpine village' resort. The proposed development would be exclusive and set its sights on attracting an international clientele. These plans, should they go ahead, will see yet another historically significant building disappear.

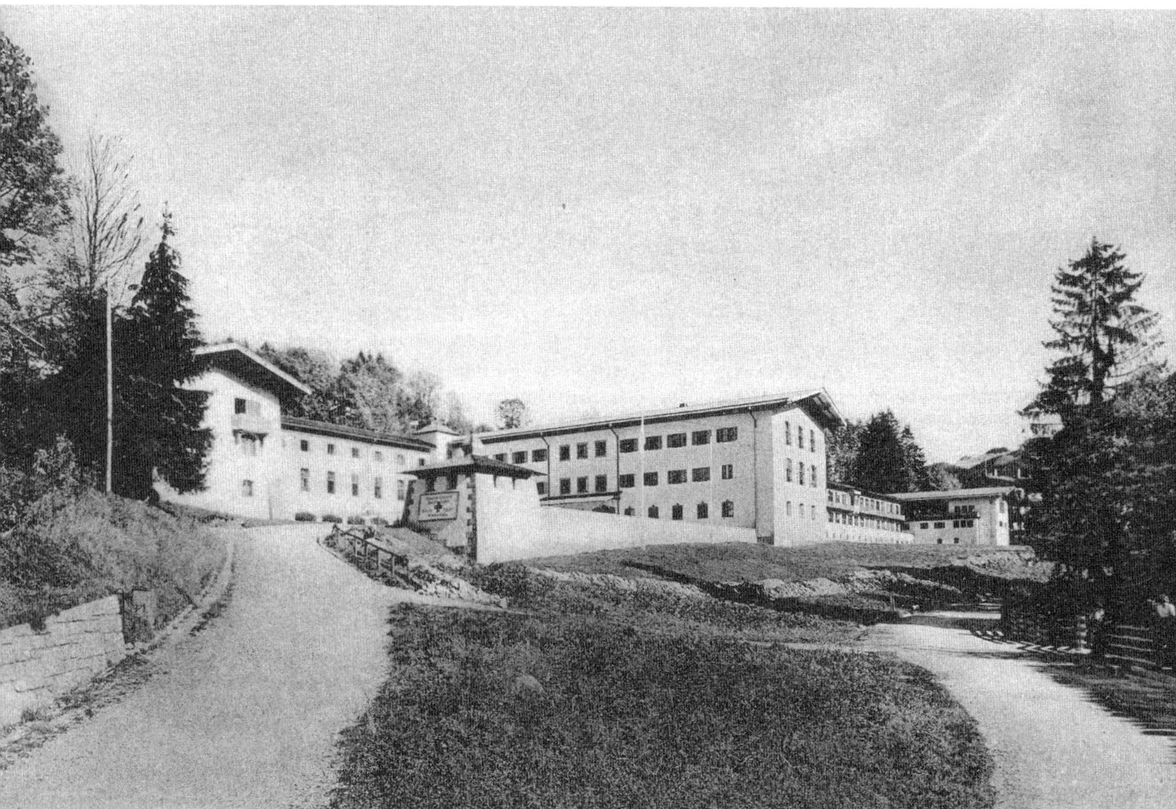

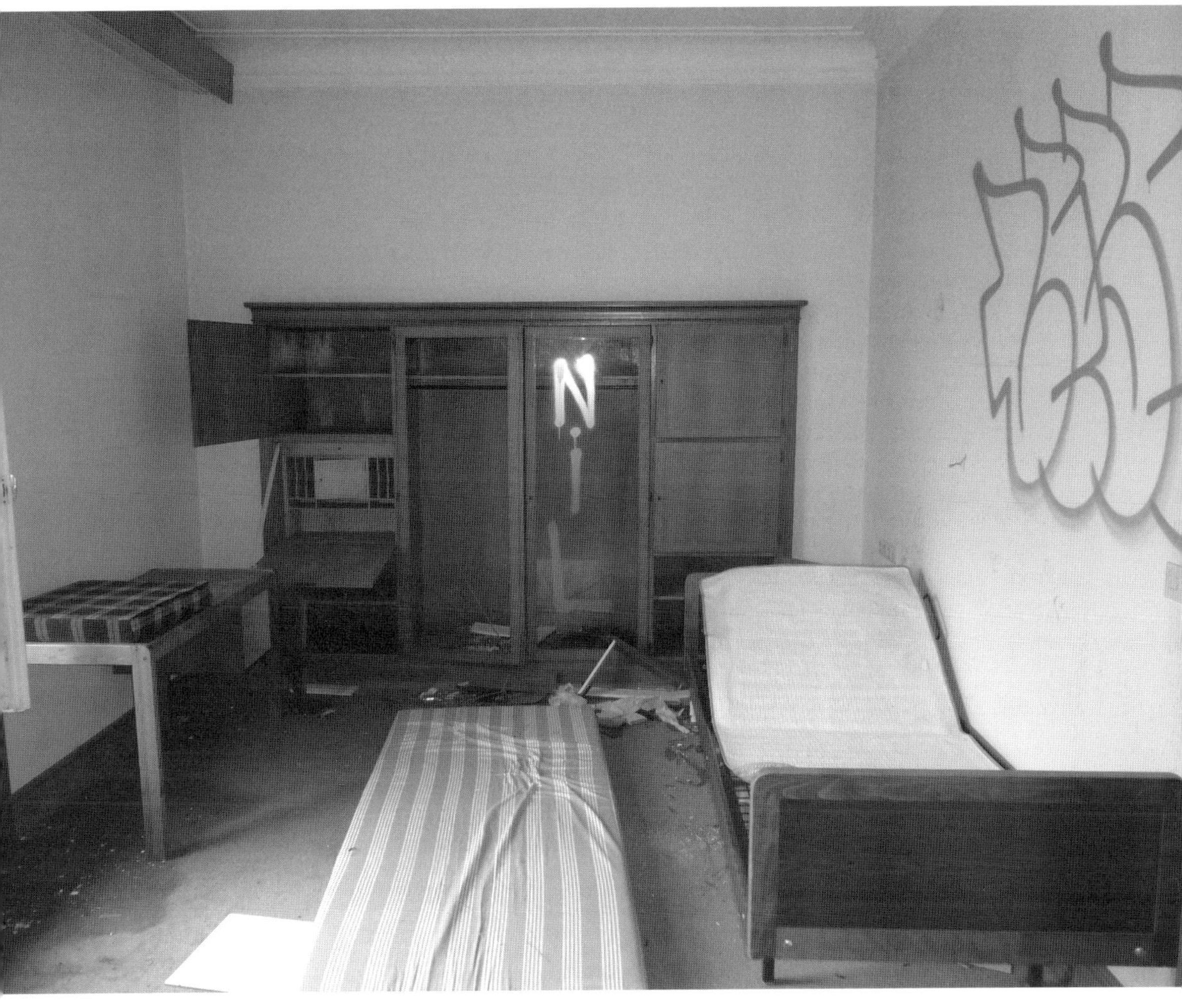

102. Hermann Göring's private room in the Dietrich Eckart Hospital as it appeared when photographed in 2015. Sporadic acts of vandalism have played their part in the deterioration of the hospital interior since its closure.

The furniture we see in the room is not Third Reich period, however, the fitted cabinet with incorporated writing desk on the opposite wall is period. On close inspection the quality of the piece makes this immediately obvious. The window on the left looked out towards the Watzmann. A door on the right led into the Reichsmarschall's private bathroom, a room of equal size to this one.

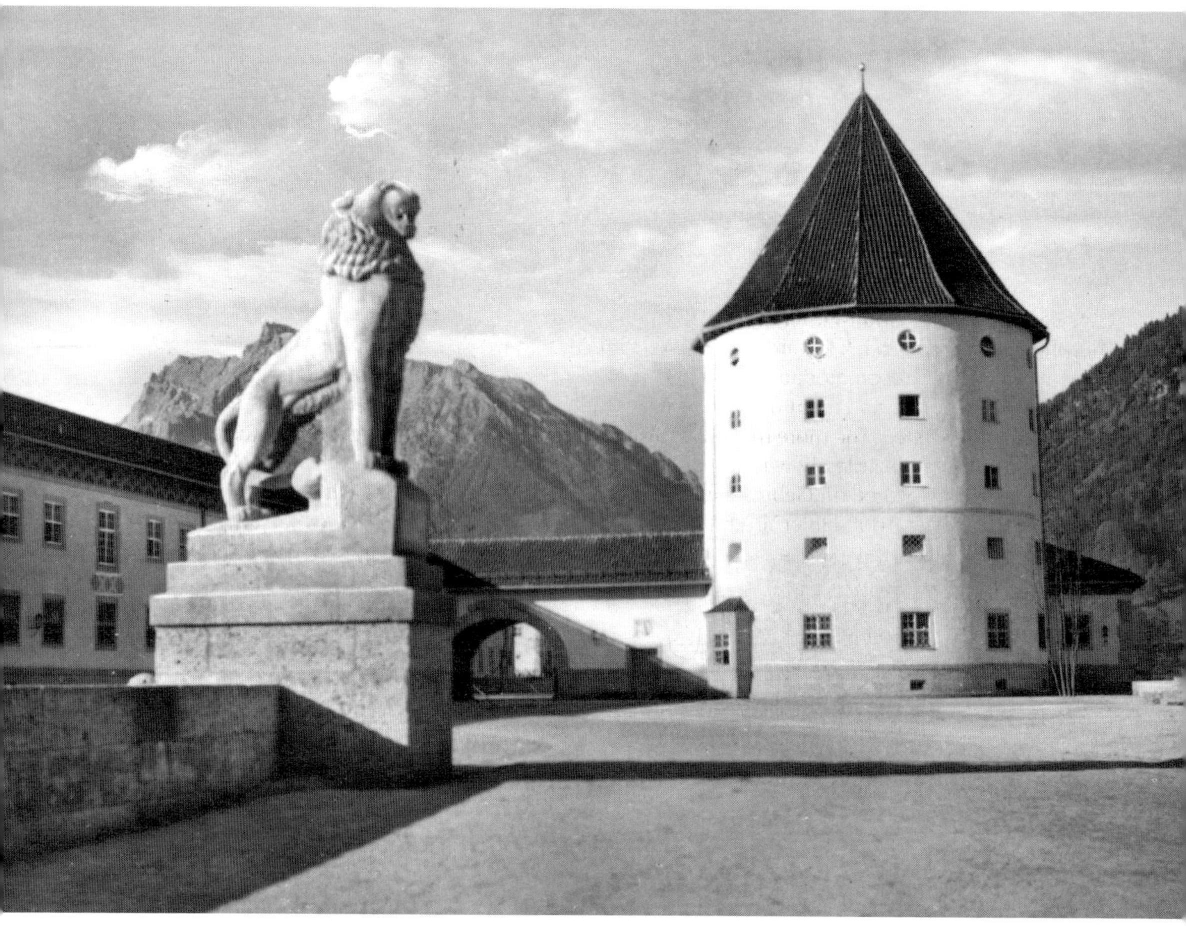

103. Barracks Berchtesgaden-Strub with Hochkalter.

This postcard shows the main entrance of the Adolf Hitler *Kaserne* (Barracks) as seen from the roadside. The imposing period stone lion standing close to the entrance now bears a plaque recognising the sacrifice of the mountain troops who died during the Second World War. Of considerable size, the complex was designed by Munich architect Bruno Biehler. Construction began in September 1937. The 2nd Battalion, *Gebirgs-Jäger* (Mountain Rifle) Regiment 100 moved into the completed barracks on 11 November 1938.

With so many members of the Nazi hierarchy spending so much time in and around the area, and given the mountainous terrain of the region, it was considered a good idea to have a specialist Alpine regiment based nearby. The role of these troops was to provide additional protection for the Nazi leaders and increased security for the area in general.

In the latter stages of the Second World War the barracks provided accommodation for high-ranking German officers. After 1945 the former Adolf Hitler Barracks were taken over by the US and put to various uses. In 1995 the departure of the Americans saw the barracks return to German control. Once again they are home to a mountain infantry regiment.

Posted in Berchtesgaden on 8 December 1942 this postcard made its way to an address in Munich. The card was sent *'Feldpost'* meaning military post by a serving soldier; perhaps a soldier based in the Adolf Hitler Barracks at the time.

104. Berchtesgaden, Adolf-Hitler-Barracks.

This photograph looks back towards the main entrance from inside the complex; this affords a look at the grounds and accommodation/administration blocks. The barracks are situated in Strub just outside Berchtesgaden and apart from the construction of some additional accommodation blocks they remain unchanged. The more recently constructed blocks follow the original architectural style and integrate almost seamlessly with the original 1930s buildings.

The barracks are located on Gebirgsjägerstrasse, off Ramsauer Straße, just a little further along the road from the former Adolf Hitler Youth Hostel.

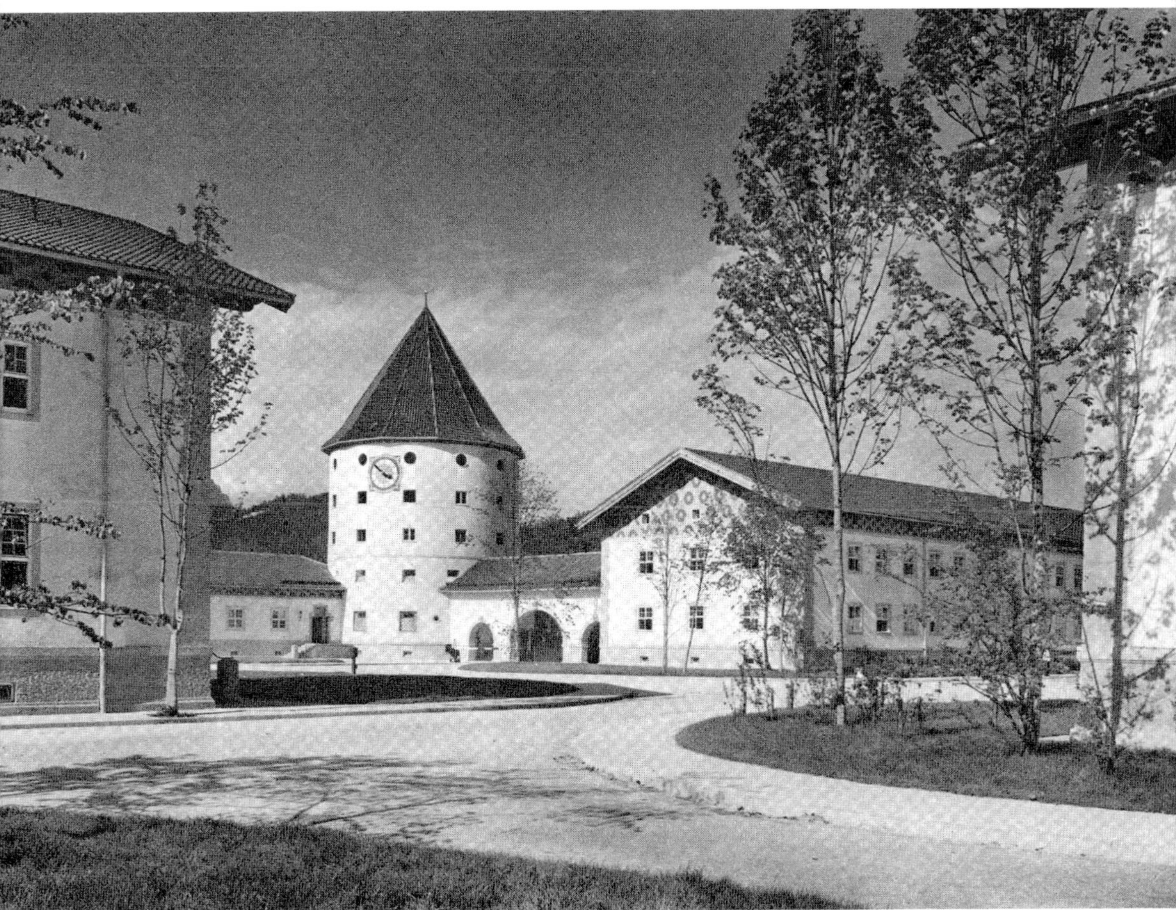

105. Adolf Hitler Jugendherberge Strub near Berchtesgaden.
Designed by architect Georg Zimmermann the foundation stone of the Adolf-Hitler-Youth-Hostel was laid on 20 April 1935, Hitler's birthday. The completed hostel complex opened on 18 October 1938 when a speech given by Reich Youth Leader Baldur von Schirach was radiobroadcast to the nation. The Adolf Hitler Youth Hostel would accommodate many thousands of members of the various youth organisations who visited this, the 'Führer's chosen homeland' through the following years.

This postcard shows the main building that stands by the roadside not far from the Adolf Hitler Barracks already discussed in postcards numbers 103 and 104. This, the main building underwent refurbishment in 2011 and now looks quite different.

The wall by the roadside on the left and the single storey wing seen on the right were removed while a number of the windows in the main building were replaced; at the same time the original interior of the building underwent complete renovation. Only one of the three original accommodation blocks close to the main building remains unchanged. The complex continues to operate as a youth hostel.

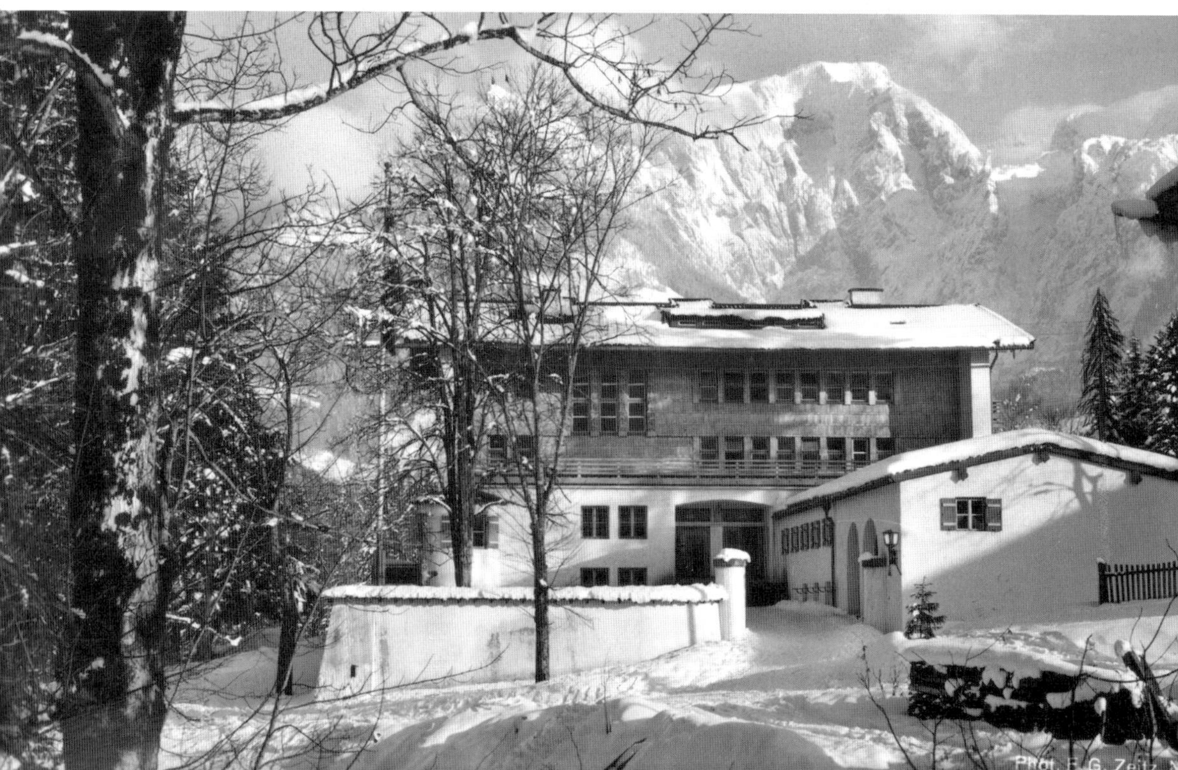

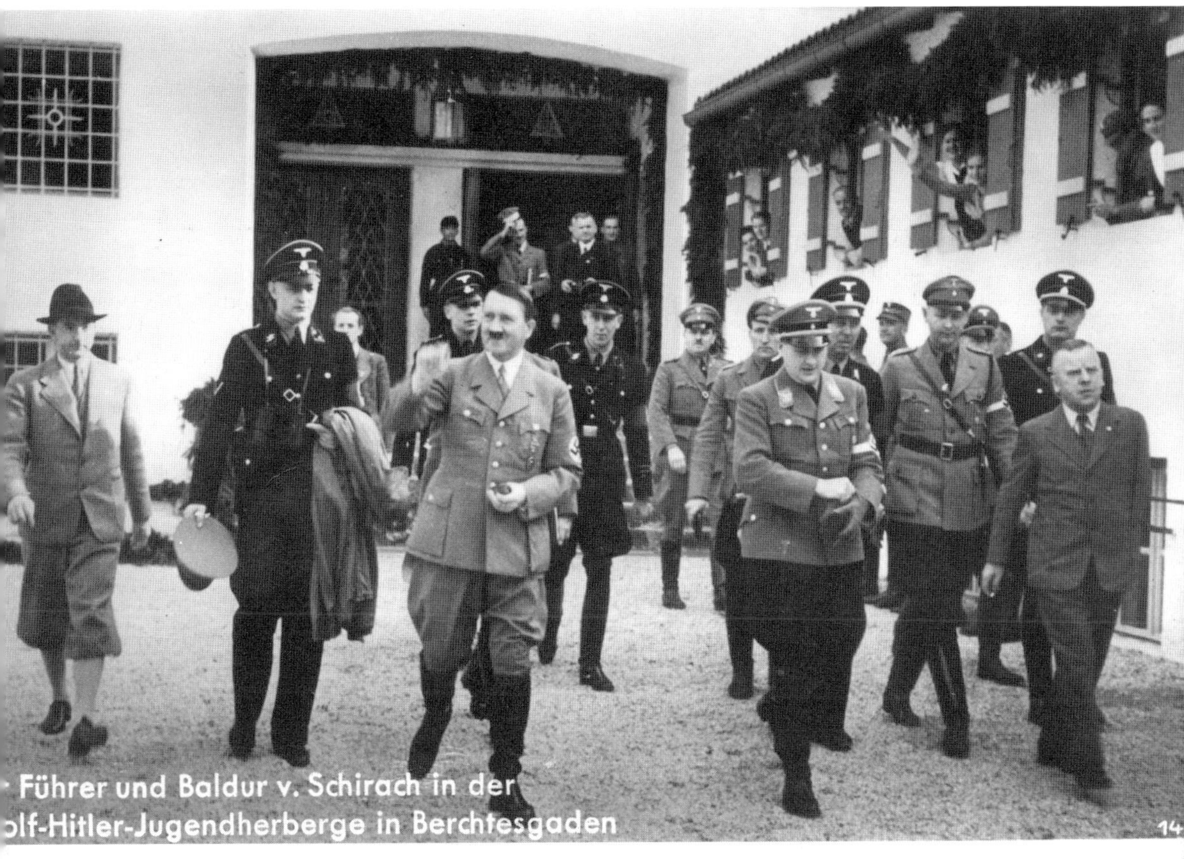

106. The Führer and Baldur von Schirach in the Adolf-Hitler-Youth-Hostel in Berchtesgaden.
Hitler, accompanied by a number of SS men, Nazi Party officials and Reich Youth Leader Baldur von Schirach (on Hitler's left) take their leave of the youth hostel near Berchtesgaden to the excited farewells of young people gathered at the windows. The SS-man behind Hitler dutifully carries the Führer's hat and coat.

The man directly behind von Schirach in SS uniform and partially obscured is SS-*Obergruppenführer* (Lieutenant-General) Julius Schaub (1898–1967) chief aide and adjutant to Hitler. Schaub held this position from 1940 until 1945. On 22 April 1945 Schaub, on Hitler's direct orders, travelled to the Berghof where, as instructed, he destroyed all the Führer's personal documents and paperwork.

Its been said that Hitler did this in an effort to spare many who had corresponded with him over the years from retribution should these documents fall into allied hands. Had that happened who knows how many reputations would have been destroyed and forever tarnished.

Posted in Berchtesgaden on 28 January 1939, little more than three months after the youth hostel opened, this postcard made its way to an address in nearby Salzburg, Austria.

107. The large day room.
This photograph shows the large communal day room in the Adolf Hitler Youth Hostel. A large picture of the Führer, the spiritual father of German youth hangs on the back wall. Many members of the various youth movements, both male and female, would have stayed in groups in the hostel. Given how much time Hitler spent in the area, the hostel's location in Strub on the outskirts of Berchtesgaden would have made this a favourite destination for young people.

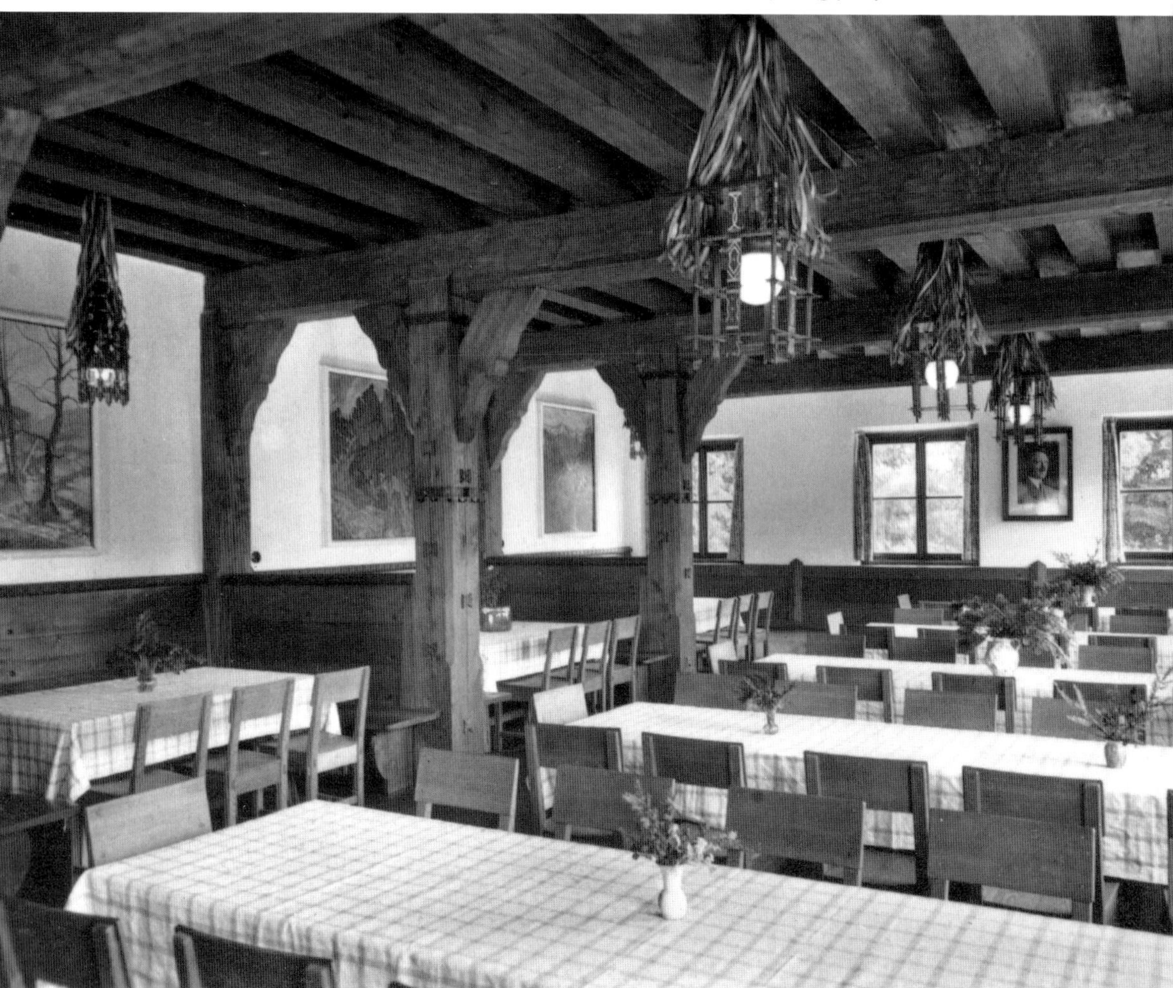

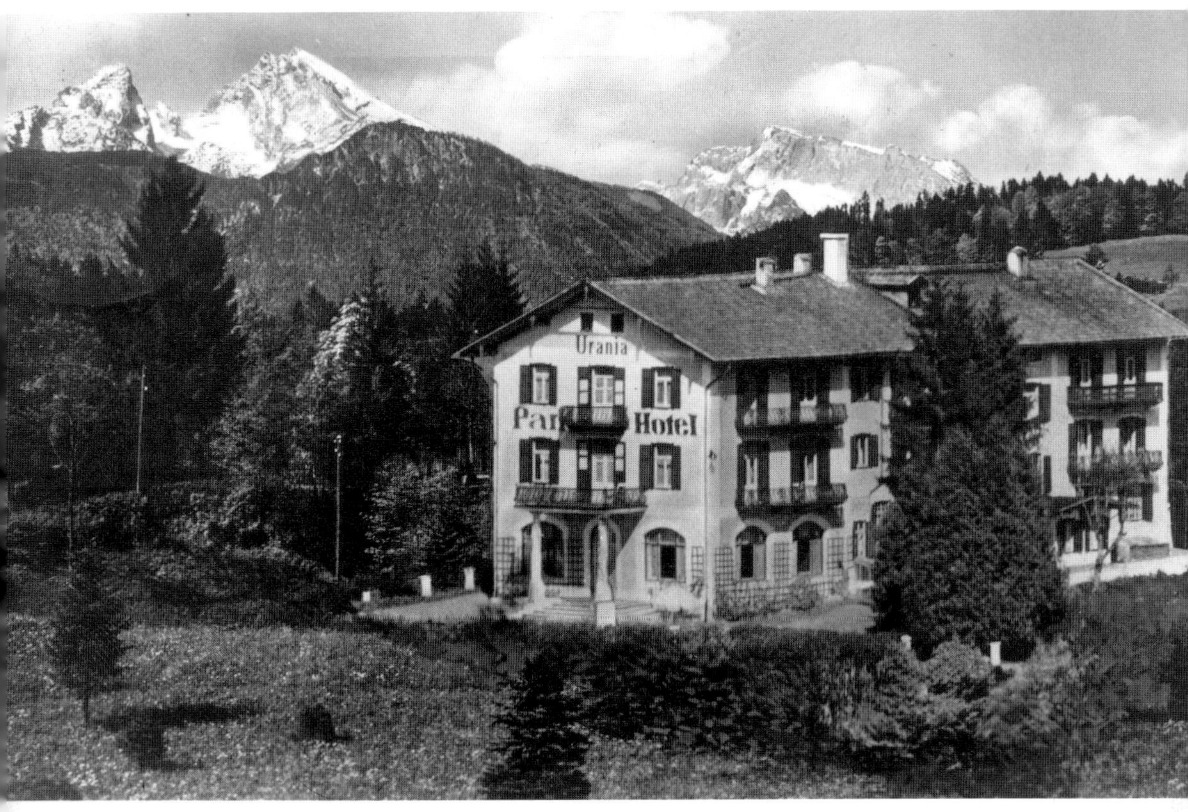

108. Recreational home for DAF Berchtesgaden.

The Urania Park Hotel, sometimes referred to as the Karlsbader Urania Pension just outside Berchtesgaden became a recreational centre for members of the DAF, (DAF; *Deutsche Arbeitsfront* – German Labour Front) during the Nazi period.

Headed by Dr Robert Ley (1890–1945) the DAF had been established in May 1933 to replace the existing German trades unions system. The DAF would become an immense organization with a staggering number of over twenty million members.

The idea was to bring all workers, from the shop floor to management level together to work for the common good. The Nazi Party sought to improve workers' conditions and productivity through numerous incentive schemes. One of these, the KdF (KdF; *Kraft durch Freude* – Strength through Joy) a subsidiary of the DAF, was a recreational organisation set up in 1933 to provide paid holiday trips for workers. By the late 1930s the KdF had become the world's largest tour operator.

As well as providing educational courses, the KdF also arranged activities for workers to enjoy during their leisure time, with sports clubs and access to subsidised tickets to various events including concerts, exhibitions, museums, the theatre and the opera.

Given Berchtesgaden's importance during the Third Reich period it is probably reasonable to assume that the Urania Park Hotel was not frequented by the rank and file of the DAF but was retained for the exclusive use of those running the organisation. This postcard bearing a special postmark requesting, 'War Relief for the German Red Cross' was posted in Munich on 28 July 1940.

109. Uncaptioned.
In this particular instance the Park Hotel, seen here in the centre in the lower foreground, is almost completely lost in this spectacular winter scene. This postcard reveals something of the incredible natural beauty of the area where the snow-covered Göll and Brett completely dwarf the hotel when photographed from this angle.

The Urania Park Hotel was located in the area of Mitterbach, just off Königsseer Straße. Situated on the outskirts of Berchtesgaden the property offered fabulous mountain views. The building was demolished in the 1960s.

Another DAF facility was located at Hallthurm. Hallthurm is approximately halfway between Bischofswiesen and Bad Reichenhall, at a point where the railway line from Bad Reichenhall to Berchtesgaden crosses the road before stopping at the small station of Hallthurm. As previously stated, the Berchtesgaden facility would have catered for the 'higher ranks' within the DAF and this was probably also the case at Hallthurm.

The former DAF Recreational Centre at Hallthurm has been extended in recent years with new buildings having been constructed in the grounds. The complex is now known as the *'Sozialtherapeutisches Zentrum Hallthurm'* (Hallthurm Social Therapeutic Centre), a centre helping those suffering with mental health issues and addiction.

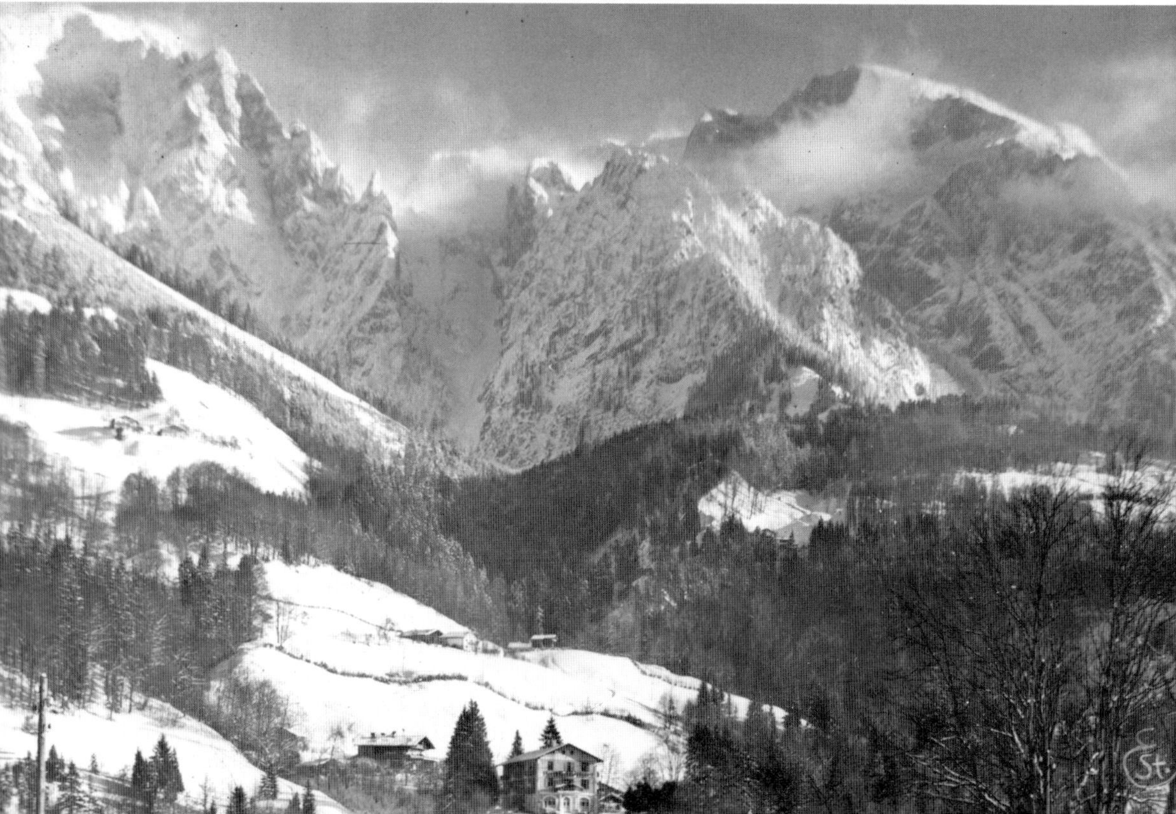

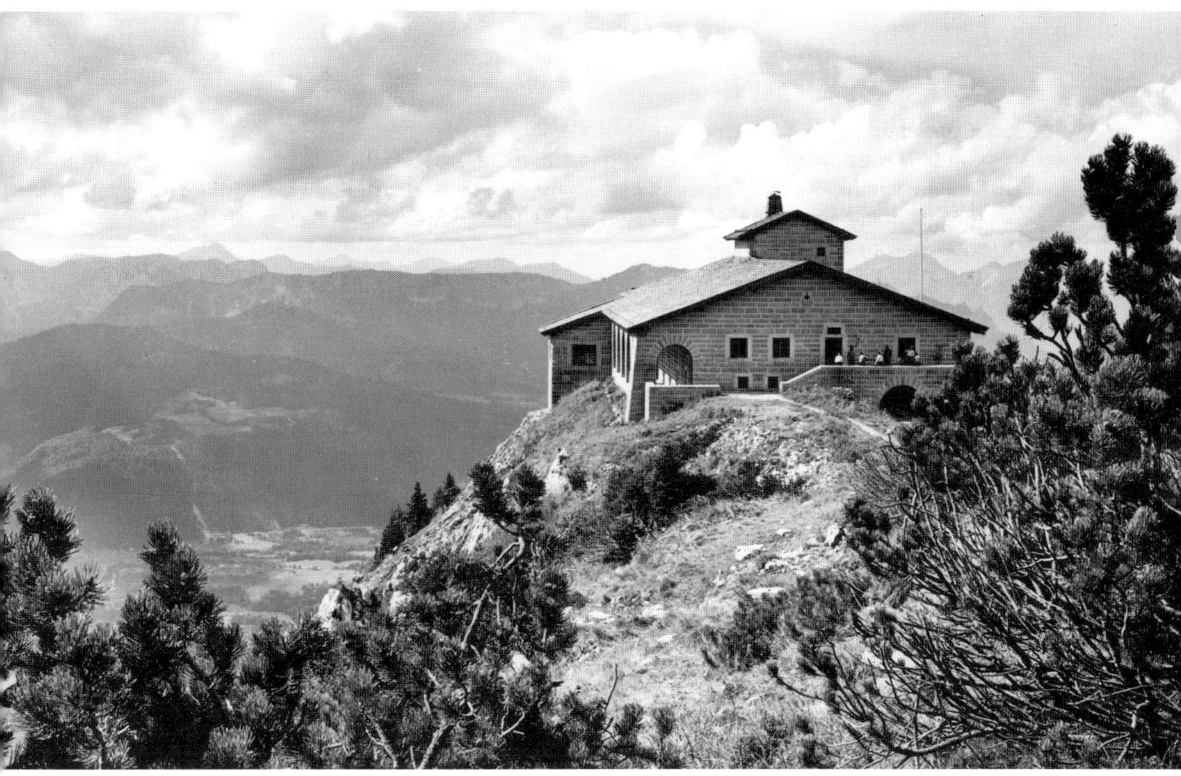

110. Berchtesgaden – The Kehlsteinhaus 1840 metres above sea level.

This one small building, originally conceived as a teahouse, is known the world over. Miraculously it survived the bombing of the area on 25 April 1945 unscathed. Perched on a rocky outcrop at 1834 metres (6017 feet) it is undoubtedly a feat of engineering and construction by any standard. The architect Roderick Fick was charged with coming up with a design that could withstand the harshest conditions in such an exposed position. The Kehlsteinhaus would be a gift from the Nazi Party to Adolf Hitler on the occasion of his fiftieth birthday on Thursday, 20 April 1939. Discussions on the intended project got underway in April 1937. *Reichsleiter* (Reich Leader) Martin Bormann who had initiated the idea would oversee the work.

As the Kehlstein Mountain was in a pristine state with no existing roads or buildings, everything, absolutely everything had to be done from scratch. Under the direction of Dr Fritz Todt, at that time Inspector General for German Roads, a new mountain road some 6.5 kilometres (4 miles) long was constructed. This incredible road began at Obersalzberg and ended some 130 metres (430 feet) below the building itself. A tunnel was then constructed to provide access to an elevator; this in turn would carry visitors up through the heart of the mountain to arrive in the Kehlsteinhaus.

It is hard to conceive the conditions under which the workers laboured to construct this incredible road and building. Nonetheless work finished ahead of schedule at the end of 1938. Adolf Hitler's first visit to the Kehlsteinhaus was on 16 September 1938. The NSDAP officially presented this extraordinary gift to the Führer on his 50th birthday on 20 April the following year. Adolf Hitler made fourteen official visits to the Kehlsteinhaus between 1938 and 1940, together with a small number of private, unofficial visits. Hitler much preferred to visit the smaller teahouse at Mooslahnerkopf below the Berghof; something he did almost daily when he was residing on the Obersalzberg.

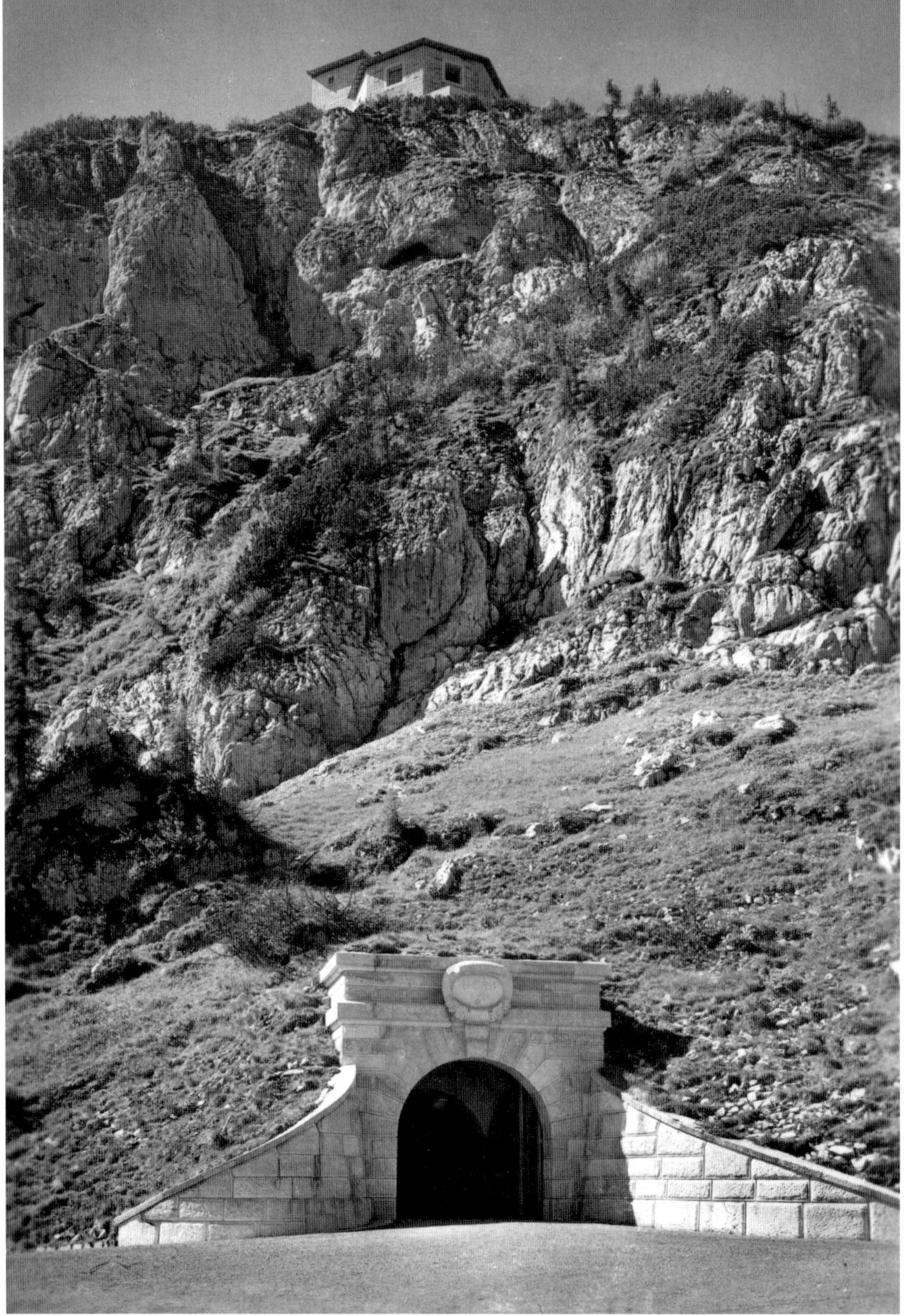

111. Hitler's Eagle's Nest (1832 m).
The entrance to the 126 metre (413 feet) long tunnel; this in turn leads to the lift that carries visitors the remaining 124 metres (406 feet) to arrive in the Kehlsteinhaus seen above. This small building receives over 300,000 visitors from around the world annually. It is open between May and October depending on weather conditions.

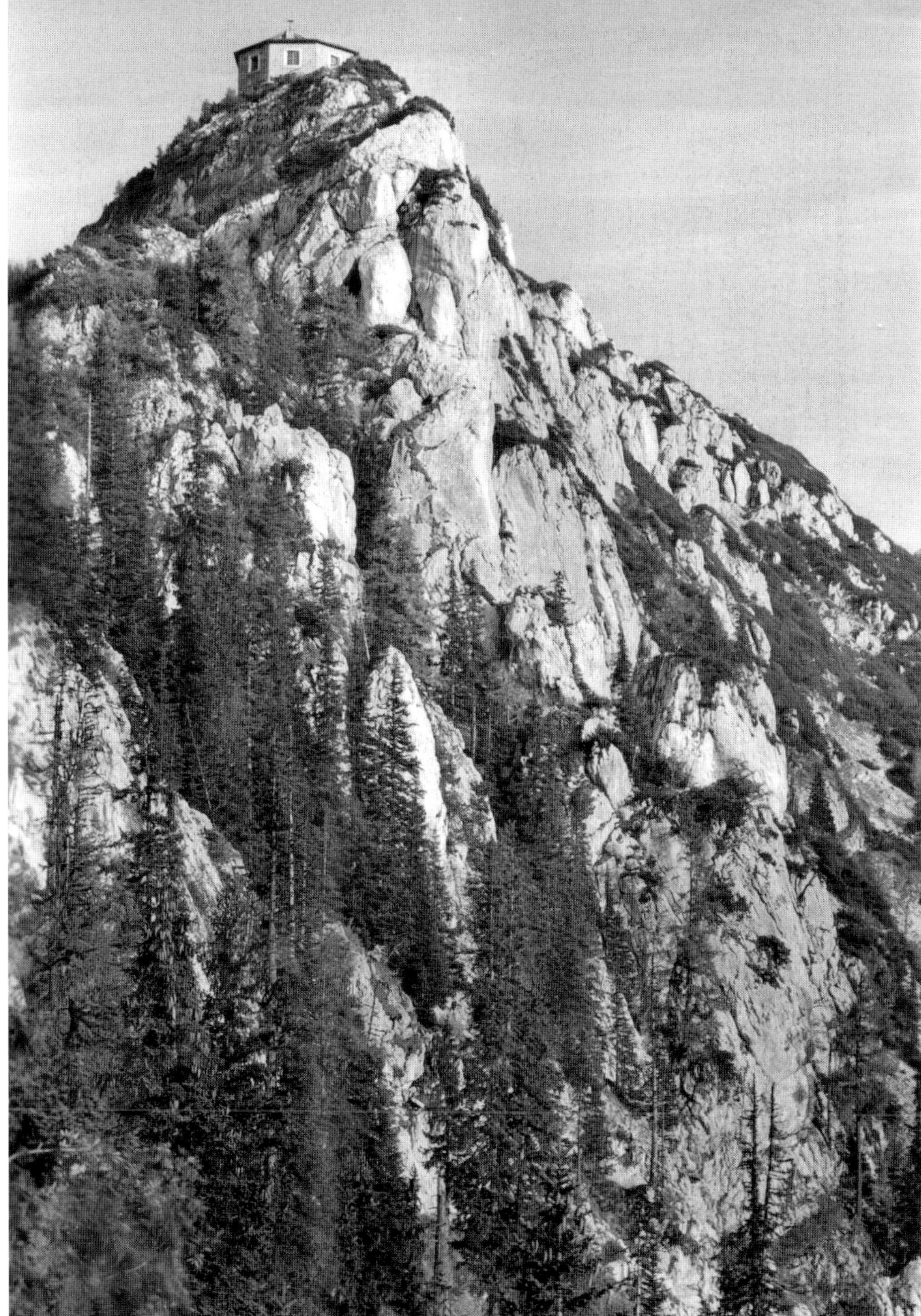

112. Kehlsteinhaus (1836m) Eagle's Nest.
In this instance the photographer has travelled to the Scharitzkehlalm to capture this spectacular image of the Kehlsteinhaus. While not often photographed from this side of the mountain this image gives a clear indication as to the enormity of the task that was undertaken to construct what was to be the ultimate birthday gift, a special present from the Nazi Party to Adolf Hitler on his 50th birthday.

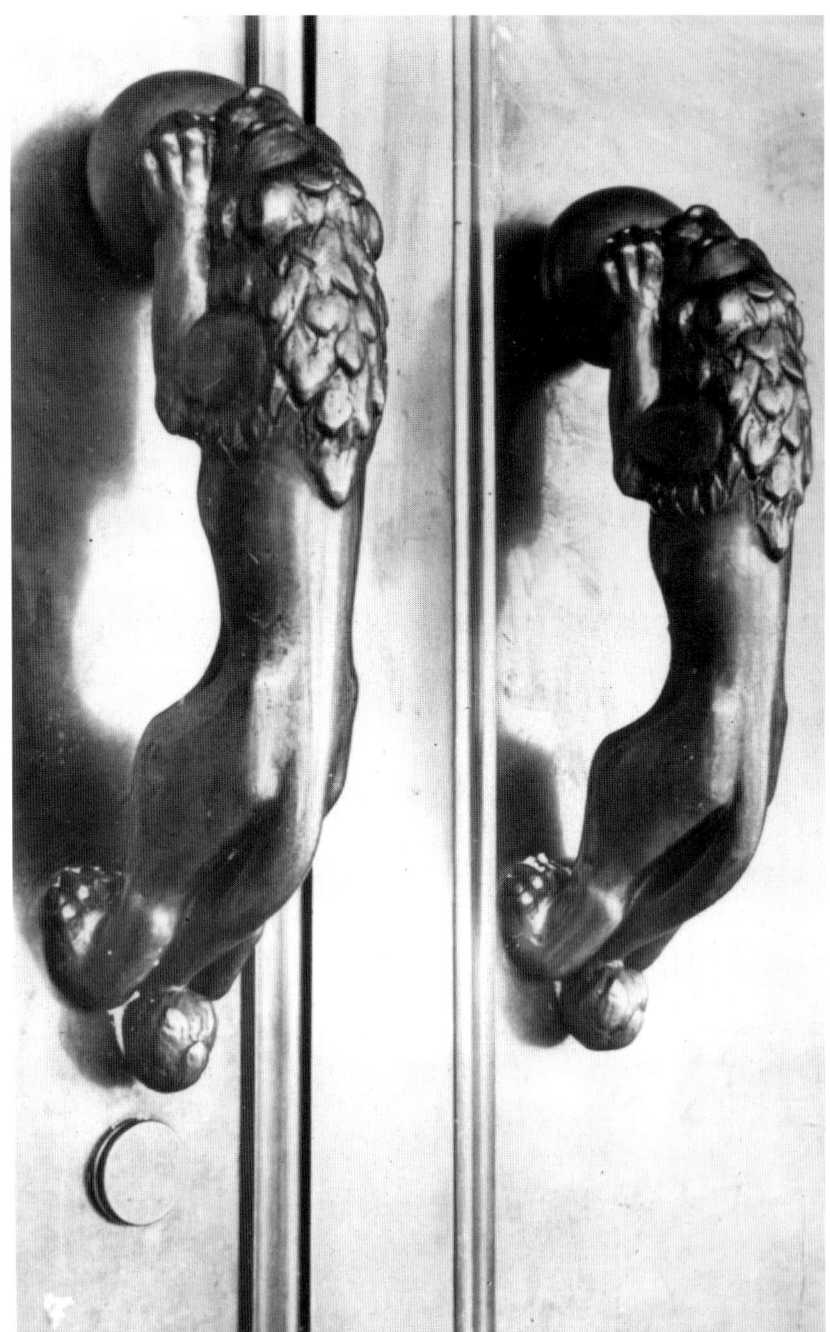

113. Reverse unmarked, source unknown.
The brass door handles on the outer doors to the entrance tunnel were in the form of two lions each holding a ball in their front paws. Designed by Professor Bernhard Bleeker the handles were taken by the Americans at the end of the war. The outer and inner doors are made of copper and brass.

114. Reverse unmarked, source unknown.

The entrance tunnel is protected by two sets of heavy double doors. This photograph looks back down the 126 metre (413 feet) long, marble-lined entrance tunnel towards the inner doors. Rather surprisingly the tunnel's original light fittings are still in place. The tunnel is lined with Kälberstein marble; the floor is formed of large granite slabs.

Originally the tunnel was heated; warm air was pumped into this tunnel from an adjacent service tunnel that runs the entire length of this, the entrance tunnel. On walking down the entrance tunnel vents placed at floor level allowed the warm air to enter this tunnel.

The original plan was for the mountain road to continue all the way up to the Kehlsteinhaus. However on reaching the last section it became clear that the terrain would not allow for a road to be built that would not be visible from below; additionally this last section was above the treeline meaning that if indeed this last section of road could be built it would certainly be visible from the valley below. This would have meant that all the effort that had been put into making the already constructed road all but invisible from below, meaningless. The problem was resolved when the tunnel and elevator option was adopted. The final cost of the Kehlsteinhaus project was some 34 million Reichmarks, at that time equivalent to 10 million US Dollars

This set of twelve black and white photographs numbers 113 to 124, each measuring 11 x 7 cms (4.5 x 3 ins) are printed on 'Agfa Brovira' paper. As Afga Brovira photographic paper was introduced in the mid 1930s there is absolutely no reason to presume that these are anything other than contemporary prints.

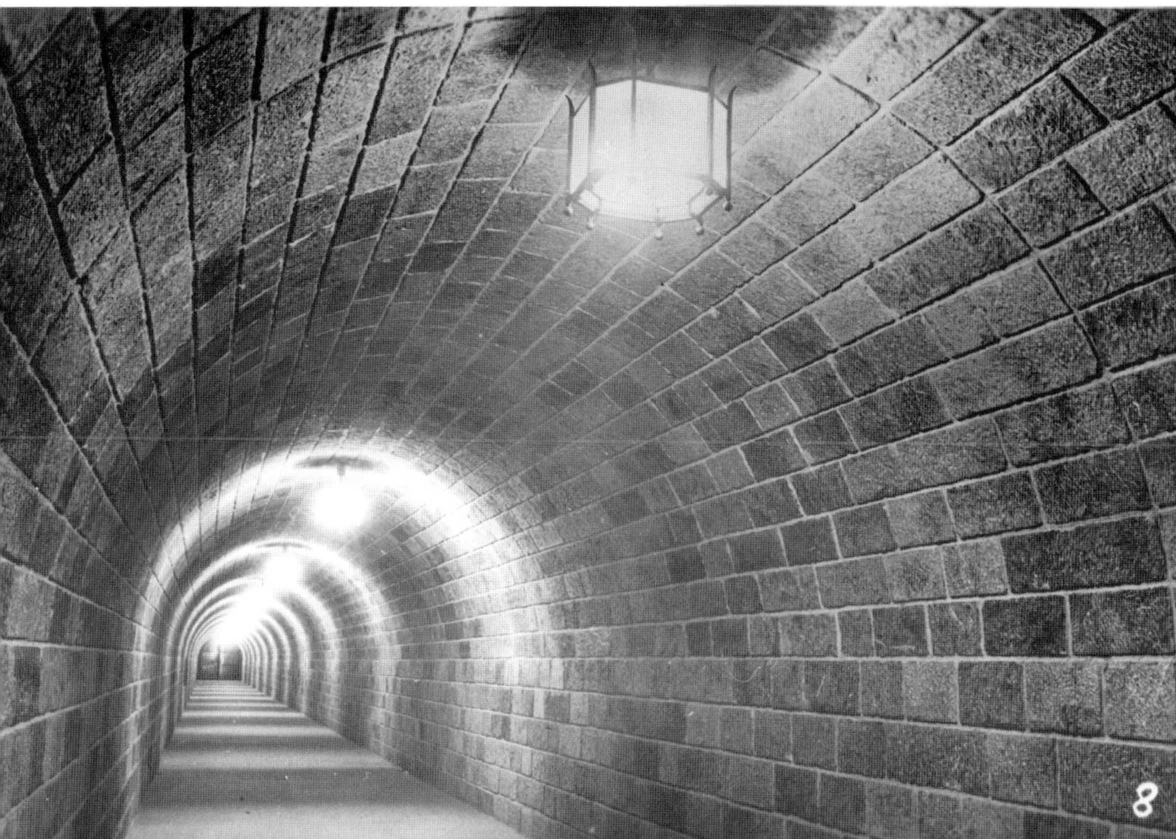

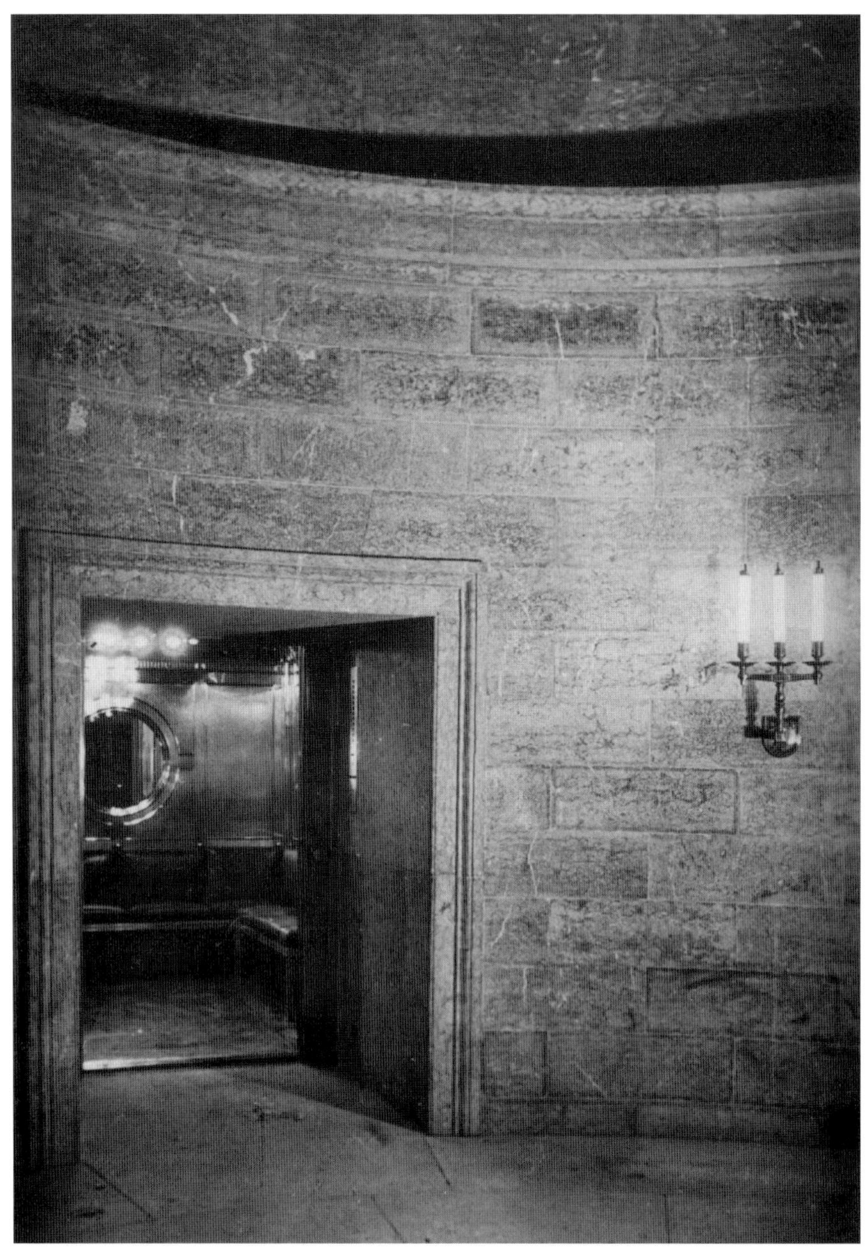

115. Reverse unmarked, source unknown.
On reaching the end of the entrance tunnel one turns right to enter this circular waiting room. This room with its high domed ceiling is lined with Ruhpoldinger marble blocks; it is interesting to note and clear to see that the blocks have been installed so that each block meets its neighbour with no mortar having been used in the joints between them. This photograph shows the lift doors open to reveal the highly polished solid brass interior of the cabin as designed by Professor Roderick Fick. Today this same lift carries as many as forty people at a time.

116. Reverse unmarked, source unknown.

The service tunnel that runs parallel to the entrance tunnel carried electric cables and the ducting for the warm air that once heated the entrance tunnel. As the photograph shows, the service tunnel was just that, a service tunnel: a tunnel with an almost rough-hewn finish.

Those visiting the Kehlsteinhaus (Eagle's Nest) today alight from the buses close to the ticket office located near the entrance tunnel. All the buildings in the parking area are post war construction; there were no buildings in this parking area during the Third Reich period. Entry to the service tunnel below is via a small metal door built into the mountainside. When coming up the mountain road and entering the parking area this door can be seen immediately before the first building on the right, the souvenir shop. The door is locked and members of the public have no access.

However, beyond this locked door and on the left hand side is another door giving access to this service tunnel. Leaving the service tunnel and moving forward along the corridor there are rooms off to the right. The first of these was the transformer room for the lift, next to this was a small room accommodating the control-panel. The next room on the right was yet another transformer room.

At the end of the corridor another metal door opens into the large engine room. The 'engine' is actually a MAN diesel submarine engine. This installation, the tunnels, the rooms and the engine were put in place as a back-up power supply. Should the electrical supply from the valley below fail, the diesel engine would provide power to the Kehlsteinhaus and the lift. The engine is maintained and could still perform its originally intended role if required.

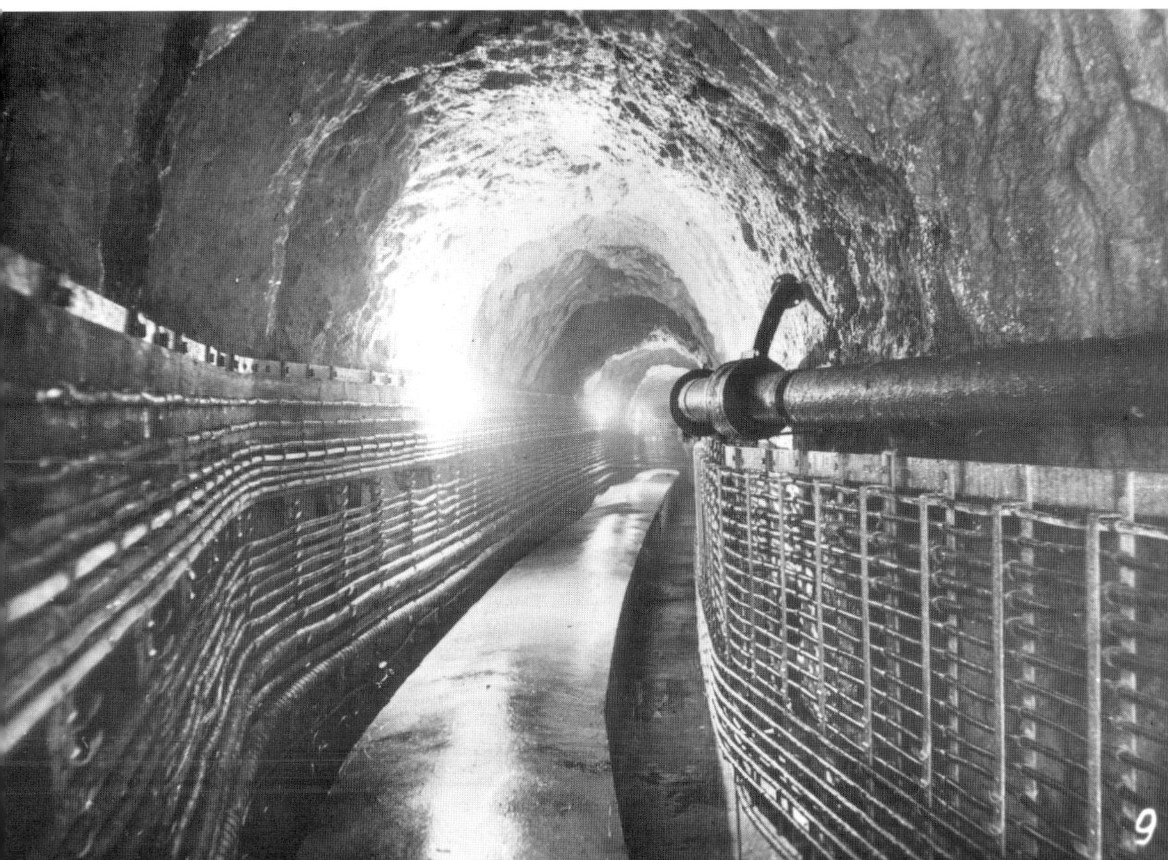

117. Reverse unmarked, source unknown.

This photograph shows the engine room. In the foreground we see the large Siemens generator, behind that stands the MAN eight-cylinder diesel submarine engine. These two main components occupy a central position in the engine room. The original 'shadow board' with all the tools required to work on the engine is still attached to the adjacent wall. This huge engine was transported up the mountain on the back of a lorry. Continuing past the engine and the generator brings you to the last rooms in this underground complex, the switchboard room and the fuel storage room. The electric cables running up the mountain from the Obersalzberg were placed below ground. The entire project had been carried out in a way so as to have the least visual impact in an attempt to leave the Kehlstein Mountain in a near natural state.

   This manufacturer's plate attached to the opposite side of the engine bears the following information.

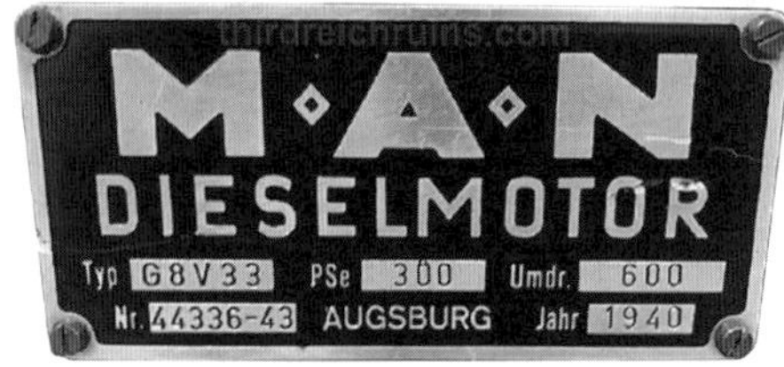

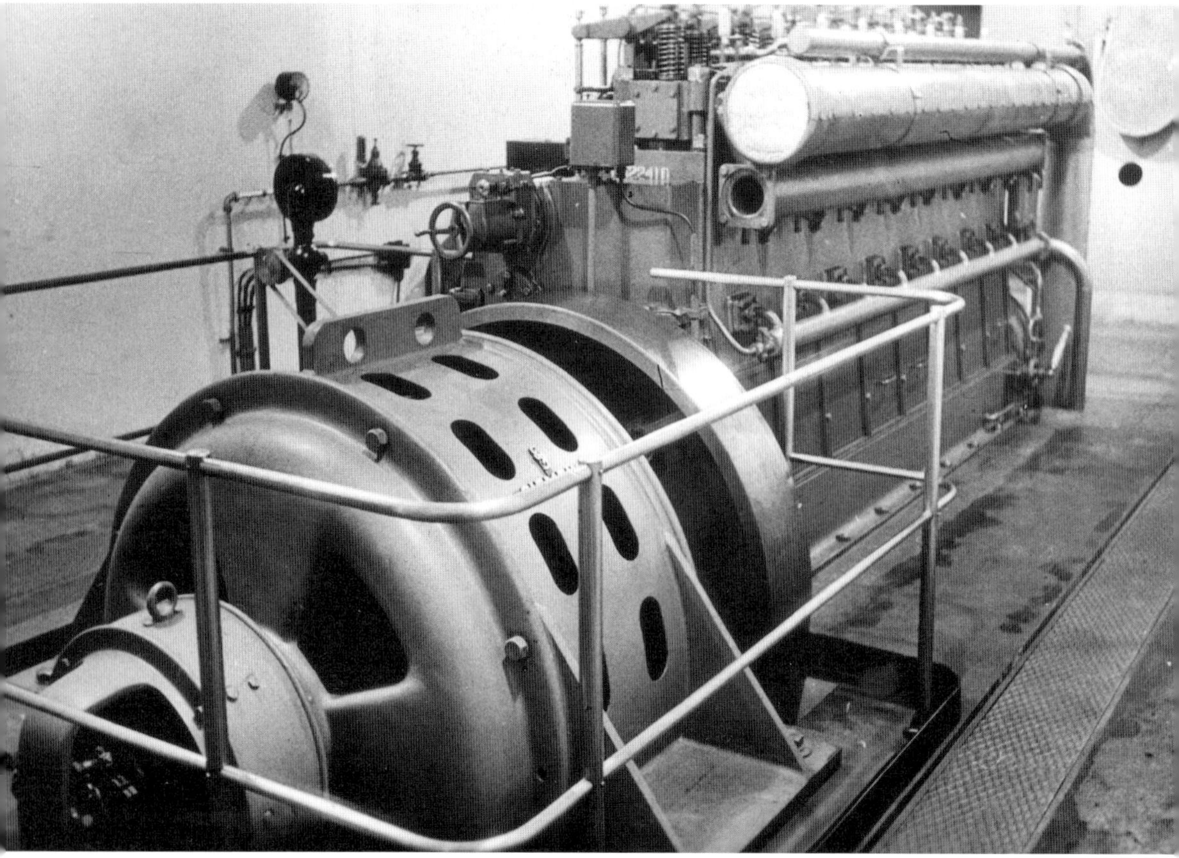

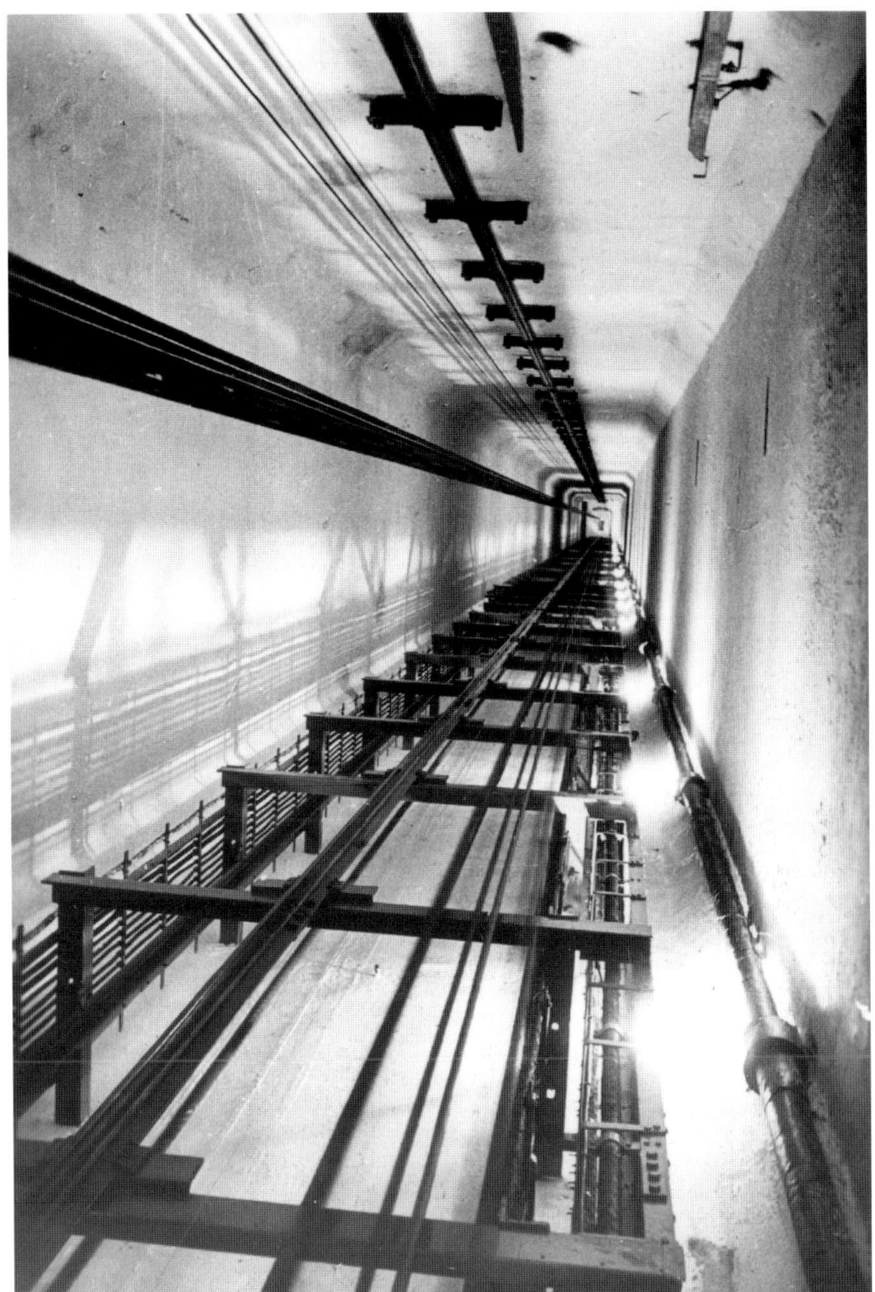

118. Reverse unmarked, source unknown.
The lift shaft is 131 metres (430 feet) deep. Using low impact charges to reduce the risk of cave in, teams working their way down through the mountain from the summit connected with teams blasting their way up from below. This is where one of the workers met his death when he fell down the shaft.

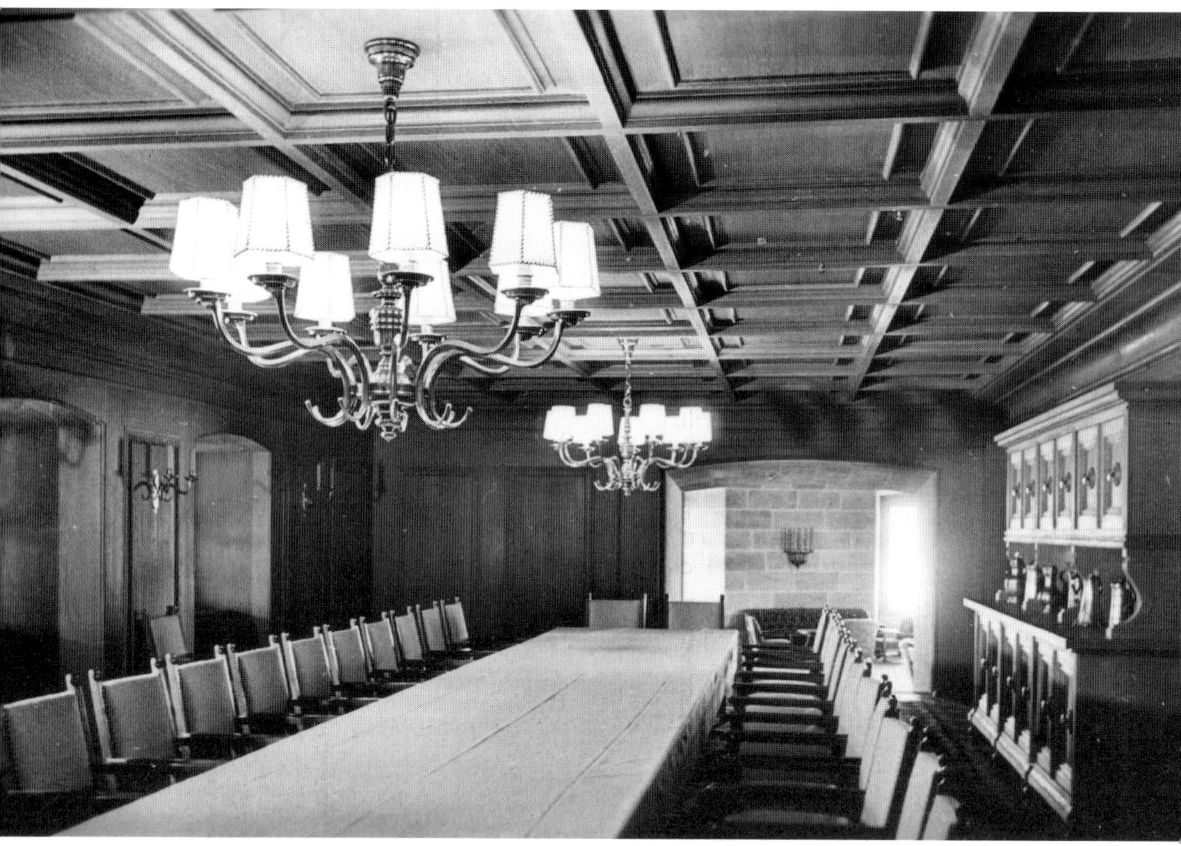

119. Reverse unmarked, source unknown.

On stepping out of the lift one enters the Kehlsteinhaus. The corridor directly in front leads towards the back of the building. The first doors on the left are the toilets, immediately past the toilets a staircase leads down to the full basement. The next door on the left and at the end of the corridor leads into what was the guardroom.

At the end of the corridor on the right and opposite the guardroom is the kitchen. The door on the right next the kitchen leads into what was Hitler's study, a room he never used; this room is now the manager's office. On exiting the lift, the door immediately to the right leads into the above room, the former dining-room. With all fittings and furnishings in place this is how the dining-room would have appeared to Adolf Hitler when he visited the building.

The wall panels are made of the highest quality sand blasted oak. The coffered ceiling is again the finest quality. The dining table seen in the photograph could seat up to thirty guests. The large oak buffet standing on the right hand side was the only piece of original furniture left in the building after the Allies had taken what they wanted. Its survival was due to the fact that it would not fit in the lift.

In 2010 the oak buffet was finally removed and placed in a Munich museum. Looking past the table we get a glimpse of the large reception room. The light fittings seen in the photograph were also taken at the end of the Second World War.

120. Reverse unmarked, source unknown.

The large circular reception room in the Kehlsteinhaus as it appeared when photographed in late 1940. The central table made of beech and walnut was manufactured by the Munich-based, Pössenbacher Company. The main focal point is the fireplace. It's said that the red Italian marble for the fireplace was a gift to Hitler from Mussolini. The thick luxurious carpet was a gift from the Japanese Emperor Hirohito. The carpet was cut into pieces by American GIs to be taken as souvenirs.

The tapestry above the fireplace, described as 'richly costumed figures in a country hunting scene' was made in the 1600s. This tapestry alone is said to have cost 32,000 Reichsmarks. The walls in the reception room are very thick. The interior walls are formed of thick limestone blocks while the outer walls were built using granite quarried near Hauzenberg in Lower Bavaria.

The heavy oak beams in the ceiling have no function other than to be visually pleasing. The beams were installed on the instructions of Martin Bormann after Hitler had remarked how he would have liked to see some beams up there.

On the occasion of his first visit to the Kehlsteinhaus on 16 September 1938, at a time when the building work had just ended Hitler was accompanied by his friend George Ward Price, a British journalist. Another early visitor was the French Ambassador, André François-Poncet. The debate continues as to whether it was Ward Price or François-Poncet who came up with the term 'Eagle's Nest' in describing the building and its incredible location.

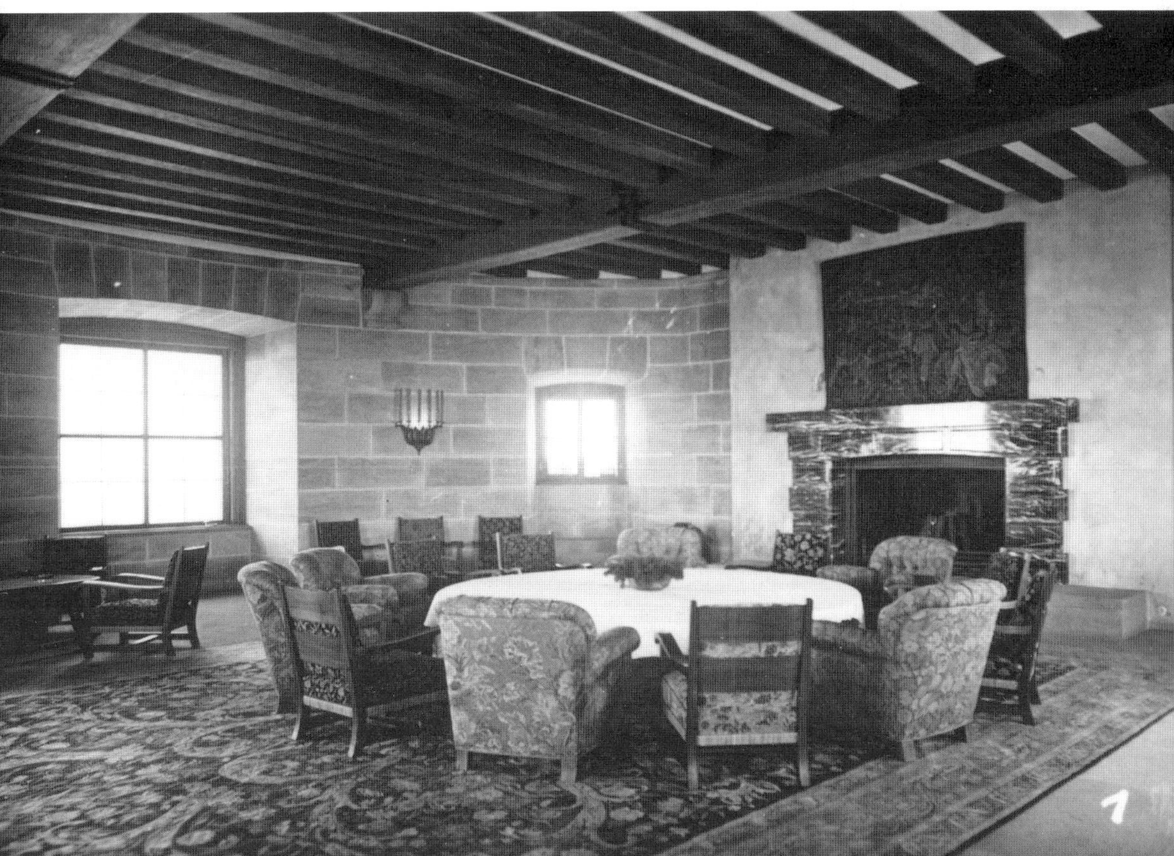

121. Reverse unmarked, source unknown.

The Scharitzkehlstüberl, often referred to as the Eva Braun room is located just off the reception room. The wall panels are made of expensive 'Zirbel' pine, also called cembra pine. The wood planks are split down the middle then opened 'butterfly' fashion so that the knots in the wood mirror each other perfectly when placed side by side in the panels. Cembra pine was used in the Berghof dining room and in some of the public rooms in Hotel Berchtesgadener Hof.

The windows in the Eva Braun room have been replaced; the original windows seen here could be lowered to provide wonderful views towards Hoher Göll, the Königssee and the Watzmann. The large tapestry seen on the right described as 'richly costumed figures in scenery' was also made in the early 1600s and cost 24,000 Reichsmarks. Both tapestries were purchased in Munich in September 1938.

Eva Braun was a regular visitor to the Kehlsteinhaus. This room is allegedly where she and her sister, Gretel, and her friends Gerda Bormann, Margerete Speer and Eva's old school friend Herta Schneider would spend time chatting and enjoying the views; when the weather was good they would sunbathe at the rear of the building.

A door to the left leads out onto the covered sun terrace, this in turn leads to the back of the building where a pathway leads to the Kehlstein summit. The original light fittings seen in the photograph are somewhat miraculously still in place.

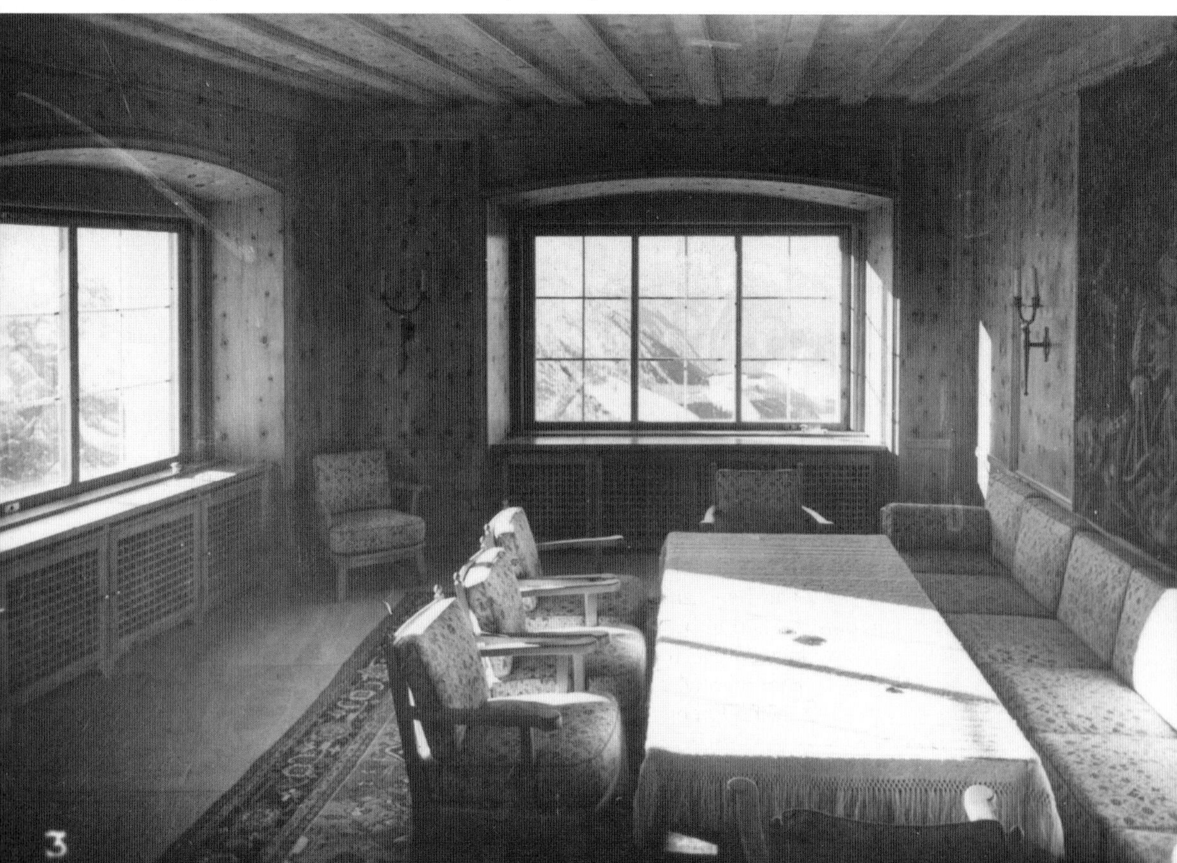

142

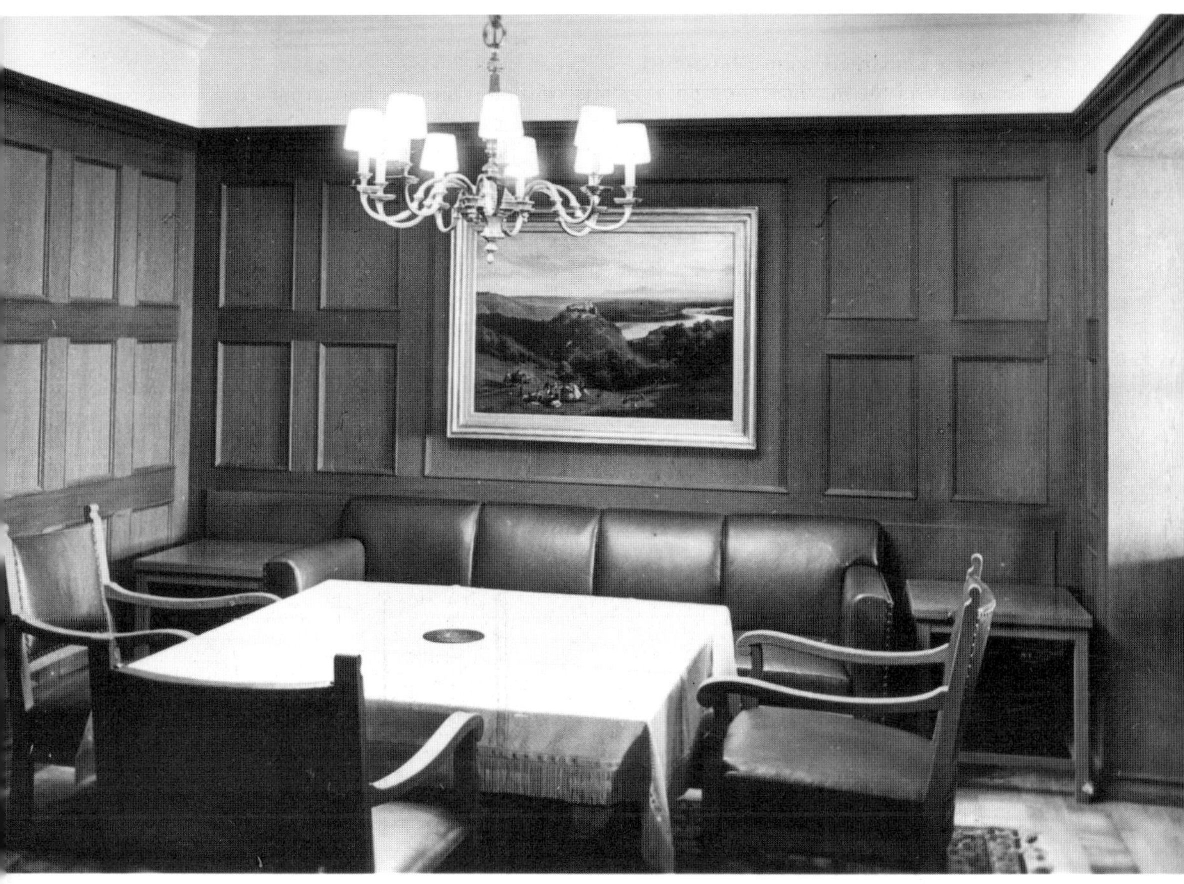

122. Reverse unmarked, source unknown.

Hitler's study was located between the dining room and the kitchen; it was a room he never used. Today this is the restaurant manager's office. The Kehlsteinhaus was a showpiece of German ingenuity, engineering and construction. The building and its location greatly impressed visiting diplomats who were taken there when meeting Hitler on the Obersalzberg.

Among those in the Nazi leadership who visited the Kehlsteinhaus were: Martin Bormann, Joseph Goebbels, Heinrich Himmler, Joachim von Ribbentrop, Robert Ley and Albert Speer. While Adolf Hitler visited the Kehlsteinhaus for the last time on Thursday, 17 October 1940 other members of the Nazi hierarchy continued to visit the building.

While some 3800 workers had been employed on the project, and given the difficulty of the terrain and the fact that they worked through the winter of 1937/38 it is surprising that only eight workers were killed. Five workers died as the result of a landslide in August 1937. One died when he fell down the lift-shaft. Another died when the Opel Blitz lorry he was driving went off the road and one died of stab wounds in the Ofneralm labour camp when he refused to pay up on a bet he'd lost.

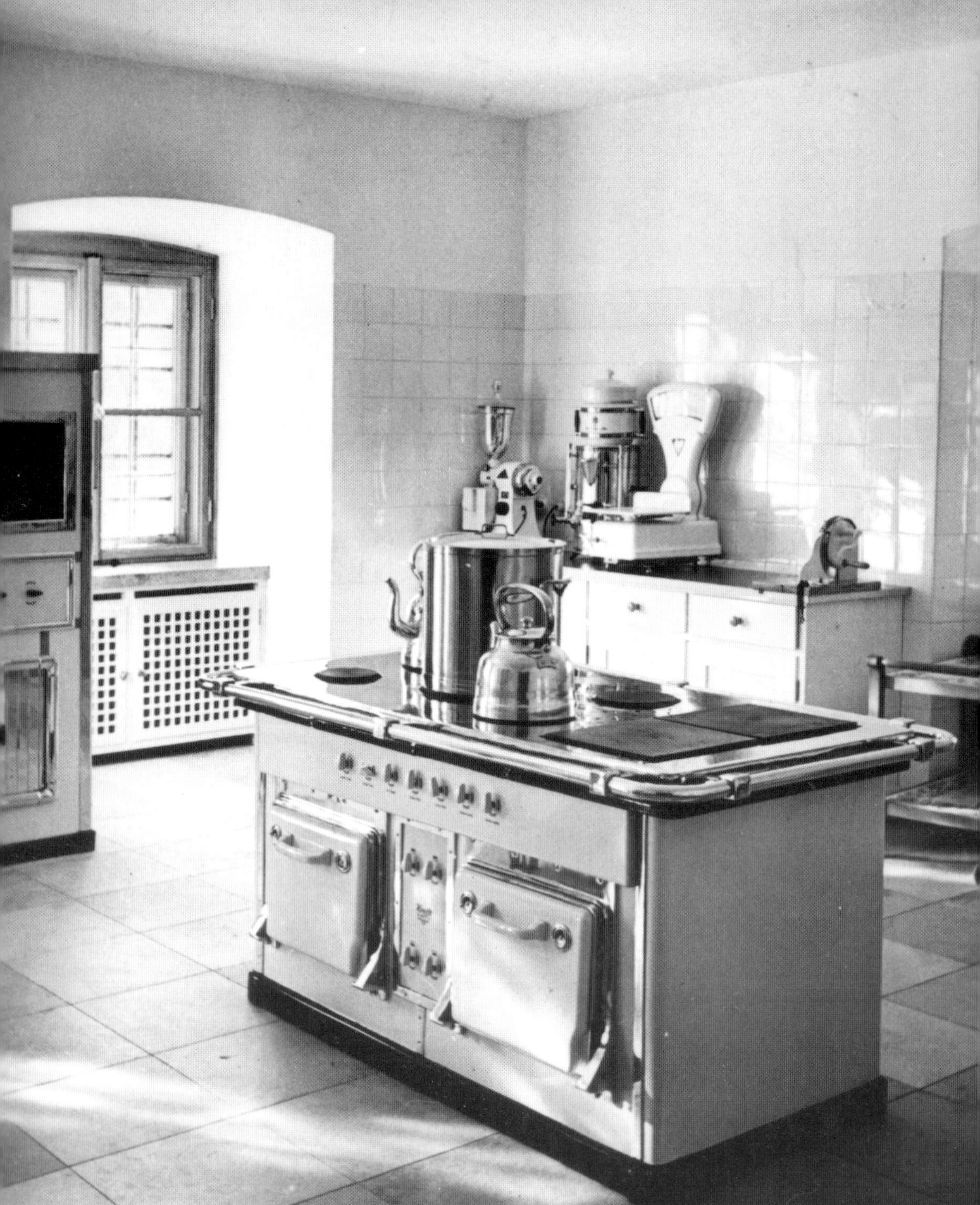

123. Reverse unmarked, source unknown.
The bright ultra-modern kitchen boasted all electrical appliances supplied by the Krefft Company. Rather strangely, apart from preparing beverages, the kitchen was only used to reheat food that had been prepared on the Obersalzberg then transported up the mountain in thermal containers.

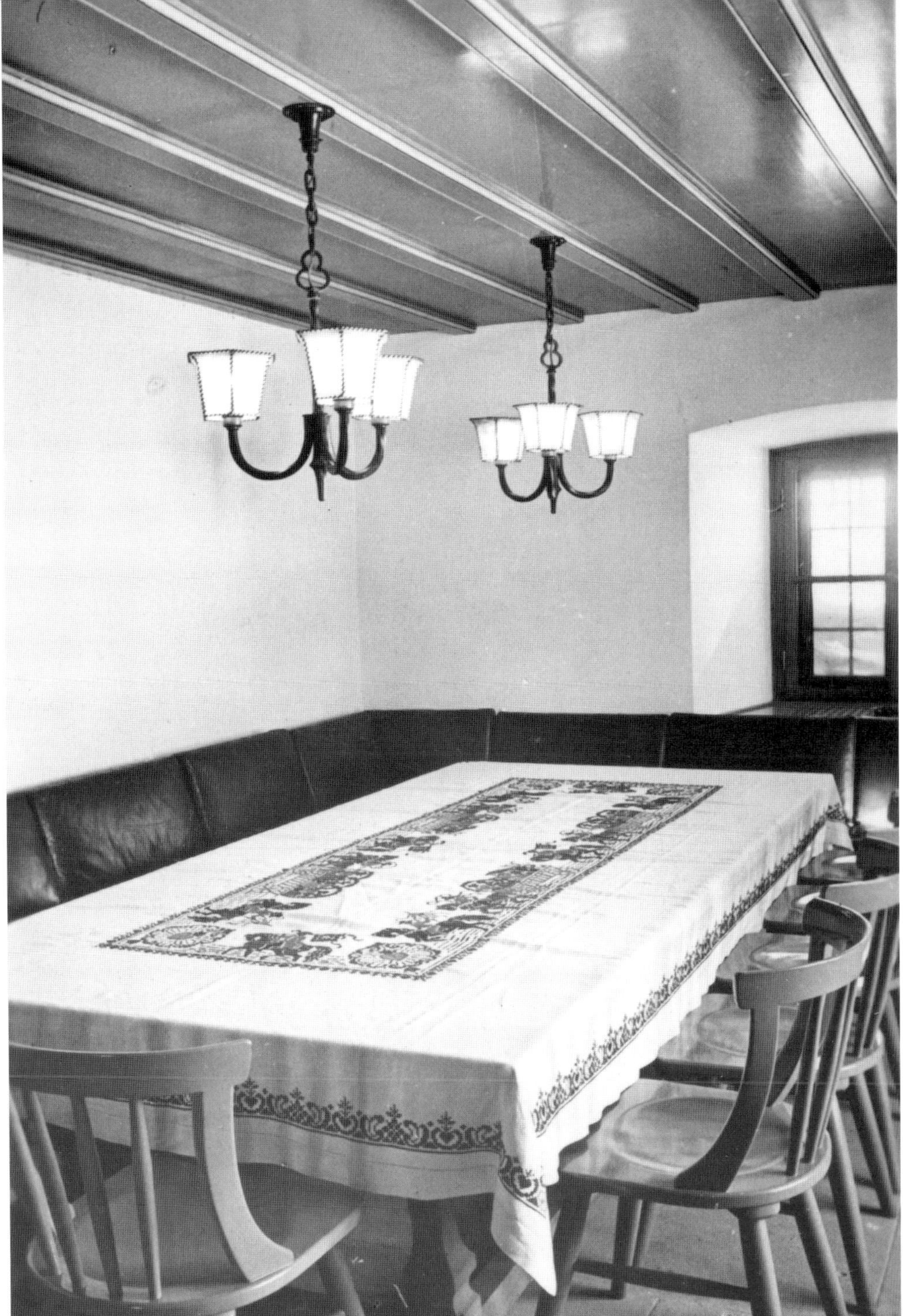

124. Reverse unmarked, source unknown.
The last room on the left of the corridor, and located opposite the kitchen, was the SS guardroom.
The room looked out on the Kehlstein summit. The guards carried out regular patrols of the perimeter
fences from here. Today the former guardroom operates primarily as a private function room.

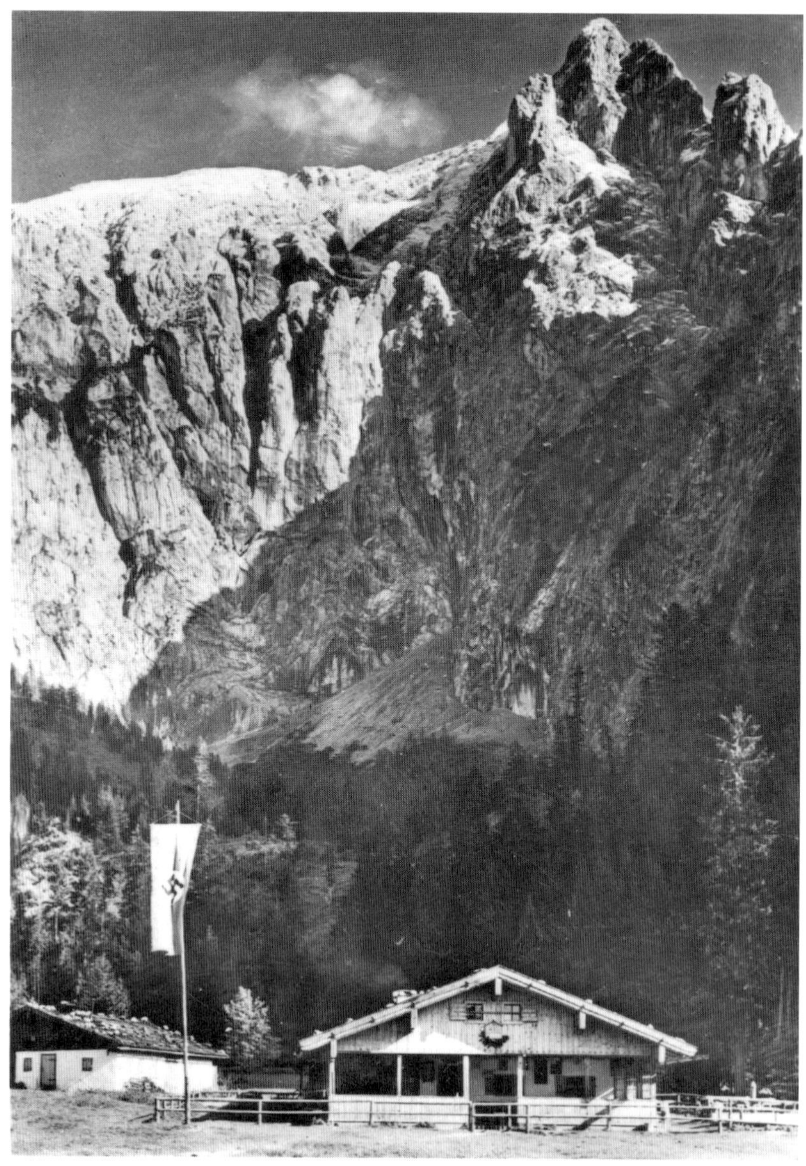

125. Scharitzkehl-Alm (1040 metres above sea level) with Hoher Göll.

Standing at 2522 metres (8274 feet) the rugged Hoher Göll provides the backdrop for this photograph of the Scharitzkehlalm. The building in the foreground is still a restaurant. This was another favourite destination for Adolf Hitler when out walking in the area. The Scharitzkehlalm was the location for one of the many labour camps accommodating the thousands of workers employed not only on the Kehlsteinhaus but also on many other construction projects taking place on the Obersalzberg.

Martin Bormann appropriated the Scharitzkehlalm as grazing land for the Gutshof cattle. The reverse bears a hand-applied rubber stamp reading 'Scharitzkehl-Alpe Berchtesgaden' informing us that this postcard was bought at the Scharitzkehlalm. It was posted in Berchtesgaden on 25 May 1935 to an address in Magdeburg.

126. Mackensen-Kaserne, Bad Reichenhall.

Constructed between 1934 and 1937 the Mackensen-Kaserne was named after the First World War Field Marshal, Anton Ludwig Friedrich August von Mackensen (1849–1945). The barracks are on Nonner Straße in the Karlstein area of Bad Reichenhall. On completion, the 3rd Battalion *Gebirgsjägerregiment* (Mountain Rifle Regiment) 100 occupied the new barracks. The 2nd Battalion of Regiment 100 occupied the Adolf-Hitler-Barracks in Strub just outside Berchtesgaden.

Given the ever-increasing risk of allied bombing and with over twenty hospitals located in and around the town the decision was taken to move all combat-ready military units housed in the barracks in Bad Reichenhall out of the town. *Gebirgsjägerregiment* (Mountain Rifle Regiment) 100 vacated their Bad Reichenhall base on 12 December 1944 taking all military equipment with them. They then moved south to set up new bases in and around Ramsau.

Bad Reichenhall was immediately declared an 'open city'. (The term 'open city' means that a city, or in this case a town, is undefended and not fortified. It is open to occupation by opposing forces with no resistance. Under International Law an 'open city' may not be bombed or be subjected to an artillery attack.) Despite this 'open city' declaration the 8th US Air Force bombed Bad Reichenhall on 25 April 1945 killing 215 people, these included men, women and children. The end of the Second World War would see the Mackensen Kaserne put to use as accommodation for displaced persons.

Posted on 31 May 1940, this particular postcard was sent by a soldier stationed at the Mackensen-Kaserne, it bears the *'Feldpost'* postmark for the barracks and was sent to an address in Graz in Austria. Additionally the soldier has placed a small 'X' on the left on the image to indicate his own accommodation block within the barracks.

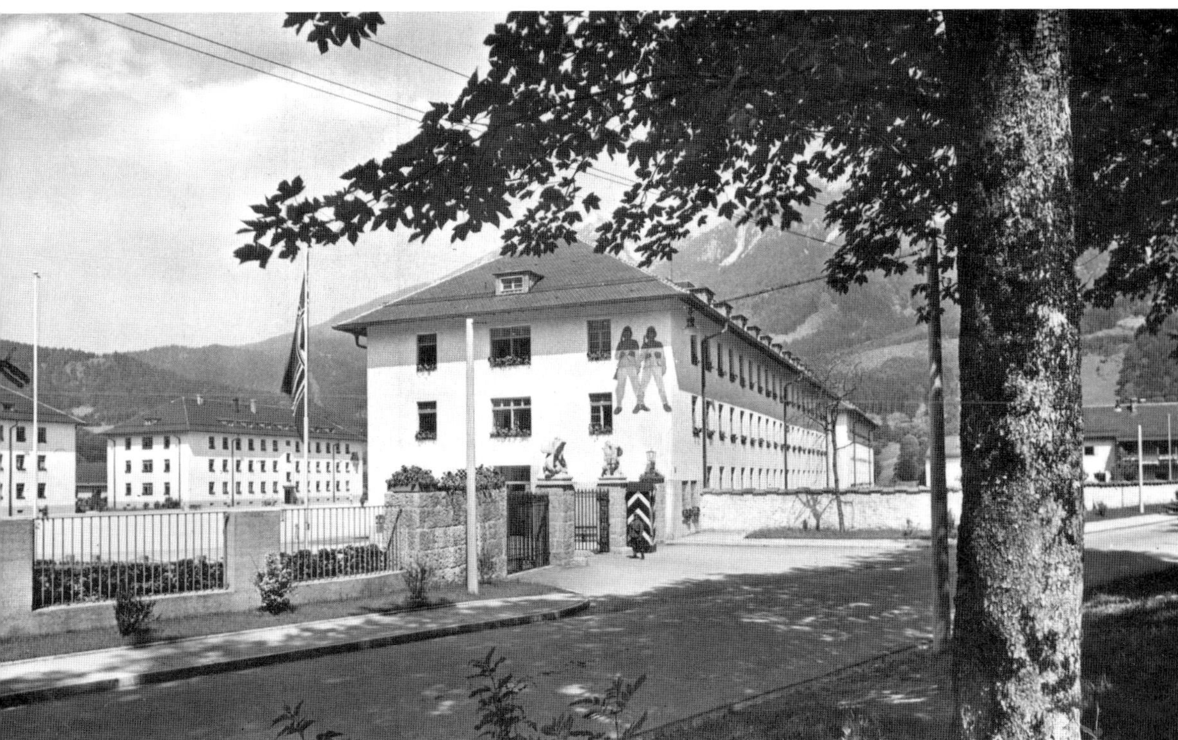

127. General-Ritter-von-Tutschek-Kaserne Bad Reichenhall.
Located on the same street as the Mackensen-Kaserne, the General-Ritter-von-Tutschek-Kaserne was named after General Ludwig Ritter von Tutschek (1860–1937). Von Tutschek commanded the 15th Bavarian Infantry Regiment at the outbreak of the First World War. He was one of the original commanders of the then newly-formed German *Alpenkorps* (Alpine Corps) on its foundation in 1915. On opening in October 1935 the barracks became home to Mountain Infantry Regiment 100. These mountain specialists were considered élite. Rather fittingly the mural on the building in the centre of the image depicts climbing soldiers.

The former Mackensen and von-Tutschek-Kaserne are now collectively known as the Hochstaufen-Kaserne and are today home to mountain infantry units of the German Bundeswehr.

These two relatively large military establishments located on the same street on the outskirts of Bad Reichenhall would have undoubtedly been priority targets for the Allied bombers that attacked the town on Wednesday 25 April 1945, and yet, rather miraculously, they emerged completely unscathed.

Bearing an Ellwangen postmark this postcard was posted on 15 April 1941. Ellwangen is a town located 124 kilometres (77 miles) southwest of Nuremberg. Exactly one week later, on 22 June 1941 German forces launched Operation Barbarossa, the invasion of the Soviet Union. The Soviet Union and Nazi Germany were diametrically opposed ideologies in every sense.

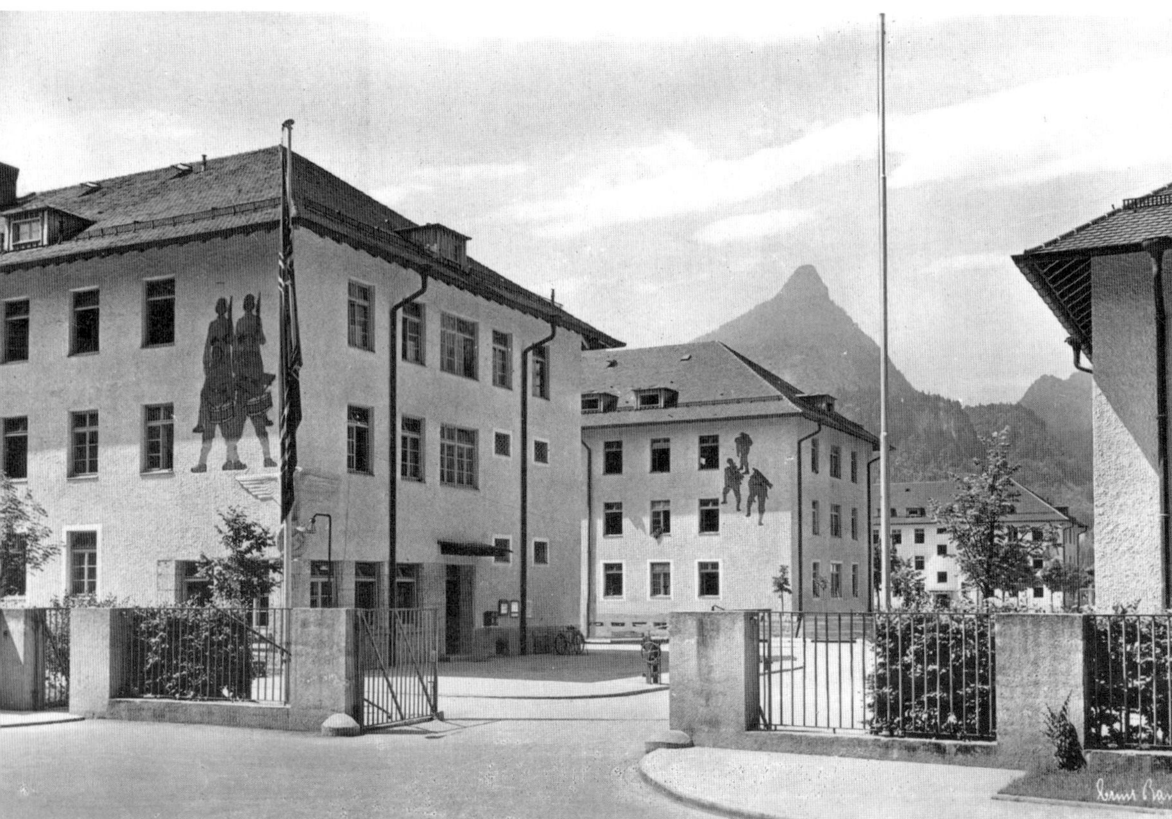

128. The eagle on the corner of the former General-Ritter-von-Tutschek-Kaserne in Bad Reichenhall as it appears today. Again as with the eagle above the main entrance to the former Reich Chancellery in Stanggass outside Berchtesgaden the swastika that once sat within the wreath held in the bird's talons has been removed, however in this instance the swastika has been replaced with an edelweiss; the symbol of German mountain infantry.

The mural showing the drummers and the eagle seen here appears in the image on the previous page, number 148. While partially obscured, the eagle can be seen on the corner of the building directly behind the flagpole. It should be noted that the Hochstaufen-Kaserne is an active military base and as such the taking of photographs is forbidden. A sign attached to the gate almost directly below the eagle provides the appropriate warning information.

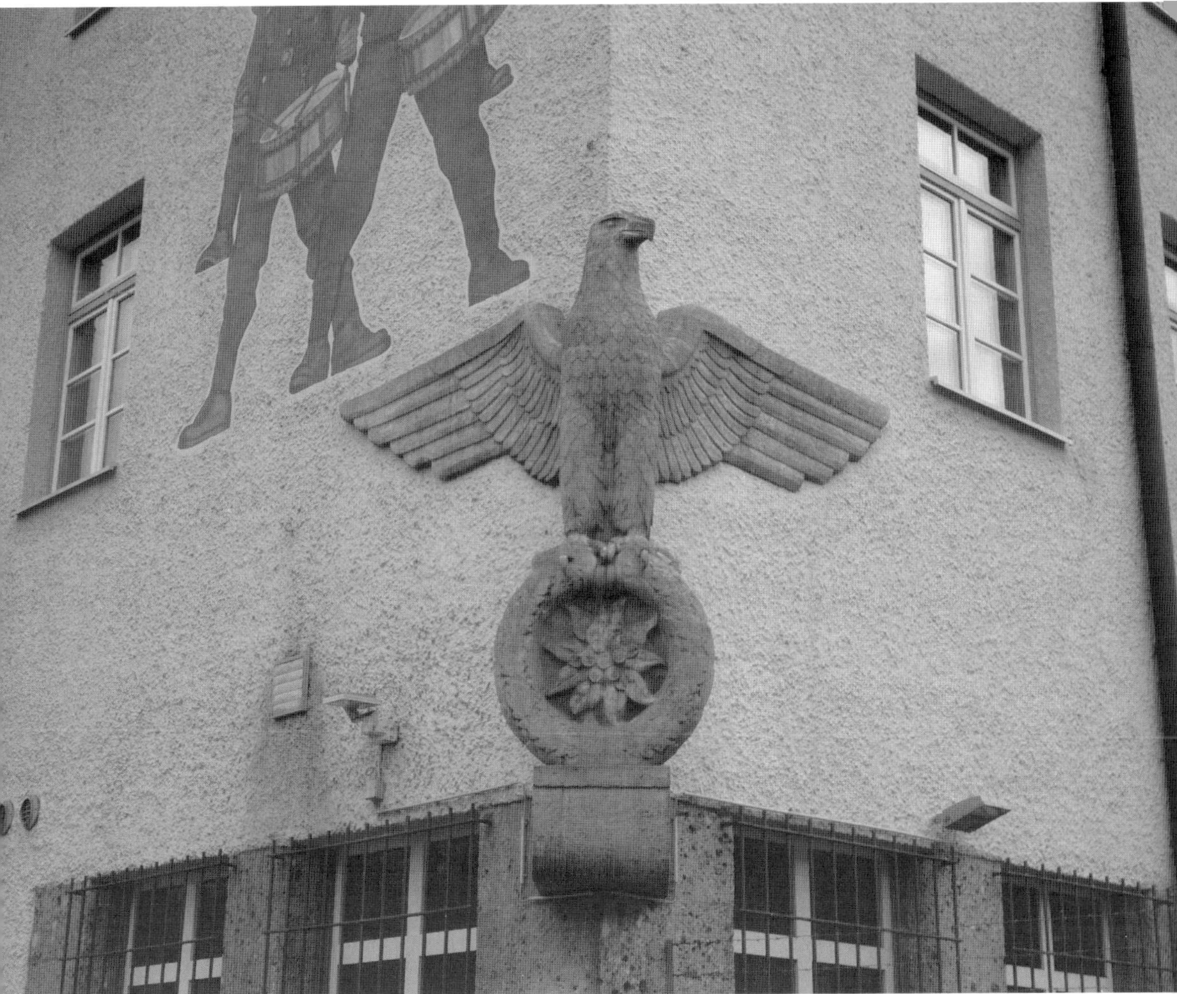

129. Städtisches Krankenhaus.

Constructed between 1928 and 1930 Bad Reichenhall's Städtisches Krankenhaus (Municipal Hospital) on Riedelstraße was designed by renowned German architect, Richard Schachner (1873–1936). Schachner is perhaps best known for his work in designing hospitals and clinics. Being a spa town, Bad Reichenhall was home to number of clinics and hospitals. During the Second World War many of these, including the Städtisches Krankenhaus became military hospitals treating wounded German soldiers. At the time of the bombing of the town on 25 April 1945 there were over twenty such hospitals located in Bad Reichenhall.

The Städtisches Krankenhaus survived the bombing of the town undamaged. This was due to its location; it was not close to the main targets. Nonetheless at least 215 people, including soldiers, men, women and children died on the day. The Städtisches Krankenhaus, also known as the Schachner building is now a listed building. The original part of the hospital seen here now operates as a retirement home. The district clinic is now housed in the later extensions that were constructed through the 1960s and 1990s.

This postcard, posted in Bad Reichenhall on 23 March 1935 was sent to an address in Neulustheim, a district in northeast Munich.

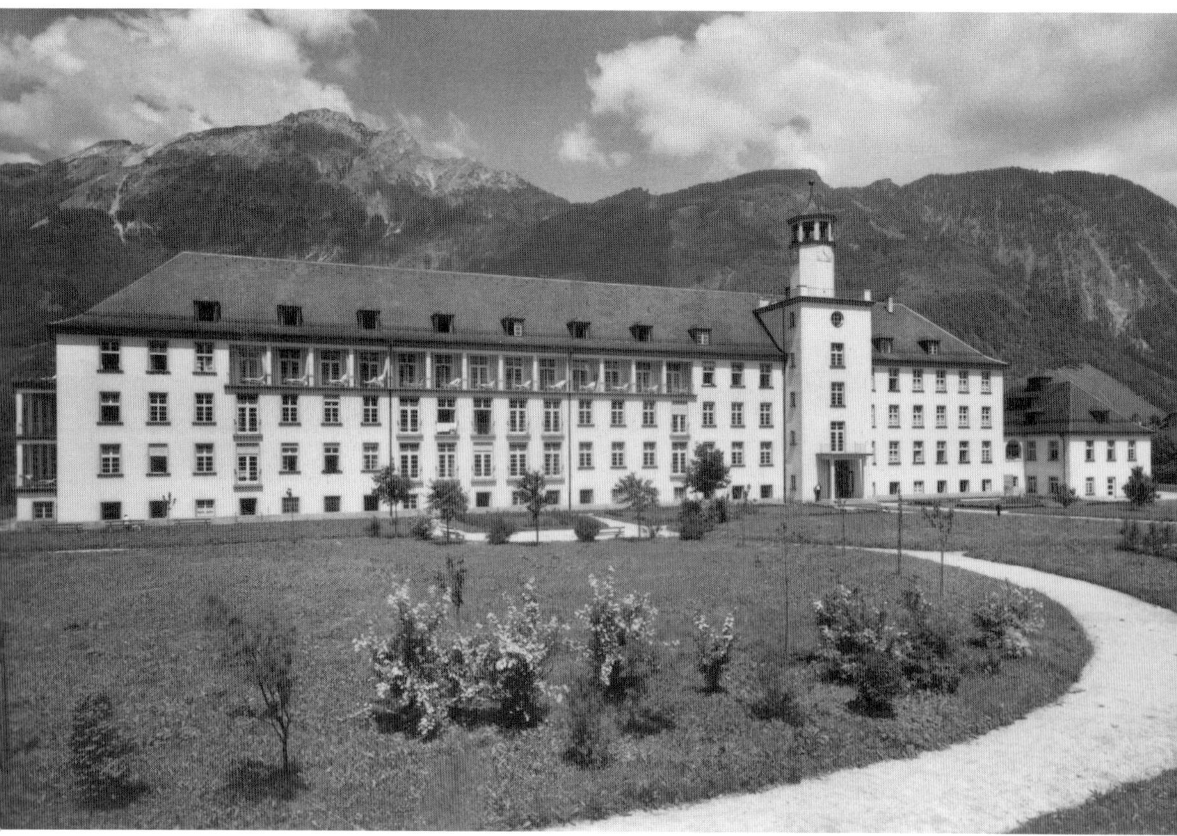

130. Bad Reichenhall Town Hall.

This postcard shows the Rathaus (Town Hall) on Rathausplatz, sometimes called the Marktplatz close to the centre of the old town.

Few photographs show the Rathaus with the Nazi flag flying on the building. Some less commonly found Third Reich period postcards showing the Rathaus have captions reading; Bad Reichenhall, Platz der S.A. (the Square of the SA, or, SA Square.)

The murals on the front of the building were painted in 1924

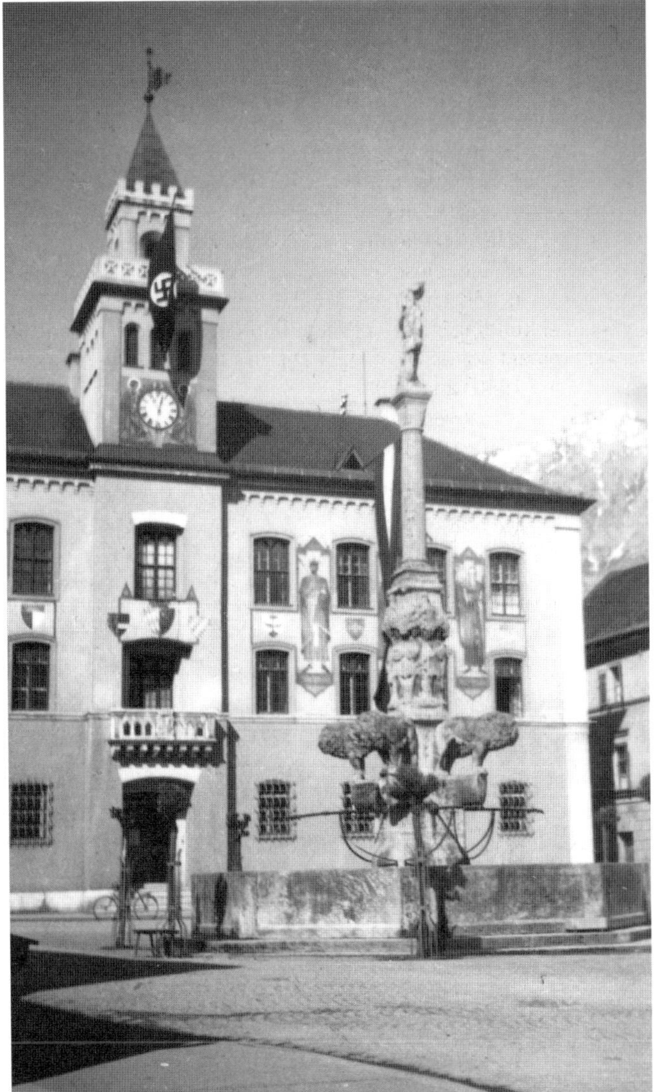

by artist Josef Hengge, the man who would paint the murals on the Berchtesgaden war memorial in 1929.

Hitler paid a number of visits to the nearby Predigstuhl Mountain Hotel that overlooks Bad Reichenhall. On Sunday 2 July 1933 the Führer gave a speech to a group of SA and SS leaders and members of the Stahlhelm organisation in the Staatliches Kurhaus on Kurstrasse. (The Stahlhelm (Steel Helmet) organisation was a veterans' group formed in December 1918. The Stahlhelm supported Hitler in the 1933 elections and in July that year the organisation was absorbed into the SA.)

The 'Wittelsbacher Brunnen' (Wittelsbach Fountain) observed in front of the Rathaus was designed by Munich sculptor, Karl Killer (1873–1948). It was erected in gratitude to the Wittelsbach family: the ancestral family of Bavaria.

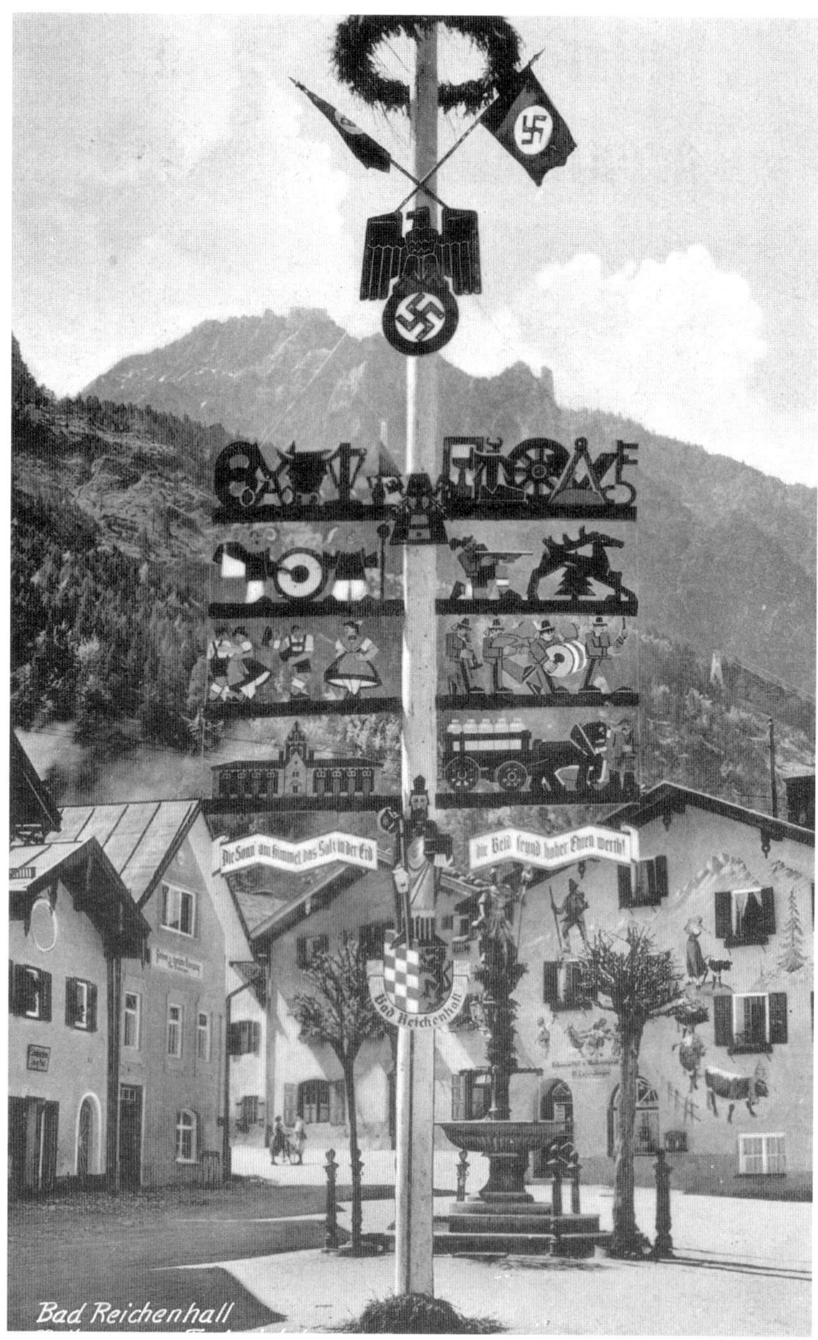

131. Bad Reichenhall. Maypole on the Florianiplatz.
Posted on 5 April 1944 to an address in Gross-Zimmern, a town east of Darmstadt, this postcard shows the annually erected maypole complete with Nazi symbolism standing in Bad Reichenhall's Florianiplatz.

152

Hitler's speeches in and around Berchtesgaden

While perhaps not comprehensive, the following is a list of dates and venues where Hitler gave speeches in and around the Berchtesgaden area. It is worth mentioning the first date on the list, Saturday, 28 April 1923. This was Hitler's first speech on the Obersalzberg. Visiting Hotel zum Türken with his friend Dietrich Eckart on the day, Hitler gave something of an impromptu speech to local people gathered in the hotel. At that point in time, Hitler, the future Fuhrer, could not have imagined that he would come to rent Haus Wachenfeld, the small Alpine chalet within sight of the hotel, or how this mountain would come to play a pivotal role in both his personal and political life, and in world events.

Saturday, 28 April 1923, Hotel zum Türken, Obersalzberg.
Spoke to local people gathered in the hotel.

Sunday, 1 July 1923, Gasthaus zur Krone, Berchtesgaden.

Sunday, 1 July 1923, Hotel Watzmann, Berchtesgaden.

Tuesday, 20 October 1924, Hotel Deutsches Haus, Berchtesgaden.
Speech to Nazi Party members.

Friday, 8 October 1926, Gasthof Neuhaus, Berchtesgaden.

Sunday, 10 July 1932, Festplatz, Berchtesgaden.

Sunday, 2 July 1933, Kurhaus, Bad Reichenhall.
Speech to SA, SS and members of the Stahlhelm.

Sunday, 6 July 1933, Obersalzberg.
Speech to Reichsleiters and Gauleiters.

Tuesday, 15 January 1935, Berchtesgaden.
Speech broadcast from Berchtesgaden Post Office on victory in Saar plebiscite.

Sunday, 13 December 1936, Obersalzberg.
Speech to SA and SS leaders.

Monday, 18 January 1937, Bischofswiesen.
Speech to construction workers.

Wednesday, 17 February 1937, Obersalzberg.
Speech to representatives of front fighters' associations from various countries.

Thursday, 20 May 1937, Obersalzberg.
Speech to construction workers on the inauguration of a new cinema/theatre hall.

Monday, 14 August 1939, Obersalzberg.
Speech to Commanders in Chief of the Wehrmacht.

Tuesday, 22 August 1939, Berghof, Obersalzberg.
Speech to fifty senior commanders on the diplomatic situation as German Foreign Minister Ribbentrop met with Stalin in Moscow.

Tuesday, 13 May 1941, Obersalzberg.
Speech to Reichsleiters and Gauleiters on the flight of Rudolf Hess to Britain three days earlier on 10 May.

Wednesday, 2 June 1943, Hotel Platterhof, Obersalzberg.
Speech to German armament industrialists.

Thursday, 22 June 1944, Hotel Platterhof, Obersalzberg.
Speech to Wehrmacht officers.

Monday, 26 June 1944, Obersalzberg.
Speech to senior officers and over two hundred armament experts about the war situation.

As Adolf Hitler left the Berghof and his beloved Obersalzberg on 14 July 1944 he could not have known that he would never return. The Führer left Berchtesgaden for the Wolf's Lair, his eastern headquarters near Rastenburg in East Prussia. Hitler was fortunate to survive the attempt on his life when, just six days later, on 20 July 1944, *Oberst* (Colonel) Claus von Stauffenberg planted a bomb that exploded at 12.42pm killing four and injuring twenty others in the briefing room at the Wolf's Lair. Hitler survived the attack with only minor injuries. Von Stauffenberg was executed by firing-squad the following day.

The Final Days

Given the importance of this region to Adolf Hitler on a personal level, notwithstanding its position as a second seat of government during the Third Reich period, its hardly surprising to find that, even as the Second World War entered its final phase, we find those remaining military units in and around the region considering the idea of making a last ditch defence of the area. The following information provided by Gerd Bartels, and additional local sources, paints a picture of uncertainty, growing anxiety and desperation.

Gerd still remembers two young soldiers from the Waffen-SS coming to their school in Bad Reichenhall in those final days. These soldiers couldn't have been more than sixteen or seventeen years old. They were looking for volunteers to come and help dig trenches and anti-tank ditches in the areas of Kirchholz and Martzoll on the outskirts of the town.

We now look at what was going on in those final days and how a number of private establishments were put to various uses as preparations were made for a battle that might, or might not take place. In the end there was no last stand, no final battle, common sense prevailed and what would have been a senseless loss of life was avoided.

On Friday, 4 May 1945 *Landrat* (District Commissioner) Karl Theodor Jacob (1908–1980) issued a leaflet telling the residents of Berchtesgaden to hang pieces of white material outside their homes and to remain calm and patient. Jacob then had a conversation with SS-*Obersturmbannführer* (Lieutenant-Colonel) Dr Bernhard Frank (1913–2011) the commander in charge of the Obersalzberg complex. Having been given Frank's personal assurance that he would not defend the Obersalzberg, Jacob then ordered Berchtesgaden's *Volkssturm* (Peoples' Army) unit to stand down. That done, he went out to meet the approaching enemy forces.

Theodor Jacob met an armoured column of the 3rd US Infantry Division north of Bischofswiesen. On being introduced to and then speaking with Lieutenant-Colonel Kenneth Wallace, commanding officer of the 1st Battalion, 7th Infantry Regiment, 3rd Infantry Division, Jacob declared Berchtesgaden an open town. Returning to Berchtesgaden, Theodor Jacob officially surrendered Berchtesgaden and Ramsau to Wallace, the surrender taking place in front of the war memorial in Berchtesgaden's Schloßplatz (Palace Square) see postcard 84 on page 106. Having accepted the surrender the 3rd Infantry Division made its way up the Obersalzberg later that day. As previously stated the local population had looted the Obersalzberg on 1 May; they'd already taken everything of value thus leaving little for the Americans to pilfer.

It was over; the town of Berchtesgaden and its population had been spared. Many of the remaining SS-men and Nazi Party officials in the area discarded their uniforms and put on civilian clothes as they attempted to 'disappear', many were successful in their flight.

132. Saalachsee, the pearl of Bad Reichenhall.

This postcard shows the Café am See at the Saalachsee on the outskirts of Bad Reichenhall. The Saalachsee is a reservoir that was created following the construction of a dam built between 1910 and 1913. The dam was built to operate a hydroelectric power plant on the Saalach River. Located near the dam, the Café am See, also known as Gaststätte Kübling is now the Wirtshaus am Saalachsee.

It was near here that Gerd Bartels and a classmate got a lift with two soldiers in a Kubelwagen. The boys were walking by the Saalachsee as they made their way home to Hintersee after being released from school following the bombing of the town on 25 April 1945. The soldiers brought the boys as far as Jettenberg where they got out. They got another lift with a soldier on a motorcycle with sidecar. He brought them as far as Hindenburglinde; the lads made what remained of their journey to Hintersee on foot.

The distance from Bad Reichenhall to Hintersee is 18 kilometres (11 miles), a long way on foot. It would have taken the boys around three and a half hours to walk the eighteen kilometres. However, with the help of the lifts they received from the soldiers it only took about an hour and a half.

Posted in Bad Reichenhall on 18 June 1941 this postcard made its way to an address in Hannover. A special postmark on the reverse promotes the 'Predigstuhl-Bahn' (Predigstuhl cable car) that transports people from the outskirts of the town to the hotel located on top of the Predigstuhl Mountain. At 1614 metres (5295 feet) above the town the hotel offers fabulous views of Bad Reichenhall and the surrounding area. The cable car, the first of its kind in Germany opened on 1 July 1928. While it's said that Hitler disliked heights the Führer would have used the cable car when he visited the Predigstuhl Hotel.

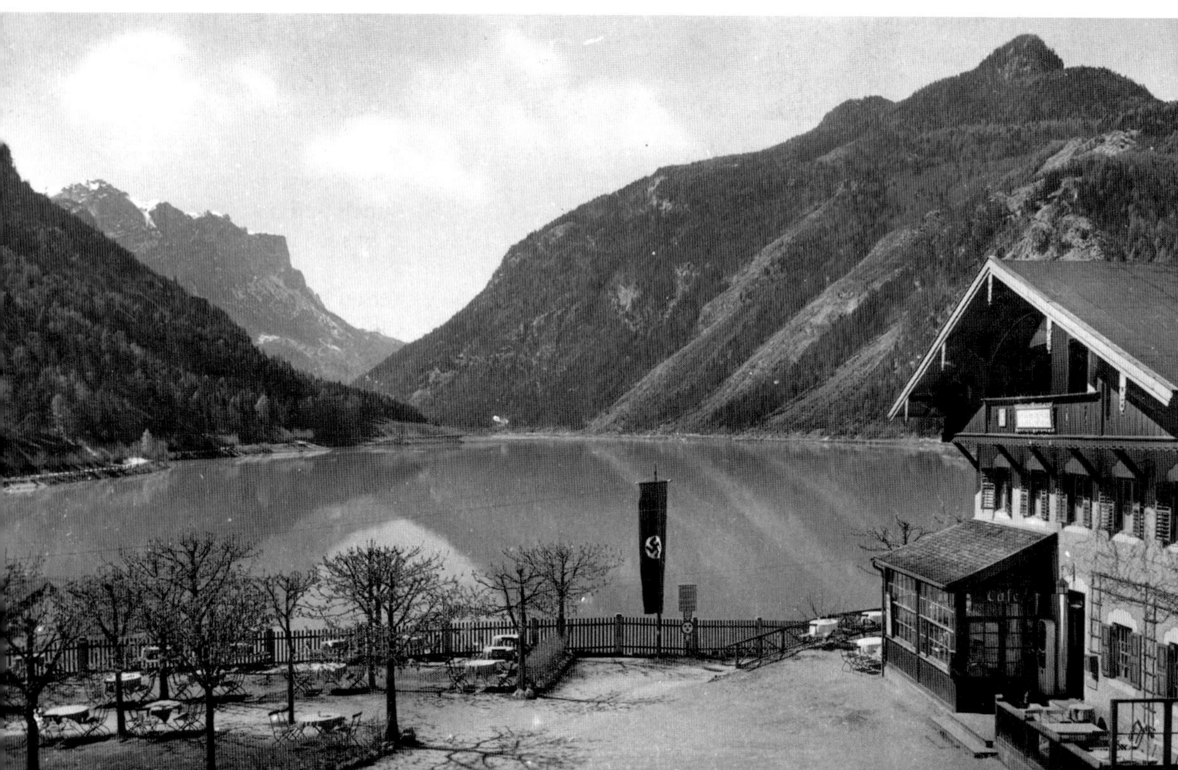

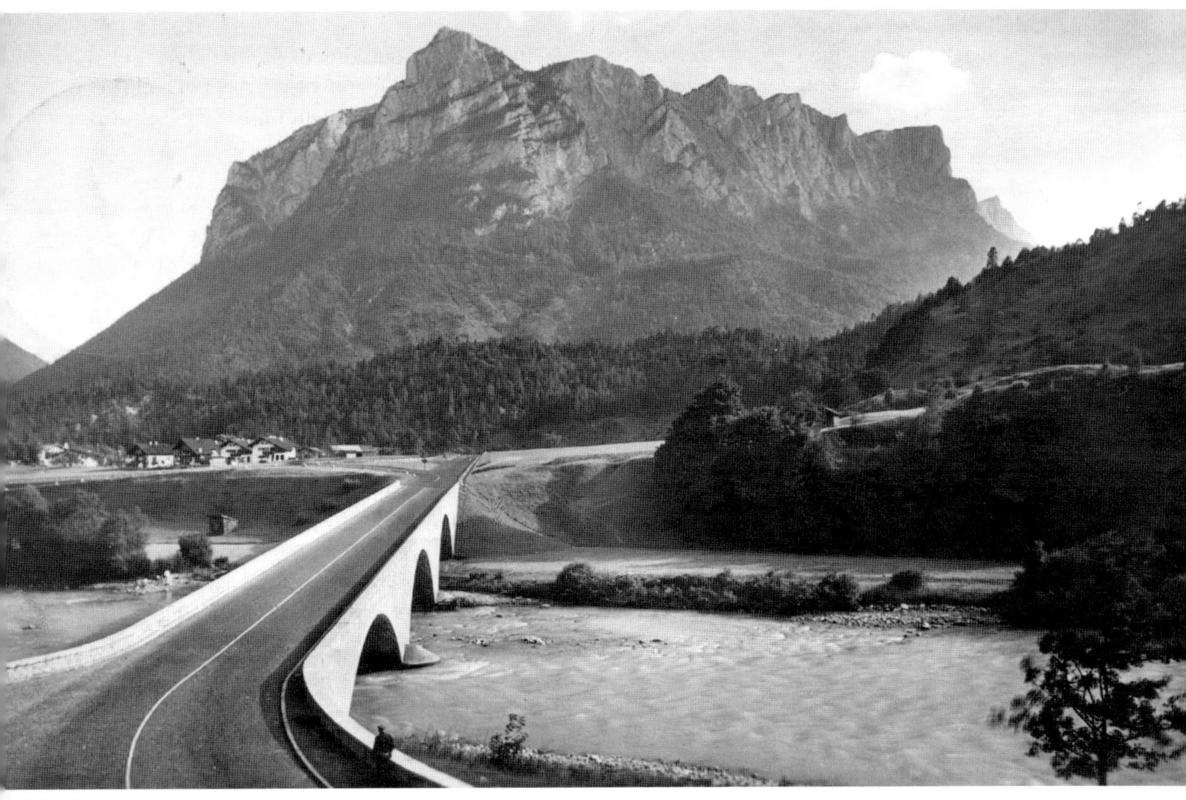

133. Deutsche Alpenstrasse near Jettenberg with Reiteralpe.

This postcard offers a fine view of the bridge over the Saalach River on the Deutsche Alpenstraße near Jettenberg. The soldiers in the Kubelwagen who picked up Gerd Bartels and his friend close to the Saalachsee dropped the lads off here. The village of Jettenberg can be seen on the other side of the bridge.

The boys found the journey in the Kubelwagen, then a short time later on the motorcycle with sidecar all very exciting. Introduced in 1940 the VW Kübelwagen was the German equivalent to the Allied Jeep. By the end of the Second World War over 50,000 of these rugged utility vehicles had been built. The mountains seen in the background are the Reiteralpe. Looking at the postcard, Hintersee is located on the opposite side of the Reiteralpe.

The Deutsche Alpenstraße remains one of Europe's most spectacular, most beautiful mountain roads; renowned for its engineering and construction it provides for some incredible scenery along its route. The Alpenstraße, and the Autobahn, the world's first nationwide motorway network constructed under the Nazis must be considered two of regime's greatest accomplishments; legacies that continue to serve the nation.

Posted in Höllriegelskreuth, an area in the southern part of Munich on 8 August 1940 this postcard made its way to an address in Berlin-Staaken. Staaken is a district on the outskirts of west Berlin.

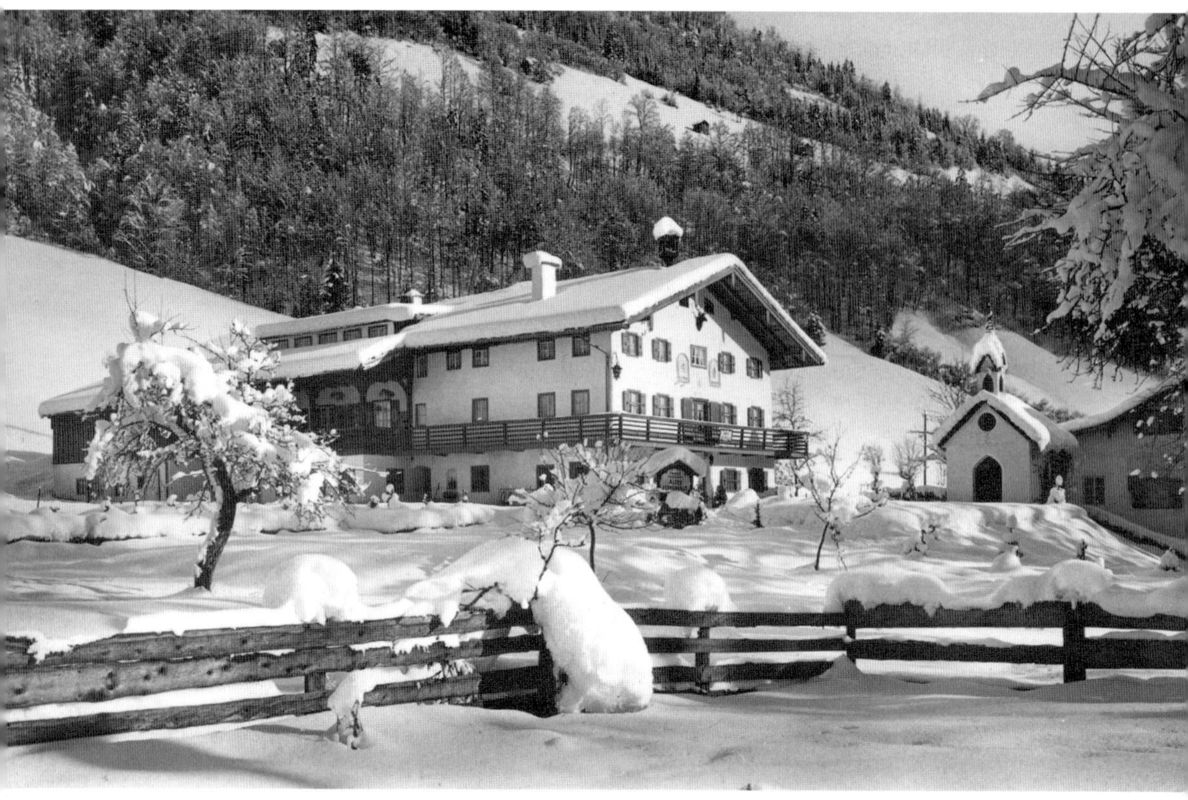

134. Altes Forsthaus Ramsau near Berchtesgaden.

This delightful scene shows the Altes Forsthaus in Ramsau. Prior to the bombing of the Obersalzberg on 25 April 1945, Dr Hans-Heinrich Lammers, Head of the Reich Chancellery and his wife Elfriede had been living in the service building of the Reich Chancellery at Stanggaß.

In the aftermath of the bombing the couple left the Chancellery complex and moved into this building, the Altes Forsthaus. Now run by the Heinrich family, the Altes Forsthaus offers traditional Bavarian food and accommodation.

Bearing a Ramsau postmark this postcard was posted on 7 August 1940 to an address in Regensburg. Located 124 kilometres (77 miles) north of Munich, Regensburg is a city full of charm and history.

135. Uncaptioned.

At the time this photograph was taken this building was known as Pension Datzmann; today it is the Alpenhotel Beslhof. While having been renovated through the intervening years the still recognizable former Pension Datzmann is located on the road leading from Ramsau to Hintersee.

On 25 September 1944 Adolf Hitler issued a decree calling for the formation of a *Volkssturm* (People's Army) to help defend the homeland. On 18 October 1944 the people of Ramsau were obliged to form their own *Volkssturm* unit. In an effort to strengthen the Wehrmacht all men aged sixteen to sixty who were not already doing military service for whatever reason and who were able-bodied were required to join the *Volkssturm*. Pension Datzmann, sometimes also called Gasthof Datzmann is where the men of the local *Volkssturm* practised shooting at the small bore shooting-range located there.

This postcard was posted in Berchtesgaden on 9 July 1932 and sent to an address in Zwickau, a city south of Leipzig. The next day, Sunday 10 July, Hitler gave a speech in the Festplatz in Berchtesgaden. Later that month, on 31 July 1932 the Nazi Party won 230 of 608 seats in the Reichstag elections. Just six months later, on 30 January 1933 Adolf Hitler would be appointed German Chancellor.

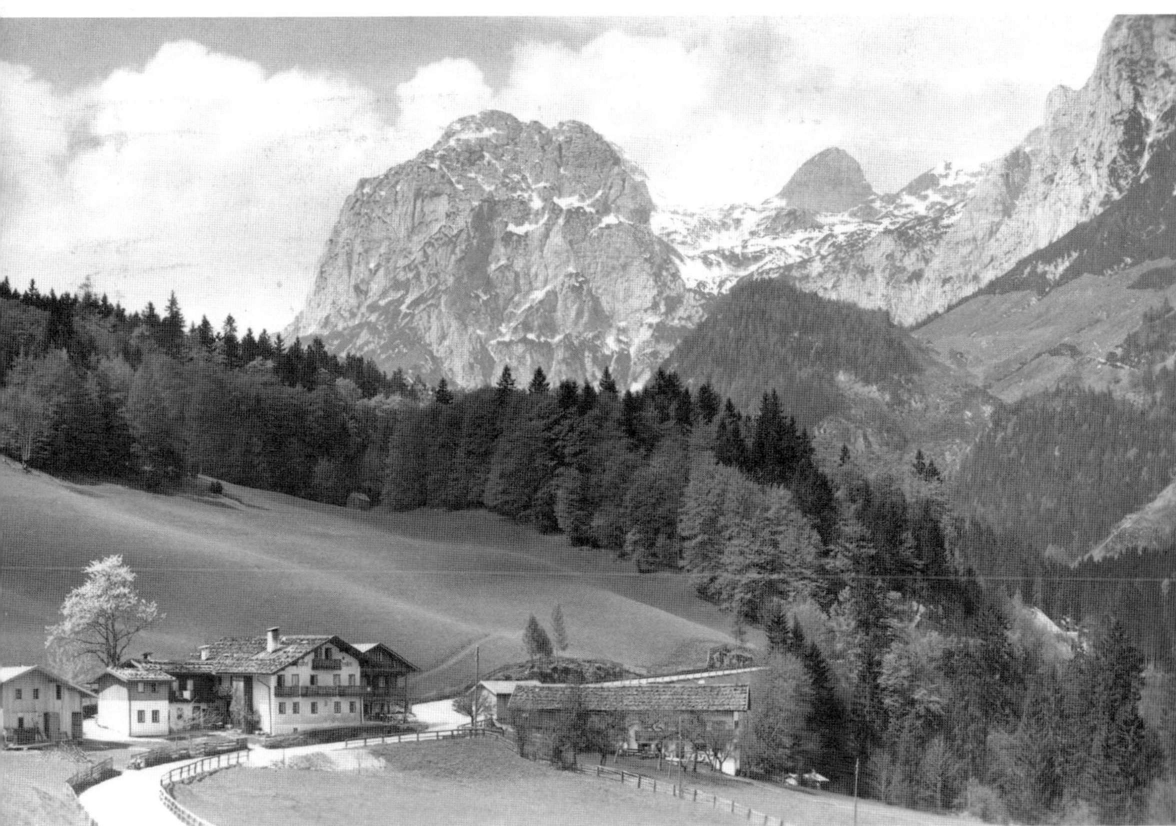

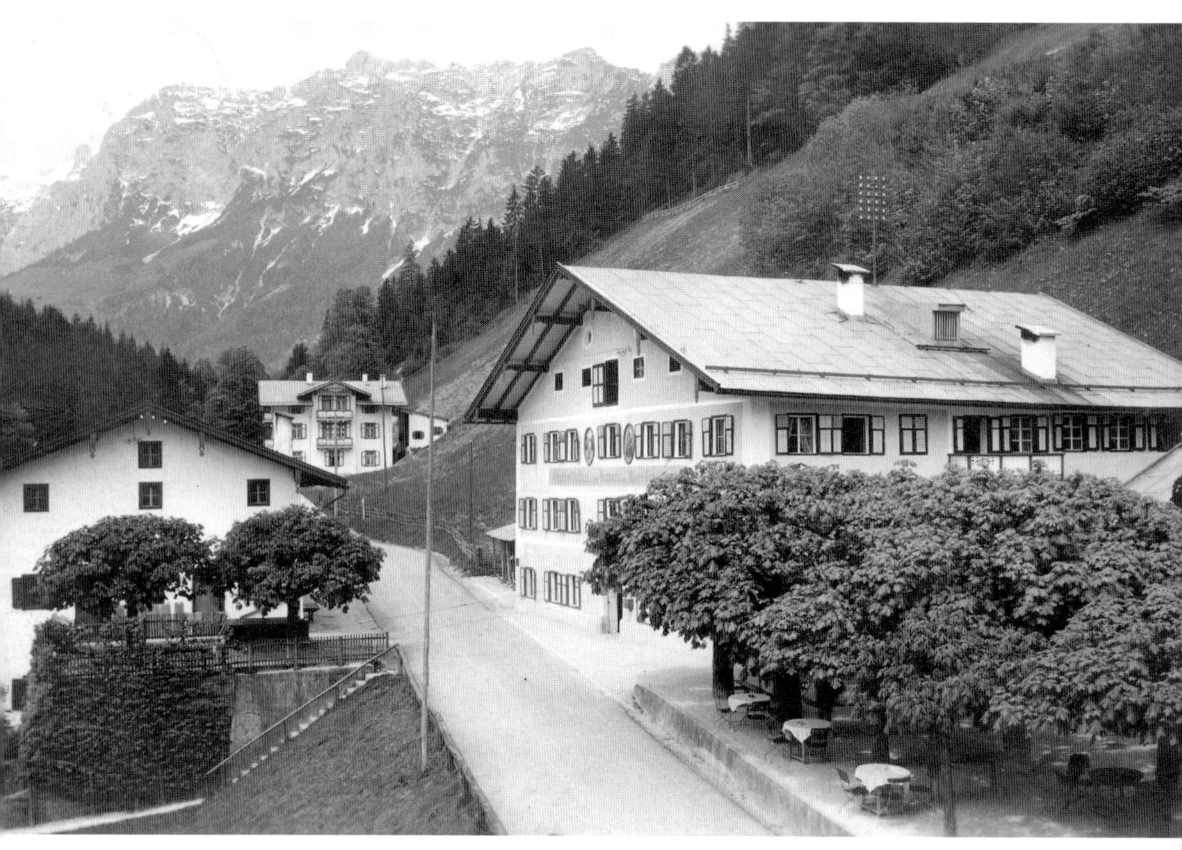

136. Uncaptioned.

This photograph shows Gasthof Oberwirt, an inn and restaurant close to the centre of Ramsau. In those final uncertain, desperate days of the Second World War this is where the men of the *Volkssturm* received military training and lessons in weapons handling. The Oberwirt is situated just a little further up the road from the previously mentioned village church of St. Sebastian.

Infantry field training took place on the Rehleggerfeld in Ramsau. Fearing aerial bombardment, slit trenches were dug at various locations. The school in Ramsau was used as a headquarters for local operations and was under the leadership of the local mayor, Josef Moser.

Posted in Ramsau on 1 July 1934 to an address in Leipzig, the sender, a guest in the Oberwirt, gives the address as; 83486 Ramsau, Oberes Gasthaus (Upper Inn), not to be confused with Gasthof Unterwirt (Lower Inn) another inn at the opposite end of the village. While Gasthof Unterwirt closed some years ago the Oberwirt continues to provide traditional Bavarian cooking and guest accommodation.

160

**137. Gasthaus and Pension Schwarzbachwacht 880 metres above sea level.
Ramsau near Berchtesgaden, (Bavarian Highlands).**

The Schwarzbachwacht, today the 'Wirtshaus Wachterl' sits by the roadside on what is today the Deutsche Alpenstraße. On 17 November 1944 and, having just bombed nearby Salzburg, a returning American bomber dropped two high explosive bombs that exploded in the forest a mere 600 metres from the building. Fortunately for the owners the dense forest absorbed the blast leaving the Schwarzbachwacht undamaged.

Even as the Third Reich was disintegrating and with only days until total collapse there were those who wanted to fight on. An SS officer at Schwarzbachwacht wanted to create a combat unit made up of retreating German soldiers and threatened to shoot those who refused to join as deserters. Fortunately another officer, Major Karl Dieterich managed to convince the men that any such action would be totally pointless, it would change nothing and only end in further unnecessary deaths for absolutely no gain. A faded, hand-applied stamp on the reverse of this postcard shows the year 1928.

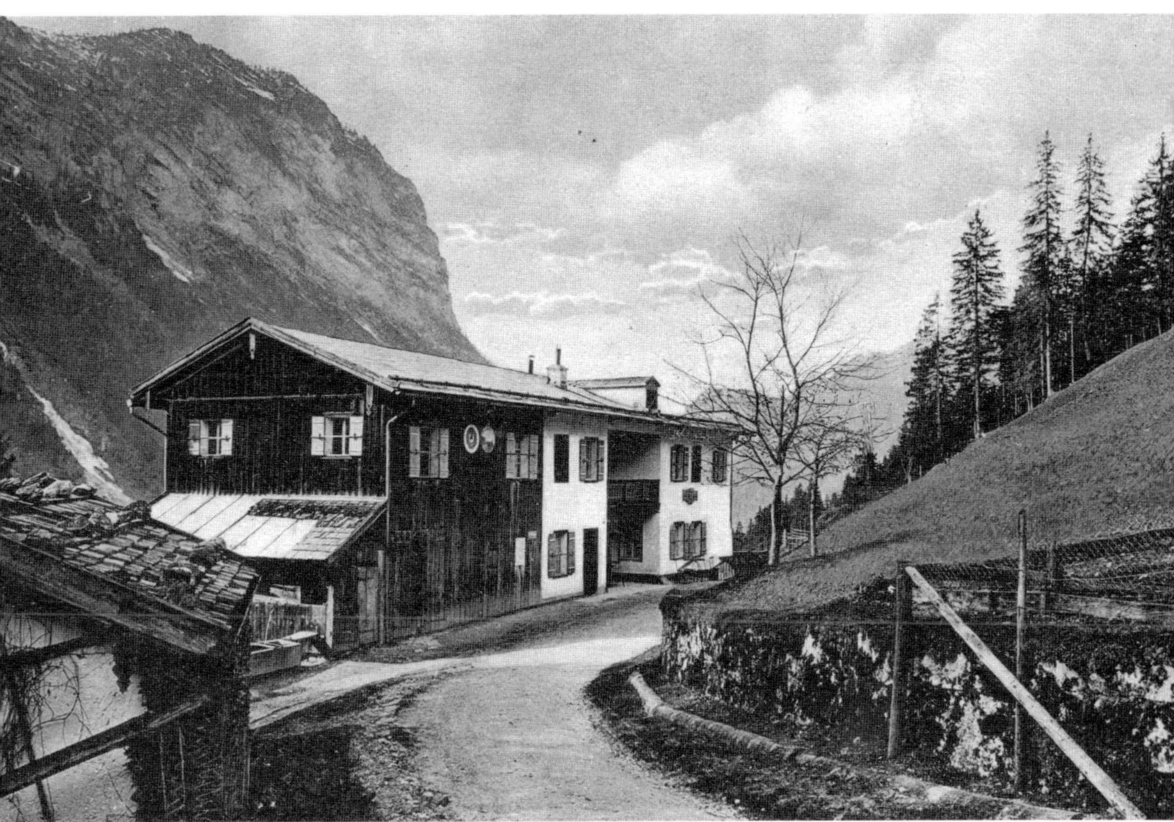

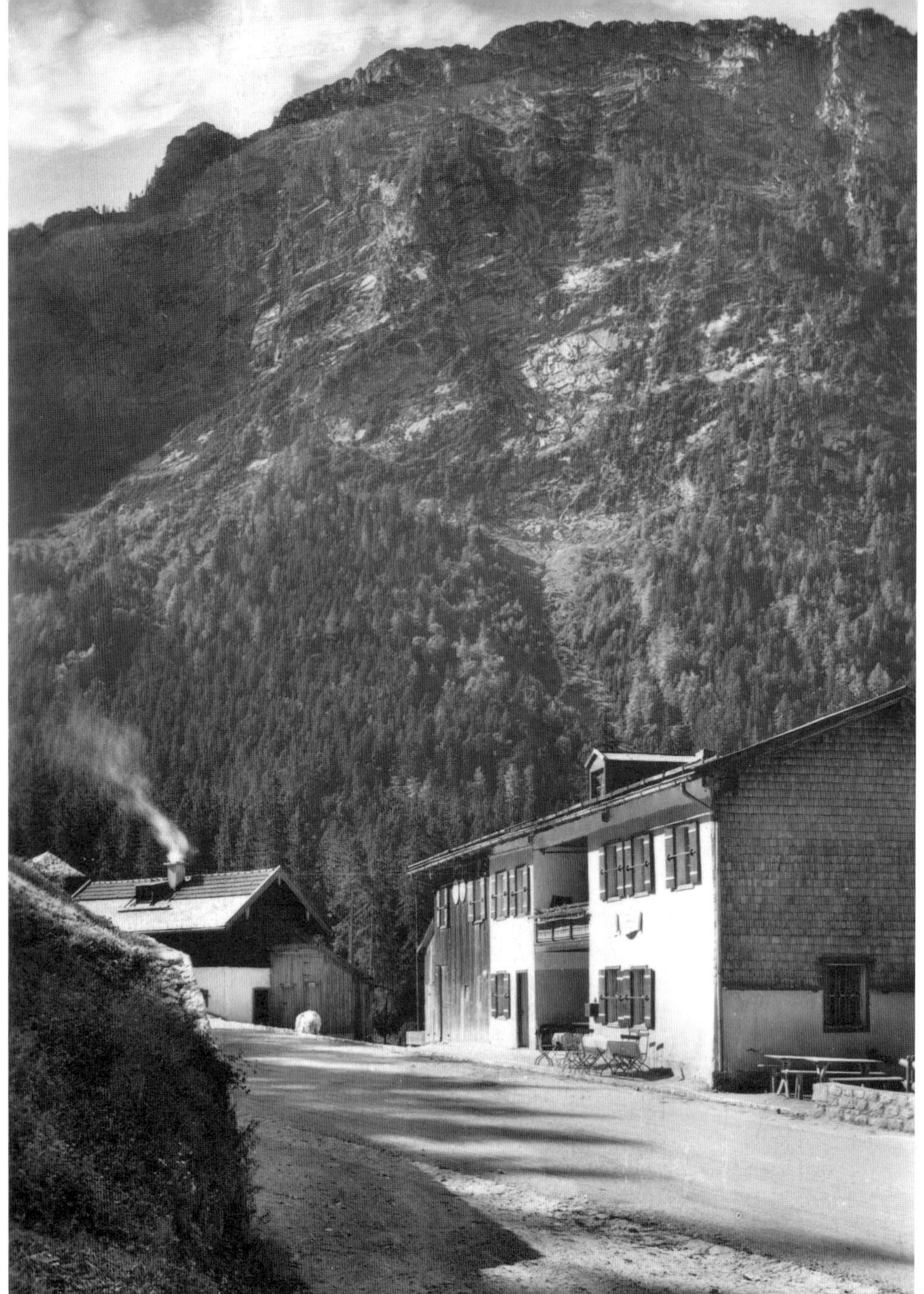

138. Alpine guesthouse 'Wachterl' on the Deutsche Alpenstraße towards Reiteralpe.
The above caption tells us the Wachterl is located on the Deutsche Alpenstraße. This photograph dating from the late 1930s has been taken from the opposite side to that seen in the previous image and shows a small section of Dr Fritz Todt's then recently completed new Alpine road. The reverse bears a hand-applied stamp reading: *Anton & Wally Maier 'Wachterl' Schwarzbachwacht, Post Ramsau.*

162

139. Haus Geiger, Berchtesgaden.
In 1865 Hugo Geiger (1828–1874), a retired Royal Bavarian Customs Service official opened a guesthouse, Haus Geiger on the outskirts of Berchtesgaden.

Later known as Hotel Geiger the popular hotel became a rest and recuperation facility for Luftwaffe officers during the Second World War.

In the final days of the war Hotel Geiger was home to Chief of the General Staff of the Luftwaffe General Karl Koller (1898–1951).

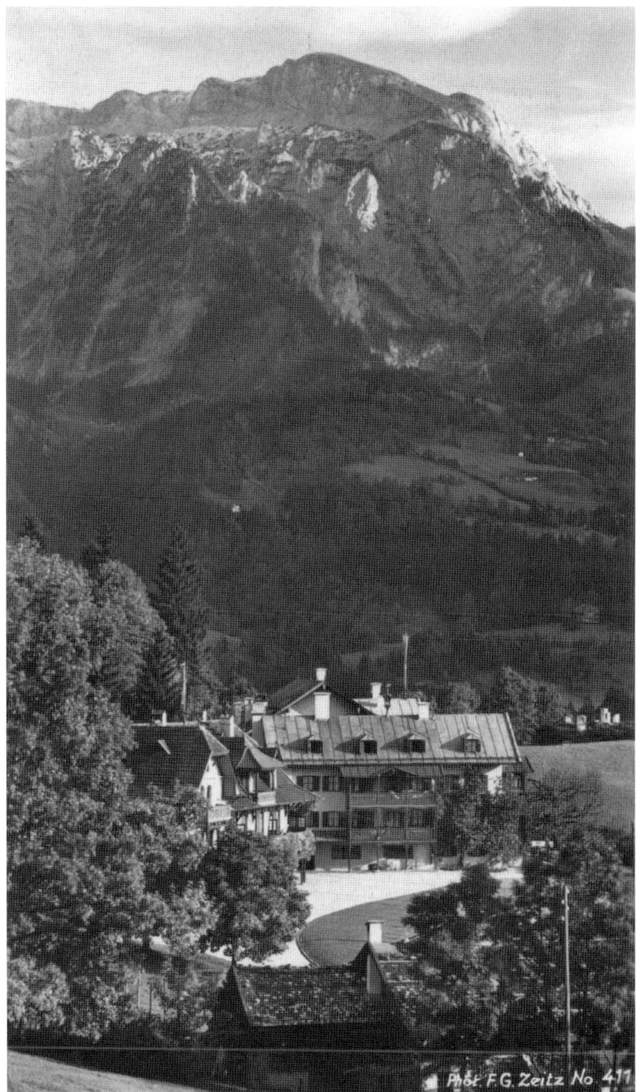

Koller had been awarded the Knight's Cross of the Iron Cross in April 1942 and the German Cross in Gold in February 1944.

Karl Koller was injured when von Stauffenberg's bomb exploded at Hitler's eastern headquarters at Rastenburg in East Prussia on 20 July 1944. Koller attended Hitler's 56th birthday celebrations in the Berlin bunker on 20 April 1945. General Koller would leave Berchtesgaden just one hour before US forces arrived in the area. He was taken prisoner by the Americans at Zell am See on 7 May 1945.

With its traditional rustic charm and wonderful mountain views Hotel Geiger remained a popular destination for visitors to the area. Sadly, in 1997, insolvency led to the hotel being closed. Following years of looting and vandalism a very dilapidated Hotel Geiger was finally demolished in 2018. A modern design hotel, the Kulturhof now occupies the site. The new buildings lack all traditional charm.

140. Haus Geiger with Göll and Brett.
This delightful postcard shows Haus Geiger and the surrounding area in the full grip of winter. The mountain on the left is the Kehlstein, and while it is impossible to make out any detail, the small snow-covered object on the top of the mountain is in fact the Kehlsteinhaus (Eagle's Nest).

The building on the left by the roadside has what appears to be a small Red Cross flag hanging just below the balcony. These flags were used to indicate military medical stations at the time. I spent many hours in the abandoned Hotel Geiger in the years prior to its demolition, and while it was in a very dilapidated state it was clear to see that it would have been a particularly charming building back in the day.

Bearing a Salzburg postmark this postcard was posted on 31 August 1944 to an address in Dessau. Dessau is a town located 69 kilometres (43 miles) north of Leipzig. Earlier that month on 16 August the Junkers Ju287, Germany's first high-speed, long-range, four jet-engine bomber had its maiden flight. On 25 August Paris had been liberated. August 1944 was a month of extremes by any standard. The following month the first V2 rocket hit London on 8 September 1944.

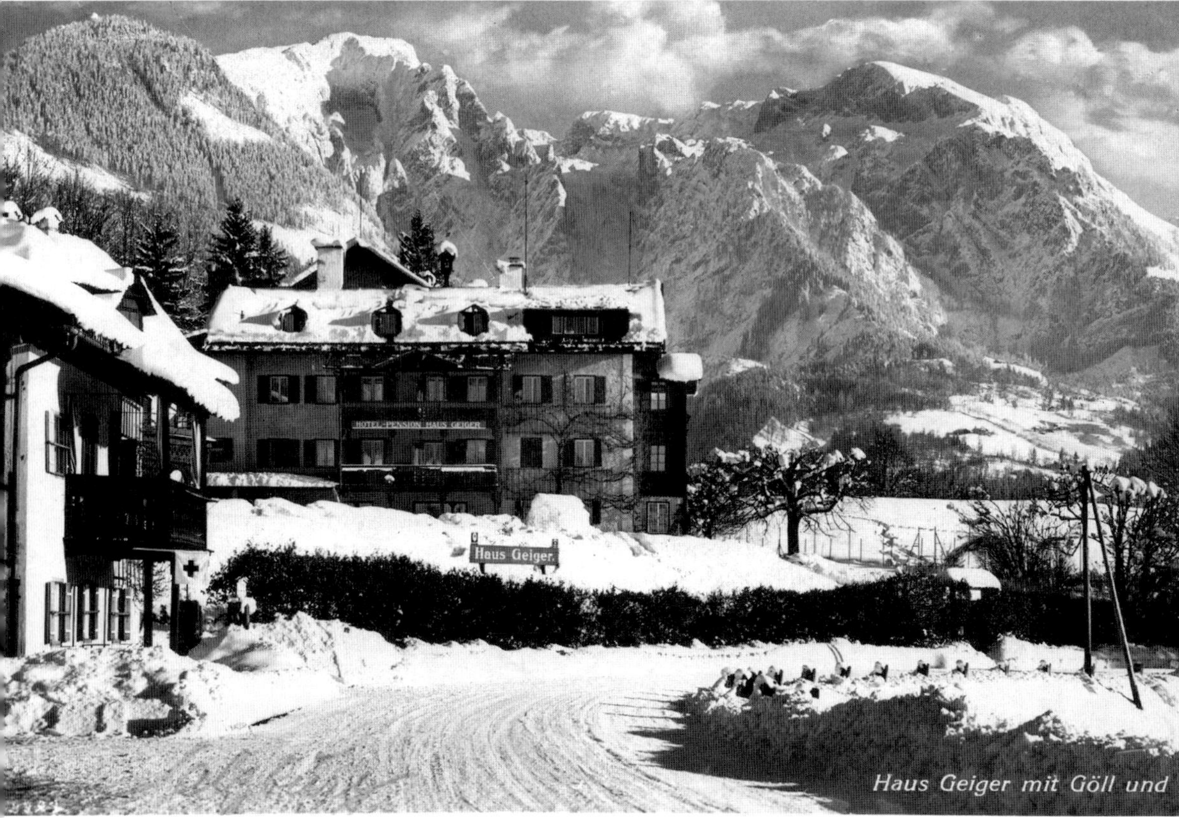

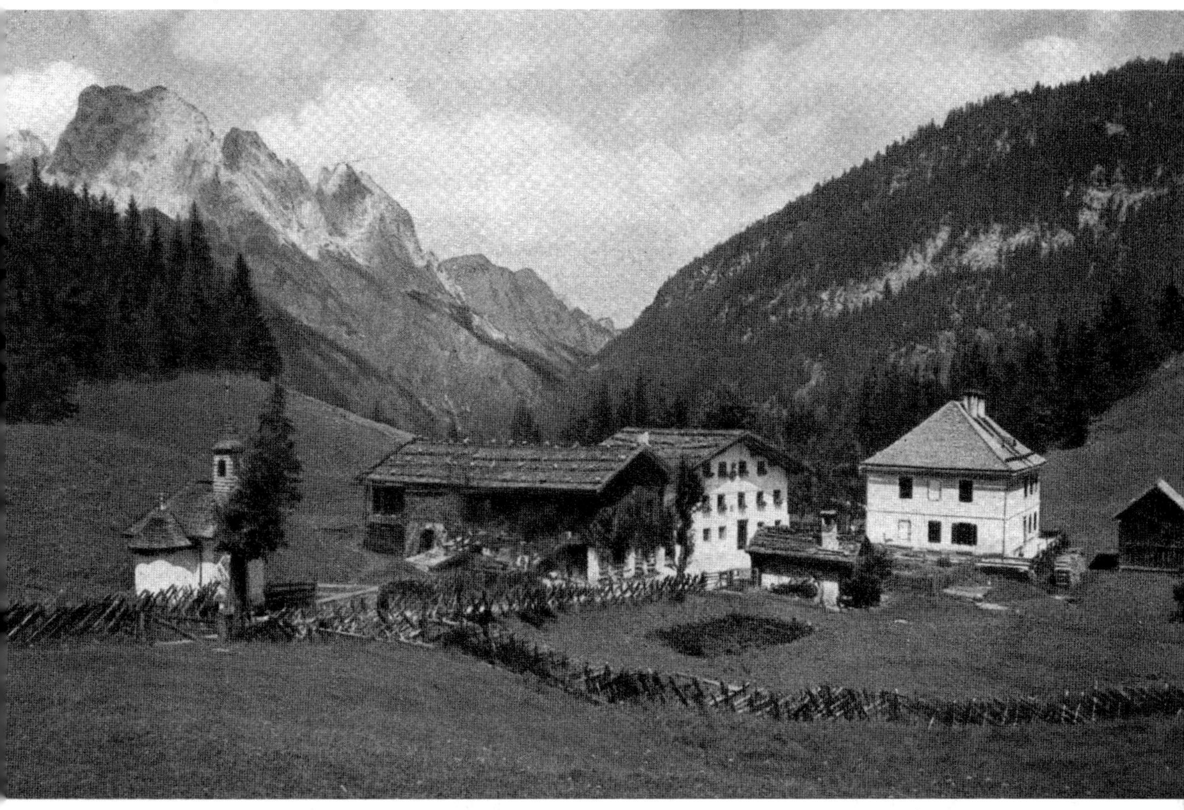

141. Hirschbühel (Mooswacht) with the Mühlsturzhorn 2288m.

This is Hirschbichl, a place also referred to as Hirschbühel or Mooswacht. It sits at the top of the ancient mountain pass leading up from Hintersee. The pass dates back to the 13th century when it was used to transport salt by mule. What was once a customs guardhouse is today an inn. Hirschbichl at 1183 metres (3880 feet) sits at the highest point on the pass. This pass, virtually unknown to the advancing allied forces was put to good use by fleeing German soldiers and SS-men as the Allies advanced towards Ramsau and Hintersee.

Some of the civil servants and military personnel who had taken up residence at Hintersee following the bombing of the Obersalzberg had important secret files and documents in their possession; documents that had been brought from Berlin to Berchtesgaden and the Obersalzberg.

As reports of allied forces moving through the Ramsau valley reached Hintersee these people used the mountain pass to move on to Hirschbichl. Having commandeered the Mooswacht Inn they spent an entire night burning top-secret documents. With time running out its said that many of these documents were packed in boxes and buried in the surrounding forest.

This postcard was posted in nearby Weißbach bei Lofer on 27 July 1937. The hand-applied 'Gasthof Hirschbühel' stamp on the reverse tells us that this postcard was purchased there.

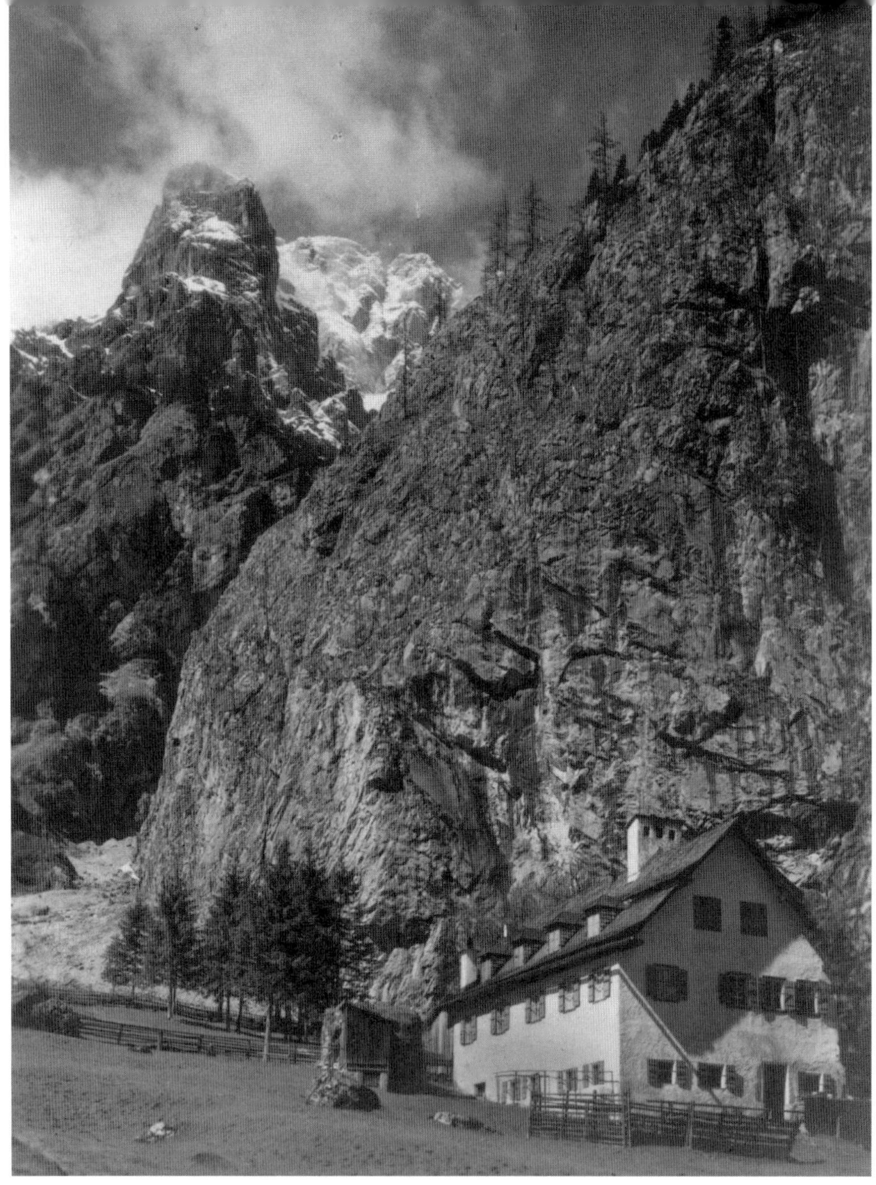

142. The Wimbach Castle in the Wimbachtal.
This photograph shows Wimbach Castle in the Wimbach valley near Ramsau. The castle was built in 1784 by the last provost of Berchtesgaden, Joseph Conrad von Schroffenberg. In 1810 the castle became the property of the Bavarian ruling Wittlesbach family. King Maximilian II (1811–64) and Prince Regent Luitpold (1821–1912) in particular, used Wimbach Castle as a hunting lodge and held organised court hunts here.

During the final desperate, uncertain days of the Second World War as the situation deteriorated and total collapse seemed imminent, peoples' concerns turned to the welfare and protection of their children. Fearing what might happen to their children many parents restricted their children to the confines of the family home, while others took them to remote Alpine huts. Those who could brought their children to Wimbach Castle where, situated at 938 metres (3075 feet) high in the Wimbach valley they felt safer. Today the former hunting lodge is the 'Berggaststätte Wimbachschloss', a mountain restaurant. This postcard was posted in Ramsau on 30 January 1934 to an address in Rotterdam, Holland.

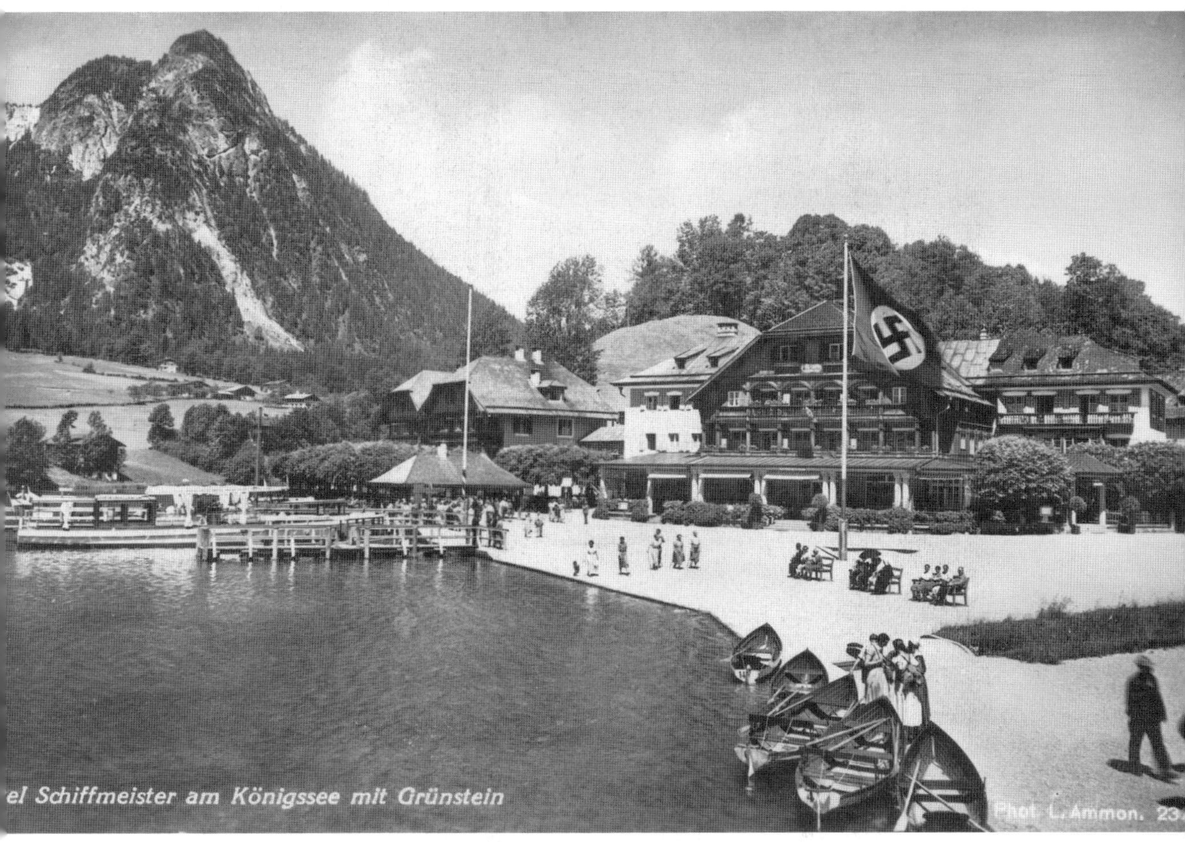

143. Hotel Schiffmeister on the Königssee with Grünstein.

The Königssee is regarded as one of the most beautiful lakes in Germany. It is long, narrow and very deep, comparable to a Norwegian fjord. Most of the lake lies within the Berchtesgaden National Park. The lake is some 7.7 kilometres (4.75 miles) in length and has a depth of around 190 metres (623 feet). With its steep forested banks and sheer rock walls it is truly magnificent. The Königssee was somewhere that Hitler and Eva Braun liked to visit in good weather.

The Grünstein dominates the background in this particular photograph; standing at 1304 metres (4278 feet) the Grünstein is a popular venue for those who prefer a more exhilarating hiking experience.

In the final days of the Second World War, Hotel Schiffmeister, the building seen directly behind the flagpole, was headquarters to *Generalfeldmarschall* (General Field Marshal) Albert Kesselring (1885–1960) then Commander-in-Chief West. Two days after the bombing of the Obersalzberg Kesselring moved into the hotel using it as his command post between 27 April and 3 May 1945 when he left for Maria Alm in Austria.

On 7 May Kesselring met with American forces at Saalfelden near Salzburg where he surrendered the southern half of all German forces. Kesselring, one of the Führer's most loyal and competent commanders, a man who was popular with all who served under him would remain loyal to Hitler; Albert Kesselring was one of the last German commanders to surrender.

Bearing a Königssee postmark this postcard was posted on 24 June 1936 to an address in Salzwedel a town 147 kilometres (91 miles) northeast of Hannover.

144. The Führer on the Königssee.

These last four postcards numbers 144 to 147, while relating to activity at or near the Königssee represent an earlier timeframe.

Hitler sits in the stern of one of the many pleasure craft that travel the lake. The Königssee has been a popular attraction with people visiting Berchtesgaden and the surrounding areas for many years. Parts of the lake are close to 190 metres (623 feet) deep. In an effort to maintain the cleanliness and purity of the water only rowing-boats and electrically powered boats are allowed on the Königssee.

Eva Braun was an altogether more frequent visitor to the Königssee. She liked to swim and practise her gymnastics on a small beach below the Königsbach waterfall on the eastern side of the lake. Eva and her friends would swim in a natural rock pool formed by the waterfall located on the slope high above the beach.

Gerd Bartels told me that a Volkswagen Beetle sits on the bottom of the lake at a depth of around 120 metres (393 feet). The story goes that in January 1964, despite being warned, a local man took his VW Beetle out onto the frozen lake. He made it all the way to St Bartholomä near the opposite end of the lake. The return journey however proved fatal. The car went through the ice near the Falkensteinwand.

The car and its driver were found some years ago during an exploration of the area using a mini submarine. Due to the depth and the limited oxygen in the water both car and driver were in a remarkable state of preservation. At the request of the unfortunate driver's family the scene was left undisturbed.

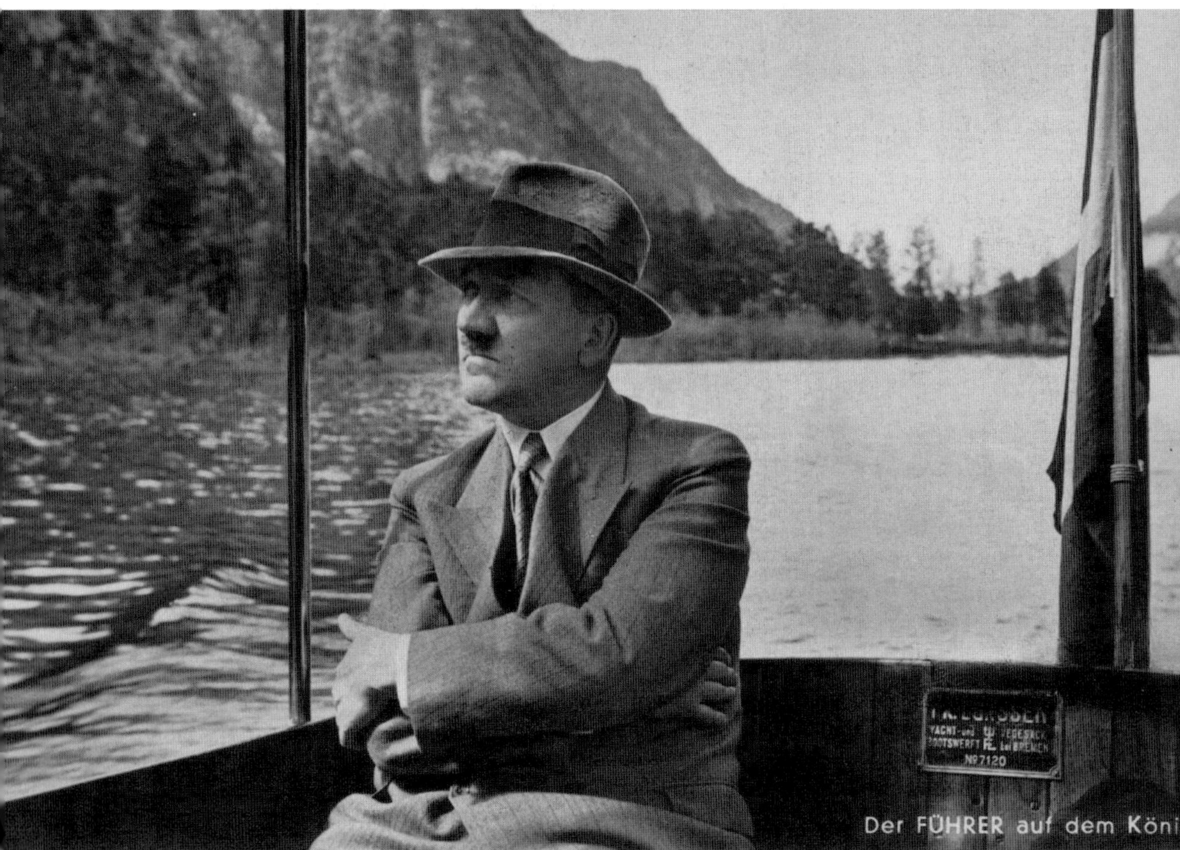

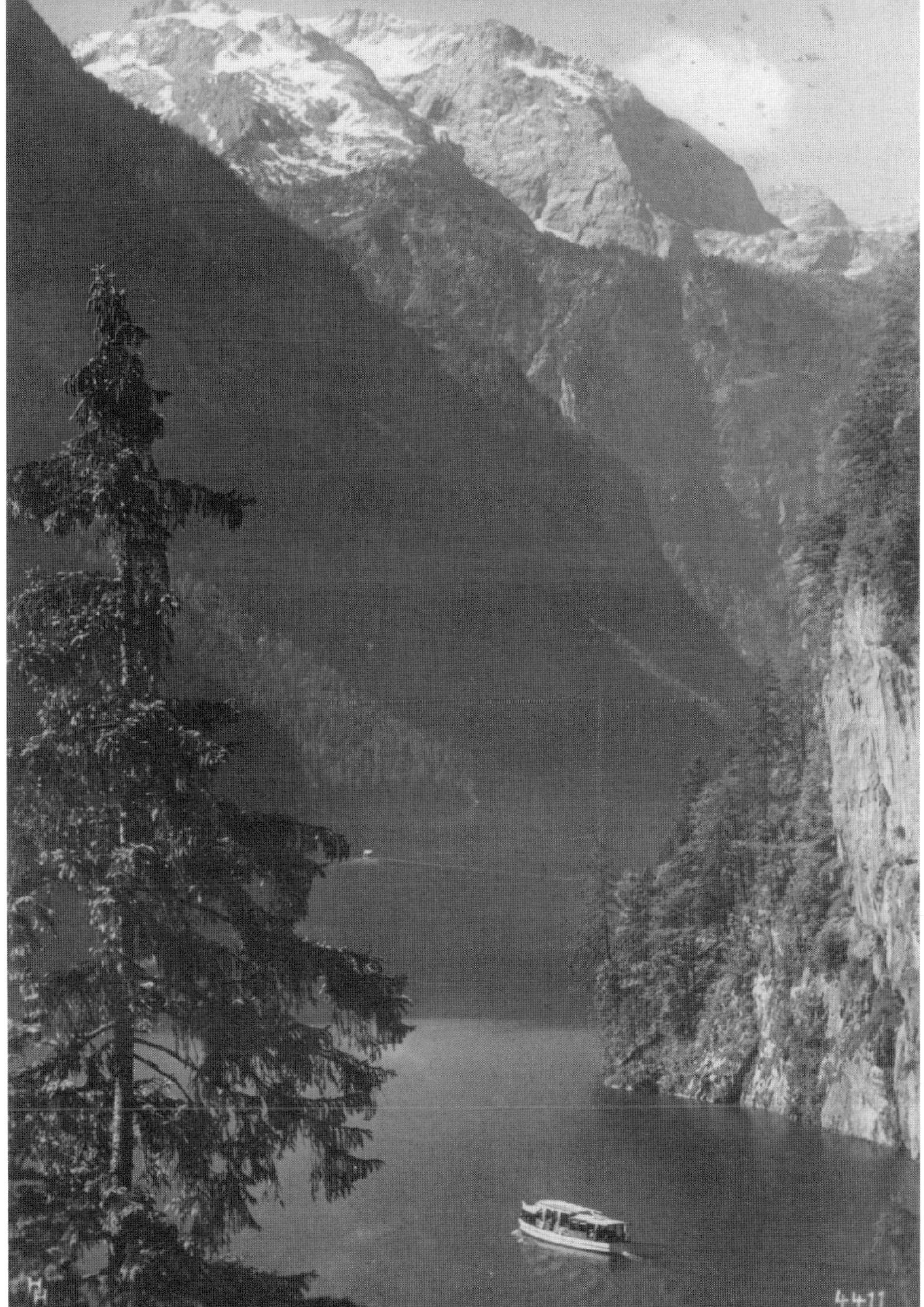

145. The Königssee near Berchtesgaden towards Funtenseetauern.
A view of the visually stunning Königssee photographed from a point high on the Malerwinkel. The sheer rock face, the Falkensteinwand mentioned in caption number 144 can be seen on the right-hand side of this image. At 2579 metres (8460 feet) the Funtenseetauern in the background is one of the Berchtesgaden massifs. This card was posted in Berchtesgaden on 4 August 1936 to an address in Leipzig.

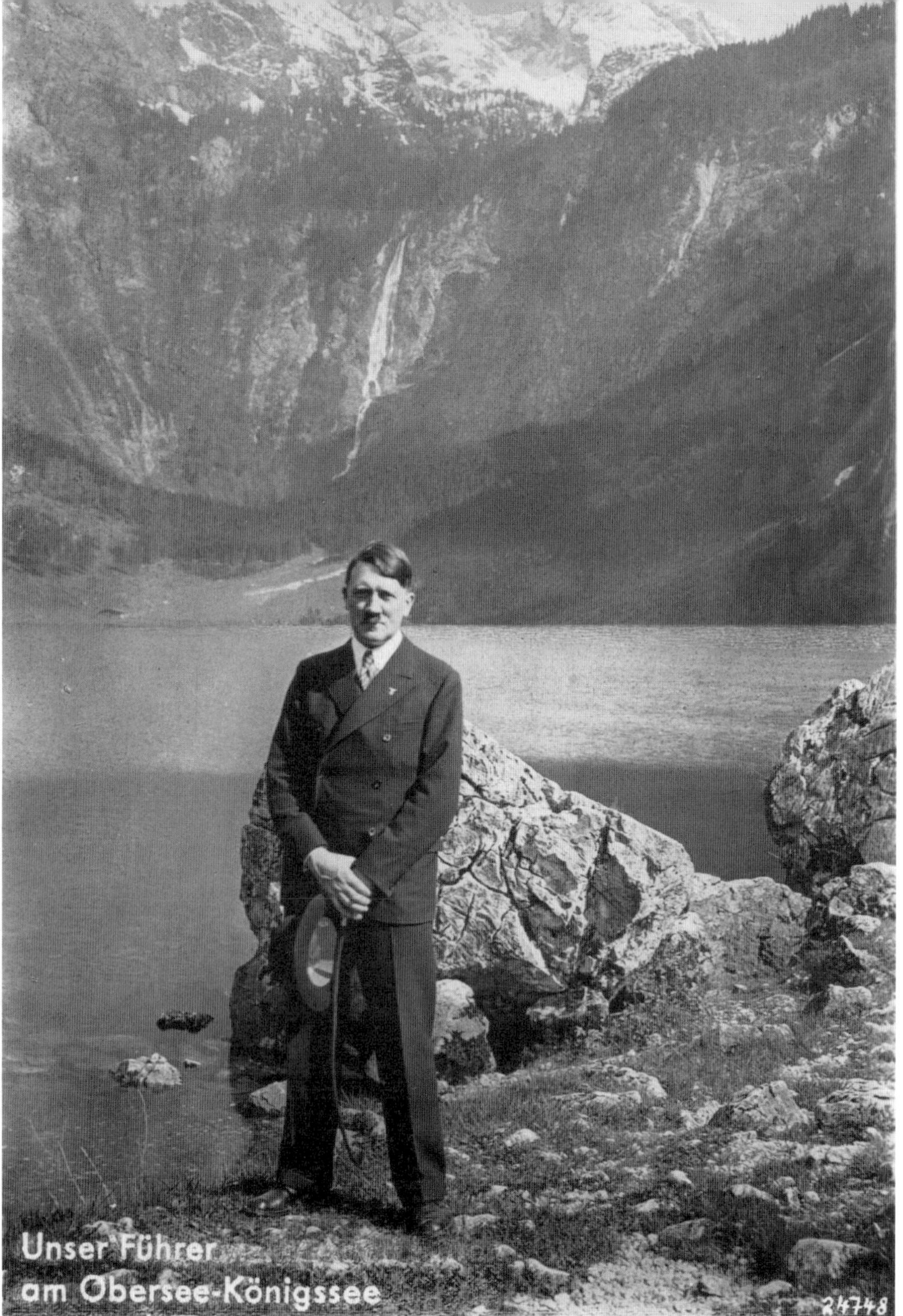

146. Our Führer at the Obersee-Königssee.

Hitler poses by the Obersee. Having travelled the length of the Königssee the boat docks at Salet. A fifteen minute walk brings you to the Obersee and the point where Hitler is seen standing. Bearing a Königssee postmark dated 12 August 1938 this postcard made its way to an address in Bad Harzburg, a spa town in Lower Saxony.

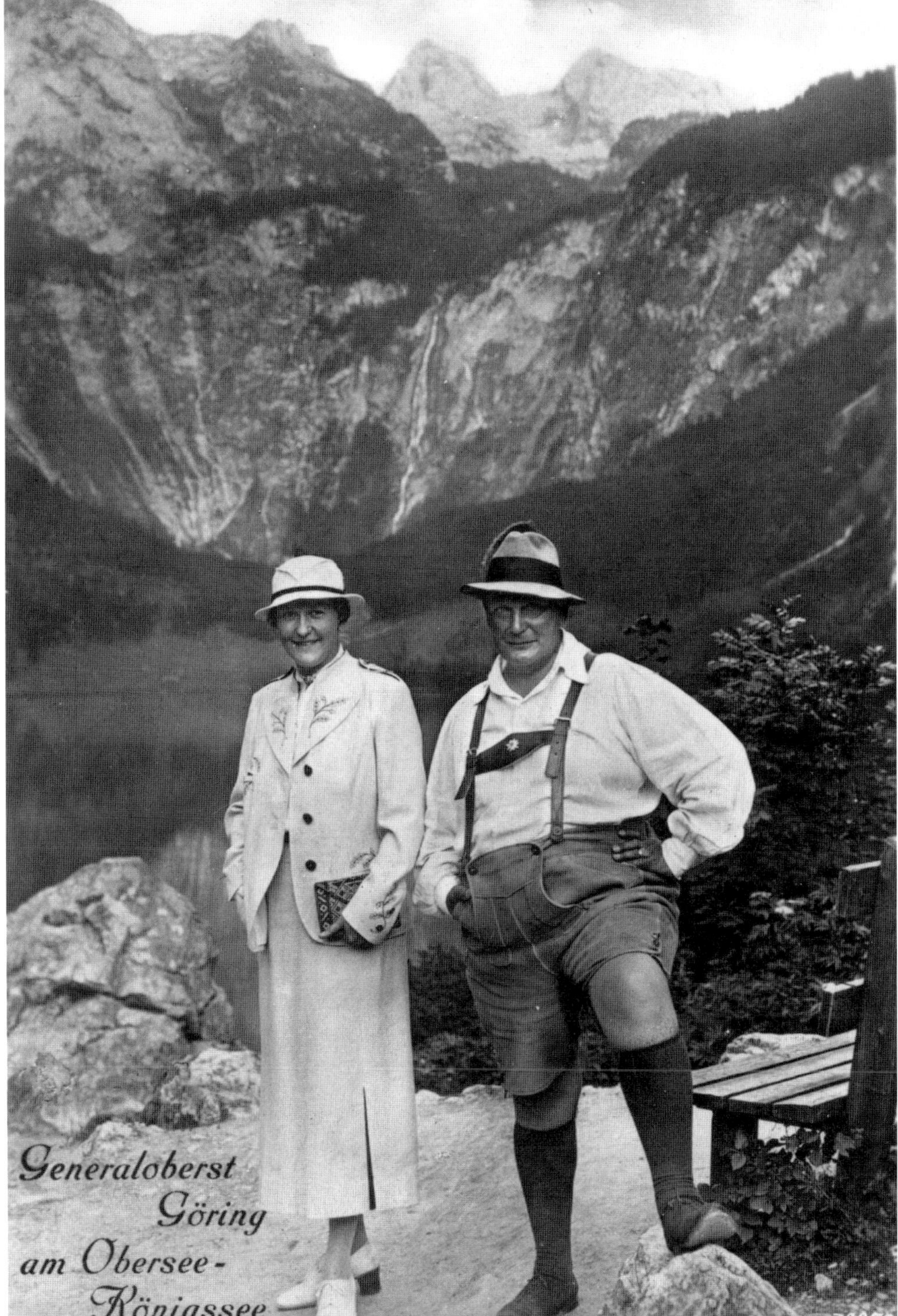

147. Generaloberst Göring at the Obersee-Königssee.
This rarely found postcard shows Hermann Göring and his wife, the actress Emmy Sonnemann at the Obersee. Göring, despite his robust build was a keen hunter and enjoyed many outdoor activities including climbing.

Salvaged Historical Artefacts

I have been exploring and researching in and around Berchtesgaden for well over thirty years. During that time I have gained access to places and people I would never have thought possible. As my work allowed a twelve-month career break I took six months off in 2009 and again in 2010 to work as a guide specializing in Third Reich history in Berchtesgaden. On retiring in early 2014 my wife and I returned to Berchtesgaden where I resumed my guiding work for the next three seasons. We returned to England at the end of 2016.

I have explored and photographed many of the buildings mentioned here numerous times. I have spent hours in Hotel Berchtesgadener Hof and more time than I care to mention in Hotel Geiger and the Dietrich Eckart Hospital, and hundreds of hours in and around the numerous sites and tunnels on the Obersalzberg.

Spending so much time in an area allows for the development of an intimate knowledge on the history and locations, from buildings to ruins and bunkers to tunnels I've gained access to some incredible places. The time I spent in the region was a continual learning experience and I have indeed been privileged to be able to spend so much time on a subject and in a place that cast its irresistible spell on me decades ago.

The next few photographs show just a few of the pieces I have managed to salvage from some of the buildings mentioned on earlier pages. I should state that no laws were broken in the recovery process. Like many before me I simply seized the opportunities as they presented themselves.

148. This complete brass door lock is from Hotel Berchtesgadener Hof. I recovered it from the building in 2006 during the early stages of demolition, at a time when the interior was being ripped out. I removed it from one of the doors that separated the main dining room from the breakfast room on the ground floor. Looking at postcard number 95, on page 116, the door in question is the first on the left.

It was sad to see the interior fittings and finishes, including oak panelling and fine Untersberg and Adnet marble being broken up and removed without any thought of either salvage or historical interest. Similarly I have complete door locks from both Hotel Geiger and the former Dietrich Eckart Hospital.

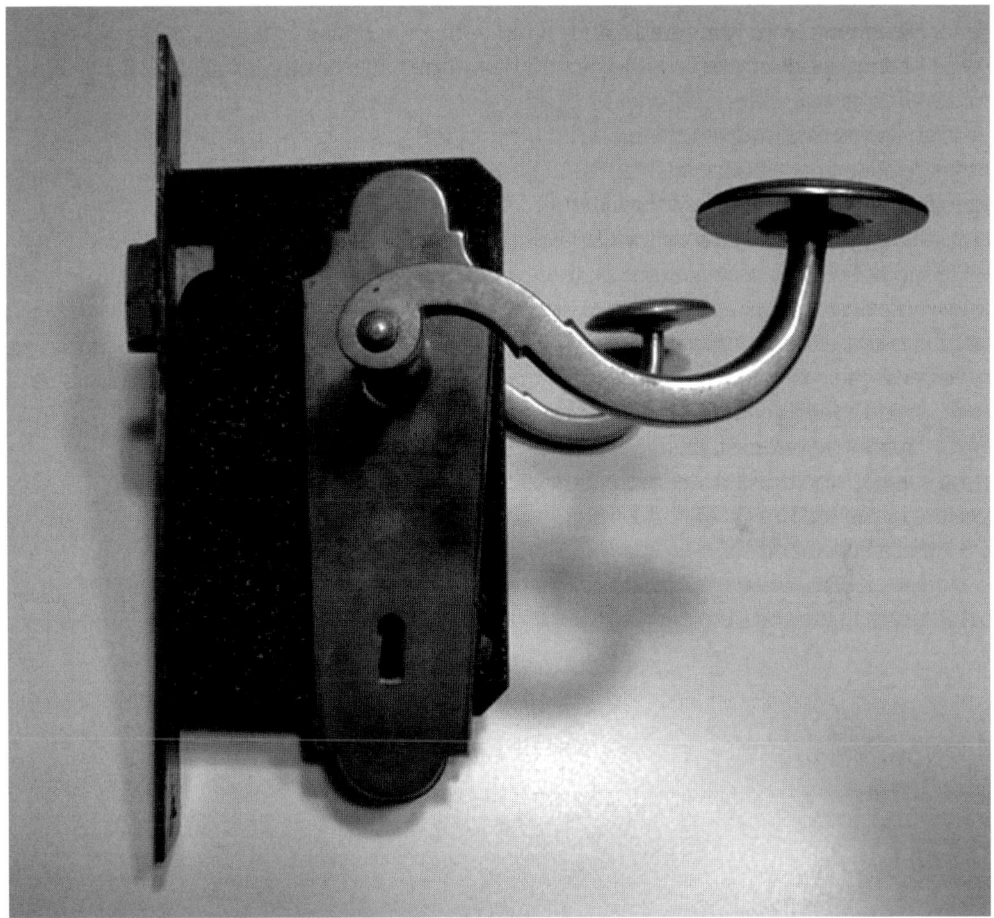

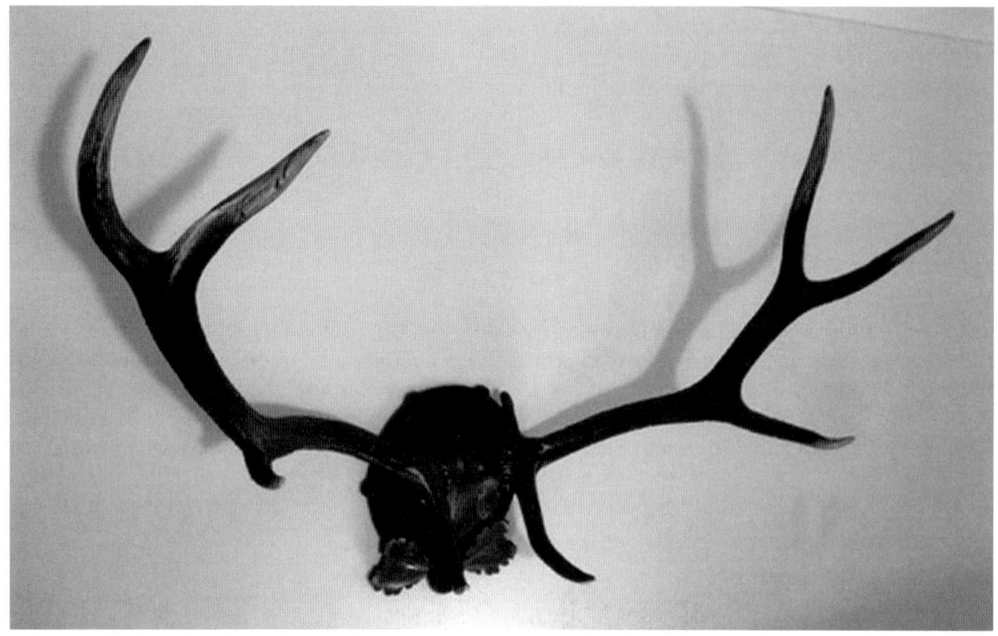

149. These antlers are from the former Hotel Post; they are over one hundred years old. Measuring 93cms (3 feet) tip to tip they hung in the hotel owned by the Weiss family for many decades. The former Hotel Post is now the *Jugendgästehaus CVJM Aktivzentrum;* (Youth Guest House CVJM Activity Centre) basically a youth hostel similar to those run by the YMCA. The building has operated as a hostel since 1981.

A friend who worked in the hostel bought the antlers in 2005 when the building was undergoing renovation and, knowing my interest, kindly gave them to me in 2016.

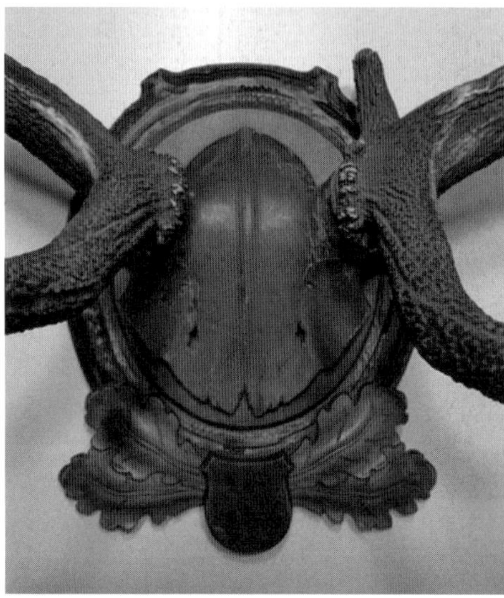

150. A close-up of the beautifully hand-carved wood base upon which the antlers are mounted. Everything, including the centre section representing the animal's skull is carved wood.

151. This hand-carved double scallop wood shell resting on a scroll is from Hotel Geiger. It was one of twenty-six such shells that formed part of the decoration around the walls in the lounge on the ground floor.

Fine wood panelling covered the walls and ceiling in the lounge. These wooden shells were fixed high up on the wall panels. This was the last remaining of the twenty-six examples when I removed it in June 2011.

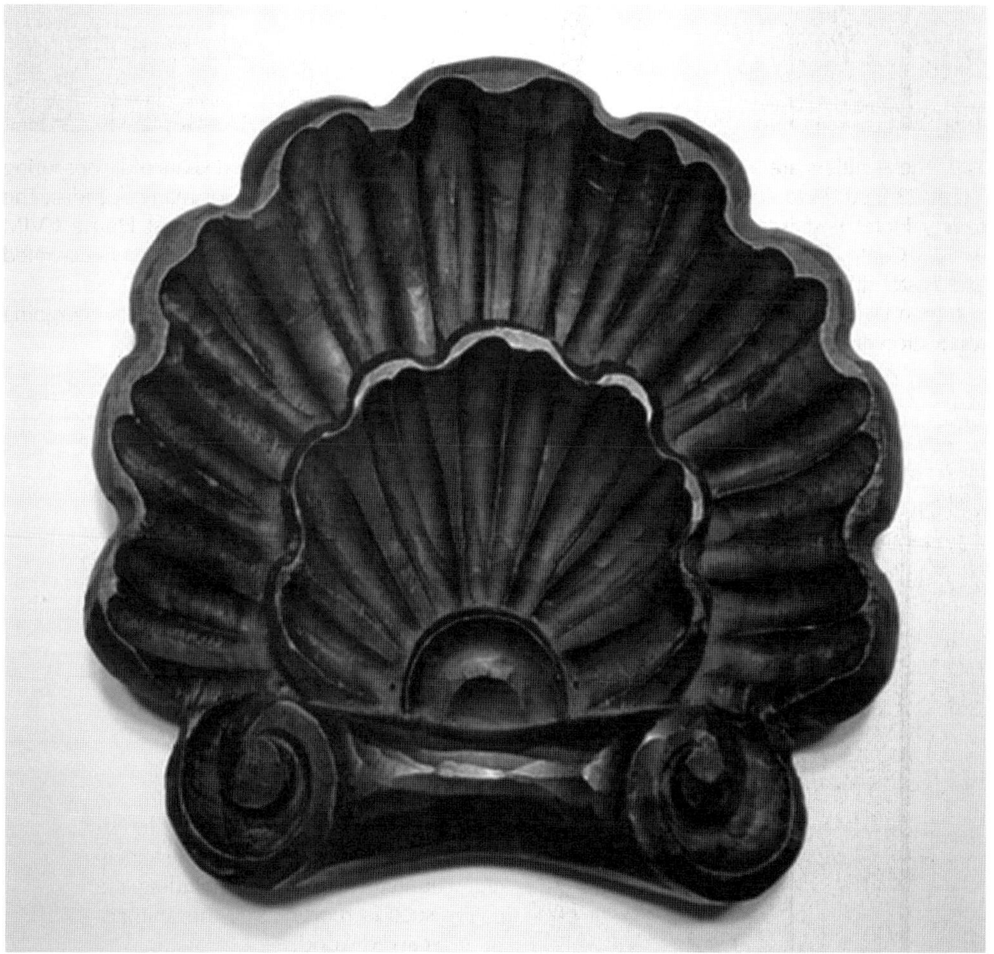

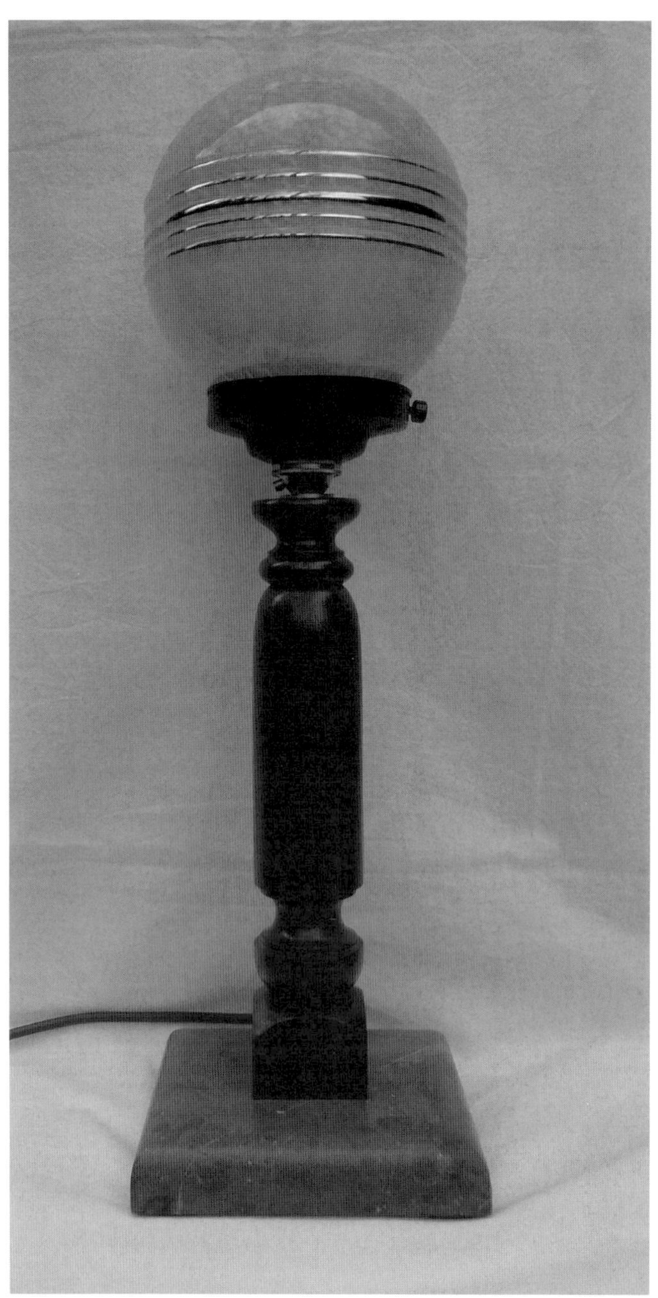

152. This desk/table lamp is made from pieces salvaged from Hotel Geiger. The heavy base is made of Untersberg marble. The windowsills in the lounge where the wooden shell was recovered were made of Untersberg marble.

Only one of the three large marble sills remained in place; this was because whoever had tried to remove it previously had used too much force and the sill had cracked and broken across the middle, front to back. I removed half of the sill and took it to a local stonemason who cut and shaped the lamp base seen here. The wood section is made from part of one of the few remaining staircase spindles in the hotel. The glass shade and its Bakelite fitting were bought in a second-hand shop.

176

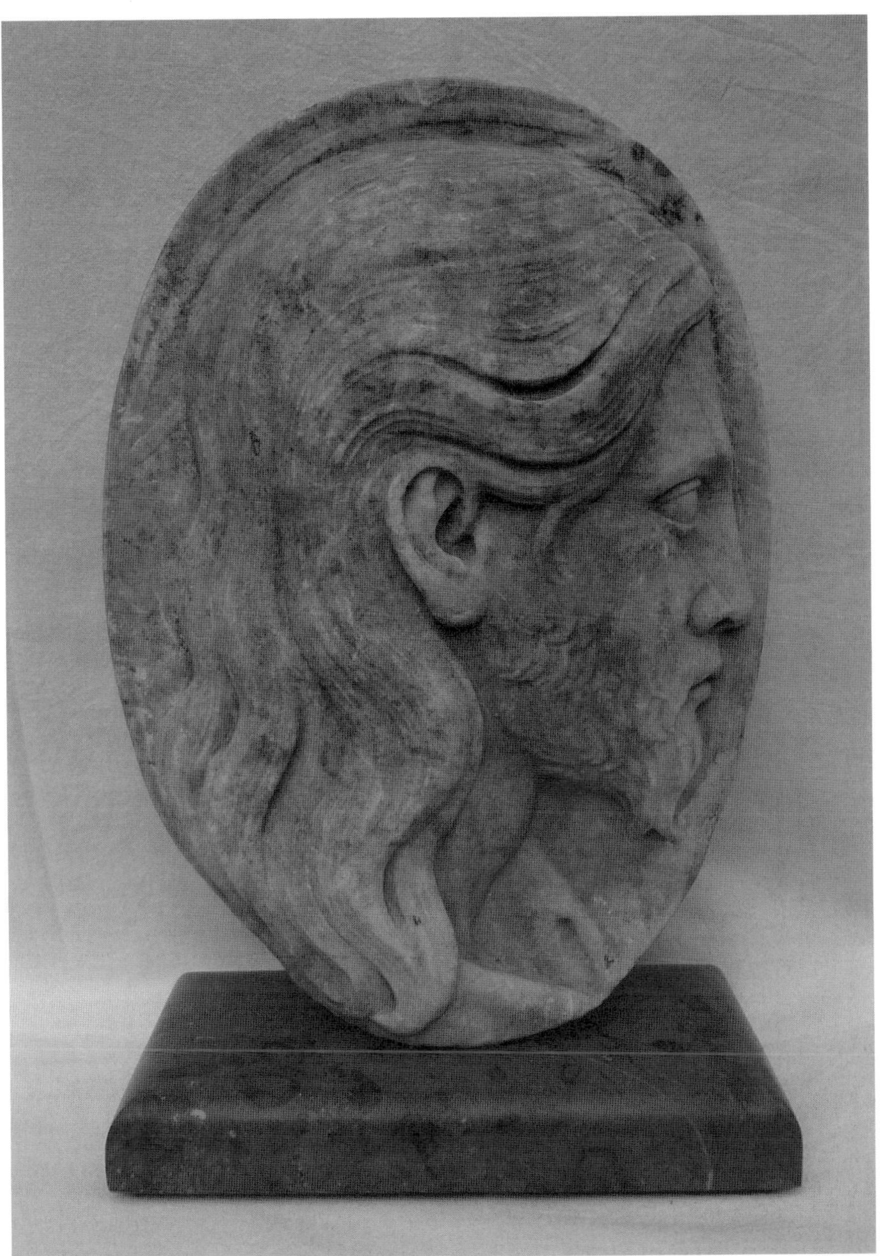

153. I like to think of this as my greatest find. This really *was* a find! It was a couple of days after Christmas 2015 and with nothing to do we decided to drive up the Obersalzberg, park near Hotel zum Türken, and walk to Mooslahnerkopf. This is one of my wife's favourite walks in the area. We drove to the Obersalzberg and parked close to the hotel, which was closed. The snow on the ground was between fifteen and twenty centimetres (six to eight inches) deep and there was no one else around.

We walked to Mooslahnerkopf where we spent some time enjoying the view across the valley to the Untersberg and Salzburg. On the way back we decided to shorten the route by walking across the golf course. Having crossed the snow-covered greens we started up the field on the other side towards the road. In doing this we passed the site of Villa Bechstein. Owned by the piano-manufacturing Bechstein family, the villa had been bought to become a Nazi Party guesthouse on the Obersalzberg. The house was within sight of the Berghof. Those who stayed there included, Joseph Goebbels, Rudold Hess, Benito Mussolini and Albert Speer.

Apart from some blast damage, the house had survived the bombing of 25 April 1945 relatively well. Having been subjected to the usual looting the property was knocked down in 1952, around the time the Berghof ruins were blown up. A draglift for skiers was installed some years ago and a section of the lift passed close to where Villa Bechstein once stood. During construction a section of the hillside had been cut away to reduce the gradient of the draglift, this again was close to the site of the villa.

We were walking up the hillside and close to this artificially created earth bank when something sticking out of the bank caught my eye and I stopped. It was getting late in the afternoon and the light was beginning to fade. As I looked closer I could hardly believe my eyes. I called out to my wife and she joined me.

What we saw was a piece of white stone poking a little way out of the earth bank with what looked like human features carved on it. I removed my gloves and taking hold of the stone I began to gently move it up and down and from side to side in an attempt to free it from the surrounding earth. To my amazement it came out easily and in one piece.

What I recovered was this finely carved piece of marble showing the features of a young man with long flowing hair and a beard. The reverse is flat with a rough chiselled finish. The piece measures 30 x 21 cms (12 x 8.5 ins). The rough finish on the reverse and having a hole in the base implies the piece was probably intended to be wall mounted. The base seen in the photograph is yet another piece of the same marble windowsill removed from Hotel Geiger that was cut and shaped by the same stonemason.

This piece can only be from Villa Bechstein. It's amazing to think that it lay buried in the ground for over sixty years until melting snow and rain water washed away enough of the soil in the earth bank to expose part of it. Friends who have looked at it have speculated that it may represent one of the muses, something to do with music given the property's connection to the Bechstein family. Others have suggested it might be religious; either way it was an incredible piece of luck to find it.

It's worth mentioning that it is forbidden to use metal detectors or to dig on the Obersalzberg. If found engaged in such activity penalties include large fines and being banned from the mountainside for a specified period, perhaps years. As for myself, there was no digging involved; the elements exposed my 'marble head' and I said thank you! Even now I sometimes wonder: did I find it, or did it find me!

Author's Comment

In addition to the information provided by Gerhard Bartels, both verbally and in document form, I should mention the work of a local resident, Karl Komposch from Ramsau. Herr Komposch was a highly respected chronicler of local history. He served in the German Army during the Second World War in Poland, France, Hungary and Bulgaria. He was wounded just before the war ended and having been held prisoner of war he eventually returned home to Ramsau in 1946. Gerd Bartels provided a document written by Karl Komposch titled:

II World War 1939–1945
End of the war in Ramsau near Berchtesgaden
(Compiled by Karl Komposch, Ramsau)

In his research Herr Komposch interviewed thirty-four local witnesses. He names eight books on the history of the area and lists a number of local institutions that he visited where he researched the archives of these organisations. Karl Komposch died on 6 October 2021; he was almost 101 years old.

Gerd Bartels approached the widow of Karl Komposch to request permission to use extracts from the abovementioned document, permission was granted. I am most grateful to Frau Komposch for allowing us to use some of the information relating to the Ramsau and Hintersee areas during the last days of the Second World War as gathered and compiled by her late husband, Karl Komposch.

Having what amounted to unrestricted access to local records and enjoying a level of personal contact with local residents, in many cases friends and neighbours, we must accept that the information gathered and compiled by Herr Komposch is certainly more detailed and more accurate than any information that might be gathered by an outsider.

The immediately recognizable Nazi flag appears in many of the photographs on the preceding pages. However, we should not presume this means that everyone who 'flew the flag' was a Nazi Party member. On 15 September 1935 the Nazi flag was officially adopted as the national flag and remained so for the duration of the regime. The national flag was everywhere; to fly one outside your home would have been considered a patriotic act in the same way that flags are to be seen outside peoples' homes in many countries today. Again, to display images of Hitler and other symbolism representative of the regime in the home was commonplace in the same way that people display pictures of leading political figures they admire today.

$\mathfrak{Statement}$

In contributing to this book and reflecting upon the events that shaped his childhood Gerhard Bartels feels that he too was a victim of the Nazi regime. As a child he was exploited in the propaganda of the time. Gerhard was not asked if he wanted to be photographed with Hitler, neither was he aware why he was being photographed nor the subsequent consequences. Heinrich Hoffmann selected Gerhard simply because he was fair-haired and blue-eyed and therefore, in the eyes of the regime, Aryan. Again, Gerhard was required by law to join the *Deutsches Jungvolk* (German Young People); failure to do so would have had repercussions.

Gerhard and his family, like many other decent people, were swept up in the 'feel-good factor' of the early years of the regime and were totally unaware of the terrible agenda that was to unfold. Gerhard's father, August Bartels, was sent to Latvia to work as a regional farmer. When fleeing Latvia in 1944 the family lost most of their possessions and were themselves lucky to escape. We must also remember how the family home and business was requisitioned in the final days of the war. During the latter years of the regime the Bartels family did all they could to help any, and all, victims they met. This dark part of German history has left its mark on all who lived through it and survived.

We must never forget that Adolf Hitler and the Nazi Party plunged the world into a war that led to the deaths of almost sixty million people. That said, we should also remember that the sins of the father should not be visited upon the children. The de-Nazification and re-education programmes that followed the Second World War have resulted in a Germany that today reflects the best ideals of a modern democratic state. As to the Bartels family, I would ask that their right to privacy be respected.

James Wilson

Appendix

The following information has been taken from the reverse of the postcards shown throughout this book. It is offered by way of acknowledgement and credit to the original photographers and publishers of these postcards. This information may be cross-referenced by using the corresponding number of each postcard caption.

1. Original-Aufnahme u. Verlag von Karl Sammüller. Tengling a. Waginger-See.
2. Druck und Verlag Photo-Kitt, München 5.
3. Verlag Philipp Krebs, Dresden A 1, Ringstr. 23.
4. Gebirgsaufnahmen von Michael Lochner, Berchtesgaden.
5. H. Gutjahr, Ramsau.
6. Aufnahme u. Verlag: F. G. Zeitz, Königssee/Obb.
7. Aufnahme und Verlag: M. Lochner Berchtesgaden.
8. Reverse unmarked, source unknown.
9. Gebr. Metz, Kunstanstalt, Tübingen. Photographiekarte chamois Bütten.
10. Gebr. Metz, Kunstanstalt, Tübingen. Photographiekarte chamois Bütten.
11. Verlag: L. Ammon, Schönau-B'gaden.
12. Gebr. Metz, Tübingen.
13. H. Gutjahr, Ramsau.
14. Photo-Hoffmann, München, Theresienstr. 74.
15. Photo-Hoffmann, München, Theresienstr. 74.
16. Photo-Hoffmann, München, Theresienstr. 74.
17. Photo-Hoffmann, München, Friedrichstr. 34.
18. Photo-Hoffmann, München, Friedrichstr. 34.
19. Photo-Hoffmann, München, Theresienstr. 74.
20. Photo-Hoffmann, München, Theresienstr. 74.
21. Nordd. Städte-Verkehrs-Werbung, Hannover-Hainholz. Ruf: 32020.
22. Photograph by author.
23. Photo-Hoffmann, München, Theresienstr. 74.
24. Photo-Hoffmann, München, Theresienstr. 74.
25. Photo-Hoffmann, München, Theresienstr. 74.
26. Photo-Hoffmann, München, Theresienstr. 74.
27. H. Gutjahr, Ramsau.
28. Verlag von Karl Ermisch, Berchtesgaden.
29. Photograph by author.
30. Phot. W. Fiß. Ramsau (Obb.)
31. Photograph by author.
32. Photograph by author.

33. H. Gutjahr, Ramsau.

34. Phot. W. Fiß, Ramsau (Obb.)

35. Orig.-Aufn. v Hans Huber Alpiner Verlag Garmisch-Partenkirchen.

36. Photo J Schmid, Berchtesgaden.

37. Aufnahme und Verlag: M. Lochner, Berchtesgaden.

38. Aufnahme der österr. Luftbild-Industrie-Salzburg.

39. 'Star' Film & Foto Berchtesgaden.

40. Aufnahme und Verlag: M. Lochner Berchtesgaden.

41. Photograph by author.

42. Photograph by author.

43. Photograph by author.

44. Photograph by author.

45. Fotobrom Riga. Latvijas vertspapiru spiestuve, Riga, Latgales iela 11.

46. Verlag Georg Preuss, Berlin S. 14.

47. Courtesy Gerhard Bartels.

48. Reverse unmarked, source unknown.

49. Verlag Intra Nürnberg. Druck: F. Willmy G.m.b.H., Nürnberg.

50. Gebr. Metz, Tübingen.

51. UTLN.

52. Photograph by author.

53. Aufnahme und Verlag: M. Lochner, Berchtesgaden.

54. Gebirgsaufnahmen von Michael Lochner, Berchtesgaden.

55. Aufnahme und Verlag F. G. Zeitz, Königssee / Obb.

56. Verlag Josef Fendt, Berchtesgaden.

57. Verlag: L. Ammon, Schönau-B'gaden.

58. Verlag von Karl Ermisch, Berchtesgaden.

59. Fot. Ernst Baumann, Bad Reichenhall.

60. Verlag von Karl Ermisch, Berchtesgaden.

61. Aufn. u. Verlag M. Lochner, Obersalzberg, Berchtesgaden.

62. Photo-Hoffman, München, Friedrichstr. 34.

63. Photohaus J. Schmid, Berchtesgaden – Fernruf 254.

64. Aufnahme und Verlag M. Lochner, Berchtesgaden. Echte Photographie.

65. Verlag: L. Ammon, Schönau-B'gaden.

66. Photohaus J. Schmid, Berchtesgaden – Fernruf 254.

67. Photo-Hoffmann, München, Friedrichstr. 34.

68. Reverse unmarked, source unknown.

69. Reverse unmarked, source unknown.

70. Reverse unmarked, source unknown.

71. Reverse unmarked, source unknown.

72. Photo Brandner, unterhalb Haus Wachenfeld. Telef. 83.

73. Verlag: L. Ammon, Schönau-B'gaden.

74. Verlag: L. Ammon, Schönau-B'gaden.

75. Alpiner Kunstverlag Hans Huber, München 19.
76. Photo-Hoffmann, München, Theresienstr. 74.
77. Photo-Hoffmann, München, Theresienstr. 74.
78. Photo-Hoffmann, München, Theresienstr. 74.
79. Verlag: L. Ammon, Schönau-B'gaden.
80. Verlag: L. Ammon, Schönau-Berchtesgaden.
81. Reverse unmarked, source unknown.
82. Verlag Schöning & Co., Lübeck.
83. Aufnahme und Verlag F. G. Zeitz, Königssee / Obb.
84. Photohaus J. Schmid, Berchtesgaden – Fernruf 254.
85. Photo J Schmid, Berchtesgaden.
86. Bro 292. Echte Fotografie.
87. Photograph by author.
88. Verlag von Karl Ermisch, Berchtesgaden.
89. Foto Kunstkarte von Karl Dietrich. Laufen u Freilassing Obb.
90. Kunst u. Verlagsanstalt Martin Herpich, München.
91. Photo-Hoffmann, München, Friedrichstr. 34.
92. Photo-Hoffmann, München, Friedrichstr. 34.
93. Photo-Hoffmann, München, Friedrichstr. 34.
94. Photo-Hoffmann, München, Friedrichstr. 34.
95. Photo-Hoffmann, München, Friedrichstr. 34.
96. Verlag: L. Ammon, Schönau-B'gaden.
97. Photograph by author.
98. Aufnahme 2 J. Schmid, Berchtesgaden. Echte Fotografie.
99. Photograph by author.
100. Photohaus J. Schmid, Berchtesgaden.
101. Photohaus J. Schmid, Berchtesgaden.
102. Photograph by author.
103. Aufnahme und Verlag: M. Lochner, Berchtesgaden.
104. Aufnahme Dr. Wiedemann. Herausgegeben vom Generalkommando VII. A.K.
105. Aufnahme und Verlag F. G. Zeitz, Königssee / Obb.
106. Photohaus J. Schmid, Berchtesgaden – Fernruf 254.
107. Reverse unmarked, source unknown.
108. Photohaus J. Schmid, Berchtesgaden – Fernruf 254.
109. Aufnahme u. Verlag Photo Steger, Berchtesgaden.
110. Aufnahme u. Verlag: F. G. Zeitz, Königssee/Obb.
111. Alpiner Kunstverlag Hans Huber, Garmisch-Partenkirchen.
112. L. Ammon, Berchtesgaden-Schönau.
113. Reverse unmarked, source unknown.
114. Reverse unmarked, source unknown.
115. Reverse unmarked, source unknown.
116. Reverse unmarked, source unknown.

117. Reverse unmarked, source unknown.
118. Reverse unmarked, source unknown.
119. Reverse unmarked, source unknown.
120. Reverse unmarked, source unknown.
121. Reverse unmarked, source unknown.
122. Reverse unmarked, source unknown.
123. Reverse unmarked, source unknown.
124. Reverse unmarked, source unknown.
125. Aufnahme und Verlag M. Lochner, Berchtesgaden.
126. Verlag Helff & Stein K. G., Leipzig-Innsbruck.
127. Verlag Helff & Stein K. G., Leipzig-Innsbruck.
128. Photograph by author.
129. Photohaus Fröhlich Bad Reichenhall.
130. Photo - Schmid - Maier - Bad Reichenhall.
131. Martin Herpich, Kunst und Verlagsanstalt, München.
132. Cosy-Verlag Alfred Gründler, Salzburg, Getreidegasse 22.
133. Verlag Helff & Stein K.G., Leipzig C1.
134. Reverse unmarked, source unknown.
135. Photographie H. Gutjahr, Ramsau (bayr. Alpen).
136. H. Gutjahr, Photogr., Ramsau, bayr. Alpen.
137. Photogr. H. Gutjahr, Ramsau.
138. Aufn. u. Verlag Georg Bichler, Fotohaus, Altenmarkt/Alz Obb.
139. Aufnahme und Verlag F. G. Zeitz, Königssee / Obb.
140. Verlag: L. Ammon, Schönau-B'gaden.
141. Eigentum u. Verlag von Jos. Schmidt, Photograph, Lofer.
142. Reverse unmarked, source unknown.
143. Verlag: L. Ammon, Schönau-B'gaden.
144. Photo-Hoffmann, München, Theresienstr. 74.
145. Orig.-Aufn. v. Hans Huber, Alpiner Verlag, Garmisch-Partenkirchen.
146. Photo Jul. Hillebrand Nachf., Königssee (Ob.-Bayern).
147. Photo Jul. Hillebrand, Königssee (Ob Bayern).
148. Photograph by author.
149. Photograph by author.
150. Photograph by author.
151. Photograph by author.
152. Photograph by author.
153. Photograph by author.

James Wilson was born in Northern Ireland in 1953.
In 1972 and following family tradition he entered the printing industry.
He moved to London in 1979 where he went on
to run his own business through the 1980s.
In 1995 he joined the Metropolitan Police Service.
He retired in 2014.
James Wilson is a Certified Specialised Guide for Third Reich Themes
with the Munich-Berlin Institute for Contemporary History.
He has worked as a specialised tour-guide on the Obersalzberg,
at the Eagle's Nest and around Berchtesgaden.

James Wilson is the author of:

Luftwaffe Propaganda Postcards, Airlife Publishing Ltd, 1996

Hitler's Alpine Retreat, Pen & Sword Books Ltd, 2005

Propaganda Postcards of the Luftwaffe, Pen & Sword Books Ltd, 2007

The Nazis' Nuremberg Rallies, Pen & Sword Books Ltd, 2012

Hitler's Alpine Headquarters, Pen & Sword Books Ltd, 2013

Dear Reader,

We hope you have enjoyed this book, but why not share your views on social media? You can also follow our pages to see more about our other products: facebook.com/penandswordbooks or follow us on Twitter @penswordbooks

You can also view our products at www.pen-and-sword.co.uk (UK and ROW) or www.penandswordbooks.com (North America).

To keep up to date with our latest releases and online catalogues, please sign up to our newsletter at: www.pen-and-sword.co.uk/newsletter

If you would like a printed catalogue with our latest books, then please email: enquiries@pen-and-sword.co.uk or telephone: 01226 734555 (UK and ROW) or email: Uspen-and-sword@casematepublishers.com or telephone: (610) 853-9131 (North America).

We respect your privacy and we will only use personal information to send you information about our products.

Thank you!